A Daily Defense

365 Days (plus one) to Becoming a Better Apologist

JIMMY AKIN

A Daily Defense

365 Days (plus one)
to Becoming a Better Apologist

Published by Catholic Answers, Inc.
2020 Gillespie Way
El Cajon, California 92020
1-888-291-8000 orders
619-387-0042 fax
catholic.com
Printed in the United States of America

Cover design by Devin Schadt

978-1-68357-004-2
978-1-68357-005-9 Kindle
978-1-68357-006-6 ePub

Introduction

The history of Christianity is one of debate. As the Gospels reveal, Jesus was challenged right from the start. Rival schools like the Pharisees and Sadducees posed pointed questions to him, trying to trap him in his words and even to get him in trouble with the authorities. Some of Jesus' most famous statements were responses to challenges from his critics:

- "What God has joined together, let man not put asunder."
- "A house divided against itself cannot stand."
- "Render unto Caesar what is Caesar's, and unto God what is God's."

Our world is very different from the one in which Jesus lived. But the more things change, the more they stay the same. If people posed challenges to Jesus, they will do so to us as well.

A disciple is not above his teacher, but every one when he is fully taught will be like his teacher (Luke 6:40).

In our religiously fragmented but highly interconnected world, people from countless perspectives pose challenges to the Faith every day—in conversations, through the mass media, and on the Internet. There is no escaping this daily onslaught.

The solution is to mount a daily defense—to respond to the many challenges that we, as believers, are presented with. Hence this book: It takes up a different challenge every day of the year (plus a bonus challenge for leap year), and shows how you can defend the Faith and give answers to those skeptical of it.

Each page is devoted to a single challenge, which is posed at the top of the page in the CHALLENGE section. The DEFENSE section that follows contains a brief summary of what you can say in response. Obviously, there is much more that can be said on each subject, but here we will cover the highlights—the key talking points. In some cases there will also be a TIP, which will frequently be a recommendation for a book where you can learn more.

Challenges to the Faith are often unexpected, and the ones in this book are arranged in a way that reflects that. Each day presents you with something new, often dealing with a very different subject, so there is constantly something fresh to learn and think about.

The book is designed so that no matter when in the year you first pick it up, you can start on Day 1 and read straight through for a whole year. It's also designed so that you can quickly find responses to challenges that people put to you. Just check the ALPHABETICAL INDEX in the back to find specific responses.

If the Faith is faced with many challenges today, the good news is that there are solid answers, so we should not be surprised or intimidated by them. Instead, we should be prepared. As St. Peter said:

> Have no fear of them, nor be troubled, but in your hearts reverence Christ as Lord. Always be prepared to make a defense to anyone who calls you to account for the hope that is in you, yet do it with gentleness and reverence (1 Pet. 3:14–15).

May God bless you and your efforts as you learn and defend his holy Faith.

—Jimmy Akin
May 13, 2016
Our Lady of Fátima

Abbreviations

CCC	*Catechism of the Catholic Church*
JD	*Joint Declaration on the Doctrine of Justification*
KJV	*King James Version*
LEB	*Lexham English Bible*
NABRE	*New American Bible: Revised Edition*
ST	*Summa Theologiae*

Spiritual or Religious?

CHALLENGE

"I consider myself spiritual rather than religious. Why isn't that enough?"

DEFENSE

Because God loves you and wants even better things for you.

When people say they are spiritual rather than religious, they frequently mean that, although they don't practice a specific religion, they recognize there is more to the world than matter; that it has a spiritual dimension. This is good! But it doesn't go very far. Wouldn't it be nice to know more about the world's spiritual dimension? In every field, having more knowledge is better, and it makes sense to ask if we can learn more about the world's spiritual dimension.

From a Christian perspective, we can learn more. God loves us and wants us to know him—not just have feelings or guesses. When he created the universe, God left evidence allowing us to learn certain things about him: "Ever since the creation of the world his invisible nature, namely, his eternal power and deity, has been clearly perceived in the things that have been made" (Rom. 1:20).

He also left evidence in the human heart: "With [man's] openness to truth and beauty, his sense of moral goodness, his freedom and the voice of his conscience, with his longings for the infinite and for happiness, man questions himself about God's existence. In all this he discerns signs of his spiritual soul. The soul, the seed of eternity we bear in ourselves, irreducible to the merely material, can have its origin only in God" (CCC 33).

Further, God has entered history, communicating with us through his prophets and, most importantly, through his Son, Jesus.

Apologetics examines and presents the evidence showing God has communicated with us, and its ultimate purpose is to help us discover God and the joy and happiness he wants us to have. "The desire for God is written in the human heart, because man is created by God and for God; and God never ceases to draw man to himself. Only in God will he find the truth and happiness he never stops searching for" (CCC 27).

Or, as St. Augustine put it: "You have made us for yourself, and our heart is restless until it rests in you" (*Confessions* 1:1:1).

TIP

A good book on the evidence for faith is the *Handbook of Catholic Apologetics* by Peter Kreeft and Ronald Tacelli.

A Stone Too Heavy for God to Lift?

CHALLENGE

"The Christian idea of an omnipotent God is logically contradictory. Can God make a stone so heavy he can't lift it? If he can then there is something he can't do (lift the stone), but if he can't, then there's also something he can't do (make the stone)."

DEFENSE

To accuse others of a logical contradiction, first you must understand their idea correctly. Otherwise you commit the straw man fallacy. This objection misunderstands omnipotence.

The term "omnipotent" means "all-powerful" (Latin, *omnis*, "all," and *potens*, "powerful"). This is often said to mean that God can "do anything," but this statement is ambiguous, and the ambiguity leads to the objection above.

What does it mean to say God can do anything? If "anything" means anything *that you can say,* then the idea would involve logical contradictions. You could, for example, say that God could make four-sided triangles, square circles, married bachelors, two-horned unicorns, and other entities whose definitions involve logical contradictions.

This is not what Christian theologians mean by omnipotence. Instead, they mean that God can do anything *that is logically possible*—that is, anything that *does not* involve a logical contradiction. This causes the objection to vanish, because if omnipotence excludes logical contradictions, then, by definition, it does not involve them.

It thus resolves the question of whether God can make a stone so heavy he can't lift it. By virtue of omnipotence, God has infinite, or unlimited, lifting power. There is no upper limit to what God can lift. Thus a stone too heavy for God to lift would have to have *more than infinite weight,* and the idea of "more than infinite" weight involves a logical contradiction.

Stones too heavy for an omnipotent being to lift fall in the same category as four-sided triangles and married bachelors. They contain logical contradictions and thus represent jibberish rather than logically possible entities.

TIP

For more, see St. Thomas Aquinas, ST I:25:3–4.

Changing God's Mind

CHALLENGE

"Why should we bother praying? If God is all-knowing, he knows what we need, and we can't change his mind because he's changeless."

DEFENSE

Prayer is not about giving God information or changing his mind. It is an activity he wants us to do because it draws us out of ourselves and builds relationships—with him and our fellow human beings. That's why he rewards it.

Jesus made the point that prayer is not about giving God information: "Your Father knows what you need before you ask him" (Matt. 6:8).

The reason God wants us to pray is that it keeps us from closing in on ourselves. He wants us to have a relationship with him—to think about him, to care about pleasing him, to love him. Humans build relationships by talking, and so God rewards us when we talk to him and relate to him in the ways we are able. He also wants us to care about one another and not to think exclusively about our own needs. Thus he rewards it when we pray for others.

This way, the people of God are built up through love and mutual concern. When we pray, we are drawn out of ourselves to care both about God and about our neighbor.

Because God already knows what we need, praying is not something that helps him. It helps us. It rescues us from thoughtlessness, and makes us better, more loving people.

It also does not change God's mind. It's true that he is outside of time and changeless, but this does not prevent him from knowing the prayers that we offer to him at particular moments in time and rewarding them.

The fact that God is changeless but gives gifts to those in time was noted by James: "Every good endowment and every perfect gift is from above, coming down from the Father of lights with whom there is no variation or shadow due to change" (James 1:17).

TIP

Notice how, by praying to God and on behalf of others, we learn to care about both, thus helping us fulfill the two great commandments: love of God and love of neighbor (Mark 12:28–34).

Why the Cross?

CHALLENGE

"The Crucifixion seems irrational. Couldn't an omnipotent God save us without Jesus dying on a cross?"

DEFENSE

God could have chosen another way to bring about the salvation of the world. According to the common view, he could simply have forgiven our sins and saved us without any earthly sacrifice. But there are reasons why he chose the Crucifixion.

By using the Crucifixion to accomplish the redemption, God drew on a theme that first-century Jews would have understood: sacrifice. In fact, this was something everybody in the ancient world understood. The impulse to sacrifice is found in cultures all over the world and is innate to human nature, providing a way for people everywhere to understand what Christ did for us.

In a sacrifice, people would bring a gift—often an animal—and offer it on an altar. The sacrifice could be a gesture of apology for having sinned or an act of thanks or reverence. Whatever its specific intent, it was meant in a general way to cultivate good relations with heaven.

In the Crucifixion, Jesus presented himself as a sacrifice on our behalf. Indeed, he was the sacrifice to which all other Jewish sin offerings pointed, "for it is impossible that the blood of bulls and goats should take away sins" (Heb. 10:4).

More fundamentally, God communicated important lessons to us. One is just how serious our sins are—given that it took the death of the Son of God to atone for them. He also showed us just how much he loves us in spite of our sins. "God shows his love for us in that while we were yet sinners Christ died for us" (Rom. 5:8; cf. CCC 604).

God also drew on a theme that had special meaning for Jews: Passover. At the founding of their nation, God led them out of slavery in Egypt through the sacrifice of the Passover lambs, when God's wrath passed over the Israelites. Now Jesus, "the Lamb of God" (John 1:29, 36), was sacrificed at Passover (John 19:14–16), so that God's wrath might pass over us and we might be led out of slavery to sin. Thus Paul can say, "Christ, our paschal lamb, has been sacrificed" (1 Cor. 5:7).

Sola Scriptura

CHALLENGE

"It is a foundational principle that you need to be able to prove your theological beliefs by Scripture alone, and Catholics can't do that."

DEFENSE

Sola scriptura may be a foundational principle of Protestantism, but not of Catholicism. Further, it does not meet its own test.

Catholics do not accept the principle of *sola scriptura* ("Scripture alone"), and so they have no need to justify their theological beliefs using only the Bible. In many apologetic discussions, it can be helpful to do so, since many Christian and non-Christian groups see Scripture, or parts of it, as an important source of information, and its role as a commonly recognized authority is helpful. But one should not fall into the trap of thinking that Catholics have that obligation.

It can also be helpful in discussions with Protestants to directly challenge *sola scriptura*, because it has a serious problem: If theological beliefs need to be proved by Scripture alone, then so does *sola scriptura*. Its advocates need to produce verses showing that every theological belief must be provable by Scripture alone, and this cannot be done. There are verses its advocates sometimes appeal to (some of which we deal with elsewhere; see Days 50 and 177), but none says or implies what is claimed.

We can point out that all such verses were written before the canon was finished. At that time, *sola scriptura* was not in operation, for Christians were bound to accept the teaching of the apostles, whether it was written or oral (2 Thess. 2:15; cf. 1 Cor. 11:2). Consequently, for a verse to prove *sola scriptura*, it would need to indicate that there would be a shift in how Christians form their beliefs in the postapostolic age.

Yet there are no verses that say things such as, "After we apostles are dead, everything we said orally loses its authority; you are to look only to Scripture," or, "We apostles have agreed to make sure all of our teachings are written down in Scripture, so use only that to settle theological questions after we are gone."

In the absence of verses saying or implying these things, *sola scriptura* does not meet its own test and thus is a self-refuting doctrine.

Miracles and Probability

CHALLENGE

"By definition, miracles are improbable. In any given instance it's very unlikely that a miracle will occur. The greater probability is the non-miraculous. We should accept the greatest probability, so we should not believe in miracles."

DEFENSE

This assumes we should refuse to believe a miracle has happened without looking at the evidence.

Supernatural interventions are not improbable by definition. They could be happening all around us, but with such regularity that we don't identify them as miracles.

Interventions we would recognize as miracles (water turning to wine, loaves multiplying, the dead rising) are rare, but this is no reason to conclude that they never happen or we should never believe in them.

For example, identical twins also are rare. For every thousand births, only about three will involve identical twins. But the fact that identical twins are rare does not mean they are not born or that we should disbelieve in them.

It is true that, if we have no further knowledge, the likelihood is that a pregnancy will *not* involve identical twins. If we had to place a bet in advance, the safe bet would be against twins. But after the birth has happened, the thing to do is to look at the evidence and see whether identical twins were born.

Miracles may be less common than twins, but the same principles apply. If we are asked whether a miracle will occur at a particular place and time, and we know nothing else, then the odds are low. If we had to place a bet, the smart bet would be that one will not. But if we know more than that, we have to incorporate that information into our assessment. If a miracle is reported to have happened, we should ask what evidence there is that it did. Uncommon events do happen, and we need to look at the evidence.

TIP

As an exercise, see how many improbable events you can name that actually happened. This will let you expand on this defense in the future.

Suffering with a Purpose

CHALLENGE

"Why would a good God allow physical evils like suffering and death?"

DEFENSE

We don't have full answers to the problem of evil in this life, but we can see that at least *some* physical evils are helpful.

God can tolerate some physical evils because good comes from them. According to John Paul II: "Certain forms of physical 'evil' . . . belong to the very structure of created beings, which by their nature are contingent and passing, and therefore corruptible. Besides, we know that material beings are in a close relation of interdependence as expressed by the old saying: 'the death of one is the life of another.' So then, in a certain sense death serves life" (General Audience, June 4, 1986).

We see this in the natural world, such as when a lion kills a zebra so that it can eat. The death of the zebra serves the life of the lion. In the same way, the living things we humans eat (whether plants or animals) sustain our lives.

The *Catechism* says:

> With infinite wisdom and goodness God freely willed to create a world "in a state of journeying" towards its ultimate perfection. In God's plan this process of becoming involves the appearance of certain beings and the disappearance of others, the existence of the more perfect alongside the less perfect, both constructive and destructive forces of nature. With physical good there exists also physical evil as long as creation has not reached perfection (CCC 310).

Pain can also play a valuable role in our lives. Some people suffer from congenital insensitivity to pain, and its results can be dramatic, even fatal. Physical pain serves as a warning system, and people without a proper pain response can be severely injured or killed. Even emotional pain can be useful. The emotion of fear alerts us to danger and motivates us to take steps to avoid it.

TIP

Although some suffering plays a valuable role in the present life, this doesn't exhaust the problem of evil. Unlike the above examples, some suffering serves no obvious purpose (see the question for Day 38). The above answer, however, provides a partial explanation of why God tolerates some suffering and how he brings good out of it.

Christianity and the Existence of Jesus

CHALLENGE

"What evidence do we have that Jesus even existed?"

DEFENSE

Apart from the references to Jesus in early Christian and non-Christian literature, the appearance and rapid spread of Christianity provide powerful evidence for the existence of Jesus.

Josephus indicates Jesus was a Jew in first-century Palestine (thus Jesus' "brother" was executed in A.D. 62; *Antiquities of the Jews* 20:9:1).

Tacitus says Jesus was "executed during the rule of Tiberius by the procurator Pontius Pilate" (*Annals* 15:44). Pilate's tenure was A.D. 26 to 36.

Writing around A.D. 110, Pliny the Younger notes he interviewed people in his province of Bithynia (in modern Turkey) who had been Christians twenty years earlier (c. 90). The movement had made such an impact on his territory that the sellers of animals for pagan sacrifices had suffered an economic downturn and pagan temples were almost deserted (*Letters* 96).

Tacitus and Suetonius speak of Christians in Rome during the reign of Nero (A.D. 54–68; *Annals* 15:44; *Lives of the Caesars*, "Nero" 16), and Suetonius appears to refer to them being there under Claudius (A.D. 41–54; *Lives of the Caesars*, "Claudius" 25).

Other first- and second-century sources show that the movement was in Syrian Antioch, Ephesus, Corinth, Thessalonica, Philippi, and many other locations.

All sources agree that Christianity was a new movement, beginning in the first half of the first century. Christian sources even admit it did not begin until the fifteenth year of Tiberius (cf. Luke 3:1), or A.D. 29.

This means that Christianity spread *extremely* quickly, and it did so in an age without telecommunications, without the printing press, and when travel was difficult and dangerous. The only way for a movement to spread that quickly, under those conditions, is if it was both organized and driven by a powerful missionary impulse.

Early Christian writings reveal quite a bit about how the movement was organized. Its initial leaders were known as "apostles," which in Greek means "sent ones." So who did the sending? The sources we have are unanimous: Jesus of Nazareth. The apostles were sent by him.

In view of the rapid spread of Christianity, there is no reason to doubt this. Movements have founders, and they preserve the memory of their founder. The appearance and growth of Christianity thus point to the existence of Jesus.

Traditions of Men versus Sacred Tradition

CHALLENGE

"Catholics should not depend on Tradition. Jesus says Tradition makes void the word of God (Matt. 15:6; cf. Mark 7:8, Col. 2:8)."

DEFENSE

Jesus did say that the Pharisees nullified God's word for the sake of their tradition, but he did not condemn tradition itself. Indeed, Scripture's attitude toward apostolic Tradition is positive.

Tradition is important to every person and every group of people. It represents our education, our culture, everything that has been handed on to us from previous generations. Tradition is—by definition—what is handed on. The term comes from the Latin word *tradere*, "to hand on."

Some traditions, like some of the Pharisees' traditions, can be harmful. Others, being of merely human origin, are not authoritative. Scripture lumps both under the heading "traditions of men."

But not all traditions are in this category. For Christians, the Faith handed down to us from Christ and the apostles is of unparalleled importance. In Catholic circles, this passing down of the Faith is referred to as "Sacred Tradition" or "Apostolic Tradition" (with a capital "T" to distinguish it from other, lesser, "lowercase" traditions).

Initially, the apostles handed on the Faith orally—by preaching—but with time some of them and their associates wrote the New Testament documents, which together with the Old Testament comprise Sacred Scripture. Since Scripture has been handed down to us from the apostles, it is the inspired, written part of Sacred Tradition.

Whether or not an item of Tradition was written in Scripture, it is still important and binding. Thus the New Testament exhorts the reader to maintain Sacred Tradition (1 Cor. 11:2; 2 Thess. 3:6), and in 2 Thessalonians 2:15, Paul tells his readers to "stand firm and hold to the Traditions which you were taught by us, either by word of mouth or by letter."

Another noteworthy passage is 2 Timothy 2:2, in which Paul instructs his protégé, "what you have heard from me before many witnesses entrust to faithful men who will be able to teach others also." Bearing in mind that Paul wrote this letter just before he died (cf. 2 Tim. 4:6–8), Paul is exhorting the transmission of Sacred Tradition across generations of Christian leaders—from his generation, to Timothy's generation, to the ones that will follow.

The Religion of Your Parents

CHALLENGE

"Most people accept whatever religion they are raised in. This means there's no particular reason to believe in religion. Further, it would be unfair of God to damn people simply because they believed what their parents taught them to believe."

DEFENSE

The fact that people tend to accept the beliefs they are raised with does not give a reason to reject belief altogether. Also, God takes into account the way people are raised.

Children have a natural tendency to accept the beliefs they are taught by their parents and their culture. This is essential to our education, since we do not have the opportunity to personally verify the vast majority of our beliefs.

This is true across all subjects, not just religion. For example, people tend to accept the ideas about the natural world that are prevalent in their culture, but this does not mean they have a reason to disbelieve in the natural world or how it works. Rather, it means they have reason to accept what they have been taught unless and until a superior case is made for another view.

Similarly, people have a reason to accept the religion they were raised in unless and until they encounter a superior case for another religion. Christianity has nothing to fear in this regard. Of all religions, it has made perhaps the most comprehensive and thorough study of the arguments and evidences that support it—a field known as Christian apologetics. This book is one example of that.

If most people remain in the religion of their birth, it is because most do not undertake a detailed study of apologetics and thus do not encounter the powerful evidences for the Christian faith.

Nevertheless, God takes into account the background with which a person is raised. He does not automatically damn people because of what their parents taught them. The Church holds that "those who, through no fault of their own, do not know the gospel of Christ or his Church, but who nevertheless seek God with a sincere heart, and, moved by grace, try in their actions to do his will as they know it through the dictates of their conscience—those too may achieve eternal salvation" (CCC 847).

Science and the Supernatural

"Science cannot accept the supernatural. The natural world is all there is."

At best, this leads to a reductionistic understanding of science.
At worst, it reflects intellectual prejudice.

The term "nature" is often used to refer to the visible world we see around us (i.e., the world detectible by the senses and by scientific instruments). The supernatural then would be anything that falls outside of the visible world.

On this understanding, the assertion that science can't accept the supernatural would mean that science cannot deal with anything outside of the visible world. It would not mean, however, that there is nothing outside the visible world. Just because we can't detect something with the senses doesn't mean that it isn't real. There could be vast realms outside the visible world that would be inaccessible to science on this understanding.

Further, those realms might be capable of interacting with the visible world, which would pose a challenge for science. We might be able to see visible effects of causes in the non-visible world, but science would not be able to explain the effects by their true causes, which it would be forbidden to discuss.

Sometimes people use "nature" to refer to everything that exists. On this understanding, one could assert that *nature* is all there is, but this also would not mean that the *visible world* is all that exists. There still could be vast realms not accessible to the senses. They might even interact with the visible world. Using "nature" to refer to everything that exists just reclassifies things that would otherwise be called supernatural as exotic parts of nature.

The claim that the visible world is all that exists is simply an assertion. It is not a scientific claim because it cannot be verified by science. If science, by its nature, is limited to examining the visible universe, then there is no way to perform a set of observations and experiments proving that there are no realms outside the visible universe. The assertion that only the visible world is real thus would be a matter of unscientific prejudice against the idea there is anything outside the visible world.

"The Word Was God"

CHALLENGE

"Jesus is not God. John 1:1 shouldn't be translated 'the Word was God' but 'the Word was a god.'"

DEFENSE

What that Gospel says about Jesus makes this translation impossible.

It is true that Greek lacks the indefinite article ("a," "an"), and so translators must decide whether to add it in English. However, one cannot simply assert that it should be added in a particular case. One needs proof from the context.

Considered apart from its context, the Greek phrase normally translated "the Word was God" (*theos ēn ho logos*) could be rendered a number of ways. However, the thing that determines which translations are accurate is the context—what else the Gospel of John has to say that has a bearing on the meaning of this phrase. When this is taken into account, it is clear that any translation of John 1:1 that would reduce the Word to the status of a created being, such as a finite "god" inferior to the true God, is inaccurate. The Gospel of John repeatedly emphasizes the full divinity of Christ.

John is explicit about the matter when he states, "This was why the Jews sought all the more to kill him, because he not only broke the sabbath but also called God his Father, making himself equal with God" (John 5:18).

Similarly, when Jesus is asked how he could have seen Abraham, he replies, "Before Abraham was, I AM" (John 8:58), using the same Greek phrase for "I AM" (*egō eimi*) used in the Greek Old Testament when God declares his name to Moses and tells him, "Say this to the people of Israel, 'I AM has sent me to you'" (Exod. 3:14). Jesus' audience understood that he was claiming to be God, "so they took up stones to throw at him" (John 8:59).

Later Jesus declares, "I and the Father are one" (John 10:30).

And after the Resurrection, Thomas declares him to be, "My Lord and my God!" (John 20:28). This reference is particularly significant, because it serves as the bookend for John 1:1's statement "the Word was God." The two declarations frame the Gospel of John's teaching on Jesus' divinity.

TIP

For a technical discussion of the grammar of the Greek phrase translated "the Word was God," see Daniel Wallace, *Greek Grammar Beyond the Basics*, 255–70.

Original Sin and Justice

CHALLENGE

"Original sin is unjust. How could a good God punish us for something done by our ancestors?"

DEFENSE

This misunderstands what original sin is. God doesn't punish us because of what Adam did.

Genesis 1 and 2 depict God creating mankind in a state that was "very good" (Gen. 1:31). "As long as he remained in the divine intimacy, man would not have to suffer or die. The inner harmony of the human person, the harmony between man and woman, and finally the harmony between the first couple and all creation, comprised the state called 'original justice'" (CCC 376). But man turned away from union with God through sin, which Genesis depicts as the act of eating the forbidden fruit (CCC 390).

If Adam and Eve had remained in original justice, their descendants would have been born in it as well. However, having lost this through sin, their descendants are born deprived of original holiness and justice. Thus we are said to be born in original sin.

However, we are not personally guilty of Adam's sin, and God does not hold us accountable for it. "Original sin is called 'sin' only in an analogical sense: It is a sin 'contracted' and not 'committed'—a state and not an act" (CCC 404). "Original sin does not have the character of a personal fault in any of Adam's descendants. It is a deprivation of original holiness and justice" (CCC 405).

Although it is not a personal fault, original sin has consequences for human nature, which is "wounded in the natural powers proper to it, subject to ignorance, suffering, and the dominion of death, and inclined to sin—an inclination to evil that is called concupiscence" (CCC 405).

The situation is like that of a rich man who gambles away his fortune and is unable to pass it on to his children. The gambler was personally at fault, but his children experience the deprivation and poverty that his actions brought about. In the same way, God gave our first parents an abundance of spiritual riches that they lost through their own folly. The fault was theirs, but we are born in spiritual poverty and out of divine intimacy.

Jesus as Messiah

"Why should I believe that Jesus is the Jewish Messiah?"

DEFENSE

The answer depends on one's viewpoint.

If one is already a believer in the Hebrew Scriptures, then one can point to various prophecies that were fulfilled by Jesus. There have been a number of understandings of the Messiah in Judaism, which makes the study of Messianic prophecy complex and beyond the scope of these daily entries.

However, it is worth pointing to a particular prophecy that was fulfilled through Jesus. The prophets declare that "the earth shall be full of the knowledge of the Lord as the waters cover the sea" (Isa. 11:9; cf. Hab. 2:14).

When these prophecies were given, the number of people who believed in the God of Abraham was vanishingly small. The vast majority of people were polytheists, and the world was covered in pagan darkness.

Today, however, the situation is very different. Half of the human race worships the God of Abraham, and virtually everyone has heard of him. By comparison to the days of the prophets, the world is now covered by the knowledge of the Lord the way the waters cover the sea.

This did not happen by accident. It is part of God's plan.

It also did not happen apart from Jesus of Nazareth. It was through him that the nations came to worship the God of Abraham. Consequently, he has a very prominent role in God's plan.

This role is linked to his claim to be the Messiah. Without this claim, the nations would not have come to believe in God through him, and he is the single most successful messianic claimant in history, such that even those who do not believe in him routinely refer to him as "Jesus Christ" (*Christos* being the Greek word for "Messiah"). As a result, his role as Messiah must be given serious and open-minded consideration.

If one is not yet a believer in the Hebrew Scriptures, or even if one is, a particularly striking proof of Jesus' role as Messiah is provided by his Resurrection. We have good evidence that this event happened (see Days 206–215), and just as miracles validate the ministries of prophets (see Day 78), this miracle validates Jesus' ministry and qualifies him to tell us what his role in God's plan is.

The Anointing of the Sick

CHALLENGE

"The sacrament of the anointing of the sick has no biblical basis; it is a human invention."

DEFENSE

The anointing of the sick is recorded in the Bible.

The practice of anointing the sick as a means of miraculous healing was already part of the Christian movement during the earthly ministry of Christ. Jesus performed many exorcisms and healings, and he commissioned the apostles to continue this miraculous ministry, using anointing as one of their methods. Thus in Mark we read how Jesus sent the Twelve on a preaching and miracle-working mission and "they cast out many demons, and anointed with oil many that were sick and healed them" (Mark 6:13).

The anointing of the sick continued to be used later in the apostolic age. Thus in the letter of James we read: "Is any among you sick? Let him call for the elders of the church, and let them pray over him, anointing him with oil in the name of the Lord; and the prayer of faith will save the sick man, and the Lord will raise him up; and if he has committed sins, he will be forgiven" (James 5:14–15).

It is this passage in particular from which the Church draws its understanding of the anointing of the sick: "The first grace of this sacrament is one of strengthening, peace, and courage to overcome the difficulties that go with the condition of serious illness or the frailty of old age. This grace is a gift of the Holy Spirit, who renews trust and faith in God and strengthens against the temptations of the evil one, the temptation to discouragement and anguish in the face of death. This assistance from the Lord by the power of his Spirit is meant to lead the sick person to healing of the soul, but also of the body if such is God's will. Furthermore, 'if he has committed sins, he will be forgiven'" (CCC 1520).

Note that James says that the sick person is to call for "the elders [Greek, *presbuteroi*] of the Church." *Presbuteros* is the Greek word from which the English word "priest" is derived. Since the anointing of the sick is part of the ministry of the *presbuteroi*, "only priests (bishops and presbyters) are ministers of the anointing of the sick" (CCC 1516).

The Practical Problems of *Sola Scriptura*

CHALLENGE

"God wants us to determine our theology by Scripture alone. Every Christian should read the Bible and decide for himself what's true."

DEFENSE

This is a view that couldn't have been entertained until the early 1500s. Until then, multiple practical problems prevented it.

Among the problems are these:

1. If every Christian is to read the Bible for himself and do the kind of study needed to decide delicate theological questions, then he must first *have* a Bible. But before the invention of the printing press (in the mid-1400s), Bibles had to be hand copied, and so they were fantastically expensive, costing far more than an ordinary person could afford. The widespread application of *sola scriptura* thus presupposes the invention of the printing press.

2. It also presupposes universal distribution of Bibles. Copies not only have to be made, they have to be put in the hands of the people who are to use them. This requires a society with a developed economy and infrastructure capable of producing the wealth needed to print and distribute millions of Bibles.

3. The recipients of these Bibles must be well educated. Illiterates can't do the kind of detailed study needed to settle numerous theological questions. *Sola scriptura* thus requires universal literacy among Christians, as well as a high level of education in the critical thinking skills needed to sort through technical arguments about biblical passages and theological propositions.

4. In addition to the Bibles, Christians would need to possess extensive scholarly support materials—commentaries, concordances, Bible dictionaries, Greek and Hebrew lexicons, and so on. No competent theologian would dream of doing his work without these resources, and they would be all the more necessary for a less-educated layman to accurately determine theological matters for himself.

Needless to say, these conditions didn't apply in the early Church or for most of Christian history (or for many Christians today).

It's easy to see why the Reformers—a group of well-educated individuals in the 1500s—got excited about the mass printing of Bibles and thought of having everyone decide his own theology. But this was not God's plan for the first Christians, or for most Christians, which means it's an anachronistic view that is not God's plan.

Abortion and Scripture

"Catholics shouldn't oppose abortion. The Bible never says
anything about abortion or when we get our souls."

This objection supposes that we need the
Bible to address the subject. We don't.

First, reason alone is capable of establishing that the unborn are innocent human beings and thus have a right to life (see Days 70, 88, 185,
191, and 202).

Second, Catholics are not Protestants and do not have to verify everything from Scripture alone (see Day 5; cf. CCC 2270–75).

Third, Scripture contains principles that apply to the question of
abortion. The most fundamental principle is in the Ten Commandments: "You shall not kill" (Exod. 20:13; Deut. 5:17). Though the
King James Version and older translations use the word "kill" in this
passage, the Hebrew term (*ratsakh*) has a more specialized meaning.
Thus many modern translations render the commandment "You shall
not murder" or "You shall not commit murder."

The Ten Commandments do not explicitly apply this principle to
unborn children, but the Bible recognizes that they are, in fact, children, and that they must be protected:

> When men strive together, and hurt a woman with child, so that
> there is a miscarriage [literally, "and her children go out"], and yet no
> harm follows, the one who hurt her shall be fined, according as the
> woman's husband shall lay upon him; and he shall pay as the judges
> determine. If any harm follows, then you shall give life for life, eye for
> eye, tooth for tooth, hand for hand, foot for foot (Exod. 21:22–24).

The fact that the unborn are, indeed, children—and that we ourselves were in our mother's wombs—comes out in a particularly
touching way in Scripture, such as when the Psalms declare:

> O Lord, you have searched me and known me! . . . For thou didst
> form my inward parts, thou didst knit me together in my mother's
> womb. I praise thee, for thou are fearful and wonderful (Ps. 139:1,
> 13–14; see also Job 31:14–15, Jeremiah 1:4–5).

Scripture also notes that the spirit is what keeps the body alive, so
that "the body apart from the spirit is dead" (James 2:26). Since a living human being is present from the moment of conception, the soul
is present from that time as well (cf. CCC 365).

The End of the World in the First Century?

CHALLENGE

"Early Christians believed that the world would end shortly after Jesus' ministry. It didn't. Therefore, Christianity is false."

DEFENSE

This overestimates belief in an imminent end. It also confuses hope and expectation with assertion.

The idea that the early Christians believed in an imminent end of the world has been exaggerated due to a misreading of key texts in the teaching of Jesus (see Days 69, 104, 154, and 167). Having said that, some did hope for or even expect an early end. Thus in 1 Thessalonians 4:17, Paul refers to "we who are alive" at the end, suggesting he hoped to be alive at the end. But he did not assert that he would be alive then. Elsewhere, he questioned whether he would be (Phil. 1:20–24, 2:17; cf. 2 Cor. 5:6–9), and by the end of his life he was certain he would not (2 Tim. 4:6–10).

This illustrates the difference between a hope or an expectation on the one hand and an assertion on the other. Early Christians like Paul may have entertained the hope that Christ would soon return, they may even have expected it, but this is not the same as asserting that it would happen then.

The Church holds that those things "asserted by the inspired authors or sacred writers must be held to be asserted by the Holy Spirit" (Vatican II, *Dei Verbum* 11), but things they merely hoped or expected and did not assert are not assertions of the Holy Spirit. As a result, Scripture can reveal the hopes and expectations of ancient writers without claiming that these would come to pass.

The book of Revelation also made it clear that a long period of time would pass before the end. Although the book stresses that most of its vision would take place soon (Rev. 1:1, 22:6), it also indicated a millennium (symbolic of a long period of time) would occur before the end (Rev. 20:1–6).

TIP

In chapter 2 of *Jesus of Nazareth*, vol. 2, Benedict XVI has an extended discussion of how the teaching of Jesus does not entail any particular time frame and points to a period of evangelizing the world before the end.

Peter's Sins

CHALLENGE

"Peter was not the first pope. Even if Jesus appointed Peter as leader of the apostles, he would have been disqualified later by his sins—particularly when he denied Jesus."

DEFENSE

Jesus foresaw Peter's denial, took it into account, and afterward confirmed him in his office.

Peter's denial was very grave. According to John, he denied being a disciple of Jesus (John 18:25). That was a public denial of the Faith (albeit an insincere one, since Peter did not abandon the Christian movement).

Despite this, Jesus had foreseen Peter's denial and told him in advance to take a pastoral role with respect to the other apostles after he repented, saying: "I have prayed for you that your faith may not fail; and when you have turned again, strengthen your brethren" (Luke 22:32). He did not say this to any of the others. Jesus thus envisioned Peter continuing to have a unique leadership role among the apostles even after his denial.

It is thus questionable whether Peter lost his leadership role even temporarily, but lest there be any doubt, Jesus afterward publicly confirmed Peter in office. In the presence of the other disciples, he asked Peter three times whether he loved him (mirroring the three denials). Jesus emphasized Peter's unique pastoral role among the disciples by initially asking him, "Do you love me more *than these*"—indicating the other disciples. When Jesus then told Peter three times to feed his sheep, the other disciples are included in that group (John 21:15–17).

If Peter's denial had cost him his office, it likely wouldn't have prevented him from being the leader of the apostles, but from being an apostle altogether. Yet this clearly did not happen. Peter continued to function as an apostle for decades. What's more, the New Testament continues to portray him as their leader. In Acts 1–12, where he served as the focus of the book, Peter is the leader and the central figure in almost every event recorded.

The Gospels also were written in the decades after Peter's denial, and the fact that three of the Gospels contain passages in which Jesus formally confers a leadership role on Peter (Matt. 16:18; Luke 22:32; John 21:15–17) indicates his leadership was still relevant in these decades.

Baptism and Salvation

CHALLENGE

"Baptism is not needed for salvation. It is a symbolic ritual that represents an inward change that has already taken place."

DEFENSE

The New Testament links baptism to salvation.

Baptism is not just a ritual. It communicates God's graces, such as the forgiveness of sins and the gift of the Holy Spirit. Thus Peter told the crowd on the day of Pentecost: "Repent, and be baptized every one of you in the name of Jesus Christ for the forgiveness of your sins; and you shall receive the gift of the Holy Spirit" (Acts 2:38).

Similarly, when he was converted to the Faith, Paul was told: "Rise and be baptized, and wash away your sins, calling on his name" (Acts 22:16).

In his letters, Peter explicitly connected baptism with salvation. Comparing baptism to how eight people were saved in Noah's Ark, he writes: "Baptism, which corresponds to this, now saves you, not as a removal of dirt from the body but as an appeal to God for a clear conscience, through the resurrection of Jesus Christ" (1 Pet. 3:21). Baptism does not save because it makes us physically cleaner, he says. Rather it "now saves you" because it involves "an appeal to God for a clear conscience," which is granted to us "through the resurrection of Jesus Christ."

The New Testament also indicates that baptism is the means by which we are regenerated or "born again." Jesus taught: "Truly, truly, I say to you, unless one is born anew, he cannot see the kingdom of God. . . . Unless one is born of water and the Spirit, he cannot enter the kingdom of God" (John 3:3, 5).

Paul agrees, saying that "he saved us, not because of deeds done by us in righteousness, but in virtue of his own mercy, by the washing of regeneration and renewal in the Holy Spirit" (Titus 3:5). Baptism thus places us in the state of salvation.

TIP

Baptism is a normative necessity but not an absolute one. To deliberately refuse baptism is to refuse salvation on the terms God offers it, but God can save those who are not baptized through no fault of their own (CCC 1257–61).

The Dating of John

CHALLENGE

"The Gospel of John is not historically reliable. It was written in the A.D. 90s and is markedly different in style and substance from the other Gospels."

DEFENSE

Actually, the Gospel of John is very historically reliable. Arguments to the contrary do not prove their case.

Even if John were written in the A.D. 90s, that's within sixty years of the events it records. Historically speaking, that is quite close to them, and it poses no barrier to the accuracy of John. But John likely was written earlier. It refers to architecture in Jerusalem as still standing (5:2), but Jerusalem was destroyed in A.D. 70. The Greek text of John 21:19 refers to the death by which Peter "*will glorify* God" (future tense), suggesting it was written before Peter's martyrdom in mid-67.

Whenever it was written, John is based on the testimony of an eyewitness (the "beloved disciple")—a point the text makes explicitly (21:24), for the ancients were as aware of the value of eyewitness testimony as we are.

John is written in a different literary style than the other Gospels, but this is not surprising. Each author has his own style, and John's is simply different than the others. This does not mean that he isn't interested in history. In fact, he records key historical facts about the chronology of Jesus' ministry that the other evangelists do not. Thus he mentions that at least three Passovers took place between the beginning and end of Jesus' ministry (2:13, 6:4, 11:55). Using this and other information, we are able to determine that Jesus' ministry lasted over three years.

John also contains significantly different material than the other Gospels, and the reason is very simple: John intends to *supplement* the other Gospels by recording things they didn't. In particular, John is supplementing Mark, and his Gospel is designed to interlock with Mark's.

TIP

For arguments on an early dating for John, see John A.T. Robinson, *Redating the New Testament* and *The Priority of John*. On the dating of Peter's martyrdom and the value of John's chronology, see Jack Finegan, *Handbook of Biblical Chronology*, 2nd ed., and Andrew E. Steinmann, *From Abraham to Paul*. On John's use of Mark, see Richard Bauckham, "John for Readers of Mark" in *The Gospels for All Christians*.

"Queen of Heaven" Condemned?

CHALLENGE

"Catholics should not regard Mary as the "Queen of Heaven." The Bible speaks of devotion to the Queen of Heaven and condemns it in unequivocal terms (Jer. 7:18, 44:17–19, 25)."

DEFENSE

The "Queen of Heaven" that Jeremiah refers to is not Mary. Therefore, he was not condemning Marian devotion.

The fact that Jeremiah was not referring to Mary is obvious, since he was writing around 600 B.C., not the first century A.D. In his day, the title "Queen of Heaven" was used to refer to various pagan deities. There were many such deities, as every pagan pantheon had a major, ruling deity who was depicted as a king in heaven. Correspondingly, various goddesses were regarded as queens in heaven.

Scholars are not sure which of these deities Jeremiah was referring to. It may have been a Canaanite goddess such as Ashtoreth (the wife of Ba'al), Asherah (the wife of El), or the warrior goddess Anat. Whichever he meant, it is clear that the condemned devotion was taking place in his own day, for Jeremiah refers to it as "what they are doing in the cities of Judah and in the streets of Jerusalem" (Jer. 7:17). He also promises that God's wrath would fall on members of his own generation as a result of this practice (Jer. 44:24–30).

The fact that "Queen of Heaven" was used for a pagan deity in Jeremiah's day does not mean that it can't also have a legitimate use. Words and phrases gain their meaning and connotations from the way they are used in a particular community, and they are not permanently ruined just because pagans once used them.

As noted, the same pagan pantheons that had Queens of Heaven also had Kings of Heaven, but that didn't stop the biblical authors from referring to the true God as a King (Ps. 29:10, 47:2, 6–7, 103:19; Isa. 6:5; Mal. 1:14; 1 Tim. 1:17; Rev. 15:3, etc.). They even used the exact title "King of Heaven" for him (Dan. 4:37; Tob. 1:18, 13:7).

The question thus is not whether "Queen of Heaven" was once used for a pagan deity, but whether it can have a different and appropriate sense. As we discuss elsewhere, it can (see Day 64).

Who Bought the Field of Blood?

CHALLENGE

"Matthew and Luke contradict each other. Matthew says that the Jewish priests bought the field of blood (Matt. 27:7–8), whereas Luke says that Judas Iscariot did (Acts 1:18–19)."

DEFENSE

Matthew and Luke are in fundamental agreement, and there are many ways the different attributions can be explained.

Both authors agree that Judas Iscariot's betrayal led to a field in the area of Jerusalem becoming known as the field of blood. Both also say that this field was paid for with the money that the chief priests had given Judas to betray Jesus. Both are thus agreed about the basic facts. How, then, can we account for the different way the two authors describe the purchase of the field?

One proposal is that the reference in Acts ("Now this man bought a field with the reward of his wickedness") is meant to be ironic rather than literal. It occurs in a speech that Peter is making, and it has been suggested that Peter merely meant that Judas got his just deserts. The money he originally meant to spend on himself ended up paying for a graveyard.

This is possible, but as we observe elsewhere (see Day 124), the biblical authors sometimes omit the agents who perform an action in order to bring out the significance of the principal figures with respect to whom the action is performed.

Thus we read that Moses built the tabernacle (2 Chron. 1:3) and Solomon built the temple (1 Kings 6:1–38), though in reality both were built by workmen acting on the leaders' behalf (Exod. 38:22–23; 1 Kings 7:13–45). Sometimes the agents get mentioned and sometimes they don't.

It is therefore possible that Matthew chose to mention the role of the priests: They were the agents who actually bought the field. By contrast, Luke wants to bring out the significance of the fact that it was Judas's money, without going into the mechanics of how the transaction was made. He thus omitted reference to the priests and only mentioned Judas.

Or this choice may have been made by someone earlier in the chain of tradition than Luke, who simply reported the tradition as he had it. Either way, it would be in keeping with the known practice of omitting agents to bring out the significance of the principals.

The Moral Argument

"Why shouldn't I believe in scientific materialism—the view that only physical matter and energy exist and that science is the key to all knowledge?"

DEFENSE

Because morality points us beyond the purely material and beyond what science is capable of establishing.

Moral values are real. Some things are objectively right and some are objectively wrong. Showing compassion for the poor and the weak is good; torturing babies for fun is evil. Belief in moral values is a human universal that exists in all cultures. It is built into human nature, and it cannot be suppressed. Even those who profess philosophies denying moral realism cannot maintain the pretense. They invariably slip back into realist thinking and language, expressing either appreciation for acts they sense are good or outrage at acts they sense are evil.

But science is not capable of establishing moral values (one of several limitations it has; see Day 333). It may be capable of studying what people *consider* morally good and bad, but it is not capable of establishing what *is* morally good and bad.

This is known in philosophy as the "is-ought problem." Certain statements are descriptive, describing the way the world *is*. Others are prescriptive, describing the way the world *ought* to be. Science is capable of investigating the former, but it does not have the ability to investigate the latter. As philosophers have often put it, you cannot derive an *ought*-statement from an *is*-statement.

The reason is that science involves an empirical methodology—one based on things that can be detected and measured by the physical senses or by physical extensions of them (e.g., telescopes, microscopes, radio wave detectors). But moral good and evil cannot be detected and measured in this way. They are non-empirical qualities. You cannot detect moral goodness with a technical instrument or torture someone in a lab and use an evil-ometer to determine how bad the act is.

We thus have good reason, based on the universal human belief in moral realism, to hold that moral values are objectively real, but they transcend the empirical. This shows that there is a transcendental realm that goes beyond the purely material and the abilities of science.

TIP

To help skeptics see the point, you may wish to propose examples of concrete things they will regard as morally evil.

Jesus' Celibacy

CHALLENGE

"The Church covered up Jesus's marriage to Mary Magdalene. The Gospel of Philip says they were married, and Jewish men didn't stay unmarried in Jesus' day, so he wouldn't have been celibate."

DEFENSE

There were celibate Jewish men in Jesus' day, and the evidence shows that Jesus stayed unmarried.

The Gospel of Philip is a second- or third-century writing in the Coptic language. It does not contain reliable history, and it does not describe Mary as Jesus' wife but as a companion, which she was, along with others (see Luke 8:1–3).

There are several women named Mary in the New Testament, and to keep them straight, they are referred to by various appellations. Normally, women were referred to by their male relations, as in "Mary, the mother of Jesus" (Acts 1:14). If Mary Magdalene were Jesus' wife, she would be referred to as "Mary, the wife of Jesus," but she is not. "Magdalene" is a place name. Magdala was a village by the Sea of Galilee, and she was "Mary of Magdala" (John 19:25, 20:1, 18). The fact that she is referred to by a place name indicates that she did not have a father, husband, or son whose name she could be called by.

There were celibate Jewish men in Jesus' time, as well as before. The prophet Jeremiah was one (Jer. 16:1–2). In the first century, celibacy was practiced among Jews both by individuals (*Life of Josephus* 2) and among groups such as the Theraputae (Philo, *On the Contemplative Life* 3[21]), the Essenes (Philo, *Hypothetica* 11:14; Josephus, *Antiquities* 18:1:5, *War*, 2:8:2), and the Christians (see Day 92). Jesus recommended celibacy as a spiritual discipline ("for the sake of the kingdom of heaven") to those who could accept it (Matt. 19:11–12). It would be surprising for Jesus to advocate celibacy this way if he did not practice it.

The New Testament never speaks of Mary Magdalene, or any other individual, as the wife of Jesus. Instead, it speaks of the entire Church as his bride (2 Cor. 11:2–3; Eph. 5:21–32; Rev. 19:6–9, 21:1–2, 9–10). This is significant because the metaphor of the Church as the bride of Christ would not have arisen if Jesus were married to an individual woman and there were a literal "Mrs. Jesus" in the early Church.

The Book of Acts and History

CHALLENGE

"Acts is not a reliable account of the history of the early Church. It is a work of ideology."

DEFENSE

Acts is an extremely reliable history. Every historian has a point of view, and the fact that Luke was writing from a Christian point of view does not mean he was inaccurate.

The book of Acts is based on the evidence of eyewitnesses, like Luke's Gospel (Luke 1:2).

It is easy to tell who the eyewitnesses in Acts were: Peter is a major source for chapters 1 to 12, Paul for chapters 13 to 28, Philip for chapter 8, and Priscilla and Aquila for chapter 18. Luke himself was an eyewitness for what scholars call the "we" passages, where the narration switches from third person to first, describing what "we" did (16:10–17, 20:5–15, 21:1–18, 27:1–28:16).

Luke's attention to detail is shown in many ways. For example, in chronicling the travels of Paul, he gives specific information about the time it took to arrive at different locations. This information is accurate, and it could not have simply been looked up in a reference work in the ancient world. This suggests Luke or someone in Paul's circle kept a travel diary. The fact that Luke does not give parallel information about travel times in the first part of the book, when Peter dominates the narrative, shows that Luke was faithful to his sources. He used the information they provided and did not invent such details.

The archaeologist Sir William Ramsay, initially a skeptic of Acts, reviewed the evidence and concluded:

> Luke is a historian of the first rank; not merely are his statements of fact trustworthy; he is possessed of the true historic sense; he fixes his mind on the idea and plan that rules in the evolution of history; and proportions the scale of his treatment to the importance of each incident. He seizes the important and critical events and shows their true nature at greater length, while he touches lightly or omits entirely much that was valueless for his purpose. In short, this author should be placed along with the very greatest of historians (*The Bearing of Recent Discovery on the Trustworthiness of the New Testament*, chapter 18).

TIP

See also Ramsay's book *St. Paul the Traveller and Roman Citizen*.

The Language of the Deuterocanonicals

CHALLENGE

"The deuterocanonical books don't belong in Scripture. They are not written in Hebrew, the language of the Old Testament."

DEFENSE

The language that a book was written in doesn't determine whether it's Scripture.

Hebrew was the national language of the Israelites for much of their history, and many Old Testament books were written in it, but the Israelites' language changed over time. Sometimes it changed through the incorporation of loanwords from other languages. Thus we find Egyptian, Akkadian, and Persian loanwords in books of Scripture written when these cultures had influence in Israel.

During the Babylonian exile (sixth century B.C.), when Jews were ruled by Aramaic-speakers, Hebrew fell out of popular use and Aramaic came into use; following the conquests of Alexander the Great (fourth century B.C.), Greek came into use by Jews—particularly among those living among Greek-speakers.

These developments led to the translation of the Hebrew Scriptures, first orally into Aramaic, and later in written form, in works known as the *targums*. They were also translated into Greek with the appearance of the *Septuagint*.

Scripture also began to be written in these languages. Ezra contains extensive passages from letters in Aramaic (Ezra 4:8–6:18, 7:12–26), much of Daniel is written in Aramaic (Dan. 2:4b–7:28), and the New Testament is in Greek.

The deuterocanonicals were written during this time of linguistic transition, and they reflect that. Deuterocanonicals written in Hebrew include Sirach (see the translator's prologue; also, versions in that language have been found), Baruch, and 1 Maccabees (noted by Origen and Jerome). Judith and Tobit were both written either in Hebrew or Aramaic (fragments of Tobit in both survive, and Jerome used an Aramaic version in composing the Vulgate). The deuterocanonical portions of Daniel were originally written in Hebrew or Aramaic, and the deuterocanonical portions of Esther were partly written in Hebrew or Aramaic and partly in Greek. 2 Maccabees was written in Greek, though it includes two prefatory letters that were likely originally in Aramaic. Finally, Wisdom was written in Greek.

Ultimately, it is divine inspiration, not original language, that determines whether a book is Scripture. If Hebrew was required, all the New Testament and even some parts of protocanonical Old Testament books would have to be struck.

The Holy Spirit Is a Person

CHALLENGE

"The Holy Spirit is not a person. Instead, it is the active power that God uses to accomplish his will. It's an impersonal force—like radio waves."

DEFENSE

Contrary to this view of the Jehovah's Witnesses, Scripture indicates that the Holy Spirit is a person, not an impersonal force.

Impersonal forces don't know things or make choices, but the Holy Spirit does both. He knows the thoughts of God (1 Cor. 2:11), and he chooses how spiritual gifts will be distributed (1 Cor. 12:11). The Holy Spirit thus has the personal attributes of intellect and will.

Scripture refers to the Holy Spirit as a Paraclete (Greek *parakletos*; see John 14:26; cf. 15:26, 16:7–8). This term, often translated as "Comforter," "Counselor," or "Advocate," refers to a *person* who is called to aid one, especially in legal settings. Scripture also speaks of Jesus, who is unmistakably a person, as a Paraclete (1 John 2:1).

Impersonal forces cannot communicate, but Scripture refers to the Holy Spirit communicating (Acts 5:32, 20:23, 21:11, 1 Tim. 4:1). Sometimes the Holy Spirit is directly quoted (Acts 8:29, 10:19, 21:11; Rev. 14:13). The Holy Spirit is even quoted using the personal pronoun *I*: "While they were worshiping the Lord and fasting, the Holy Spirit said, 'Set apart for me Barnabas and Saul for the work to which I have called them'" (Acts 13:2).

This is particularly significant because the Holy Spirit is directly quoted in the historical narrative of Acts. He is quoted just like other persons, and the quotation cannot be dismissed as symbolic. This is straightforward historical narrative.

Scripture thus depicts the Holy Spirit with intellect and will, as a person who—like Jesus—assists Christians, and as a person who communicates and does so using the personal pronoun *I*. The claim the Holy Spirit is an impersonal force is not supported by the text.

TIP

Jehovah's Witnesses deny that Christ is God. When they go door knocking, they're usually well coached on how to discuss their views on this, but they are less prepared to discuss the personhood of the Holy Spirit. This can be a fruitful topic of discussion, given the biblical evidence discussed above.

Spirituality and Organized Religion

"It is enough to simply be spiritual. There is no need to be religious or to belong to an organized religion."

This presupposes that we don't know which religion is true.

If we knew little about the supernatural world—perhaps simply that it exists—it might make sense to hold to only a general spirituality. However, if we know more, the situation changes. The more we know, the more we are obligated to believe. If we know enough to show that a particular religion is true, we are obligated by our knowledge of the truth to embrace that religion. And if the religion we know to be true is organized, we are obliged to embrace organized religion.

Individuals vary in what they know. Some may know only enough to justify a general spirituality, but this is not the case for everyone.

An extensive body of evidence supporting the Christian faith exists. This evidence is documented by the field known as Christian apologetics, and some of it is found in this book. Those aware of this evidence and the truth of the Christian faith are obliged to accept it. For them, merely being spiritual is not enough. They are obliged by their knowledge of the truth to become Christian.

Christianity is an organized religion and has been since the beginning. It was founded by Jesus, who appointed twelve apostles to be its first leaders (Matt. 10:1–4, Mark 3:13–19, Luke 6:12–16). They then appointed other leaders, and the Christian faithful have an obligation to respect their leaders (1 Thess. 5:12; Heb. 13:17).

Having more knowledge—and thus more truth—is good. We apply this principle in every other field, and it is true in religion and spirituality as well. The fact that God has revealed more about himself also gives us greater reason to love and appreciate him and what he has done for us.

Those who have only a general spirituality should consider: "Suppose it were possible to know more. Wouldn't you want to know? Wouldn't that be a good thing?" Asking these questions can be an invitation to study the Christian faith and the evidence supporting it.

A Continuing Papacy

CHALLENGE

"Even if we admit that Peter was leader of the Twelve, and thus of the Church in Jesus' absence, there's no reason to infer that his office would be passed on in future generations."

DEFENSE

The biblical background to Peter's office—as well as common sense—indicate his leadership function would continue.

When Jesus conferred Peter's leadership function on him in Matthew 16:18, he said he would give him the keys of the kingdom. This invokes an Old Testament background that informs the nature of Peter's office. Evangelical scholar F.F. Bruce writes:

> And what about the "keys of the kingdom"? The keys of a royal or noble establishment were entrusted to the chief steward or major domo; he carried them on his shoulder in earlier times, and there they served as a badge of the authority entrusted to him. About 700 B.C. an oracle from God announced that this authority in the royal palace in Jerusalem was to be conferred on a man called Eliakim: "I will place on his shoulder the key to the house of David; what he opens no one can shut, and what he shuts no one can open" (Isa. 22:22). So in the new community that Jesus was about to build, Peter would be, so to speak, chief steward (Walter Kaiser, et al., *Hard Sayings of the Bible*, on Matt. 16:18–19).

Isaiah 22:15–25 involves more than Eliakim. It is a succession passage in which the current chief steward of the house of David—a man named Shebna—is to be replaced by Eliakim. This illustrates the ongoing nature of the office. It was not a temporary one. As long as the house of David endured, kings employed chief stewards to manage affairs on their behalf. This is part of the background to Peter's office. By appointing Peter the chief steward of the house of the New David, Jesus is instituting an office meant to exist as long as the house of the New David—i.e., the Church—exists.

Common sense also indicates this would be a continuing office. If Jesus deemed that his Church needed a central leader at the very beginning, when it was tiny and organizational demands were small, the need for this office would scarcely evaporate as the Church grew larger and organizational demands increased. The need for a leader would grow, and Jesus foresaw and planned for this.

Literal versus Non-literal Accounts

CHALLENGE

*"If you admit non-literal accounts into the Bible,
how do you know that it isn't all non-literal?"*

DEFENSE

Just because the Bible contains one kind of material doesn't mean
it can't contain other kinds, or that we can't tell the difference.

It would be the fallacy of hasty generalization to conclude that just because some passages are non-literal, they all must be. We don't make this kind of mistake with other literature. For example, if you walk into a library and notice that it has fiction shelves, you don't thereby conclude that *all* the books in the library must be fiction. Typical libraries have both fiction and nonfiction.

This analogy is closer to the Bible than may at first be obvious. Although the Bible is printed in a single volume today, it is a library of books that were written over a period of more than a thousand years. Like a modern library, the Bible has books of different types. Some are historical, some poetic, some prophetic, and some fall into other categories.

The different types of books do not prevent us from being able to distinguish them. In a modern library, a biography does not read like a novel, and in the Bible a poetic book does not read like a historical one. It is even possible to identify which passages of a book belong to which genres, as when the Gospels switch between biographical material about Jesus and his parables or his prophecies.

Sometimes the genre of a biblical book is not immediately obvious because of cultural differences between then and today. We have a native faculty for identifying the genres of books written in our own culture because we are used to reading them and we understand their cultural references. We have less of a faculty for identifying the genres of biblical books because they were written in a different culture, do not always follow the same conventions, and contain unfamiliar references.

However, a close study of the books and the culture they were written in can compensate for this. That is a major function of biblical scholarship. It is thus possible to identify the clues in a text that told the original audience what kind of literature they were reading (see Days 181, 196).

Calling Priests "Father"

CHALLENGE

"Catholics shouldn't call priests 'Father.' Jesus said, 'Call no man your father on earth, for you have one Father, who is in heaven' (Matt. 23:9)."

DEFENSE

Jesus was using hyperbole. Other passages in the New Testament indicate that Christ's ministers have a form of spiritual fatherhood.

Hyperbole is exaggeration to make a point. It is a common feature of biblical speech, as when Jesus says his disciples must "hate" their family members (Luke 14:26; a non-hyperbolic paraphrase of this passage is given in Matt. 10:37).

Jesus does not *literally* mean that you can't call anyone on earth "father." If he did, then we could not call our own biological fathers by this term, which would be absurd. It would also rob our understanding of God's Fatherhood of its earthly frame of reference (CCC 41, 238–39).

Jesus' point is that we must not confuse the type of Fatherhood God has—which is ultimate—with any other form of fatherhood, which is limited and provisional. He uses hyperbolic language to make this point in a striking, memorable way, but he does not expect hyperbole to be taken literally.

Thus other passages in the New Testament indicate that Christ's ministers have a role as spiritual fathers. Paul refers to how he became the spiritual father of the Corinthians (1 Cor. 4:14–15). He refers to the Galatians as his little children (Gal. 4:19) and to Timothy (1 Cor. 4:17; 1 Tim. 1:2, 18; 2 Tim. 1:2, 2:1), Titus (Titus 1:4), and Onesimus (Philem. 10) as his spiritual sons. Peter refers to Mark as his spiritual son (1 Pet. 4:13), and John refers to his readers as his little children (1 John 2:1; 3 John 4).

This is a standard mode of speech in the New Testament, shared by multiple authors, including eyewitnesses of Jesus (Peter and John). This widespread practice among the apostles further underscores the hyperbolic nature of Christ's statement.

The pattern also strongly indicates the role that Christ's ministers have as spiritual fathers, and if someone has a particular role, it is truthful to refer to him by that role. God does not object to that, and the Church follows the apostolic example when it refers to the spiritual fatherhood of priests.

John the Baptist and Reincarnation

CHALLENGE

"John the Baptist was the reincarnation of the prophet Elijah. When the disciples ask Jesus why the scribes say that Elijah must come before the Messiah, Jesus says he already had come. 'Then the disciples understood that he was speaking to them of John the Baptist' (Matt. 17:13). Also, Luke says John the Baptist will have the spirit of Elijah (Luke 1:17)."

DEFENSE

John the Baptist functioned symbolically as a new Elijah, but he denied actually being Elijah in person (John 1:21).

The New Testament repeatedly states that we will be resurrected, not reincarnated. Jesus' Resurrection is recorded in all four Gospels (Matt. 28:6–7; Mark 16:6, 14; Luke 24:5, 34; John 21:14), and it sets the pattern for ours (1 Cor. 6:14). Thus he is referred to as "the firstborn of the dead" (Col. 1:18; Rev. 1:5). The New Testament is emphatic about our resurrection (1 Cor. 15), stating that "it is appointed for men to die once, and after that comes judgment" (Heb. 9:27).

In Matthew, when the disciples ask their question about Elijah, they have just seen Jesus transfigured along with Moses and Elijah (Matt. 17:1–9). Elijah—not John the Baptist—had just appeared to them, and they were wondering if this was the fulfillment of the prophecy that Elijah would return before the Messiah (Mal. 4:5–6).

John the Baptist could not be the reincarnation of Elijah because Elijah never died. Instead, he was taken up to heaven in a whirlwind (2 Kings 2:1–15). At that time, Elijah's servant, Elisha, asked that he be allowed to inherit a double portion of Elijah's spirit, which he did (2 Kings 2:10–11, 15). Elisha could not have been the reincarnation of Elijah because they lived at the same time. For Elisha to inherit a double portion of Elijah's spirit meant that he was able to inherit Elijah's role as a prophet; he had the same prophetic spirit, not the same individual soul.

When Luke's Gospel says John the Baptist "will go before [Jesus] in the spirit and power of Elijah" (Luke 1:17), it is saying that John the Baptist will inherit Elijah's function and strength as prophet the way Elisha did.

Whom Did Jesus Pray To?

CHALLENGE

"On various occasions in the Gospels, Jesus prays (e.g., Matt. 26:36; Luke 3:21; John 11:41). If Jesus was God, this makes no sense. How could he pray to himself?"

DEFENSE

He wasn't praying to himself. He was praying to his Father.

People do talk to themselves from time to time, but this is not what Jesus was doing.

The Father, the Son, and the Holy Spirit are each God, but they are distinct, divine persons. The doctrine of the Trinity is that there is one God in three persons.

Consequently, it was natural for Jesus as one divine person to speak to his Father as another divine person—at least after Jesus became incarnate as a man and took on human modes of communication.

By praying, he was not giving the Father information that the Father did not already have. The same is true of us when we pray, as Jesus pointed out (Matt. 6:8). Prayer is not about giving God information, but about relating to him in a way suited to human nature (see Day 3). Having taken on human nature, it was natural for Jesus to relate to God in this manner. In doing so, he also set an example for us.

The passages in which Jesus prays are useful for showing the error of certain heresies that misunderstand the Trinity.

In the third century, a priest named Sabellius taught that there is only one person in the Godhead, and that the Father, Son, and Holy Spirit are not distinct persons but modes in which that single, divine person acts. In the ancient Church, this view was known as Sabellianism or modalism.

In the twentieth century, a similar view came to be taught in certain Pentecostal circles. "Oneness Pentecostals" hold to a "oneness doctrine," which agrees with Sabellianism that there is only a single, divine person in the Godhead.

The passages in which Jesus prays to the Father show the error of these views, since they illustrate the fact that the two are distinct persons and thus that there is more than one person in the Godhead.

How Did the Field of Blood Get Its Name?

CHALLENGE

"Matthew and Luke contradict each other. Matthew says the field of blood got its name because it was bought with blood money (Matt. 27:6–7), but Luke says it was because people knew that Judas died a gruesome death there (Acts 1:18–19)."

DEFENSE

Names can have more than one significance, and the two explanations are compatible.

The fact that Matthew and Luke record different expressions of the tradition regarding Judas's fate indicate that both were in circulation.

Some people—aware of Matthew's tradition—knew the priests bought the field and called it "field of blood" because it was bought with blood money. Others—aware of Luke's tradition—knew about Judas's bloody fate and called it "field of blood" for that reason. Some Jerusalemites may have been aware of both versions—like modern readers are—and called it "field of blood" for *both* reasons.

There are parallels to this elsewhere in the Bible. The biblical authors and their audiences often saw a single name as having more than one significance.

For example, the name of the city Be'er-sheva can mean "Well of the Seven" or "Well of the Oath," and the author of Genesis preserves more than one tradition regarding its significance. He notes that at this location Abraham dug a well, gave Abimelech seven lambs, and swore an oath with Abimelech (Gen. 21:30–32). He also notes that Isaac later dug a well and swore an oath with Abimelech there (Gen. 26:31–33). Ancient readers of Genesis were thus aware of both traditions and saw them as complementary explanations for the name of Be'er-sheva: It was called that for *both* reasons.

Similarly, the field of blood was so called *both* because it was bought with blood money and because of Judas's death. (Note that Luke says Judas bought a field, that he died a bloody death, and that people thus called the place "field of blood," but he doesn't say Judas died there. He may or may not have.)

One explanation would have originated first, but both were in circulation in the first century, and both contributed to why people called the field what they did.

Do the Saints Pray for Us?

CHALLENGE

*"Catholics should not ask the saints for intercession.
We have no evidence they pray for us."*

DEFENSE

We have evidence the saints pray for us, including Scripture.

First, we may infer from the fact that the saints are in heaven that they would pray for us. Being in heaven means being united with God, who is love (1 John 4:8–9, 16). When united with God, we will be transformed to be like him (Rom. 8:29; 1 Cor. 15:49–52; 2 Cor. 3:18; 2 Pet. 1:4; 1 John 3:2), for "nothing unclean shall enter" the heavenly city (Rev. 21:27).

Being thus transformed by the love of God, the saints are filled with love and so care about others. It is natural when you care about someone to pray to God for that person. We can thus infer that, just as God loves us and provides for us, the saints love and pray for those on earth.

We also have direct evidence of their intercession in Scripture. Judah Maccabee had a vision of two men who had died. The first was the former high priest Onias, and in the vision, "With outstretched arms Onias was praying for the entire Jewish nation" (2 Macc. 15:12). When he saw the second man, Judah was told, "This is God's prophet Jeremiah, who loves the Jewish people and offers many prayers for us and for Jerusalem, the holy city" (2 Macc. 15:14).

2 Maccabees is not in the Protestant canon, but it is in the Catholic canon, so it is legitimate for Catholics to appeal to it to inform their faith. Even for Protestants, 2 Maccabees attests the pre-Christian Jewish belief in the intercession of the saints.

The book of Revelation, in the Protestant and Catholic canons, also shows the saints and angels interceding in heaven. In Revelation 5:8, we see the twenty-four elders, who appear to represent the leaders of the people of God in heaven, offering incense to God, which we are told represents the prayers of the saints. In Revelation 8:3–4, we see an angel offer incense to God, incense mingled "with the prayers of all the saints upon the golden altar" in heaven. Guardian angels also intercede (Matt. 18:10).

One or Two in the Gospels?

CHALLENGE

"How can you trust the Gospels when they can't even agree on whether Jesus exorcized one demoniac or two, healed one blind man or two, rode on one animal or two, or had his Resurrection announced by one angel or two?"

DEFENSE

These incidents are not contradictions; they are reports that mention different details.

It is true the Gospels sometimes report an incident and mention only a single demoniac (Mark 5:2; Luke 8:27), blind man (Mark 8:22–23, 10:46; Luke 18:35), animal (Mark 11:2; Luke 19:30; John 12:14), or angel (Matt. 28:2; Mark 16:5), while other reports mention two demoniacs (Matt. 8:28), blind men (Matt. 9:27, 20:30), animals (Matt. 21:2), or angels (Luke 24:4; John 20:12).

These are not contradictions, because in none of these cases does an evangelist say there was *only* one of the things in question present. The evangelist may mention only one, but that leaves open the possibility—confirmed by one or more of the other evangelists—that there was more than one present.

It has often been noted that if several people witness a car accident, they will each observe and report different details when they recount it later. This phenomenon may be partly responsible for cases mentioned above. For example, if Matthew was an eyewitness to a particular event he may have remembered seeing two demoniacs, blind men, and so on, while noneyewitnesses like Mark and Luke were dependent on sources who may have mentioned only one.

There also may be another phenomenon at work: dramatic simplification. Because books then were fantastically expensive (a copy of the Gospel of Matthew could have cost the ancient equivalent of more than $1,500), ancient authors worked under pressure to keep their books short. This could result in them presenting only an incident's essentials, which could have the added benefit of making the story more focused and compelling.

If on a single occasion two people asked Jesus for a particular favor, like healing, or if two angels showed up to deliver a single message, the essence of the event could be communicated to the audience if only one was mentioned. After all, Jesus did grant a person's request for healing, and an angel did show up to deliver a message. The mention of a similar companion in both cases was not essential.

Suffering with No Clear Purpose

CHALLENGE

"The Christian God can't exist. Why would a good God allow innocent people to suffer and die with no clear purpose?"

DEFENSE

God can bring good from evil and he can more than compensate us.

The faculties that allow suffering—such as the pain receptors in our nervous systems—have a purpose, which is to help us avoid danger (see Day 7), but sometimes they are triggered in situations where they don't help—resulting in apparently purposeless suffering.

Fortunately, God can bring good out of every tragedy, and faith tells us he will (Rom. 8:28; CCC 324). However, there is more that can be said.

For a person with an atheistic perspective, death is the ultimate end. If someone has suffered unjustly in this life, that's it. The person is just out of luck. Nothing can ever make up for the suffering he experienced.

But from a Christian perspective, death is not the end. It's a transition, and we will exist forever. That means that no matter what we have suffered in this life or how short our life was, God can make it up to us. Indeed, he can do far more. Paul says: "I consider that the sufferings of this present time are not worth comparing with the glory that is to be revealed to us" (Rom. 8:18).

Elsewhere he says, "So we do not lose heart. . . . For this slight momentary affliction is preparing for us an eternal weight of glory beyond all comparison, because we look not to the things that are seen but to the things that are unseen; for the things that are seen are transient, but the things that are unseen are eternal" (2 Cor. 4:16–18).

This is part of what makes it possible to live with the mystery of evil. I may experience evil in this life. From an earthly perspective, I may suffer, but I can endure that if I know that death is not the end and God will more than compensate for what I have suffered innocently. I don't have to know all the reasons why this or that evil occurs, as long as I know that God will make everything right in the end.

The Concept of the Trinity

CHALLENGE

"The concept of the Trinity makes no sense. How can God be one and three at the same time?"

DEFENSE

The doctrine of the Trinity does not say that God is one and three in the same sense. He is one God and three Persons.

"The supreme being must be unique, without equal . . . . If God is not one, he is not God" (CCC 228). Yet God is also Father, Son, and Holy Spirit. "The Trinity is One. We do not confess three Gods, but one God in three persons" (CCC 253).

It is not surprising that the doctrine of the Trinity is difficult to understand. God is infinite and we are finite. It is natural that our minds would have difficulty grasping what a being so far above us is like. Our minds are designed principally to interact with the world in which we live, and in this life we do not meet beings that are trinities. That's outside our experience. We would not even know God is a Trinity unless he had revealed it (CCC 237).

Nevertheless, God designed our minds to understand at least some aspects of his mystery, and we can see that the concept of the Trinity does not involve a logical contradiction.

This is possible because the category *being* and the category *person* are distinct—something we can see in things we are familiar with (CCC 40–41). In life, we encounter many beings, or things that exist. Some are impersonal (not persons), such as rocks and trees and snowflakes. Other beings are personal. You, me, and everyone we know are persons. This shows that there is a distinction between *being* and *person*.

This distinction is important, because if some beings are less than one person (in fact, zero persons), and if some beings are exactly one person, then there is no contradiction in the idea of a being that is more than one person.

Thus God—the supreme being and thus the ground of all being—is three persons. This may be difficult to envision in this life. God is not yet part of our experience in the way he will be in the next life (CCC 163), but even now we can see that there is no contradiction.

Four Hundred Silent Years?

CHALLENGE

"The deuterocanonicals are not genuine Scripture. There was a period of 400 'silent years' between Malachi and the New Testament when God didn't give any prophetic word. The deuterocanonicals even refer to 'the time that prophets ceased to appear' (1 Macc. 9:27)."

DEFENSE

The lull in prophetic activity is no indicator of whether books from this period are genuine Scripture.

First, the lull that 1 Maccabees refers to was temporary. Even the people living then expected new prophets to appear (1 Macc. 4:46, 14:41).

Second, there have been other lulls in prophetic activity; this was not the first. Similar ones are referred to in 1 Samuel 3:1 (during Samuel's boyhood, "the word of the Lord was rare in those days; there was no frequent vision"), Psalm 74:9 ("there is no longer any prophet"), and Lamentations 2:9 (Zion's "prophets obtain no vision from the Lord").

Third, the lulls were not total. Thus during the time of Samuel's boyhood, visions were *rare*, not non-existent. In the period before the writing of the New Testament, Anna served as a prophetess, and Simeon, Zechariah, Mary, and Joseph had revelations (Luke 2:36, 2:25–26, 1:11–20, 26–37; Matt. 1:20–23, 2:13, 19–20). There may not have been major prophets, but there were ongoing visions and revelations, including during the period of the Maccabees (2 Macc. 3:24–28, 5:2–4, 15:12–16).

Fourth, these lulls did not prevent the writing of Scripture about or during them. If they prevented the writing of Scripture *about* them, then 1 Samuel would not be Scripture, and if it prevented the writing of Scripture *during* them, then Psalm 74 and Lamentations would not be Scripture.

The view that the non-unique lull during the time of the Maccabees prevented Scripture from being written about or during this period is false. It is based on a misunderstanding of the connection between prophets and the writing of Scripture. Although all authors of Scripture are vessels of divine inspiration, they are not all individuals who function professionally as prophets, like Isaiah, Daniel, or Hosea. Thus, a lull in prophetic activity cannot be read as a cessation of Scripture writing. If it did, then parts of the canon that all Christians and Jews accept would have to be struck.

"Absent from the Body"

CHALLENGE

"Paul said that to be absent from the body is to be present with the Lord. Therefore, there is no room for purgatory."

DEFENSE

This challenge is based on a misquotation and several problematic assumptions.

Here is the passage on which the argument is based:

> So we are always of good courage; we know that while we are at home in the body we are away from the Lord, for we walk by faith, not by sight. We are of good courage, and we would rather be away from the body and at home with the Lord. So whether we are at home or away, we make it our aim to please him. For we must all appear before the judgment seat of Christ, so that each one may receive good or evil, according to what he has done in the body (2 Cor. 5:6–10).

Paul doesn't say that being absent from the body is being present with Christ. That's a misquotation. He says that *while* we are in the body we are away from the Lord and that we would *rather* be away from the body and with the Lord, but he doesn't say that one condition *is* the other.

Consider: When we are at work we are away from home, and we might wish to be away from work and at home instead. But this does not mean that being away from work is the same thing as being at home. There are many other places one can be. Even going straight home from work doesn't mean you will be there instantly.

This challenge also has two problematic assumptions: (1) that purgatory takes time (we don't know that it does; it may happen in a flash), and (2) that it is not something that happens when we encounter Christ. Benedict XVI challenged these ideas in his encyclical *Spe Salvi* (sections 47–48) and proposed the possibility that purgatory simply *is* a transforming encounter with Christ that can't be reckoned in earthly time.

Finally, Paul says we strive to please Jesus "for we must all appear before the judgment seat of Christ." Elsewhere he links the judgment of Christ to purgatory (1 Cor. 3:11–15).

What Happened at Jesus' Tomb?

CHALLENGE

"The Gospel accounts of what happened at Jesus' tomb contradict one another."

DEFENSE

They do not contradict. They agree on all the core facts, and the differences in detail are due to the literary choices that ancient authors regularly made.

All four agree that women went to Jesus' tomb after the Sabbath, around dawn on the first day of the week (Matt. 28:1; Mark 16:1–2; Luke 24:1; John 20:1). The stone was rolled away, the body was gone, and they encountered an angel (Matt. 28:2–7; Mark 16:4–7; Luke 24:2–7, 10; John 20:1, 11–13).

The evangelists do mention different details. All the Gospels indicate Mary Magdalen was among the women, but Matthew, Mark, and Luke mention her companions. Which ones are mentioned was likely determined by who an evangelist knew to be there, who he thought his audience would recognize, and who he wanted to emphasize.

Matthew and Mark mention one angel, while Luke and John indicate there were two. The formers' omission of the second angel is an omission, not a contradiction (see Day 37). Mark refers to "a young man . . . in a white robe," but leaves it to the reader to infer that he was an angel. The others make this explicit, and also take note of his clothing, which is described as "white as snow" (Matthew), "dazzling" (Luke), and simply "white" (John).

The evangelists record different parts of the angels' message. Matthew and Mark mention that Jesus will appear to the disciples in Galilee (see Day 115), while Luke and John omit this.

Matthew mentions the guards at the tomb, which he previously mentioned in Matthew 27:62–66. He also records that an angel rolled back the stone. This is implicit in the other three. The way Matthew records the angel's action could be read as a flashback (i.e., what happened before the women arrived). Even without this reading, the evangelists were not bound to record events in chronological order (see Day 89).

John mentions that between the time the women first visited the tomb and the angelic encounter, Peter and John visited the tomb. Peter's visit is also confirmed in Luke 24:12.

Such variations are choices that an ancient author would be expected to make. None involve contradictions.

Statues of Saints

CHALLENGE

"The Catholic use of statues of saints is idolatry."

DEFENSE

Idolatry involves worshipping a statue as a god.
That's not what Catholics do with statues.

Statues of saints do not represent gods. They represent human beings or angels united with God in heaven.

Even the least learned practicing Catholics are aware that statues of saints are not gods, and neither are the saints they represent. If you point to a statue of the Virgin Mary and ask, "Is this a goddess?" or "Is the Virgin Mary a goddess?" you should receive the answer "no" in both cases. If this is the case for the Virgin Mary, the same will be true of any saint.

As long as one is not confusing a statue with a god, it is not an idol, and the commandment against idolatry is not violated.

This was true in the Bible. At various points, God commanded the Israelites to make statues and images for religious use. For example, in the book of Numbers the Israelites were suffering from a plague of poisonous snakes, and God commanded Moses to make a bronze serpent and set it on a pole so that those bitten by the snakes could gaze upon the bronze serpent and live (Num. 21:6–9). The act of looking at a statue has no natural power to heal, so this was a religious use. It was only when, centuries later, people began to regard the statue as a god that it was being used as an idol and so was destroyed (2 Kings 18:4).

God also commanded that his temple, which represented heaven, be filled with images of the inhabitants of heaven. Thus he originally ordered that craftsmen work images of cherubim (a kind of angel) into curtains of the Tent of Meeting (Exod. 26:1). Later, carvings of cherubim were made on the walls and doors of the temple (1 Kings 6:29–35).

Statues were also made. The lid of the Ark of the Covenant included two statues of cherubim that spread their wings toward each other (Exod. 25:18–20), and the temple included giant, fifteen-foot tall statues of cherubim in the holy of holies (1 Kings 6:23–28).

Since the Ascension of Christ, the saints have joined the angels in heaven (CCC 1023), making images of them in church appropriate as well.

Mark and Luke Not Eyewitnesses

*"How can the Gospels of Mark and Luke be accurate?
Neither Mark nor Luke was an eyewitness of Jesus."*

DEFENSE

You don't have to be an eyewitness to write an accurate biography.

Today biographers don't have to know the person they are writing about. They don't even have to be alive at the same time as their subject. Consider all the recent biographies of Abraham Lincoln. No modern authors were eyewitnesses of Lincoln, yet people don't discount their biographies on that basis. What matters is that a biographer has access to reliable sources, and both Mark and Luke did.

According to the first-century figure John the Presbyter, who was likely one of the authors of the New Testament and who is sometimes identified as the apostle John, Mark served as Peter's interpreter (cf. 1 Peter 5:13) and wrote his Gospel based on his knowledge of Peter's preaching (see Eusebius, *Church History* 3:39:14–15). Based on the unusual prominence of Peter in Mark's Gospel, scholars have generally agreed that this is correct. Richard Bauckham has even argued that Mark uses a literary device known as *inclusio* to signal the fact that Peter stands behind the information in his Gospel (see *Jesus and the Eyewitnesses*, chapters 6–7). Mark is thus based on eyewitness testimony.

Similarly, Luke informs us at the beginning of his Gospel that the information in it was "delivered to us by those who from the beginning were eyewitnesses and ministers of the word" (Luke 1:2). We can even tell which eyewitnesses much of the information came from. First, Luke used Mark as one of his sources, so some of his material came from Peter through Mark. Second, Luke spent several years with Paul in Rome (Acts 28:16, 30), where Peter also spent the later part of his ministry. Peter thus served as a major source for Acts 1–12 (see Day 26), and Luke likely derived some of the material in his Gospel directly from Peter as well.

We can also detect other sources. For example, Luke preserves traditions derived from the Virgin Mary, and he signals this by noting how Mary "kept all these things, pondering them in her heart" (Luke 2:19, cf. 2:51).

Confessing to a Priest

"Why should we confess our sins to a priest? We should go to God directly."

We can and should ask God directly for forgiveness, but Scripture also reveals that it is his will—in some cases—that we approach his ministers in confession.

Prayer may be sufficient for the forgiveness of daily, venial sins, but Jesus indicated that some sins are more serious by instituting the sacrament of confession to deal with them.

After rising from the dead, he told the disciples, "As the Father has sent me, even so I send you." Then he breathed on them, and said, "Receive the Holy Spirit. If you forgive the sins of any, they are forgiven; if you retain the sins of any, they are retained" (John 20:21–23).

Previously, God had sent Jesus to forgive sins on earth (Matt. 9:6), and people glorified God "who had given such authority to men" (Matt. 9:8). Now Jesus shares this authority with his ministers.

Notice that he gives them the power to forgive *or retain* (not forgive) sins. The decision whether to forgive or retain a sin is serious, and Christ's ministers must not make it in an uninformed manner. To perform their role, they need to be properly informed.

In particular, ministers need to know: (1) that we have committed a particular sin, and (2) that we are genuinely repentant. Since they have no way of knowing these things apart from our informing them, we are obliged to confess. Thus we have the sacrament of confession.

John 20:21–23 is also the background we need when reading the same author's affirmation that, "If we confess our sins, he is faithful and just, and will forgive our sins and cleanse us from all unrighteousness" (1 John 1:9).

Historically, penance has been celebrated in different forms. Early in Church history, it was common for it to be celebrated publicly, with Christ's minister presiding over the service. Such public confession is envisioned in the exhortation, "Therefore confess your sins to one another" (James 5:16), which is done in the presence of "the elders of the church" (James 5:14)—the elders being the priests. In Greek, "elder" is *presbuteros*, from which we get the English word "priest."

The *Kalam* Argument

CHALLENGE

"What possible reason do you have for thinking that God exists?"

DEFENSE

Here's one: the universe had a beginning.

This is known as the *kalam* cosmological argument. (*Kalam* is an Arabic word meaning "discourse.") It can be framed as follows:

1. Everything that has a beginning has a cause.
2. The universe has a beginning.
3. Therefore, the universe has a cause.
4. The universe is the realm of space and time.
5. A cause transcends the thing it causes.
6. Therefore, the cause of the universe transcends space and time.
7. God is the spatially and temporally transcendent cause of the universe.
8. Therefore, God exists.

The premises of this argument are lines 1, 2, 4, 5, and 7. The conclusions (lines 3, 6, and 8) follow from them.

Line 1 is validated by experience. Everything we see that has a beginning also has a cause.

Line 2 is sometimes supported by philosophical arguments attempting to show that the universe could not have an infinite past. Some philosophers have found these arguments persuasive, but others, myself included, have not. I agree with St. Thomas Aquinas that, although God *did* create the universe with a finite history, he could have created it with an infinite history if he chose (ST I:46:2).

A more promising basis for line 2 is found in modern science, which points to the origin of the world, including space and time, in an event approximately 13.7 billion years ago known as the Big Bang. Multiple lines of evidence point to the reality of this event. The results of science are always provisional, and so it is possible that one day the Big Bang could either be disproved or proved not to be the actual beginning of the universe. However, the Big Bang is well supported science and our best understanding at present. Its implications therefore should be taken seriously.

Line 4 is established by observation. The universe is characterized by space and time, and, so far as we can tell, it is coextensive with space and time. Further, physics supports the idea that space and time began with the Big Bang.

Line 5 is based on the fact that nothing is its own cause. Therefore, causes must transcend their effects. Line 7 is true by definition.

Objections to the *Kalam* Argument

CHALLENGE
"The kalam *argument for God's existence is flawed: (1) Quantum physics
shows that things can begin without a cause; (2) the argument deals
with the visible universe, but there may also be other universes; (3) if all
things must have a cause, then God would need a cause, too; and
(4) God can't be his own cause because that would be nonsensical."*

DEFENSE
None of these objections overturn the *kalam* argument.

First, quantum physics does not show things can begin without a cause. It has provided evidence that apparently empty space contains energy that can give rise to briefly existing pairs of what are known as "virtual particles" in events known as "quantum fluctuations."

However, these fluctuations and particles behave in a lawlike manner. Because of the limits imposed on our ability to observe subatomic phenomena (by Heisenberg's Uncertainty Principle), we must describe their behavior in terms of probability, but it is clear there are laws—and if laws then *causes*—governing these events. Any phenomenon describable in terms of laws is subject to causation, and that includes the phenomena studied by quantum physics.

Second, although some physicists have speculated about the possibility of other universes, we do not presently have evidence that any other universes exist.

Even if other universes do exist, that does not undermine the *kalam* argument. God can make any number of universes he chooses. In order to undermine the *kalam* argument, one would have to show not only that other universes exist, but that our universe was born from a series of previous universes that stretch back infinitely far in time, so that there was no original beginning.

One can speculate about prior universes, but we have no proof of them. The evidence we have currently shows a single universe beginning in the Big Bang.

Third, the claim is not that everything has a cause. If this were the case then God would require a cause. Instead, the claim is that everything *that has a beginning* has a cause. Since God transcends space and time, he does not have a beginning. As a timeless, eternal Being, God does not require a cause.

Fourth, God is not his own cause. The idea of self-causation is incoherent. Therefore, God has no cause.

Praying for the Dead

CHALLENGE

"The Catholic practice of praying for the dead is unbiblical."

DEFENSE

The practice is not just Catholic and it *is* biblical.

First, it isn't only Catholics who pray for the dead. Except in the Protestant community, prayer for the dead is universal among Christians. Further, prayer for the dead has been practiced by Jews since before the time of Christ and continues to be practiced by them today.

In Scripture, Judah Maccabee and his men were retrieving the bodies of fallen comrades when they discovered the men who had fallen were wearing pagan amulets, and so "they turned to prayer, beseeching that the sin which had been committed might be wholly blotted out" (2 Macc. 12:42).

Protestants may not regard this passage as Scripture, but Catholics do, and it is thus legitimate for them to appeal to it. Whether one regards it as Scripture or not, it constitutes evidence of prayer for the dead among Jews before the time of Christ, and Jews continue to pray for the dead today, particularly using a prayer known as the Mourner's Kaddish.

The New Testament also contains a plausible instance of prayer for the dead. After praying for the household of a man named Onesiphorus, Paul goes on to pray "may the Lord grant him to find mercy from the Lord on that Day" (2 Tim. 1:18). Paul twice mentions "the household of Onesiphorus" (2 Tim. 1:16, 4:19), but does not greet him with the rest of his household and speaks of him only in the past tense. Many scholars have concluded that Onesiphorus had passed away and thus Paul was praying for the departed.

Many Protestants, too, spontaneously ask God to bless their departed loved ones. Thus the Protestant apologist C.S. Lewis writes: "Of course I pray for the dead. The action is so spontaneous, so all but inevitable, that only the most compulsive theological case against it would deter me. . . . At our age the majority of those we love best are dead. What sort of intercourse with God could I have if what I love best were unmentionable to Him?" (*Letters to Malcolm: Chiefly on Prayer*, 107).

It is a natural human impulse to pray for our loved ones, even when they have passed from this life.

How the Star of Bethlehem Moved

CHALLENGE

*"The star of Bethlehem is a myth.
No star leads people from place to place."*

DEFENSE

The star of Bethlehem did not lead the Magi.

Some propose that the star was a supernatural phenomenon, making it capable of leading the Magi. However, this proposal is unnecessary. The text doesn't claim the star led anybody.

When the Magi arrive in Jerusalem, they say, "Where is he who has been born king of the Jews? For we have seen his star in the East" (Matt. 2:2). This passage has been understood two ways: (1) the Magi were in the east when they saw the star, and (2) they saw the star when it rose over the eastern horizon (as stars typically do).

On neither interpretation did the star lead the Magi. They recognized that its appearance implied a Jewish royal birth, and they therefore went where one would expect such a baby to be found: King Herod's palace in Jerusalem. If the star were leading them, they would have gone straight to Bethlehem. The fact that they had to stop and ask where to find the baby shows they weren't being led.

Once told where to look for the child, they set out on the road to Bethlehem, which is about six miles south of Jerusalem. Again, they are not following the star. They are already on their way when, by a providential coincidence, they see the star again.

"The star which they had seen in the East went before them, till it came to rest over the place where the child was. When they saw the star, they rejoiced exceedingly with great joy" (Matt. 2:9–10). Their rejoicing at seeing the star again indicates they recognized the coincidence. They weren't expecting it.

All the text implies is that the star was in the southern sky in front of them as they traveled to Bethlehem, and when they got there it was, from their perspective, vertically above the Holy Family's home. That fits the natural motion of a star, which would sweep out an arc in the sky of 15 degrees per hour as they went to Bethlehem.

The text thus indicates that the second sighting of the star was providential, but it does not suggest that the star moved in an unusual way.

Sola Scriptura and the Bereans

CHALLENGE

"We should form our theological beliefs by Scripture alone, following the example of the Bereans, who 'were more noble than those in Thessalonica, for they received the word with all eagerness, examining the scriptures daily to see if these things were so' (Acts 17:11)."

DEFENSE

This seriously misreads the passage regarding the Bereans.

The context for the Berean incident is found in Acts 17:1–10. When Paul and Silas initially visited the Macedonian city of Thessalonica, they began preaching and making converts, which led to conflict with some in the Jewish community: "And taking some wicked fellows of the rabble, they gathered a crowd, set the city in an uproar, and attacked the house of Jason, seeking to bring them out to the people" (Acts 17:5).

They then dragged Jason and some of the new Christians before the city authorities, charging them with sedition against Caesar (Acts 17:6–7). The situation was so alarming that the Thessalonian Christians hurriedly sent Paul and Silas away by night (when traveling was not safe) to the nearby city of Berea. The non-Christian Jews in Thessalonica remained so opposed to Paul that they sent men to pursue him to Berea and incite the crowds against him, forcing him to flee at once to Athens (Acts 17:13–15).

That is the background against which the statement that the Bereans were more "noble" (other translations: "open-minded") than the Thessalonians. The contrast is not between credulous Thessalonians, who accepted whatever Paul said without evidence, and skeptical Bereans, who demanded proof from Scripture. It is between actively hostile Thessalonians and Bereans who "received the word with all eagerness" (Acts 17:11).

This is no prooftext for *sola scriptura*. Paul's message did not include merely things found in the Old Testament Scriptures. It included the many new elements of the Christian faith. What the Bereans did was confirm the basic elements of his message (i.e., the fact that Jesus fulfilled messianic prophecy) and then proceeded to accept all the new, unwritten teachings that were part of it (e.g., baptism, the Eucharist, the inclusion of Gentiles in God's people without circumcision).

In short, they accepted the whole of apostolic Tradition after confirming the core elements of the Christian message with Scripture. To follow their example, we should do the same.

God Sending People to Hell

CHALLENGE

"I don't see how a loving God could send someone to hell. Why would he want to punish one of his creatures for all eternity?"

DEFENSE

God doesn't want people to go to hell. He "desires all men to be saved and to come to the knowledge of the truth" (1 Tim. 2:4), but we can reject his offer of salvation.

Although Scripture and the Church use the language of punishment in connection with hell, this has to be properly understood.

"It is not a punishment imposed externally by God but a development of premises already set by people in this life . . . 'Eternal damnation,' therefore, is not attributed to God's initiative because in his merciful love he can only desire the salvation of the beings he created. In reality, it is the creature who closes himself to his love. Damnation consists precisely in definitive separation from God, freely chosen by the human person and confirmed with death that seals his choice for ever. God's judgment ratifies this state" (John Paul II, General Audience, July 28, 1999).

Consequently, "God predestines no one to go to hell; for this, a willful turning away from God (a mortal sin) is necessary, and persistence in it until the end" (CCC 1037).

It is not that God chooses to send a person to hell. The person chooses to remain separate from God, to reject his offer of love and forgiveness, and God respects the person's choice. He will not force a person into union with him if that person chooses to be separate.

At the end of life, our choice becomes definitive. We will not change our mind after death, which is why both heaven and hell last forever (cf. CCC 1035).

But as long as we are still alive, we can still choose to turn to God, no matter what we have done, no matter how bad our sins have been. "There is no offense, however serious, that the Church cannot forgive. There is no one, however wicked and guilty, who may not confidently hope for forgiveness, provided his repentance is honest. Christ who died for all men desires that in his Church the gates of forgiveness should always be open to anyone who turns away from sin" (CCC 982).

Apostolic Traditions Outside Scripture

CHALLENGE

"If we're not supposed to determine our religious beliefs by Scripture alone, name some apostolic Traditions that aren't in the New Testament."

DEFENSE

Which examples one will find persuasive depends on one's theological viewpoint, but there are some that should be convincing to all traditional Protestants.

One is that there are to be no more apostles. The college of apostles did not continue past the first century. The task of shepherding the Church devolved from the apostles upon their successors, the bishops, but the two offices are not identical (CCC 860–62).

The cessation of the apostles did not have to be. Although membership in the Twelve required being an eyewitness of Jesus' ministry (Acts 1:21–26), there were other apostles, such as Barnabas and Paul (Acts 14:14). Paul, in particular, wasn't an eyewitness; Jesus only appeared to him later (Acts 9:1–9; cf. 1 Cor. 9:1). The fact that Jesus did this for Paul means he could have continued appearing and making new apostles down through history, but he didn't. Some individuals in history have claimed to be new apostles, but orthodox Christians have rightly rejected their claims.

Related to the passing of the apostles is the fact that public revelation has ceased (CCC 66), and thus the canon of Scripture is closed. There are to be no more books of Scripture. This also did not have to be. God could have continued to inspire authors, enabling them to write new books of the Bible. The authors wouldn't even have to be apostles, for some of the original New Testament authors (e.g., Mark and Luke) were not apostles.

Yet Christians recognized that just as the apostles ceased, so did the writing of Scripture. Of course, individuals have claimed to receive new books of Scripture (e.g., Joseph Smith), but, again, orthodox Christians have rightly rejected these claims.

The closing of the age of the apostles and the age of Scripture are elements of the deposit of faith, or apostolic Tradition, but they are not attested in Scripture. The Bible nowhere says or implies that Jesus will not continue to appear to people and create new apostles. Neither does it say or imply that God will not continue to inspire authors to write new books of Scripture. These are thus elements of apostolic Tradition not in Scripture.

Repentance and Salvation

CHALLENGE

*"It isn't necessary to turn away from sin to be saved. The Greek
word for repentance simply means 'change your mind.' As long
as you change your mind and recognize that you are a sinner,
God will forgive you even if you don't turn away from sin."*

DEFENSE

The Greek word for "repentance"—*metanoia*—does come from roots
that can mean "change" (*meta-*) and "mind" (*nous*), but the roots of a
word do not determine its meaning. The way a word is *used* does.

Scripture makes it clear that if we wish to be saved from our sins, we
need to turn from them—not just recognize them as sins.

John the Baptist said: "Bear fruit that befits repentance, and do not
presume to say to yourselves, 'We have Abraham as our father'; for I tell
you, God is able from these stones to raise up children to Abraham. Even
now the axe is laid to the root of the trees; every tree therefore that does
not bear good fruit is cut down and thrown into the fire" (Matt. 3:8–10).

This fruit involves turning away from sin and doing right, as John
emphasized to the tax collectors and soldiers who wanted to know
what implications repentance had for their lives.

"Tax collectors also came to be baptized, and said to him, 'Teacher,
what shall we do?' And he said to them, 'Collect no more than is appointed you.' Soldiers also asked him, 'And we, what shall we do?' And
he said to them, 'Rob no one by violence or by false accusation, and be
content with your wages'" (Luke 3:12–14).

Repentance does not mean a commitment to live in sinless perfection, for, as the New Testament tells us, "we all make many mistakes"
(Jas. 3:2), and "If we say we have no sin, we deceive ourselves, and the
truth is not in us" (1 John 1:8). However, it does mean that we must
will to turn from sin and, by the grace of God, to break with it fundamentally, even if we still wrestle with it during the course of this life.

TIP

If the meaning of a word was determined by its roots rather than its
usage, the English word *nice* would mean "ignorant," since it comes
from the Latin *nescius,* whose roots mean "not knowing."

Baptism in Jesus' Name

CHALLENGE

"Christians shouldn't baptize using the Trinitarian formula. The Bible speaks of baptizing in Jesus' name (Acts 2:38, 8:12, 16, 10:48, 19:5)."

DEFENSE

These verses refer to the *type* of baptism, not the words used in the rite.

Jesus indicated the words to be used in baptism, saying: "Go therefore and make disciples of all nations, baptizing them in the name of the Father and of the Son and of the Holy Spirit" (Matt. 28:19).

Referring to Christian baptism by these words would be very clunky, so there was a need for a shorter way to refer to it.

In part, this was because there were multiple baptisms in the New Testament period. Chief among these were ceremonial washings performed by non-Christian Jews (Lev. 14:8, 15:5–27, 16:4, 24–28, 17:15–16, 22:6; Num. 19:7–8, 19; Deut. 23:11), the baptism of John the Baptist (Matt. 3:13–14, 21:25; Acts 1:22, 10:37, etc.), and the baptism of Jesus (Matt. 28:19; Mark 16:16; John 4:1–2; Acts 2:38; Rom. 6:3–4, etc.). In addition, there were baptisms practiced by heretical sects and even pagans.

Consequently, there needed to be a way to refer to the Christian rite in just a few words. Since it was associated with Jesus, Luke refers to it as baptism "in the name of Jesus Christ" (Acts 2:38, 8:12, 10:48) and "in the name of the Lord Jesus" (Acts 8:16, 19:5).

But the Trinitarian formula was used in these cases, as shown when Paul baptizes some men in Ephesus. They had been evangelized by Apollos, who initially knew only John's baptism (Acts 18:24–25). After Apollos departed (19:1), Paul met them and asked an important question: "'Did you receive the Holy Spirit when you believed?' And they said, 'No, we have never even heard that there is a Holy Spirit.' And he said, 'Into what then were you baptized?' They said, 'Into John's baptism'" (19:2–3).

The fact that they had not heard of the Holy Spirit immediately caused Paul to question what baptism they had received. If it were Christian baptism, it would have used the Trinitarian formula and thus referred to the Holy Spirit. The only way they could have failed to hear of the Holy Spirit was if they had not received Christian baptism—and this proved true: They had received John's. Paul then gave them Christian baptism.

Jesus' Sacrifice and Penance

CHALLENGE

*"The value of Christ's sacrifice was infinite. He paid it all.
Thus there is no role for penance in the Christian life."*

DEFENSE

The value of Christ's death on the cross was infinite—more
than enough to pay for all the sins of mankind. But even after
God has forgiven the eternal consequences of our sins, he
still wants us to experience *some* negative consequences.

When a child misbehaves, there need to be consequences. If parents
never applied any discipline, the child would never learn his lesson.
Scripture uses parental discipline as an image to express how God
relates to us: "The Lord disciplines him whom he loves, and chastises
every son whom he receives" (Heb. 12:6). He "disciplines us for our
good, that we may share his holiness" (Heb. 12:10).

That's why we do penance. If we learn how to say no to ourselves,
we'll be better able to say no to temptation.

Christ expects us to do penance. When Jesus was asked why his disciples did not fast, he said they would fast in the future (Mark 2:18–20).
Thus he told the disciples, "*When* you fast, do not look dismal, like the
hypocrites" (Matt. 6:16). He didn't say, "*if* you fast," but "*when* you fast."
In Acts, the early Christians put this into practice (Acts 13:2, 14:23).

By practicing fasting and other forms of penance, we embrace spiritual discipline that will, as Hebrews says, help us grow in holiness.

Penance also provides us with the opportunity to express sorrow for
our sins. We have an innate need to mourn when something tragic has
occurred, and that includes our own sins. To insist a person not feel
or show any grief for sin would be unnatural and would short-circuit
responses that God built into us. There is "a time to weep . . . a time
to mourn" (Eccles. 3:4).

TIP

The first-century document known as the *Didache* (DID-ah-KAY) indicates it
was common for first-century Christians to fast twice a week: "Let not your
fastings be with the hypocrites, for they fast on the second and the fifth
day of the week [Monday and Thursday]; but keep your fast on the fourth
and on the preparation day [Wednesday and Friday]" (8:1–2).

Can the Saints Hear Us?

CHALLENGE

"We have no evidence the saints are aware of our prayer requests. How would they even know? They are not omniscient."

DEFENSE

We have evidence they are aware of our prayers.

You don't have to know everything to know some things, so the saints don't have to be omniscient to be aware of our prayer requests.

We do not know much about how the human intellect works in heaven, but the fact that heaven is a higher state than this life suggests we will have more rather than less awareness. This is also suggested because we will be made "partakers of the divine nature" (2 Pet. 1:4) and transformed to be like God by virtue of the beatific vision (1 John 3:2).

Scripture does not give many pictures of what life in heaven is like, but it shows saints and angels aware of what is happening on earth (Rev. 6:9–11, 7:13–14, 11:15–18, 16:5–6, 18:20).

The common understanding is that the saints are aware of our prayer requests through union with God. It is reasonable to suppose that, in the perfect state of heaven, people will have whatever information is relevant to them. Thus God can make a saint aware that someone is asking for his intercession.

However saints and angels are aware of our prayer requests, Scripture indicates that they are. In Revelation 5:8, the twenty-four elders, who appear to represent the leaders of the people of God in heaven, offer incense to God. We are told that the incense is "the prayers of the saints." In Revelation 8:3–4, an angel offers incense that is mingled with "the prayers of all the saints."

At that time, the term "saint" was commonly used to refer to living Christians (2 Cor. 1:1; Eph. 1:1; Phil. 1:1). It is natural to see these passages as depicting the inhabitants of heaven presenting the prayer requests of the saints on earth to God. This is surely part of what 8:3 means by the reference to the prayers of "all the saints."

TIP

If it is suggested that these passages don't deal with prayer requests made to those in heaven, then our point is made even stronger, for the passages would show that those in heaven were aware of prayer requests that weren't even addressed to them!

Supernatural Realms

CHALLENGE

"The idea of supernatural realms like heaven and hell is scientifically absurd."

DEFENSE

On the contrary: scientists themselves propose the possibility of realms with properties different from those of our world.

Contemporary scientific literature is filled with proposals that our universe might be just one realm among a much larger collection. This set of realms—referred to as the "multiverse"—is often proposed as a way of explaining why our universe has multiple properties that seem finely tuned to allow for the existence of life.

Scientists recognize that it would be very unlikely for a single universe to have such properties purely by chance. Consequently, some propose that there are a vast number of universes, each of which has different properties, making it probable that at least one would have the properties needed for life to exist. (An alternative would be to say that our universe was *designed* to have these properties.)

It is even proposed that these realms may interact with one another (e.g., "brane cosmology" proposes that our universe may have begun when two such realms collided, producing the Big Bang).

Thus far we do not have scientific evidence that any such realms exist, but the fact that scientists are proposing them shows that it is not scientifically absurd to suggest the existence of realms outside the visible world that have different properties than it does, or that are capable of interacting with it.

Indeed, even before contemporary physics, such realms were being discussed. In 1884, Edwin Abbott published a landmark book called *Flatland: A Romance of Many Dimensions,* in which he contemplated the way worlds with different numbers of dimensions might interact. Abbott proposed many examples whereby a visitor from a higher dimension could be capable of producing effects that, from an ordinary perspective, would be regarded as miraculous. Indeed, the parallels to religion are so clear that one character in the novel ends up being commissioned as an "apostle" to preach "the Gospel of the Three Dimensions."

This is *not* to say that supernatural realms such as heaven and hell are simply other dimensions or other universes on the model of those proposed by modern physicists or by authors like Abbott. However, this does show the intellectual defensibility of the idea that realms with different properties might exist and might interact with our own.

Madonna-and-Child Images

CHALLENGE

*"The pagan roots of Christianity are shown by the popular
Madonna-and-Child images depicting Mary and the baby
Jesus. Similar images depicting a goddess and her child
are found in pagan religions all over the world."*

DEFENSE

Images of the Madonna and Child neither date from the
origin of Christianity nor prove it has a pagan origin.

Images of Mary and the baby Jesus did not become common in Christian art until the fifth century. There are a few possible examples of them from the second to the fourth centuries, but none from the first. These images do not go back to the founding of Christianity and thus cannot show it to have pagan origins.

The most they could show is that at some point Christian artists drew on themes that were already present in pagan art, but there is nothing sinister or surprising about mother and child images. They appear in every culture because of a simple fact: There are mothers with children in every culture!

What's more, you don't have to be a goddess to be represented in such images. Today, every mother has photos of herself holding each baby she has had, and before the invention of photography, families could have drawings or paintings of such scenes.

The depiction of mothers with children is a natural expression of mankind's artistic impulse. Motherhood is a profound aspect of the human experience, and it is naturally reflected in a culture's art.

In cultures that believed in goddesses, it was natural to depict some of them with their children, but that is not what is happening in Madonna and Child images. Although Jesus is God, Mary is a human being—not a goddess.

She is a noteworthy biblical figure who is mentioned in multiple books of the New Testament, and it is natural that she would find a place in Christian art. One of the easiest ways to indicate her identity in a work of art is to depict her with her even more famous Son. The fact that two Gospels have infancy narratives in which people visit Mary and the child Jesus (Matt. 2:11; Luke 2:16) made it certain that such images would be depicted in Christian art.

Praying Directly to God

CHALLENGE

*"Catholics should not ask the saints for intercession.
Why do that when you can pray directly to God?"*

DEFENSE

If this proved anything, it would prove too much.
It would wipe out much of Christian prayer.

We can and should pray directly to God—the source of all gifts (James 1:17). However, it does not follow that you should pray *only* to God. This is a "both/and" situation, not an "either/or" one.

We naturally sense that it is helpful to have others praying for us, and down through the ages Christians have asked one another for their prayers. But this would be impossible if God wanted us to make requests only of him. The objection thus would prove too much.

In truth, God desires that we pray for each other. This is illustrated by the Lord's Prayer, in which we pray for ourselves and others ("Give us this day our daily bread," "Forgive us our debts," "Lead us not into temptation"; Matt. 6:11–13); by Jesus' exhortation to pray even for our enemies (Matt. 5:44); and by Paul's exhortation, "I urge that supplications, prayers, intercessions, and thanksgivings be made for all men" (1 Tim. 2:1).

God also desires that we ask others for their intercession, as illustrated by Paul's requests for his readers to pray for him (Rom. 15:30; 2 Cor. 1:11; Eph. 6:18–19; 1 Thess. 5:25; 2 Thess. 3:1–2)—a request also made by the author of Hebrews (13:18). Asking the saints for their intercession merely extends the principle. We may ask Christians in heaven for their intercession for the same reason we ask Christians on earth: It helps to have others praying for you, to not be alone in prayer. This is particularly the case when one's prayer partners are righteous, for "the prayer of a righteous man has great power in its effects" (James 5:16b). None are more righteous than those with God in heaven.

TIP

Scripture nowhere prohibits asking the saints for their intercession. Things that are not prohibited by Scripture and that have a rational basis are permitted under Christian liberty, and this practice qualifies on both counts. Opponents of the practice should ask whether they're seeking to limit the "freedom which we have in Christ Jesus" (Gal. 2:4).

"Why Have You Forsaken Me?"

CHALLENGE

"How could Jesus be the Son of God if he prayed, 'My God, my God, why have you forsaken me'? An all-good God couldn't forsake Jesus, so either Jesus made a mistake by thinking his Father had forsaken him or his Father made a mistake by actually doing so."

DEFENSE

Abandonment can be understood in different senses.
Jesus knew he would be vindicated, and his words prove it.

First, abandonment can be understood in a relative sense—as allowing a person to experience a particular bad thing. The Father certainly allowed his Son to experience suffering on the cross, so he could be said to have abandoned him *to that suffering,* but not abandoned him in any more fundamental sense. God did no wrong in this, for it was suffering with a purpose (namely, the redemption of mankind).

Jesus' prayer was not a literal request for information. He already knew why he was going to the cross (John 3:16, 6:51, 10:18). Instead, it was merely an expression of the anguish he was feeling as the suffering was transpiring.

Jesus also knew that this suffering would be temporary, for he had already predicted his crucifixion, death, and resurrection (Matt. 16:21, 17:22–23, 20:18).

His awareness of the vindication that the Resurrection would bring shows that he knew he was not abandoned in any fundamental sense but was experiencing only temporary suffering.

This is proved by the words he spoke from the cross: "My God, my God, why have you forsaken me?" (Matt. 27:46; Mark 15:34). This is the opening line of Psalm 22, which Jesus is applying to his current situation. In this psalm, the psalmist is suffering, and aspects of the psalm closely reflect Jesus' situation on the cross, including being mocked by those around him (Ps. 22:7; Matt. 27:39; Mark 15:29), having his hands and feet pierced (Ps. 22:16), and having lots cast for his garments (Ps. 22:18; Matt. 27:35; Mark 15:24).

The psalmist goes on to express confidence that God will deliver him from his present situation (Ps. 22:22–26) and that this will lead to all the nations worshipping God (Ps. 22:27).

By quoting the first line of the psalm, Jesus invoked the whole, including God's deliverance of the suffering one, who is only seemingly abandoned and will actually be delivered.

The Age of Miracles

"God doesn't give private revelation or perform any miracles today. These stopped with the first century: 'As for prophecies, they will pass away; as for tongues, they will cease; as for knowledge, it will pass away. For our knowledge is imperfect and our prophecy is imperfect; but when the perfect comes, the imperfect will pass away' (1 Cor. 13:8–10)."

This argument mistakes the time frame Paul is discussing.

He says these will pass away "when the perfect comes." To claim that happened in the first century, you have to identify what "the perfect" was. Suggestions include the death of the last apostle and the writing of the last book of Scripture.

Paul speaks of "our knowledge" being imperfect, but he is not thinking it will be perfect at the close of the apostolic age or the writing of the last book of Scripture—neither of which he mentions.

He writes: "When I was a child, I spoke like a child, I thought like a child, I reasoned like a child; when I became a man, I gave up childish ways" (1 Cor. 13:11). He describes our present knowledge as "childish" compared to how we will come to know God. But the Faith had already been "once for all delivered to the saints" (Jude 3) in Paul's day, and his knowledge was not childish compared to what was known in A.D. 100, by which time the canon was completed.

He also writes: "For now we see in a mirror dimly, but then face to face. Now I know in part; then I shall understand fully, even as I have been fully understood" (1 Cor. 13:12). Paul did not understand the Faith "dimly" compared to how it would be understood a few decades later.

Finally, the one who has fully understood him is God, and thus it is God who he refers to seeing "face to face." He thus expects perfect knowledge to arrive at the Second Coming, when we will see God (1 John 3:2). *That* is when these gifts will pass away.

The standing New Testament instructions on how we are to discern miracles say to take an open-minded but critical approach: "Do not quench the Spirit," writes St. Paul, "do not despise prophesying, but test everything; hold fast what is good" (1 Thess. 5:19–21).

Crosses and Crucifixes

CHALLENGE

"Catholics should not use crucifixes because Jesus is no longer on the cross."

DEFENSE

The reason that the cross is important is because of the Crucifixion.

This objection has more to do with group identity markers than serious theological reflection. Every group has practices that mark its identity with respect to other groups (e.g., circumcision and keeping kosher among Jewish people).

In Western Europe at the time of the Reformation, Protestants began to distinguish themselves from Catholics by certain practices. One was an avoidance of three-dimensional images of Jesus, though two-dimensional images (e.g., paintings and illustrations) were retained. The aversion to three-dimensional images of Christ led to the use of bare crosses, without the figure of Christ.

There is nothing wrong with bare crosses. They were used long before the Reformation, and they are still used in Catholic circles. The reasons for them are not theological or ideological but practical (e.g., a cross may be too small to accommodate a figure of Christ) or artistic (e.g., so that a cross can be specially decorated).

There is also nothing wrong with crucifixes, which depict Jesus hanging on the cross. They are more vivid reminders of what Jesus did for us.

The cross was not important for its own sake but because Jesus died on it. Thus, Protestants also create paintings and illustrations of Jesus hanging on the cross. This reveals that the objection sometimes made to crucifixes is not based on an aversion to depicting Jesus on the cross. A three-dimensional depiction of the Crucifixion is not intrinsically any different than a two-dimensional depiction, which suggests that the Protestant preference for bare crosses over crucifixes is a matter of culture rather than theological principle.

True, Jesus is not on the cross today, but that is irrelevant. Today, the cross on which Jesus hung no longer exists as a single object, and it is questionable whether it ever stood without Jesus on it. Frequently the patibulum (the horizontal bar of a cross) was a separate piece of wood that was raised onto the stipes (the vertical pole) at the time of Crucifixion and then taken down when the victim was dead.

All Christian crosses—whether bare or not—recall the Crucifixion. It's just a question of how vividly you want to do this.

"Works of the Law"

CHALLENGE

"Paul teaches we are saved by faith alone: 'We hold that a man is justified by faith apart from works of law' (Rom. 3:28)."

DEFENSE

Paul says that we are justified by faith apart from "works of the law." That's not the same thing.

Works of the law refer to acts undertaken to obey the Law of Moses, the fundamental law of Judaism. Thus, after saying we are justified apart from works of the law, Paul asks, "Or is God the God of Jews only? Is he not the God of Gentiles also?" (Rom. 3:29). He then refers to circumcision—the most famous requirement of the Law of Moses—saying God "will justify the circumcised on the ground of their faith and the uncircumcised through their faith" (Rom. 3:30).

Elsewhere, Paul raises the question of Jews and Gentiles and says that "a man is not justified by works of the law but through faith in Jesus Christ" (Gal. 2:16). Just before this, he referred to the Jerusalem council and noted his companion Titus was not required to undergo circumcision, though he was Greek (Gal. 2:1–10).

This event is described in Acts. It occurred when "some men came down from Judea and were teaching the brethren, 'Unless you are circumcised according to the custom of Moses, you cannot be saved'" (Acts 15:1). The resulting council reiterated that Gentile Christians did not need to be circumcised and become Jews.

That's what Paul is talking about in Romans and Galatians. He is stressing that you don't have to be circumcised, become a Jew, and obey the Mosaic Law to be saved.

Thus he says: "I testify again to every man who receives circumcision that he is bound to keep the whole law. You are severed from Christ, you who would be justified by the law; you have fallen away from grace. For through the Spirit, by faith, we wait for the hope of righteousness. For in Christ Jesus neither circumcision nor uncircumcision is of any avail, but faith working through love" (Gal. 5:3–6).

TIP

This challenge commits the fallacy of hasty generalization. It's like saying that because you need flour and not cement to make a cake, you *only* need flour (not eggs, water, sugar, and so on).

Mary as Queen of Heaven

CHALLENGE

"There is no biblical basis for regarding Mary as the Queen of Heaven. The term is not found in the Bible, and Catholics shouldn't use it."

DEFENSE

Many terms are not found in the Bible, yet they have a biblical basis. The Marian title "Queen of Heaven" is one such term.

Just because a term is not found in the Bible does not mean it is "un-biblical" (contrary to Scripture). It can have a solid scriptural basis. For example, the terms "Trinity," "original sin," and even "Bible" are not found in Scripture, but each describes a biblical reality.

Mary's role as queen is based on her Son's role as king.

Jesus serves both as David's successor as king of Israel (Luke 1:32; John 1:49, etc.) and as the universal, spiritual king, whose "kingdom is not of this world" (John 18:36), who sat down in heaven with his Father "on his throne" (Rev. 3:21), and who is thus the heavenly "king of kings" (Rev. 17:14, 19:16).

In view of Jesus' kingship, Christians naturally reflected on what this had to say about the royal status of his mother. If Jesus is king, it is natural to view Mary in regal terms.

This is particularly the case in light of the way the concept of queen-ship worked in ancient Israel. At the time, a king might have many wives (Solomon is said to have had seven hundred wives and three hundred concubines; 1 Kings 11:3), but he only had one mother, and it was to her that royal authority accrued.

In the house of David the king's mother was known as the *gebirah* (Hebrew for "lady" or "great lady"). This term is sometimes translated "queen" or "queen mother." The *gebirah* had a distinct office that allowed her to exercise royal authority greater than that of the king's wives.'

If Jesus is the new Davidic king, then it is natural to see Mary as the new Davidic *gebirah*.

Since Jesus now exercises his kingship in heaven, and since Mary is also in heaven, it has been natural to apply the term "Queen of Heaven" to her.

TIP

For information about how the office of *gebirah* worked in Israel and surrounding nations, see Roland de Vaux, *Ancient Israel: Its Life and Institutions*, 117–19.

God's Eternity, Knowledge, and Free Will

CHALLENGE

"If God is outside of time and knows everything that we're going to do, then we don't have free will."

DEFENSE

Knowing about an event does not mean causing it. God can know about things people choose without depriving them of free will.

It's true that God is outside of time and knows both our past and future choices, but this does not determine them.

Consider: You know about many events in the past—in your personal history, your family history, and world history. But your knowledge did not force any of them to happen. They occurred, for whatever reason, and you just happen to know about them.

Some occurred because of the choices of others. For example, your father may have chosen to enter a particular trade. But your knowledge of his trade does not reach back in time and force him to make this choice. It doesn't deprive him of free will.

You might object that we are talking about the past, but the same applies to the present and the future. Suppose that you know of a place where, right now, someone is singing a song. Your knowledge does not force the person to sing.

Or suppose that you are standing on top of a building, and you see two cars about to collide in the street below. Your knowledge of what is about to happen does not cause it. The choices of the drivers were what led to the accident.

Whether we are talking about the past, the present, or the future, knowledge of an event does not force it to happen or deprive those involved of free will.

Neither does God's knowledge of events. God dwells in an eternal now outside of time. All times are equally present to him, and he knows what people choose to do in those times, but his knowledge of what people choose does not make their choices unfree any more than our knowledge of their choices does.

"An Eye for an Eye"

CHALLENGE

"The Old Testament laws stating that people should be punished in an 'eye for an eye' fashion are cruel."

DEFENSE

Properly understood, these passages expressed a principle of justice and sought to promote the common good.

Three passages mention the "eye for an eye" principle: Exodus 21:22–25, Leviticus 24:17–21, and Deuteronomy 19:16–21. The first deals with the case of men who are fighting and accidentally injure a pregnant woman, causing miscarriage. The second deals with a man who attacks and maims another. The third deals with a witness who lies in court to harm an innocent person. In each passage a similar formula occurs: "you shall give life for life, eye for eye, tooth for tooth, hand for hand, foot for foot, burn for burn, wound for wound, stripe for stripe" (Exod. 21:23–25).

Note that these passages are intended to be used by a court when a crime has been committed. They aren't instructions telling people to take personal revenge. The point of having a court system is to *prevent* people from doing that by seeing that justice is done when an innocent party is harmed.

If people take their own revenge, they often do so excessively. A person who has been wounded or has seen a loved one wounded may *kill* the perpetrator. Courts exist to keep this from happening. To do their job properly, courts need to be seen as administering justice fairly. If they are seen as being too lenient, people may take matters into their own hands. Thus the "eye for an eye" passages. They direct courts to let the punishment fit the crime, which is a fundamental principle of justice. This promoted the common good and order of society by discouraging people from taking their own revenge.

In a world without an extensive prison system, this may have literally meant "an eye for an eye," though not always. Numbers 35:31 specifies that no ransom can be accepted in a case of murder, suggesting that in lesser cases the guilty party could pay compensation. A person thus might avoid "an eye for an eye" if he provided appropriate compensation to the injured party.

Justice can also be tempered by mercy in other ways. Thus Jesus counseled individuals to "turn the other cheek" rather than pressing for "eye for an eye" justice (Matt. 5:38–39).

The Sacrament of Confirmation

CHALLENGE

"The sacrament of confirmation is an invention of men with no biblical basis."

DEFENSE

The sacrament of confirmation is recorded in Scripture.

The laying on of hands is used in several Christian rites, including healing (Mark 6:5; Acts 28:8) and ordination for ministry (Acts 6:1–6, 13:2–3). It is also used in Christian initiation.

The book of Hebrews lists the laying on of hands among the "elementary doctrines of Christ"—basic things a convert would need instruction on—alongside repentance, faith, baptism, the resurrection of the dead, and eternal judgment (Heb. 6:1–2).

We see it used in Christian initiation in Acts 8, where Philip the evangelist (cf. Acts 6:5, 21:8–9) converts a number of Samaritans. Although he baptized them (Acts 8:12), he did not have the ability to lay hands on them. Thus two apostles—Peter and John—came from Jerusalem and prayed "that they might receive the Holy Spirit; for it had not yet fallen on any of them, but they had only been baptized in the name of the Lord Jesus. Then they laid their hands on them and they received the Holy Spirit" (8:15–17).

We see the same in Acts 19, where Paul administers Christian baptism to a group and then lays his hands upon them, which results in the Holy Spirit coming upon them (19:5–6).

The Holy Spirit is associated with and received in baptism (Matt. 3:11; Mark 1:8; Luke 3:16; John 1:33; Acts 2:38; 1 Cor. 12:13), but the passages above show there was also a laying on of hands for further strengthening with the Holy Spirit as part of Christian initiation.

The passages also show this laying on of hands was distinct from baptism and that not all ministers performed it. Philip the evangelist baptized but did not lay on hands, while higher-ranking ministers, such as Peter, John, and Paul, both baptized and laid on hands.

"Very early, the better to signify the gift of the Holy Spirit, an anointing with perfumed oil (chrism) was added to the laying on of hands" (CCC 1289). This rite is today known in the West as confirmation and in the East as chrismation.

Today as then, not all ministers are able to celebrate it. Bishops—the successors of the apostles—are able, as are priests under certain conditions, but other ministers are not.

Praying to Mary in the New Testament

CHALLENGE

"If praying to Mary is good, why don't we see it in the New Testament?"

DEFENSE

We would not expect to.

Not every teaching has to be present in Scripture (see Day 5), and not every practice consistent with Christian liberty has to be documented in the New Testament. It took time for Christians to work out the implications of the deposit of faith Jesus gave the apostles.

Scripture shows an awareness that we can pray for the dead (2 Macc. 12:42 and, quite possibly, 2 Tim. 1:18) and an awareness that those in heaven intercede for the living (2 Macc. 15:12, 14; Matt. 18:10; Rev. 5:8, 8:3–4). It was not long before Christians took the natural step of asking those in heaven to pray for them (see Jimmy Akin, *The Fathers Know Best,* chapter 52).

Whether this practice was already in use in the first century, we do not know, but if it was, we still would not expect to see references to Marian prayers in the New Testament. Its documents are not private devotionals and are not the type of literature we would expect to contain such references. The Gospels are set during the life of Christ, when Mary was clearly still alive, and Revelation is a prophetic work that records almost nothing of John's life outside the vision.

We do find references to personal prayer in Acts and the epistles, but there is a good reason they, too, wouldn't include Marian prayers: Mary was probably still alive. According to the Protoevangelium of James (chapters 8–9), Mary was betrothed to Joseph when she was twelve. This was a common age for girls to be married (boys typically married in their teens). The Talmud describes the onset of puberty as the preferred time for a daughter to be married (*b. Sanhedrin* 76a-b).

If Mary was thirteen when Jesus was born, then, based on the traditional date of his birth in 3–2 B.C., Mary would have been born around 15 B.C. She would be seventy in A.D. 55 and eighty in 65. Acts was written in A.D. 60, and the New Testament epistles were written between the late 40s and the mid-60s. It is thus quite possible that Mary had not reached the end of her earthly life.

"This Generation Will Not Pass Away"

CHALLENGE

"Jesus said of the end of the world, 'This generation will not pass away before all these things take place' (Mark 13:30; cf. Matt. 24:34, Luke 21:32). But Jesus' generation died, and the end of the world has not happened. Therefore, Jesus prophesied falsely, and so can't be God."

DEFENSE

"These things" does not refer to the end of the world.

Jesus gives a number of warnings concerning events that the disciples will face before the fulfillment of his words. This statement occurs after Jesus made a prediction about the temple: "Do you see these great buildings? There will not be left here one stone upon another, that will not be thrown down" (Mark 13:2).

Afterward, "as he sat on the Mount of Olives opposite the temple, Peter and James and John and Andrew asked him privately, 'Tell us, when will this be, and what will be the sign when these things are all to be accomplished?'" (Mark 13:3–4).

The disciples did not ask about the end of the world, but the destruction of the temple. Jesus answered that his generation would not pass away before the temple was destroyed, and he was correct. The Gospels record the speech occurring just before the Crucifixion, which most likely took place in A.D. 33. The temple was destroyed in A.D. 70 by forces under the command of the Roman general Titus. There would have been many people of Jesus' generation who were still alive when the temple was destroyed.

TIP

Luke introduces Jesus' speech on the Mount of Olives the same way, with the disciples asking when his prediction about the temple would be fulfilled (Luke 21:7–9). In Matthew, they ask about the temple, but they also ask, "and what will be the sign of your coming and of the close of the age?" (Matt. 24:3). These added questions may refer to the end of the world. However, Matthew *also* has a great deal of material at the end of his account that is not in Mark or Luke and that seems to deal with the end of the world (Matt. 25:1–46). This suggests the additional material deals with the additional questions, and the statement about "this generation" still refers to the destruction of the temple.

Abortion as a "Religious Issue"

CHALLENGE

"Abortion is a religious issue, and those who disapprove of abortion must not impose their religious beliefs on others."

DEFENSE

Abortion is not a "religious issue." It is a human-rights issue.

Even if abortion were a religious issue, there is no reason why religious people should set aside their moral values on this topic or any other. Religious values have played an indispensable role in issues from caring for the poor and the sick to ending slavery and tyranny. To suggest that religious people should not bring their values to bear on public issues also misunderstands the nature of democracy, which exists precisely to *allow* people to express their views on how society should be run.

But the truth is that abortion is not a religious issue. When people say it is, they imply that it is a matter of faith rather than reason. This is false. A powerful case against abortion can be made without bringing religion into the discussion. Unborn children simply *are* innocent human beings, and their innate right to life must be respected like that of any other innocent human being (see Days 88, 185, 191, 202).

It is a scientific fact that the unborn are living human organisms. This is not a religious claim. It does not depend on the teaching of any church or spiritual leader. It is a matter of basic biology, and only deliberate self-deception could allow one to avoid this fact.

Once you recognize that, the question is what you will do in response: Will you acknowledge the right to life possessed by all innocent human beings? Or will you begin the rationalizations people engage in when they wish to deprive an entire class of human beings of their right to life—whether that class be unborn children, the mentally retarded, Jews, or anyone else.

In other words, the question is whether you will side with those who justify and commit genocide or with those who seek to protect innocent human beings.

From a moral perspective, the correct choice is obvious, but too many today use the claim that abortion is a "religious issue" simply to shut down rational discussion of the subject and evade the clear implications of the facts.

Translations of Translations?

CHALLENGE

"The Bible has been translated over and over again in history. That's like making a photocopy of a photocopy—eventually, the image becomes blurry. Why should we trust the Bible, considering how many times it has been translated?"

DEFENSE

Modern Bible translations are made directly from the original languages, not other translations.

There have been many translations of the Bible, but the major translations published today are not based on other translations.

The books of the Bible were originally written in three languages—Hebrew, Aramaic, and Greek. These are not mysterious, lost languages. Each is well understood. Knowledge of them has survived down through history. In fact, there are people today who speak dialects of these languages as their native tongues. Hebrew is commonly spoken in modern Israel, Aramaic in various Middle Eastern communities, and Greek in Greece.

Languages change over time, but scholars have access to extensive collections of ancient manuscripts—as well as modern reference works—that enable them to understand these languages and to translate the books of the Bible directly from them.

These languages are not particularly difficult, and there are many introductory textbooks and courses that let anyone who wants to learn them do so.

The fact that knowledge of these languages is so widely available means that the major translations serve as a check on one another. As long as no translation has a monopoly, readers can check other translations to see how they render a passage.

There will always be oddball, eccentric translations of the Bible (just as there can be for secular works written in other languages), but these are usually produced by single, eccentric individuals. By contrast, the major translations of the Bible are made by teams of scholars who develop a consensus about how to render a text. They thus do not reflect the views of any single translator.

Many Bible commentaries and other reference works discuss translation issues extensively, allowing individuals to see arguments for and against different ways of rendering a passage.

Finally, modern Bible software is designed to let even an individual who does *not* know these languages to examine the original language text, look up the meaning of words, understand the grammar, and make an informed assessment.

Deuterocanonicals and Prophecy

CHALLENGE

"The deuterocanonical books aren't Scripture because they aren't prophetic. None of them claim to be written by a prophet, contain predictive prophecy, or contain messianic prophecy."

DEFENSE

The criterion by which a book is to be evaluated for the canon is whether it is divinely inspired, not whether it is "prophetic" in those senses. Further, claims about the deuterocanonicals not containing any prophecy are inaccurate.

Books are Scripture if they are divinely inspired (2 Tim. 3:16). They do not have to have someone who functions as a prophet as their author (Luke, for example, was not known as a prophet, but he wrote at least two books of Scripture—his Gospel and Acts). Despite this, the book of Baruch is attributed to the same Baruch who served as the prophet Jeremiah's scribe in writing the book of Jeremiah (Bar. 1:1; cf. Jer. 32:12, 36:17–18). Also, Baruch 6—also known as the Letter of Jeremiah—is attributed to Jeremiah himself (Bar. 6:1).

Books do not have to contain predictive prophecy to be Scripture. Many do not contain forecasts of specific, future events in the literal sense of the text (i.e., the sense intended by the human author, apart from additional, spiritual meanings intended by the Holy Spirit). Ruth, Proverbs, Song of Songs, and Ecclesiastes are examples of books that do not contain predictive prophecy.

However, the deuterocanonicals do contain predictive prophecy. This is true both of prophecies already fulfilled (see 2 Macc. 15:13–29) and prophecies still in the future (see Bar. 4:21–5:9; Tob. 14:5–7; 2 Macc. 7:23, 12:43). These reflect the same types of prophecy found in the protocanonical books of Scripture.

Messianic prophecy is usually found in the spiritual sense of Old Testament texts. For example, "Out of Egypt I called my son" (Hos. 11:1b) literally applies to the nation of Israel (see Hos. 11:1a), but in the spiritual sense it also contains a messianic prophecy (Matt. 2:15). The deuterocanonicals contain messianic prophecies of this sort that are just as clear as those found in the protocanonicals. For example, Wisdom 2:12–23 contains a meditation on how the wicked plot against a righteous man who regards himself as God's son. They condemn him to a shameful death, but they do not recognize the secret purposes of God, who created man for incorruption. This is a clearer messianic prophecy than most.

The Argument from Change

"What proof do you have that God exists?"

One popular proof proceeds from the existence of change in the universe.

The argument can be framed this way:

1. Some things in the world change.
2. Everything that changes is caused to do so.
3. Nothing is its own cause.
4. Therefore, things that change are caused to do so by something else.
5. There cannot be an infinite regress of such causes.
6. Therefore, there is an ultimate, unchanging cause of change.
7. God is the ultimate, changeless cause of change
8. Therefore, God exists.

The premises of this argument are lines 1, 2, 3, 5, and 7. The conclusions (lines 4, 6, and 8) follow from them.

Line 1 is proved by observation: we see constant change in the world around us.

Line 2 is a truth of metaphysics. It is also verified by observation. Whenever we see something change, there is a cause for this change. Line 3 is a truth of metaphysics. The idea of one thing ultimately being its own cause is incoherent.

Line 5 is a truth of metaphysics. Consider an analogy: if a painting is being made then paint is being applied to a canvas. The paint is moved by the bristles of a brush. The bristles are moved by the wood of the first inch of the handle to which they are attached. The wood of the first inch of the handle is moved by the wood of the second inch, which is moved by the wood of the third inch. However, the handle cannot go on forever. Ultimately, the handle is moved by an artist. To suggest otherwise would be to suggest "that a brush can paint by itself, provided it has a very long handle" (Antonin Sertillanges, quoted in Reginald Garrigou-Lagrange, *God: His Existence and His Nature*, 265). In the same way, there cannot be an infinite regress of simultaneous causes.

Line 8 is true by definition.

This is a version of St. Thomas Aquinas's "first way" of demonstrating God's existence (ST I:2:3). It's sometimes called the argument from "motion," since Aquinas refers to what we call change as motion.

Objections to the Argument from Change

CHALLENGE

"The argument from change (see Day 73) is flawed: (1) The future already exists, so time and change are illusions; (2) some things cause themselves to change, as when an animal opens its eyes; (3) there could be an infinite regress of prior causes; (4) there could be a causal loop where an event in the future causes a change in the past; and (5) God would need a cause."

DEFENSE

None of these objections overturn the argument from change.

First, although modern physics commonly proposes time is another dimension, like the dimensions of space, and the future already exists, this does not make time or change illusory. Things are different at one moment in time than another, so change occurs across time, even if all history exists at once from God's eternal perspective.

Second, apparent cases of self-motion disintegrate on close analysis. When an animal opens its eyes, the eye is not the cause of its own opening. The eyelids are moved by muscles, which are activated by neurons, which fire based on processes taking place on the subatomic level in the animal's nervous system.

Third, Aquinas agrees there could be an infinite regress of prior historical states (ST I:46:2). However, we are discussing what causes a change *at the moment it happens*, not about the history leading up to that moment. If a painting is being made, an artist needs to be applying paint to canvas *at that moment*. There cannot be an infinite series of *simultaneous* causes of the painting any more than an infinitely long brush could paint by itself.

Fourth, although physicists have speculated about the possibility of events in the future producing effects in the past, at present we have no evidence this happens. Further, as in the previous example, we are not talking about events elsewhere in history (either the past or the future). We are discussing what causes the change *at the moment it takes place*. Even if an artist traveled from the future to make a painting, the painting is still being made in the present and requires a cause at that moment.

Fifth, God does not require a cause because, per the argument, God is changeless and the argument only proposes that things that change need causes.

Infant Baptism and the New Testament

CHALLENGE

*"Infant baptism is unbiblical. One requirement for baptism
is to have belief in Jesus, which infants don't have."*

DEFENSE

The New Testament nowhere restricts baptism to people who
are above a certain age. In fact, we read of entire households
being baptized, and there are indications that baptism was
given to the children of believers, regardless of their age.

The New Testament never establishes an age requirement for baptism. Most of the people we see being baptized in its pages are adults, but this is because Christianity was a new movement, and most of its converts would naturally have been adults.

The New Testament also records entire households being baptized (Acts 10:47–11:17, 16:15, 30–34, 18:8, 1 Cor. 1:16). This establishes the principle that whole households were baptized at once, and it does not exclude young children. In fact, Luke records: "Now they were bringing even infants to [Jesus] that he might touch them; and when the disciples saw it, they rebuked them. But Jesus called them to him, saying, "Let the children come to me, and do not hinder them; for to such belongs the kingdom of God. Truly, I say to you, whoever does not receive the kingdom of God like a child shall not enter it" (Luke 18:15–17).

Christians, reflecting on this passage, recognized that if the kingdom belongs to children—"even infants"—then they are appropriate recipients of baptism, just like adults who are willing to receive the kingdom like a child and be baptized.

Further, the Jewish expectation at the time was that the children of believers would share in the blessings of the covenant along with their parents. Thus on Pentecost Peter told the crowds: "Repent, and be baptized every one of you in the name of Jesus Christ for the forgiveness of your sins; and you shall receive the gift of the Holy Spirit. For the promise is to you and to your children" (Acts 2:38–39).

As the Christian initiation ritual, baptism is the Christian equivalent of circumcision, the Jewish initiation ritual. Paul explicitly identifies baptism as "the circumcision of Christ," telling his readers: "In [Jesus] also you were circumcised with a circumcision not made by hands, by the removal of the body of the flesh, by the circumcision of Christ, having been buried with him in baptism" (Col. 2:11–12, LEB).

Infant Baptism in the Early Church

CHALLENGE

"Infant baptism is an invention of men not practiced by the early Christians."

DEFENSE

Infant baptism was practiced from the beginning of Church history. The principles behind it are articulated in the New Testament, and we have explicit documentation of it from the second century on.

We observe elsewhere the biblical principles behind infant baptism (see Day 75).

One is that baptism is the Christian initiation ritual and its equivalent of circumcision. This led some in the early Church to discuss whether baptism should be performed on the eighth day after birth—the time circumcision was performed (Lev. 12:2–3).

Around A.D. 253, Cyprian of Carthage reported the results of a council that held that baptism should *not* be delayed until the eighth day but given even sooner: "But in respect of the case of the infants, which you [Fidus] say ought not to be baptized within the second or third day after their birth, and that the law of ancient circumcision should be followed, so that one who is just born should not be baptized and sanctified within the eighth day, we all thought very differently in our council. For no one agreed with the course you thought should be taken; rather we all judge that the mercy and grace of God is not to be refused to anyone born of man" (*Letters* 58:2).

Other records show infant baptism was performed in the second century. St. Irenaeus of Lyons was clear that being regenerated or "born again" happened in baptism: "As we are lepers in sin, we are made clean of our old transgressions by means of the sacred water and the invocation of the Lord; we are spiritually regenerated" (*Fragments from the Lost Writings of Irenaeus* 34 [c. A.D. 190]).

Irenaeus further indicated that this was done for infants when he wrote: "For [Jesus] came to save all through himself—all, I say, who through him are born again to God—infants, and children, and boys, and youths, and old men" (*Against Heresies* 2:22:4 [c. A.D. 189]). As someone who grew up in a Christian home, Irenaeus himself was likely baptized as an infant around the year A.D. 140, less than fifty years from the apostolic age.

The Priesthood of All Believers

CHALLENGE

"Catholic ministers should not be called priests. All Christians are priests. Peter says his readers are 'a royal priesthood, a holy nation' (1 Pet. 2:9)."

DEFENSE

Christians are priests, but Scripture indicates that there is also a special, ministerial priesthood.

The Church agrees that, by baptism, Christians have a share in Christ's priesthood (CCC 1141, 1268, 1546; cf. 1174, 1322). This is commonly referred to as "the common priesthood of all the faithful" (CCC 1535). However, certain members of the faithful are ordained to a greater participation in Christ's priesthood by the sacrament of holy orders. This is known as the ministerial priesthood (CCC 1547). Christ—the source of the common and ministerial priesthoods—is our high priest (CCC 1544). The Church thus understands there to be a threefold structure: the common priesthood of all, the ministerial priesthood of the ordained, and the high priesthood of Christ.

This is what we see in the New Testament. The common priesthood is referred to in 1 Peter 2:9. The ministerial priesthood is referred to in Romans 15:16, where Paul speaks of how he is a minister of Christ "in the priestly service of the gospel of God." The ministerial priesthood is also referred to in passages that speak of ordained Church leaders known as "elders" (Acts 14:23; 1 Tim. 5:17; Titus 1:5; James 5:14). Finally, the high priesthood of Christ is referred to in passages such as Hebrews 3:1, 4:14–15, 5:5, 6:20, and 9:11.

This was also the pattern in the Old Testament. Peter was quoting from the Septuagint version of Exodus 19:6, where God told the Israelites that, if they kept his covenant, they would be to him "a royal priesthood and a holy nation" (Greek, *basileion hierateuma kai ethnos hagion*). There was thus a common priesthood of the Israelites, but that did not stop God from also appointing a ministerial priesthood from the sons of Aaron (Exod. 28:1), with Aaron as the high priest (Ezra 7:5). Rather than undermining the idea of a ministerial priesthood, Peter's citation of Exodus supports it by invoking for the Church the same priestly concepts that applied to Israel.

TIP

It is hard to object to Catholics calling their ministers "priests" since this term is derived from the Greek word *presbuteros* ("elder, presbyter"). The New Testament elders or presbyters gave English the word "priest."

The Concept of Revelation

CHALLENGE

"The concept of revelation is irrational. Why should we believe something just because an alleged prophet says so?"

DEFENSE

The concept of revelation is not irrational.
In fact, it's something we use all the time.

Something is revealed if it is disclosed to us by another rather than being personally verified. Sometimes this is also referred to as accepting a claim "on authority."

C.S. Lewis writes:

> Believing things on authority only means believing them because you have been told them by someone you think trustworthy. Ninety-nine per cent of the things you believe are believed on authority. I believe there is such a place as New York. I have not seen it myself. I could not prove by abstract reasoning that there must be such a place. I believe it because reliable people have told me so. The ordinary man believes in the solar system, atoms, evolution, and the circulation of the blood on authority—because the scientists say so.
>
> Every historical statement in the world is believed on authority. None of us has seen the Norman Conquest or the defeat of the [Spanish] Armada. None of us could prove them by pure logic as you prove a thing in mathematics. We believe them simply because people who did see them have left writings that tell us about them: in fact, on authority. A man who jibbed at authority in other things as some people do in religion would have to be content to know nothing all his life" (*Mere Christianity*, chapter 2).

The concept of revelation is thus rational. The question is how it functions in a religious context.

According to the Judeo-Christian view, God has given revealed information to prophets, who he authorized to communicate it to others. In doing so, he was sensitive to the question of how one would know if a prophet is reliable, and the Bible contains tests by which true prophets can be discerned. These include whether a prophet can produce a miracle to validate the claim that he is in contact with the supernatural (Deut. 18:21–22) and whether his message is consistent with prior divine revelation (Deut. 13:1–4; 1 Cor. 12:3).

From a Christian point of view, the Resurrection of Jesus was a key miracle validating Jesus' message (Acts 17:31).

The Dating of Acts

CHALLENGE

"Acts isn't reliable history. It was written long after the events."

DEFENSE

The date that the book of Acts was written does not pose a problem for its historical reliability.

We observe elsewhere the general subject of Acts' reliability (see Day 193).

Raymond Brown proposed a late date for Luke and Acts of A.D. "85, give or take five to ten years" (*An Introduction to the New Testament*, 226, 280). If so, Acts would have been written approximately fifty-two years after the earliest events it describes and twenty-five years after the latest. All of that is within living memory. However, Acts was probably written earlier, for its narrative suddenly stops while Paul is under house arrest, awaiting trial before Nero.

Paul's journey to Rome is a major theme in the book, set up as early as Acts 9:15–16. It comes into focus when Paul announces he must see Rome after visiting Jerusalem (Acts 18:21). He insists on going to Jerusalem, knowing he will be arrested (Acts 20:22–23, 21:10–14). When that occurs (Acts 21:33), the story of his journey to Rome takes over the narrative and dominates the last seven chapters of the book (one fourth of its twenty-eight chapters).

Yet it ends inconclusively, with Paul spending two years under house arrest, with no word of what happened at his trial. Given the amount of drama building up to the trial, this would make no sense if the result of Paul's trial were known. If he was condemned, Luke would have the story of his glorious martyrdom, or of his innocent suffering on account of Christ, to record. If he was acquitted (as other sources suggest he was on this occasion), Luke would have recorded his glorious vindication.

The logical explanation for why the book includes neither of these is that the trial had not yet happened, and that tells us when Acts was published: two years after Paul's Roman imprisonment began. Many scholars think Paul's imprisonment began around A.D. 60, giving us a date of 62 for Acts. A stronger case, though, is that it began in 58, giving us a date of 60 for Acts (see Jack Finegan, *Handbook of Biblical Chronology*, 2nd ed., and Andrew Steinmann, *From Abraham to Paul*).

TIP

For more on the dating of Acts, see John A.T. Robinson, *Redating the New Testament*.

Anathema

CHALLENGE

"The Catholic Church says Protestants are damned. The Council of Trent contains many canons saying that if someone endorses a particular Protestant belief, 'Let him be anathema' (damned by God)."

DEFENSE

This fundamentally misunderstands what an anathema was. It reads a non-Catholic understanding of the term into Catholic documents.

In Church documents, the term "anathema" does not mean "damned by God." It refers to a form of excommunication that used to be practiced.

When a person was excommunicated by anathema, a series of procedures had to be followed, including the local bishop warning the person he was committing a grave ecclesiastical crime and imperiling his soul. If he failed to repent, an ecclesiastical court would try and convict him, then the bishop would hold a public ceremony where he was excommunicated (cf. 1 Cor. 5:1–5, 1 Tim. 1:20). If he later repented, the bishop would perform another public ceremony, lift the excommunication, and welcome him back (cf. 2 Cor. 2:6–8).

When Trent used the formula "Let him be anathema," it indicated bishops could apply this form of excommunication to Catholics in their flocks who committed certain offenses.

The penalty did not take effect automatically. Thus, it never applied globally to Protestants. Not only were Protestants *not* subjects of Catholic bishops, the bishops had better things to do than conduct endless court procedures and ceremonies concerning people who were not part of the Catholic community.

In practice, the penalty of anathema was imposed rarely and only on those who continued to assert their Catholic identity. Eventually, it became so infrequent that it was abolished and does not exist today. The current *Code of Canon Law* (1983) does not contain the penalty of anathema, and it abrogates all penalties it does not contain (cf. canon 6).

Excommunication still exists and is still applied if a Catholic embraces a heresy (canons 751, 1364; cf. canons 11, 1321–23, 1330). However, the form of excommunication known as anathema no longer exists. But even when it did, anathema did not judge the state of a person's soul—something only God knows. It was a disciplinary measure intended to protect the Catholic community and to wake a Catholic up to the spiritual danger he was in.

Undercutting Evangelization?

CHALLENGE

"The Catholic claim that it's possible for non-Christians to be saved undercuts the basis of evangelization."

DEFENSE

The duty to evangelize is not based on the idea that it's impossible to be saved without explicitly embracing the Christian faith.

We have a duty to evangelize because Jesus told us to: "Go therefore and make disciples of all nations, baptizing them in the name of the Father and of the Son and of the Holy Spirit, teaching them to observe all that I have commanded you" (Matt. 28:19–20), and, "Go into all the world and preach the gospel to the whole creation" (Mark 16:15).

It is God's will we evangelize, and regardless of the reasons for this, a sense of duty and gratitude should motivate us to preach the gospel. It so happens God has given us insights into why it is his will we evangelize, and not all of these are connected with the next life. Simply knowing the truth about God is good, and preaching the truth about the Creator to creation is a worthwhile activity regardless of what happens in the next life. Further, the Christian faith is not exclusively concerned with the afterlife. Being a Christian brings blessings in this life as well, and it is worthwhile to share the gospel with others for that reason.

Of course, one's response to the gospel *does* affect salvation, and this is a powerful motive to evangelize, but it is not the only one.

Further, it doesn't have to be *impossible* for a person to be saved for there to be a salvation-based motive for evangelization. If becoming a Christian makes it easier or more likely for him to be saved, that is reason to share the gospel with him.

There are spiritual dangers in the world: "Very often, deceived by the Evil One, men have become vain in their reasonings, and have exchanged the truth of God for a lie, and served the creature rather than the Creator. Or else, living and dying in this world without God, they are exposed to ultimate despair" (CCC 844).

If a person has a clearer understanding of the truth and greater access to the means of grace that the Christian faith offers, then he will be better prepared to overcome those dangers and be saved.

Annulments and Divorce

*"The Church is hypocritical in its opposition to divorce.
Annulments are just the Catholic equivalent."*

DEFENSE

Annulments are not the same thing as divorce, and the Church's
teaching on annulments is rooted in the teaching of Jesus.

A divorce claims to sever a marriage bond that really existed, while
an annulment is a finding that there never was an actual marriage in
the first place.

This is why, when a civil court is asked to grant a divorce, the spouses
don't have to prove anything about the time they were married (other
than that they *were* married). One spouse simply has to show that, after
the marriage, one party did something that gave the other cause for the
divorce (e.g., adultery, abuse, abandonment)—or, in an age of no-fault
divorce, simply that they no longer wish to be married.

By contrast, when a Church tribunal is asked to grant a declaration
of nullity (known as an annulment), it must investigate the circumstances that applied *at the time of the wedding*, to see whether there were
any factors present that would have prevented a valid (actual) marriage
from coming into existence.

The fact that not all marriages are valid is clear from the teaching of Jesus, who stated: "Whoever divorces his wife and marries another, commits adultery against her; and if she divorces her husband
and marries another, she commits adultery" (Mark 10:11–12; cf. Luke
16:18). Jesus indicates that, in these cases, the second marriages are not
valid. When the parties have sex, they are committing adultery against
their first spouses, to whom they are actually still married. Thus some
marriages (like the first ones) are valid, while other marriages (like the
second ones) are not; they are null, and so in these cases the Church
can issue a decree of nullity, or an annulment.

There can be a variety of factors that cause a marriage to be null
from the beginning. Already being married is only one of them. However, the purpose of an annulment is not to dissolve a marriage that
exists but to show that—despite appearances—it did not really exist.

TIP

For more information on the Church's teaching on divorce, see Day 132.

Non-Christian Eyewitnesses?

CHALLENGE

"If Jesus existed, why don't we have statements about him from non-Christian eyewitnesses of his ministry?"

DEFENSE

Because we would not expect to.

Based on events like the feeding of the five thousand and the four thousand (Matt. 14:13–21, 15:32–38), we may estimate that the number of people who were eyewitnesses of Jesus' ministry was in the tens of thousands. However, the vast majority were not among his constant companions and only encountered him on one or a handful of occasions. They were thus unlikely to leave a written account.

Further, the vast majority of them—like the vast majority in first-century Palestine—belonged to the rural lower class and were illiterate. The ancient Mediterranean world had a primarily oral culture, and most could not write, especially in rural places like Galilee. Consequently, information about popular figures like Jesus was primarily passed on by oral tradition.

Those most interested in passing on traditions about a teacher—whether in oral or written form—were his disciples, who in this case would be Christians, the people that this challenge is excluding. Non-Christians would have little interest in passing on Jesus' traditions, much less writing them down.

The number of people who were eyewitnesses of Jesus, non-Christian, able to write, and motivated to write about him was probably very small. It probably included only a few people, like the governor Pontius Pilate, the high priest Caiaphas, and some in their circles. Some of these people probably did write about Jesus. In particular, Pilate likely recorded Jesus' execution in government records. However, we have no records from any of these people—about *anything*. All the primary source Roman records perished, as did any kept by the Jewish authorities (lost when the Romans burned the Jerusalem temple in A.D. 70).

We know about people in this period (e.g., popular Jewish figures such as Honi the Circle Maker, Judas the Galilean, Theudas, and the revolutionary known as "the Egyptian") not because we have eyewitness accounts, which are rare, but because they are mentioned by ancient historians and other writers.

The same types of sources that speak of them also speak of Jesus. In fact, our evidence for Jesus is even better, as in his case we do have statements by eyewitnesses, such as his Christian followers Matthew and John.

Peter in Galatians

CHALLENGE

"Peter didn't have a special role among the apostles. Paul doesn't show him special respect in his letter to the Galatians. He even opposed Peter 'to his face' (Gal. 2:11)."

DEFENSE

On the contrary, his letter to the Galatians shows that Paul acknowledged Peter's unique role in the Church.

Paul's critics had apparently accused him of trying to please men by preaching a watered-down gospel that did not require circumcision. Thus he stresses that he is not trying to please men and that his gospel is not of human origin (Gal. 1:10–12).

He then recounts a series of incidents to illustrate his assertion. Peter figures in each incident.

First (Gal. 1:13–24), he recounts how after his conversion he did not consult with anyone, though "after three years I went up to Jerusalem to visit Cephas [i.e., Peter], and remained with him fifteen days" (Gal. 1:18).

Second (Gal. 2:1–10), he recounts how he returned for the Jerusalem council, and when he did so the other apostles "saw that I had been entrusted with the gospel to the uncircumcised, just as Peter had been entrusted with the gospel to the circumcised (for he who worked through Peter for the mission to the circumcised worked through me also for the Gentiles)" (Gal. 2:7–8). He also notes that "James and Cephas and John . . . were reputed to be pillars" (Gal. 2:9).

Third (Gal. 2:11–16), he recounts how "when Cephas came to Antioch I opposed him to his face, because he stood condemned. For before certain men came from James, he ate with the Gentiles; but when they came he drew back and separated himself, fearing the circumcision party. . . . But when I saw that they were not straightforward about the truth of the gospel, I said to Cephas before them all, 'If you, though a Jew, live like a Gentile and not like a Jew, how can you compel the Gentiles to live like Jews?'" (Gal. 2:11–12, 14).

Each incident shows Peter's unique role: Paul went to visit Peter, not the other apostles. Peter had a special mission to the Jews that paralleled Paul's mission to the Gentiles. Peter was recognized as a pillar. And, in the ideal test case of whether Paul would bend the gospel to please men, Paul was willing to stand up even to the most authoritative Church leader: Peter.

Descended from David *How?*

CHALLENGE

"Jesus' genealogies contradict each other. Matthew says that Jesus descended from David's son Solomon (Matt. 1:6), but Luke says it was David's son Nathan (Luke 3:31). Similarly, Matthew has him descended from Zerubbabel's son Abiud (Matt. 1:13), whereas Luke says it was Zerubbabel's son Rhesa (Luke 3:27)."

DEFENSE

Jesus was descended from David and Zerubbabel by more than one line.

Normally, a person has two parents, four grandparents, eight great-grandparents, and so on. But this doubling pattern does not go back indefinitely.

Marriages usually occur within the same community (a village, region, tribe, or nation). People in a community tend to be related. Consequently, the number of ancestors is less than what the doubling pattern would predict. In a small community, an individual may occupy more than one slot in a family tree.

Suppose William has a son named Henry, who has descendants, and several generations later, one named Elizabeth is born. Suppose William also has a daughter named Adela, who also has descendants. Because of intermarriage in the community, Elizabeth is also one of Adela's descendants. Genealogists would say Elizabeth is descended from William by the Henry "line" and the Adela "line."

This describes the British royal family. Queen Elizabeth II descends from William the Conqueror (c. 1028–1087) by the line of King Henry I and the line of St. Adela of Normandy, both of whom were William's children. In fact, Elizabeth II is descended from William by multiple lines (at least eight through Adela alone). William the Conqueror thus appears in multiple slots in Elizabeth II's family tree.

The same was true for David and Zerubbabel concerning Jesus, who descended from David by both the Solomon and Nathan lines and from Zerubbabel by both the Abiud and Rhesa lines. This is not unexpected. David lived a millennium before Jesus. Matthew records twenty-seven intervening generations, so according to the doubling pattern, Jesus would have at least 67,108,864 ancestors in David's generation.

There were not that many Israelites alive in David's generation, so, since David was one of Jesus' ancestors, David filled multiple slots in Jesus' family tree, and Jesus was descended from David by multiple lines. The same is true of Zerubbabel, though to a lesser degree, since Zerubbabel lived only half a millennium before Jesus (for more, see Day 95).

God and the Burden of Proof

CHALLENGE

"The burden of proof is on those who believe in God. Atheists don't have to prove God doesn't exist; believers have to prove he does."

DEFENSE

This misunderstands the burden of proof.

The concept is borrowed from civil law, where it refers to the obligation a party has to provide sufficient evidence for a claim or lose his case. U.S. law establishes a presumption of innocence, according to which a prosecutor must prove the accused is guilty of an offense or the accused will be acquitted and be legally treated as innocent. The presumption of innocence is a choice our society has made to favor the accused, lest prosecutors use the power of the state to falsely convict large numbers of innocent people and bring about a reign of terror.

However, the burden of proof works differently in other settings, such as philosophical or religious discussions.

From a logical point of view, it does not matter whether one is arguing for a proposition (*P*) or for its denial (*not-P*). In the absence of evidence, neither is more probable than the other. Consequently, as long as things remain in the abstract, nobody has a burden of proof.

The burden is created when one person begins asserting either *P* or *not-P*. If he wants to convince a person of a proposition or its denial, then he needs to offer that person reasons why. The philosophical burden of proof thus does not intrinsically fall on either party. It is something that you assume when you try to convince someone else of a position.

All of this applies to situations where one is making a claim about whether something exists. Until you consider the evidence, neither the proposition "X exists" nor the proposition "X does not exist" can be deemed more probable than the other, and it doesn't matter what X is. As long as you have no evidence favoring the existence or non-existence of X, both propositions are equally probable.

Thus if a theist wants to convince a non-theist that God exists, he needs to provide arguments for his position, and if an atheist wishes to convince a non-atheist that God does not exist, he similarly needs to offer arguments for his position. The burden of proof is assumed by whoever is trying to convince the other.

Too Many Rules

CHALLENGE

"The Catholic Church has too many rules."

DEFENSE

This is a cliché and does not stand up to examination.

First, how many rules is "too many"? People never propose a number for how many would be appropriate. They just repeat a stock claim to criticize the Church.

Second, the rules the Church has are much fewer than those of any group of comparable size.

The Church has a billion members, the large majority of whom belong to its Latin rite. The main legislation governing the Latin Rite is the *Code of Canon Law*, which is one volume that runs a little over 500 pages in a standard English edition.

By comparison, the United States has around 300 million citizens, but the main federal legislation governing it—the United States Code—is thirty-four primary volumes in its 2012 edition, totaling more than 45,000 pages!

Third, most laws the Catholic Church has exist to deal with situations an ordinary member will rarely encounter. Such situations happen, but so infrequently that an ordinary Catholic is not expected to know the details of the laws dealing with them. They can be briefed as the situations arise (e.g., what you need to do when being confirmed, a once-in-a-lifetime experience).

An ordinary Catholic is expected to know comparatively few rules, such as the Ten Commandments and the five precepts of the Church (CCC 2041-43). They should also know how to prepare for the sacraments they regularly receive (primarily confession and the Eucharist). This doesn't include everything a Catholic needs to know, but it does indicate the relative modesty of the rules that apply to an ordinary member's experience.

Fourth, Catholics should know basic moral principles, but so should everyone. Everybody should be a moral person.

This leads to the real reason that the "too many rules" charge is made. It isn't about the number of rules. Instead, it is about *specific moral rules*. Almost invariably, the person making the charge doesn't like one or more rules of a moral nature—usually dealing with personal gratification (e.g., don't have sex outside of marriage, don't abuse alcohol or drugs).

But these are basic moral principles that belong to human nature. The Catholic Church is merely pointing them out, and the "too many rules" charge is a smokescreen to mask personal temptations.

Justifications for Abortion

CHALLENGE

"Abortion is justified in some cases. It may not be a good time for a mother to have a baby. She may be young, still in school, poor, or unmarried. She may have as many children as she can care for, or the child could be a product of rape or incest."

DEFENSE

These represent good reasons not to *have* a baby, but they are not good reasons to *kill* a baby.

Suppose the child were already born. Would *any* of these reasons be a legitimate reason for the mother to kill her child? A mother cannot kill her newborn because she is young, in school, or unmarried. Neither can she do so because she is poor or has other children. If these are not adequate reasons for a mother to kill her child *after* birth, then they are not adequate reasons for her to kill her child *before* birth. They are just rationalizations.

Instead, mothers in difficult situations must be helped. They must receive the care and assistance they need as they carry the child to term, as well as *after* the birth, whether they choose to raise the child or pursue adoption.

Similarly, the fact that a person was conceived by an act of rape or incest would not justify killing him *after* birth, and so it does not justify killing him *before* birth, either. Rape and incest are horrible crimes. Those who commit them must be brought to justice, and their victims must receive compassion and care. But adding a new victim through a new act of violence does not make things better. It makes them worse.

Even when conceived by an act of rape or incest, unborn children are innocent human beings. It is immoral to kill them because of crimes committed by one or both of their parents. Killing people because of what their ancestors did, even their most immediate ancestors, is barbaric.

The circumstances in which these children were conceived make their situations very sensitive, but killing them does not help either them or their mothers, who need compassionate care and support.

TIP

This defense offers a useful, general test for justifications of abortion. If someone proposes a reason to have an abortion, ask if that reason would justify killing a child *after* birth. If not, it does not justify killing a child *before* birth.

Chronology in the Gospels

CHALLENGE

"The Gospels sometimes record the events of Jesus' ministry in different order and thus contradict one another."

DEFENSE

These are not contradictions. Ancient authors had the liberty to record events chronologically or non-chronologically.

Even in our modern, time-obsessed world, biographers have liberty to arrange material in non-chronological ways. A biography of Abraham Lincoln might devote a chapter to his thoughts on slavery and race relations rather than breaking this material up and covering it repeatedly throughout a chronological account of his career. Similarly, Jesus' ethical or prophetic teachings might be put together in single sections of a Gospel, as with the Sermon on the Mount (Matt. 5–7) and the Olivet Discourse (Matt. 24–25).

In the ancient world, people usually did not have day-by-day records of a person's life. The memory of what a great man did persisted, but not precisely when he did things. Recording material in a non-chronological order was thus expected. This was true even of the most famous men in the world. See Suetonius's *The Lives of the Twelve Caesars*, which records the words and deeds of the Caesars without a detailed chronology.

Ultimately, *what* a great man said and did was considered important, not precisely *when* the events happened. That's *why* the former were remembered and the latter was not.

Jesus gave his teachings on many occasions, but without having a detailed chronology available, the evangelists sequenced them according to topical and literary considerations. The same was true of many individual deeds Jesus performed (e.g., healings).

This is not to say that the evangelists give us *no* chronological information. Some events obviously occurred before or after others. Thus his baptism (with which he inaugurated his ministry) is toward the beginning of the Gospels and the Crucifixion is at the end.

Sometimes chronological details were remembered, such as the fact that Jesus performed a particular healing on the Sabbath (Mark 3:1–6), that John the Baptist's ministry began in the fifteenth year of Tiberius Caesar (Luke 3:1–3), or that certain events in Jesus' life took place on major Jewish feasts (John 2:13, 6:4, 7:2, 10:22, 11:5). It is thus possible to glean chronological information from the Gospels.

Symbolic Language in Genesis 1

CHALLENGE

"Genesis 1 is inaccurate. Modern science reveals that the world was created over eons, not six days."

DEFENSE

Genesis 1 uses symbolic language. "God himself created the visible world in all its richness, diversity, and order. Scripture presents the work of the Creator symbolically as a succession of six days of divine 'work'" (CCC 337).

The Church acknowledges the value of scientific studies. "The question about the origins of the world and of man has been the object of many scientific studies, which have splendidly enriched our knowledge of the age and dimensions of the cosmos, the development of life-forms and the appearance of man. These discoveries invite us to even greater admiration for the greatness of the Creator" (CCC 283).

A careful reading of Genesis 1 shows it uses symbolic language. It says that initially "the earth was without form and void" (Gen. 1:2). During the six days of creation, God solves both these problems. First, he gives the world form by separating day from night (day 1), sky from sea (day 2), and the waters of the sea so dry land appears (day 3). Second, he revisits these realms and populates them so they are no longer "void" (empty): He populates day and night with the sun, moon, and stars (day 4), sky and sea with birds and fish (day 5), and land with animals and man (day 6). Then he rests on the seventh day. Genesis 1 thus takes the work of the Creator and symbolically fits it into the structure of a Hebrew week.

A clue that this is literary rather than literal is the fact that the sun is not created until day 4, yet the day/night cycle was established on day 1. The ancients knew the presence of the sun is what makes it day, so the creation of the sun on day 4 shows the audience the text is symbolic.

John Paul II stated: "The Bible itself speaks to us of the origin of the universe and its makeup, not in order to provide us with a scientific treatise but in order to state the correct relationship of humanity with God and the universe. Sacred Scripture wishes simply to declare that the world was created by God" (Address to the Pontifical Academy of Sciences, October 3, 1981).

How Do You Know It Isn't All Symbolic?

CHALLENGE

"By allowing Catholics to interpret the six days of Genesis 1 in a symbolic way (CCC 337), the Church sets a dangerous precedent that could undermine the Faith. If this is symbolic, how do you know other things—such as the Resurrection—aren't?"

DEFENSE

Everyone recognizes that Scripture contains symbolism. It's a matter of correctly identifying it.

It can be tempting to reflexively classify things in Scripture as literal (or symbolic) to avoid sorting out the difference, but we must undertake this task.

Humans use both literal and symbolic speech, and we constantly discern the difference, often without being conscious of it. If someone says we need to "roll out the red carpet" for a dignitary, English speakers intuitively recognize this is a non-literal way of saying he needs to be given a special welcome. It is an expression known for its non-literal use in English.

When we encounter writing from other cultures, it can be harder to tell literal from symbolic since we are less familiar with their literary conventions, but it can be done. All recognize that the biblical prophets used symbols and Jesus told parables. This shows we can learn to recognize non-literal forms in Scripture.

Often symbols are identified by cues in the text that reveal they are not literal. For example, the creation of the sun on the fourth day, when the sun's presence is what makes it day, is a cue the days of Genesis 1 are not literal (see Day 90). No human witnessed the creation of the world, and Genesis, written somewhere around 1000 B.C., was penned long after the event. Genesis 1 is more likely to be non-literal than a text written soon after an event and using eyewitness testimony.

The latter is what we have with the Resurrection of Jesus. The New Testament was written within a few decades of the Resurrection and was composed by or in consultation with eyewitnesses (cf. Luke 1:2, John 21:24). It also contains emphatic statements about the Resurrection's reality (cf. 1 Cor. 15:1–20).

We need have no fear that recognizing parts of Scripture are symbolic will undermine the Faith any more than Jesus' use of parables does.

The Practice of Celibacy

CHALLENGE

"The practice of celibacy is unbiblical. Paul describes forbidding marriage as a 'doctrine of demons' (1 Tim. 4:1–3)."

DEFENSE

Celibacy is grounded in Scripture, including the writings of Paul.

Celibacy is the state of being unmarried. This is not the condition most people are called to, but it is for some. In the Latin Church, most ordained ministers are celibate, as are many in Eastern Catholic Churches (CCC 1579–80).

This is a matter of discipline rather than doctrine, and it could change for sufficient reason. However, being unmarried allows clergy to fully consecrate themselves to Christ and his service. It also conforms them to the model of life adopted by Christ during his ministry and by all the saved in the next life (Matt. 22:30).

The way the discipline has been practiced has varied in different periods, but it is far from unbiblical. Although Jesus recognized marriage as a good instituted by God (Matt. 19:4–6), he was celibate (see Day 25), and he recommended celibacy to those who could accept it (Matt. 19:10–12).

Celibacy is also discussed by Paul. He indicates that he was celibate and wished everyone was, though he acknowledged it is not everyone's calling (1 Cor. 7:7, cf. vv. 1–9). In view of the conditions of his day, he counseled the unmarried to remain as they were, noting it would spare them worldly troubles and allow them to be single-minded in their devotion to Christ. Yet he acknowledged that it was not sinful for them to marry (1 Cor. 7:25–38). He also appears to recommend celibacy to Timothy as a minister (2 Tim. 2:3–4).

With this background, we can understand what Paul means when he refers to forbidding marriage as a "doctrine of demons." He is not condemning celibacy, which he both practiced and recommended. He is condemning the idea that *nobody* should marry, that marriage is somehow immoral (a view endorsed by some heretics).

In the same letter, Paul endorses vows of celibacy. When discussing an order of consecrated widows, he said, "Refuse to enrol younger widows; for when they grow wanton against Christ they desire to marry, and so they incur condemnation for having violated their first pledge" (1 Tim. 5:11–12). He therefore recommended that younger widows remarry and avoid violating the consecrated widow's vow of celibacy (vv. 14–15).

Cursing the Fig Tree

CHALLENGE

"Jesus displayed gratuitous malice when he cursed a fig tree for not having fruit when it wasn't even the season for figs."

DEFENSE

Jesus didn't display gratuitous malice. He was teaching a lesson.

"Seeing in the distance a fig tree in leaf, [Jesus] went to see if he could find anything on it. When he came to it, he found nothing but leaves, for it was not the season for figs" (Mark 11:13).

The fig tree was known to produce fruit before putting forth leaves (Pliny the Elder, *Naturalis Historia* 16:49). Seeing a fig tree in leaf, Jesus had reason to suppose it had put forth figs earlier than usual. By its leaves, the tree made an outward show indicating fruit, but there was none. Jesus therefore used it to teach a lesson.

On other occasions, Jesus criticized Jewish leaders of making a false, outward show of spirituality (Matt. 23:5–7, 25–28). He also used fruit to symbolize the results of true spirituality (Matt. 7:16–20, 12:33, 13:23, etc.). In particular, he indicted the chief priests and Pharisees for failing to produce spiritual fruit, saying: "I tell you, the kingdom of God will be taken away from you and given to a nation producing the fruits of it" (Matt. 21:43).

By cursing the fig tree and causing it to wither, Jesus symbolized the fate of spiritual hypocrites and the judgment coming upon the Jewish leadership.

This is confirmed in Mark's account. Scholars have noted that Mark often sequences material so that two halves of a story are interrupted by something important that sheds light on them. Places where Mark sandwiches material this way are known as "Markan sandwiches."

The cursing of the fig tree is such a case: Jesus first curses the fig tree (Mark 11:12–14), then he clears the temple of those abusing its holiness (11:15–19), and then the disciples return and see the fig tree withered (11:20–21). The Jewish authorities, despite their outward religiosity, had allowed the temple to be corrupted, and juxtaposing Jesus' judgment on the temple with the cursing of the fig tree reveals the message that the latter teaches. It also foretells the doom of the Jewish authorities and the temple itself (Mark 12:1–12, 13:1–2).

Miracles and Science

"Miracles are part of a prescientific worldview. Today we understand that the universe operates by the laws of nature, not miracles."

DEFENSE

The ancients knew as well as we do that nature obeys particular laws. The idea that there is no room for miracles today reflects a bias against miracles, not real science.

People in the ancient world were more in touch with nature than we are. They knew it behaved according to regular cycles and that things happened in predictable ways. They knew that the sun rises every day, that they could use the motions of the stars at night to predict the seasons and the correct times for planting crops, and they were aware that stones fall down rather than up, and so on.

They also were aware that virgins do not give birth, that water does not turn into wine, that loaves do not spontaneously multiply, and that people who have been dead for several days do not come back to life—much less ascend into heaven. It was precisely because they knew the regularities of nature that they were able to identify the latter events as miracles.

The difference between then and now is that we have a more detailed knowledge of the regularities of nature. We have precise measurements of many of them, and these allow us to describe them with mathematical formulas. Some are so well established we refer to them as scientific laws.

But these "laws" are merely descriptions based on observations of how nature *usually* works. Nothing says the world *always* acts that way. Science is based on observation, and the only way we could know that the world always behaves a certain way would be to observe the entire history of the universe and see what nature does at each moment, but we can't do that.

Consequently, the idea that nature must *always* behave in the ways that it *normally* behaves goes beyond what science can establish. It's a philosophical *assumption*, not a scientific fact. The open-minded way to approach this issue would not be to make that assumption but to look at the evidence, acknowledging that nature normally works in certain ways but leaving open the possibility that unusual, miraculous events might occur.

TIP

A good book on this subject is C.S. Lewis's *Miracles*.

The Judgment of Jeconiah

CHALLENGE

"Jesus is disqualified from being the Messiah since he descends from the last king of Judah, Jeconiah (Matt. 1:12). God judged Jeconiah so that 'none of his offspring shall succeed in sitting on the throne of David, and ruling again in Judah' (Jer. 22:30)."

DEFENSE

There are multiple flaws with this argument. Here are several.

First, Jesus was not descended from David only by the line of Jeconiah. He was also descended through the line of Nathan (Luke 3:31; see Day 85). It may have been questions among some Jews about whether a descendant of only Jeconiah could be the Messiah that prompted Jesus' family to preserve the memory of the Nathan line. The presence of both genealogies in Scripture shows that, regardless where a Jew fell on the Jeconiah question, Jesus had a qualified lineage either way.

Second, the prophecy need mean no more than Jeconiah's immediate sons wouldn't be kings because the Babylonian Exile would go on for too long (cf. Jer. 22:25–28).

Third, one of Jeconiah's grandsons—Zerubbabel—received ruling authority in Judah, being made its governor (Hag. 1:1). (On Zerubbabel's lineage, see 1 Chron. 3:17–19; there may be a levirate marriage involved since Zerubbabel's father is usually said to be Shealtiel, though here he is said to be son of Pediah; both were sons of Jeconiah, and thus Zerubbabel was his grandson).

Fourth, the language used concerning Zerubbabel suggests a reversal of God's judgment. God told Jeconiah, though you "were the signet ring on my right hand, yet I would tear you off" (Jer. 22:24), but he told Zerubbabel he will "make you like a signet ring; for I have chosen you, says the Lord of hosts" (Hag. 2:23). The image of making one of Jeconiah's descendants again like a signet ring suggests a restoration of the family to divine favor.

Fifth, multiple Jewish sources indicate Jeconiah (also called Jehoiachin) repented and the curse was lifted. The *Jewish Encyclopedia* (1906 ed.) notes: "Jehoiachin's sad experiences changed his nature entirely, and as he repented of the sins which he had committed as king he was pardoned by God, who revoked the decree to the effect that none of his descendants should ever become king" (s.v. "Jehoiachin").

Sin and Mary's Humanity

"How could the Virgin Mary be sinless? She's human like everyone else."

DEFENSE

Despite our state in the present life, being human does not mean being a sinner.

If being human did entail sin, then God would have built sin into human nature, which would make him the author of evil. Instead, human nature was damaged because of the misuse of free will—which is itself a good, as it enables people to freely choose love.

Because human nature does not entail sin, it is possible for humans to be free of sin. Thus Adam and Eve were sinless before the fall of man.

There was a time in all of our lives when, in spite of our fallen nature, none of us had commited personal sin. Paul notes that in the womb Jacob and Esau "were not yet born and had done nothing either good or bad" (Rom. 9:11).

And there will be a time in the future when, if we die in God's friendship, we will all be sinless, for we will not continue to sin in heaven, because "nothing unclean shall enter it" (Rev. 21:27). Instead, we will have "the holiness without which no one will see the Lord" (Heb. 12:14), for "when he appears we shall be like him, for we shall see him as he is" (1 John 3:2). All the saved will be given this gift of total holiness, and because of her special role in God's plan of the ages, Mary was given it early.

Jesus Christ—the Second Adam (1 Cor. 15:45)—was free of all sin (2 Cor. 5:21; Heb. 4:15; 1 Pet. 2:22; 1 John 3:5). In the same way, Mary—the Second Eve (CCC 411, 494)—was also preserved from all sin. This gift was given to her because of what Christ did on the cross. It was applied to her early to make her holy in a special way and thus a more fitting mother for the Son of God.

Consequently, Mary's holiness "from the first instant of her conception comes wholly from Christ: She is redeemed, in a more exalted fashion, by reason of the merits of her Son" (CCC 492).

Human nature thus does not entail sin—which can give us all hope of one day being free of it!

The Growth of Science

CHALLENGE

"The superiority of science to faith is shown by the fact that, in the last few centuries, most discoveries have been made by science, not faith."

DEFENSE

It is a mistake to assume that a certain field is superior because it is currently experiencing a growth spurt.

Every field of study experiences more and less productive periods, but this does not show one field to be superior to another. To the extent that they reveal truth to us, they are all important, regardless of the rate of new discoveries being made in them.

Further, the fact that a field is presently experiencing growth does not mean this will continue indefinitely. Physicist Lee Smolin argues in *The Trouble with Physics* that physics has been experiencing a dry period for decades, with few new, fundamental discoveries to match previous ones. Similarly, in *The End of Science*, science writer John Horgan argues that science is approaching fundamental limits that will impede major new discoveries.

We will have to wait to see whether these difficulties can be overcome, but they serve as warnings that an indefinitely long, high rate of scientific discovery is not to be taken for granted.

Ultimately, it is a form of chronological snobbery to assume that a field is superior just because it is growing at the moment. What matters is whether it reveals truth to us, not its growth rate.

This is particularly true with respect to religion. If the Christian claim is true, then we already have the basic data we need to work with. The Faith has been "once for all delivered to the saints" (Jude 3), public revelation has ended, and the deposit of faith is closed (CCC 66). God may have chosen to give us this information before the rise of science because, unlike science, it concerns our eternal destiny and is therefore more essential for us to have.

However that may be, the Christian claim implies that we should not expect radical new discoveries regarding the Faith, but a gradual refinement of points as we better appreciate the data God has given us.

The present state of affairs is thus consistent with the Christian claim, and, regardless of their respective rates of growth, both science and faith make important contributions to humanity.

"There Be Gods Many"?

CHALLENGE

"We may only be supposed to worship one God, but the Catholic belief that only one God exists is false. Paul writes, 'though there be that are called gods, whether in heaven or in earth (as there be gods many, and lords many), but to us there is but one God, the Father . . . and one Lord Jesus Christ' (1 Cor. 8:5–6, KJV)."

DEFENSE

This passage refers to pagan deities.

Mormonism holds a position known as "henotheism" (Greek, *hen,* "one," and *theos,* "god"), according to which only one god is to be worshipped by a people as its patron deity, though many gods exist. They see this position reflected in 1 Corinthians, which they typically quote from the King James Version. According to Mormonism, the only god people on earth have dealings with, though, is God the Father.

This does not fit what Paul is saying. He is writing in the context of the Greco-Roman world, where people worshipped many gods and goddesses (e.g., Zeus, Apollo, Osiris, Isis), though Jews and Christians denied their existence. This is confirmed by multiple points.

First, Paul refers to those "called" gods—indicating that he does not view them as real gods. More modern translations commonly render this "so-called gods."

Second, he identifies some of these alleged deities as being "on earth" (Greek, *epi gēs*). This is a reference to idols.

Third, he does not say "but we only worship one God." Instead, he says, "to us there is but one God"—i.e., Christians only believe one God exists.

Fourth, the broader context confirms this. The preceding verse states: "As concerning therefore the eating of those things that are offered in sacrifice unto idols, we know that an idol is nothing in the world, and that there is none other God but one" (1 Cor. 8:4, KJV; cf. vv. 7–10). This shows that Paul is referring to pagan deities when he speaks of there being "gods many, and lords many"—the false gods worshipped by pagans—the truth being that "there is none other God but one."

TIP

Scripture elsewhere is clear that only one God exists (see Day 166).

Imputed versus Infused Righteousness

CHALLENGE

"God imputes righteousness to us; he doesn't infuse it, as the Catholic Church teaches."

DEFENSE

This involves several misunderstandings.

The words "impute" and "infuse" are derived from Latin terms—*imputare* and *infundere*—that respectively mean "to reckon" and "to pour in/on."

The image of God imputing righteousness suggests a legal or commercial context where God either legally declares us righteous or credits righteousness to our commercial accounts. The image of God infusing righteousness suggests a context in which God pours righteousness into us like water into a vessel. Despite the way this challenge is posed, Catholics don't deny God imputes righteousness to us. They have the same verses saying this in their Bibles that Protestants do (e.g., Gen. 15:6, Rom. 4:3–6, Gal. 3:6, James 2:23).

Also, the image of infused righteousness isn't frequently used in Catholic documents. It's only mentioned once in Trent's Decree on Justification (chapter 16), and not at all in the Joint Declaration on the Doctrine of Justification and its Annex. The Church more commonly uses the language of infusion concerning the Holy Spirit and the theological virtues of faith, hope, and charity (cf. Acts 2:17–18, Rom. 5:5, Titus 3:6).

Ultimately, both the images of imputation and infusion can be used to describe God's saving action. They don't need to be understood as mutually opposed, so we need to be on guard against mere quarrels about words (1 Tim. 6:4; 2 Tim. 2:14).

Although Catholics don't deny God reckons people righteous, they do understand God's word as effectual, so it brings about the effect God declares (Isa. 55:11). Thus, when God reckons or declares people righteous, they become objectively (metaphysically) righteous (see Day 350).

This does not mean their behavior instantly changes (though God does begin a work of sanctification that leads them to behave more righteously over time). It does mean that they "are made innocent, immaculate, pure, guiltless, and beloved of God, heirs indeed of God, joint heirs with Christ; so that there is nothing whatever to hinder their entrance into heaven" (Trent, Decree on Original Sin 5).

This point is frequently misunderstood in Protestant apologetics, which often claims that the idea of infused righteousness means a person is not made perfectly righteous when he is first justified. He is (see Day 257).

The Mathematics of the Last Day

CHALLENGE

"Christianity proposes that a number of implausible things will happen at the end of time: Everyone who ever lived will be resurrected (John 5:28–29); the faithful from all history will be gathered to Christ (1 Thess. 4:16–17); the New Jerusalem will be a cubic city 1,500 miles long, tall, and wide (Rev. 21:16). The math for these claims doesn't add up."

DEFENSE

These objections falsely presume that the world will continue to operate the way it presently does.

Paul compares the difference between our present bodies and our resurrected bodies to the difference between a seed and the plant that grows from it (1 Cor. 15:37–44). He also suggests we will not need to eat (1 Cor. 6:13–14).

At the end of time there will be a renovation of the world order that is comparable only to its original creation. Thus Scripture speaks of there being "a new heaven and a new earth" (Rev. 21:1). We should not assume the new order will be subject to the same limitations of space and time the present order is. Even now, God is not bound by these limitations, as shown when Jesus' body appears in many locations at once in the Eucharist or passes through physical barriers (John 20:19). In the next age, everyone's bodies will be similarly free of limitations (Phil. 3:20–21).

The general resurrection will be a major miracle, but God is omnipotent and his infinite (unlimited) power is not taxed by the size of a particular miracle. If he could create the entire universe, he can fundamentally restructure its laws and contents to accomplish these things.

The next age transcends what we can imagine, and we should recognize the symbolic nature of the images used to describe it. They are hints meant to convey a much greater reality (see Days 198, 201). In particular, numbers in Revelation are symbolic, as shown in the case of the 12,000 stadia by the fact that the next verse says the wall of the city is 144 cubits (216 feet) high (Rev. 21:17). Why would a city 1,500 miles tall need a wall only 216 feet tall to protect it?

The Pope and the Antichrist

CHALLENGE

"The pope is the Antichrist."

DEFENSE

This claim does not fit the biblical evidence;
it is based on unbiblical polemics.

Although the Antichrist is sometimes associated with figures like the "man of sin" (2 Thess. 2:3–10) and the beast of Revelation (Rev. 13:1–18), there are only four passages in the New Testament that explicitly speak of the "antichrist": 1 John 2:18, 22, 4:3, and 2 John 7. To understand the role of the Antichrist, we must look to these passages.

According to them, the Antichrist "denies the Father and the Son" (1 John 2:22), the "spirit of antichrist" "does not confess Jesus" (1 John 4:3), and the Antichrist does "not acknowledge the coming of Jesus Christ in the flesh" (2 John 7).

These passages indicate that the Antichrist denies the coming of Jesus in the flesh. This could be construed several ways: (1) Jesus was a mere man and not God Incarnate (the early heresy known as Ebionism), (2) the humanity of Jesus was only an illusion (the early heresy known as Docetism), or (3) Jesus was not the Messiah (as in non-Christian Judaism).

None of these descriptions fit the popes, who have consistently maintained that Jesus was the Messiah, that he was God, and that he was fully God and fully man. Even a cursory reading of papal teaching provides abundant evidence for this. In fact, the popes have been among the most vigorous defenders of orthodoxy on these points.

The evidence is so extensive that it is amazing anyone could make the papal Antichrist claim, and its existence calls for an explanation.

The ultimate explanation is one of necessity: Prior to the Protestant Reformation, it was universally recognized in Western Christendom that the Catholic Church was the Church of Christ, governed by the pope as the authentic representative of Christ. Critics of the papacy thus needed to provide an alternative explanation of what the pope's role was and how he could achieve such prominence if he were not Christ's representative. They therefore asserted that he was the archenemy of Christ, the Antichrist (*Smalcald Articles* 2:4:10, 14; *Westminster Confession* 25:6).

This may have been a polemically useful claim, but it does not fit the biblical data—a fact most Protestant scholars recognize today.

Science and Scripture

"Science is superior to faith, as shown by the way Christians adapt parts of the Bible to the findings of science."

DEFENSE

All truth is God's truth, and the fact that we learn new things in one field does not mean it is superior to another field.

This is true within the scientific disciplines themselves. What is learned in one field has ripples that affect others. For example, a discovery in physics may impact astronomy or chemistry. The reverse is also true. The scientific fields thus exist in a state of creative tension with respect to one another, and this is true of every other area of study, including theology. Yet this does not mean that one form of study is superior to another. They are all explorations of different aspects of the truth.

When we learn something new in one field, it is natural to seek to relate it to other fields, including religion. If a scientific discovery is well established and seems to contradict a common religious view, it is natural to revisit that view and see if we have understood the matter correctly (see Day 184).

Thus when astronomical discoveries suggested that the earth might not be the center of the universe, or paleontological and biological discoveries suggested that the earth might be much older than commonly thought and that biological evolution occurs, it was natural to revisit certain texts of Scripture to see whether they had been understood correctly.

In both cases, a careful reading showed that they were not, in fact, in conflict with the new scientific perspectives. Passages that talk about the sun rising and setting merely describe natural phenomena according to the language of appearances and do not imply the motion of the sun around the earth any more than we do today when we speak of "sunrise" and "sunset." Similarly, long before the rise of modern science, perceptive exegetes like St. Augustine had pointed out features of Genesis 1 that indicated its days were not literal (see Day 90; cf. St. Augustine, *The Literal Meaning of Genesis* 1:10[21–22]).

Investigating the proper way to harmonize Scripture and science is no different in principle than investigating how to harmonize the discoveries of physics with those of astronomy. The findings of every field are properly understood in harmony with the others.

Necessary for Salvation?

CHALLENGE

"Why should dogmas like the Assumption of Mary be necessary for salvation? That makes no sense."

DEFENSE

A belief can be related to salvation in more than one way.

Some are directly related. Thus, "whoever would draw near to God must believe that he exists and that he rewards those who seek him" (Heb. 11:6). The belief that God exists and that he will bless those who attempt to please him are directly related to salvation. So are belief in Jesus as Savior (Acts 4:12), and the means by which we receive salvation, such as the need for repentance, faith, and baptism (Mark 1:14–15; 1 Pet. 3:21).

We may refer to beliefs directly connected with salvation as soteriological beliefs, since soteriology is the branch of theology that studies salvation (Greek, *sōtēria,* "salvation"). Beliefs that belong to other branches of theology are non-soteriological, in that they are not directly connected with salvation. However, this does not mean that they are irrelevant to having faith.

"Faith is the theological virtue by which we believe in God and believe all that he has said and revealed to us, and that Holy Church proposes for our belief, because he [God] is truth itself" (CCC 1814).

A non-Catholic may not agree with the Catholic understanding of the Church's role in communicating God's teachings, but he should be able to agree with the principle that having faith in God means accepting what God reveals because he is all-knowing and utterly truthful. To put it simply: You don't have faith in God if you refuse to believe what you know God says.

This is why non-soteriological beliefs can be relevant to salvation. Suppose a person knows for a fact that God has taught something—say, the existence of angels. This is not a soteriological belief, but it is something God has taught, and to say, "Yes, I know God teaches that angels exist; I just don't believe it," means one does not have faith in God.

Faith in God *is* ordinarily required for salvation, so to deliberately reject something you know God has revealed—whether the existence of angels, the Assumption of Mary, or anything else—undermines faith itself.

Non-soteriological beliefs are thus important not because they are directly connected with salvation but because God has revealed them.

Jesus' Prophecy Unfulfilled?

CHALLENGE

"If Jesus' speech on the Mount of Olives referred to the destruction of the temple in A.D. 70 (see Day 69), then he falsely prophesied that he would return before then, saying that people 'will see the Son of man coming in clouds with great power and glory' (Mark 13:26; cf. Matt. 24:30, Luke 21:27)."

DEFENSE

There are other ways of understanding this passage.

Material in the Gospels is not always chronological. The evangelists had the freedom to arrange material by other criteria, such as topic. They could have grouped a saying about the Second Coming with other prophetic statements because they all involve prophecy. If Jesus originally made this statement in a different context, then its fulfillment would not be governed by the statements about the temple.

But this may not be a reference to the Second Coming. The Bible describes God and the Son of Man "coming" in different ways. Thus God is depicted as riding the clouds when he comes in judgment on a people (Ps. 104:3; Isa. 19:1–2; Jer. 4:13–14). This may be the kind of "coming" Jesus had in mind—a visitation of divine judgment on Jerusalem in A.D. 70.

His statement also reflects Daniel 7:13–14, where the Son of Man is brought before God *in heaven* to receive his kingdom. The prophecy thus may refer to Jesus ascending into heaven (Acts 1:9), where he received his kingdom (Acts 7:55–56) and where he now reigns (1 Cor. 15:24–26). Both explanations may apply. Jesus may invoke Daniel 7's imagery to indicate he will be reigning with God in heaven and this will manifest in divine judgment on Jerusalem with the destruction of the temple.

Theologians have also explored the idea of an *adventus medius* ("middle advent") of Christ between the First and Second Comings. This is a spiritual "coming" of Christ in which he is preached to the world to prepare for his definitive, final coming. If this is what Jesus refers to, he might have in mind the evangelization that would lead many to recognize him as the Son of Man and also the authority of his kingdom (cf. Matt. 24:31, Mark 13:27).

TIP

Benedict XVI discusses the *adventus medius* in the epilogue of his book *Jesus of Nazareth*, vol. 2.

Peter in Antioch and Papal Infallibility

CHALLENGE

"The pope can't be infallible. Paul opposed Peter at Antioch 'because he clearly was wrong' (Gal. 2:11, NABRE)."

DEFENSE

This involves a straw man argument.

The Church holds the pope engages the Church's infallibility "when, as supreme pastor and teacher of all the faithful—who confirms his brethren in the faith—he proclaims by a definitive act a doctrine pertaining to faith or morals" (CCC 891).

To proclaim a doctrine "by a definitive act" means he has to use language that indicates the matter is permanently settled. To define a matter means to completely end it (Latin, *definire,* "to define," from *de-,* "completely," and *finis,* "end").

Peter was not attempting to do this at Antioch. Indeed, he wasn't proclaiming a doctrine at all. He simply stopped eating meals with Gentiles in order to keep harmony between Jewish and Gentile Christians (Gal. 2:12). He knew that Gentile Christians did not need to be circumcized and become Jews. It was through him that God made this point (Acts 10), he defended it more than once (Acts 11:1–18, 15:7–11), and Paul acknowledged that Peter knew this (Gal. 2:15–16).

Paul thought that, in context, Peter's attempt to accommodate Jewish sensibilities sent the wrong signal, and he criticized him on that ground, but the fact remains that Peter was not proclaiming a teaching—much less claiming to settle the matter definitively. A pope's choice of lunch companion does not engage the Church's infallibility.

To work, this objection would have to vastly expand the number of situations in which papal infallibility applies—way beyond the situations the Church claims it applies in. It therefore commits the straw man fallacy by attacking a position the Church does not hold.

Paul held that Peter made a mistake in this situation, but popes can make mistakes—except in the content of their teaching when they definitively proclaim a doctrine of faith or morals. That didn't happen here.

Further, since the greater charism of inspiration entails the lesser charism of infallibility, if the Antioch incident meant Peter couldn't exercise the Church's infallibility, it would also prevent him from writing 1 and 2 Peter as inspired Scripture.

TIP

After Acts 15, Paul also accommodated Jewish sensibilities by circumcizing Timothy (Acts 16:3). The objection thus would similarly endanger Paul's letters as Scripture.

Matthew's Missing Generations

CHALLENGE

"Matthew's genealogy of Jesus omits some generations and thus is wrong."

DEFENSE

In Israelite genealogies, it was permitted to skip generations.

Hebrew and Aramaic don't have terms for "grandfather," "great-grandfather," "grandson," "great-grandson," and so on. Any male ancestor was called a father (Hebrew, *'ab,* Aramaic, *'ab, 'abba*), and any male descendant was called a son (Hebrew, *bēn,* Aramaic, *bar*).

Thus, prophesying the birth of Jesus, Gabriel tells Mary, "The Lord God will give to him the throne of his father David" (Luke 1:32). David lived a millennium before Jesus, yet he is called Jesus' father. Similarly, both Jesus and Joseph are called "son of David" (Matt. 1:20, 9:27). This made it possible to skip generations in genealogies, whether they ran forward ("Joram was the father of Uzziah") or backward ("Uzziah was the son of Joram").

Richard Bauckham notes:

> That a family descended from one of the sons of David had at least an oral genealogy must be considered certain. This does not, of course, mean that it would be a complete genealogy. Oral genealogies, like many of those in the Old Testament, regularly omit generations, since their function is not to preserve the memory of every name in the list but to link the family with an important ancestor who gives it its place in the community (*Jude and the Relatives of Jesus in the Early Church*, 341).

Matthew skips generations for literary purposes, grouping his genealogy in three sets of fourteen generations (Matt. 1:17). The reason may be to stress Jesus' connection with David. In Hebrew and Aramaic, *David* (DVD) adds up to fourteen (D = 4, V = 6, D = 4).

Matthew would have expected his readers to recognize that the generations he skips are recorded in the Old Testament. In 1:8, he says Joram was the father of Uzziah (aka Azariah), but 1 Chronicles 3:11–12 shows three generations between the two. The missing names are Ahaziah, Joash, and Amaziah. These three figures were *kings of Israel.* Their stories are told between 2 Chronicles 22 and 25.

When Matthew skips three Jewish kings in the line of David—well known to the audience from the Old Testament Scriptures—he expects his readers to recognize the literary device he is using in the genealogy.

The Word of God

CHALLENGE

"Catholicism is false because it bases its teachings on things other than the Bible—the word of God."

DEFENSE

Catholicism bases its teachings on the word of God, which is not limited to the Bible.

The Church acknowledges that "Sacred Scripture is the word of God inasmuch as it is consigned to writing under the inspiration of the divine Spirit" (Vatican II, *Dei Verbum* 9). However, even a cursory reading of Scripture shows that the word of God is not limited to Scripture.

In the very first chapter of the Bible, we read about the power of God's creative word, as he says things like, "'Let there be light'; and there was light" (Gen. 1:3). This understanding is confirmed by the Psalms, which state: "By the word of the Lord the heavens were made" (Ps. 33:6). This exercise of God's creative word occurred before the existence of man and the writing of Scripture, making it clear that the reality of God's word goes beyond Scripture.

Even after God began to communicate his word to men, it often was not in the form of Scripture. Thus the Bible records the word of God being given to prophets who wrote no Scripture at all, such as Samuel (1 Sam. 9:27), Shemaiah (1 Kings 12:22), and John the Baptist (Luke 3:2).

Similarly, the oral apostolic preaching of the Christian faith is spoken of as the word of God (Acts 4:31, 6:7, 16:6).

Most fundamentally, Scripture reveals that Jesus is the Word of God (John 1:1–18, Rev. 19:13).

All this makes it clear that the word of God is a complex, multifaceted reality that includes but goes beyond Scripture, which is the portion of God's word that was consigned to writing under divine inspiration.

Our proper response to the word of God is to accept the whole of it as authoritative, for "man shall not live by bread alone, but by every word that proceeds from the mouth of God" (Matt. 4:4; cf. Deut. 8:3). It would be wrong to close our ears to God's word when it is found outside of Scripture. Thus Paul tells his readers to "stand firm and hold to the traditions which you were taught by us, either by word of mouth or by letter" (2 Thess. 2:15).

The Coexistence of Science and Religion

CHALLENGE

"Science and religion seem antagonistic. How can they coexist?"

DEFENSE

We elsewhere cover the fact that the two fields aren't intrinsically hostile (see Day 266). This, plus the fact that they largely deal with different subjects, makes their coexistence possible.

Scripture does not dwell on the details of creation for, when inspiring the biblical authors, the Spirit of God "did not wish to teach men these facts that would be of no avail for their salvation" (St. Augustine, *The Literal Meaning of Genesis* 2:9:20).

Similarly, Cardinal Caesar Baronius is credited with saying, "The Holy Spirit's intention was to teach us how to go to heaven, not how the heavens go" (quoted in Galileo Galilei, *Letter to the Grand Duchess Christina*). According to John Paul II:

> The Bible does not concern itself with the details of the physical world, the understanding of which is the competence of human experience and reasoning. There exist two realms of knowledge, one which has its source in revelation and one which reason can discover by its own power. To the latter belong especially the experimental sciences and philosophy. The distinction between the two realms of knowledge ought not to be understood as opposition. The two realms are not altogether foreign to each other, they have points of contact. The methodologies proper to each make it possible to bring out different aspects of reality (Address to the Pontifical Academy of Sciences, October 31, 1992).

The same point was made by evolutionary biologist Stephen Jay Gould, who argued that science and religion each have a magisterium (teaching authority) with respect to their fields of study, but these largely do not overlap, stating:

> This resolution might remain all neat and clean if the non-overlapping magisteria (NOMA) of science and religion were separated by an extensive no man's land. But, in fact, the two magisteria bump right up against each other, interdigitating [i.e., weaving their fingers together] in wondrously complex ways along their joint border. Many of our deepest questions call upon aspects of both for different parts of a full answer—and the sorting of legitimate domains can become quite complex and difficult ("Nonoverlapping Magisteria," available online).

Who Wrote the Gospels?

CHALLENGE

"Matthew, Mark, Luke, and John didn't really write the Gospels. We have no idea who actually did. They are anonymous, and names weren't attached to them until the second century."

DEFENSE

The evidence suggests Matthew, Mark, Luke, and John did write the Gospels.

Ultimately, the important thing is not who wrote the Gospels but whether they are reliable.

Anonymity is no barrier to reliability, and there are many anonymous works that scholars rely on for knowledge of the ancient world. For example, scholars use the *Itinerarium Burdigalense*, an important travel narrative from A.D. 333–334 that was written by an unknown individual called only "the Pilgrim of Bordeaux."

The names of the Gospel authors may not be listed in the text of the works, but the Gospels were not anonymous in the sense that their authors were unknown to the original audience. Luke writes to his patron Theophilus (Luke 1:3, Acts 1:1), and Theophilus knew who Luke was. John expressly identifies its author as the beloved disciple (John 21:20–24), whose name was known to the intended audience. Similarly, the authors of Matthew and Mark were known to their original audiences.

The names attached to the Gospels were not of second-century origin. They were in use in the first century. Had the Gospels circulated without names for an extended period, they would have come to be called different things, the same way that there are multiple titles for many ancient works. However, they didn't. In ancient documents they are *always* referred to as the Gospels of Matthew, Mark, Luke, and John.

When the Gospels were read in church, the congregation needed to be told what was being read, and there needed to be a way to distinguish them from each other, since so much of their content was similar, with each telling the story of Jesus. The churches chose to refer to them by their authors. This need to distinguish them existed as soon as there was more than one Gospel, and so the names were used immediately, not at a later date. This is a strong indication that the names are accurate (see also Day 146).

TIP

For more on the first-century origin of the names, see Martin Hengel, *Studies in the Gospel of Mark*, chapter 3.

Adding to Scripture

CHALLENGE

"Catholics' use of Tradition and the Magisterium is wrong. In the Bible, God says we must neither add to nor take away from Scripture (Deut. 4:2, 12:32; Rev. 22:18–19)."

DEFENSE

These passages do not prove what is claimed.

The two from Deuteronomy deal with the Israelites' observance of the Mosaic Law. The first says: "You shall not add to the word which I command you, nor take from it; *that you may keep the commandments of the Lord your God which I command you*" (emphasis added).

The second reads: "*Everything that I command you you shall be careful to do*; you shall not add to it or take from it" (emphasis added).

These exhortations do not mean there are no sources of revelation outside the Law. If they did, they would cancel the rest of the Old Testament and the New Testament.

They would also contradict Deuteronomy itself, which says: "The Lord your God will raise up for you a prophet like me from among you, from your brethren—him you shall heed" (Deut. 18:15). Here Deuteronomy specifically foretells the arrival of additional sources of revelation (prophets), which the Israelites are to heed.

The passage in Revelation reads: "I warn every one who hears the words of the prophecy of this book: if any one adds to them, God will add to him the plagues described in this book, and if any one takes away from the words of the book of this prophecy, God will take away his share in the tree of life and in the holy city, which are described in this book."

"This book" is a reference to the book of Revelation, not the entire Bible. This is indicated by the parallel passage at the beginning, where John was told, "Write what you see in a book and send it to the seven churches" (Rev. 1:11).

It is also indicated by the reference to "the prophecy of this book"—Revelation being a prophetic book. And it is indicated by the Greek word used here for "book": *biblion*. This was the normal word for a scroll. Revelation fit into a scroll, but the entire Bible never did. It was far too long and consisted of a library of scrolls.

The warning is thus against tampering with the content of Revelation. It does not say there are no authorities besides Scripture.

The Eucharistic Sacrifice

CHALLENGE

"Catholicism is wrong to say the Eucharist involves a sacrifice. Jesus was sacrificed 'once for all' (Rom. 6:10; Heb. 7:27, 9:12, 26, 10:10; 1 Pet. 3:18)."

DEFENSE

Jesus died only once, but this does not exhaust his sacrificial ministry.

Hebrews acknowledges Christ's once-for-all death on earth as well as his ongoing sacrificial ministry in heaven, saying the heavenly things must be purified "with better sacrifices" (plural) than those offered in the earthly temple (Heb. 9:23; cf. George Wesley Buchanan, *The Anchor Bible: To the Hebrews*, 162).

Protestant historian J.N.D. Kelly writes that in the early Church the Eucharist was regarded as a sacrifice:

Malachi's prediction (1:10–11) that the Lord would reject Jewish sacrifices and instead would have "a pure offering" made to him by the Gentiles in every place was seized upon by Christians as a prophecy of the Eucharist. The *Didache* indeed actually applies the term *thusia*, or sacrifice, to the Eucharist. . . .

It was natural for early Christians to think of the Eucharist as a sacrifice. The fulfillment of prophecy demanded a solemn Christian offering, and the rite itself was wrapped in the sacrificial atmosphere with which our Lord invested the Last Supper. The words of institution, "Do this" (*touto poieite*), must have been charged with sacrificial overtones for second-century ears; Justin at any rate understood them to mean, "Offer this." . . . The bread and wine, moreover, are offered "for a memorial (*eis anamnēsin*) of the passion," a phrase which in view of his identification of them with the Lord's body and blood implies much more than an act of purely spiritual recollection (*Early Christian Doctrines*, 196–197).

The sacrifice of the cross was unique because it was offered "in a bloody manner" (i.e., by Christ dying), but it is perpetuated in the Eucharist, in which he does not die. The eucharistic sacrifice is the same as the sacrifice of the cross in that the offering (Christ's body and blood) and the primary sacrificing priest (Christ) are the same (CCC 1367). Today, the Eucharist is "the body and blood of Christ enthroned gloriously in heaven" (Paul VI, *Credo of the People of God*), where Jesus offers himself to the Father as "a living sacrifice"—as Christians are called to do (Rom. 12:1).

The Magisterium and the Word of God

CHALLENGE

"The Catholic Church is wrong to teach that its Magisterium is superior to the word of God."

DEFENSE

The Church teaches that the Magisterium *serves* the word of God.

During his earthly ministry, Jesus commissioned his apostles and others to teach in his name, telling them: "He who hears you hears me, and he who rejects you rejects me" (Luke 10:16).

He further commissioned this teaching authority to continue to the end of the world, saying: "Go therefore and make disciples of all nations, baptizing them in the name of the Father and of the Son and of the Holy Spirit, teaching them to observe all that I have commanded you; and lo, I am with you always, to the close of the age" (Matt. 28:19–20). Today this teaching authority, known as the Magisterium (from the Latin, *magister,* "teacher"), is exercised by the bishops, the successors of the apostles.

Although it was established by Christ, the Church does not regard the Magisterium as superior to the word of God but as its servant. Vatican II taught: "This teaching office is not above the word of God, but serves it, teaching only what has been handed on, listening to it devoutly, guarding it scrupulously and explaining it faithfully in accord with a divine commission and with the help of the Holy Spirit, it draws from this one deposit of faith everything which it presents for belief as divinely revealed" (*Dei Verbum* 10).

The idea that the Magisterium is superior to the word of God is false. It plays a subordinate role in helping the faithful identify and understand the word of God. Thus the Magisterium helped the Church discern the canon of Scripture—which books were divinely inspired and which were not. It similarly helps the Church discern which Traditions are of apostolic origin and which are not. And it helps the Church understand the contents of both Scripture and Tradition.

However, in all these things, the Magisterium is a guide and not a source. The source is the word of God, as expressed in Scripture and Tradition. The Magisterium is subordinate to these, as illustrated by the fact that it is the word of God that gives the Magisterium its authority (see the verses above), not the other way around.

Too Exclusive?

"How can Catholics and other Christians be so exclusive when it comes to salvation? The idea that God would damn people to hell just because they never heard of him is abhorrent."

That's not the teaching of the Catholic Church.

The Church holds that "those who, through no fault of their own, do not know the gospel of Christ or his Church, but who nevertheless seek God with a sincere heart, and, moved by grace, try in their actions to do his will as they know it through the dictates of their conscience—those too may achieve eternal salvation" (CCC 847).

Although a person who knows the truth of the Faith is obliged to embrace it—to do otherwise would be to knowingly and deliberately reject the truth—God is not going to send people to hell merely because they are not Christian or Catholic.

We need not fear that someone will be damned simply because they never heard of Jesus. According to the above, for people to be lost they would need to:

- reject the gospel or the Church through their own fault,
- refuse to sincerely seek God,
- refuse to be moved by God's grace, or
- refuse to do God's will as they understand it according to their conscience.

Ultimately, the same principle applies to everyone: "God predestines no one to go to hell; for this, a willful turning away from God (a mortal sin) is necessary, and persistence in it until the end" (CCC 1037).

God "desires all men to be saved and to come to the knowledge of the truth" (1 Tim. 2:4), but even if they are hindered from arriving at a full knowledge of the truth in this life, he still has ways of reaching them with his grace: "Since Christ died for all, and since all men are in fact called to one and the same destiny, which is divine, we must hold that the Holy Spirit offers to all the possibility of being made partakers, in a way known to God, of the Paschal mystery [i.e., Jesus' saving death on the Cross]" (CCC 1260).

Thus the Church acknowledges that the kind of prayer by which one "walks with God . . . is lived by many righteous people in all religions" (CCC 2569).

Too Inclusive?

"The Catholic Church is too inclusive when it says non-Christians can be saved. Jesus said, 'I am the way, and the truth, and the life; no one comes to the Father, but by me' (John 14:6), and Peter declared, 'There is salvation in no one else, for there is no other name under heaven given among men by which we must be saved' (Acts 4:12)."

DEFENSE

Salvation is through Christ alone, but that does not mean that only Christians can be saved.

When Peter says that salvation is not found in anyone besides Jesus, he asserts that there is no Savior besides Jesus; when Jesus says no one comes to the Father but by him, he refers to his unique role in God's plan and, implicitly, to his atoning death on the cross. However, neither Jesus nor Peter says one must consciously embrace the Christian faith or be damned. Indeed, we have good reason to think that some individuals will be saved who do not consciously embrace Christianity in this life.

For example, there is a stage in everyone's life when we are incapable of understanding the Christian message because we are too young. Unless we are willing to consign all infants and small children to hell (or at least all unbaptized ones), then we must be prepared to say that it is possible for them to be saved despite their lack of conscious faith in Jesus.

Similarly, righteous Jews before the time of Christ did not know that Jesus of Nazareth would be the Messiah and thus did not have conscious faith in him. It certainly was not commonly expected that the Messiah would be the Son of God or die for the sins of the world. Yet we have the explicit testimony of Scripture that many were saved despite their lack of conscious faith in Jesus (Matt. 8:11; Heb. 11).

This means that people can be *saved through Jesus* (who is "the way, the truth, and the life") without consciously understanding in this life that he is the means by which they are saved.

The same principle applies to others who do not know the truth of the Christian faith through no fault of their own (see Day 113). We even have hints of this when Paul says that God "overlooked" times of Gentile ignorance (Acts 17:30) and that non-Christian Gentiles may find that their consciences excuse them on the day of judgment (Rom. 2:15–16).

Where and When Jesus Appeared to the Disciples

CHALLENGE

"The Resurrection accounts are contradictory. Luke indicates that Jesus appeared to the disciples in Jerusalem on the same day, but Matthew and Mark indicate he appeared later in Galilee."

DEFENSE

This is not a contradiction. Jesus appeared in both places.

Paul indicates that Jesus made multiple post-Resurrection appearances (1 Cor. 15:5–8). In Acts, Luke indicates he appeared repeatedly over a period of forty days (Acts 1:3). Consequently, the evangelists needed to make choices about what appearances to include in their Gospels.

Luke chose appearances Jesus made the same day in the Jerusalem vicinity (Luke 24:13–44), while Matthew chose one in Galilee (Matt. 28:16–20). Mark also indicates Jesus appeared in Galilee (Mark 14:28, 16:7), but his original ending (which may be paralleled in Matthew) has apparently been lost.

There is no contradiction. During his ministry, Jesus visited both Galilee and the Jerusalem area, and he did the same after the Resurrection. John thus records appearances in both places (John 20:19–29, 21:1–23).

After visiting Galilee, the disciples were back in the Jerusalem area before the Ascension (Luke 24:50–53, Acts 1:9–12), when Jesus again appeared there.

The Gospels thus indicate (1) shortly after the Resurrection, Jesus appeared to the disciples, who were still in Jerusalem, (2) he later appeared to them in Galilee, and (3) toward the end of the forty days he appeared to them again in the Jerusalem vicinity. He told them to remain in the city until the descent of the Holy Spirit on Pentecost, when they began their major evangelistic work (Luke 24:49, Acts 1:4, 2:1–47).

This is why Luke focuses on the appearances in and around Jerusalem. He is planning to chronicle, in Acts, how the Christian faith began spreading in stages, "in Jerusalem and in all Judea and Samaria and to the end of the earth" (Acts 1:8). Pulling the literary focus away from Jerusalem to Galilee would distract from the events he will chronicle, since the apostles made Jerusalem their home base for many years and it became the epicenter of Christian evangelization (Acts 1–12).

Matthew and Mark, not planning on writing sequels to their Gospels, focused on an appearance in Galilee, bringing closure on a literary level by taking us back to where Jesus' ministry began.

John, supplementing the synoptic Gospels, records additional appearances in both places.

Divine Freedom

"The idea that God is free makes no sense. Anyone all-knowing would see the best solution to every problem. Anyone all-good would implement that solution. Therefore, God has no freedom."

DEFENSE

This presupposes that there is a best solution to every problem, but often this is not the case.

Sometimes there are many solutions, all of which are equal. If the problem is to pick a random number between one and ten, there are ten possible solutions. If it is to be a random number, there are no criteria by which to judge one number better than another. Therefore, all choices are equal.

Sometimes one choice is better than another, yet there is no best choice. This happens when there are an infinite (unlimited) number of choices that can be ranked in order. The second choice may be better than the first, the third choice better than the second, and so on, but since the number of choices is unlimited, there is no final, best choice.

This is the situation with respect to God and the universe. The Church holds he created the universe freely, without any compulsion (CCC 317). If he chose not to create, then there would be no created goodness. He also could create an infinite number of possible universes, which we could rank by the amount of created goodness they would contain.

God thus has a range of choices. At one end of the spectrum there is the decision not to create a universe, representing no created goodness, then a universe with a small amount of created goodness, a universe with a greater amount, a universe with a greater amount still, and so on. But there is no maximum amount of created goodness. "With infinite power God could always create something better" (CCC 310).

This means there is no "best of all possible worlds." God could always make a world a little bit better. The idea of a *best* world that infinite creative power could make is logically contradictory, like a square circle or a four-sided triangle (see Day 2).

God has an unlimited number of creative options, but no best option. He is therefore free to choose among the alternatives, including not creating at all.

TIP

For more, see St. Thomas Aquinas, ST I:25:6.

Four-Legged Insects?

CHALLENGE
"Leviticus mistakenly describes insects as having four legs, but everyone knows they have six."

DEFENSE
Everyone *does* know they have six. The Hebrews knew it, too.

Little boys everywhere have the curiosity and cruelty needed to count and pull off the legs of insects. Hebrew boys were no exception. Even for children who don't do this, the discovery that insects have more legs than the four we see on other animals is a notable discovery everyone makes in childhood.

So what does Leviticus 11:21 mean when it refers to insects that walk "on all fours" (Hebrew, *'al 'arba'*)?

In English, walking "on all fours" is a standard idiom based on the fact that most animals we interact with walk on four legs rather than standing erect and walking on two. Describing the crawling motion of insects, an English speaker might use the standard expression "on all fours" rather than switching to the awkward, unfamiliar phrase "on all sixes." If queried, "Don't you mean on all sixes?" he might reply, "It's just an expression. Don't be a pedant" (or he might use a less polite word than "pedant"). A Hebrew speaker might say the same thing, and "on all fours" may be nothing more than an expression to describe insects' movement that is not meant literally.

We also need to comment on Leviticus 11:23's reference to insects that have "four legs" (Hebrew, *'arba' raglayim*). Here it is noteworthy that the word for "legs" is in the dual number. This is a grammatical feature of Hebrew that English doesn't have. In English, we have two grammatical numbers: singular (for one item) and plural (for more than one item), but Hebrew also has a dual number for referring to things that come in pairs, like hands, eyes, and lips. Thus some scholars have taken the phrase as meaning "four *pairs of* legs."

This would not be a reference to the eight legs that spiders have—not because spiders aren't insects in modern animal taxonomies (which the ancient Hebrews didn't have), but because the verse is referring to winged insects. However, insects do have another pair of appendages—their antennae—and these are sufficiently leglike that they might be described that way phenomenologically.

In any event, Hebrews could count and knew insects have six legs.

Faith and Reason

CHALLENGE

"Christianity is irrational, for it requires faith, and faith is opposed to reason."

DEFENSE

On the contrary, "faith and reason are like two wings on which the human spirit rises to the contemplation of truth" (*Fides et Ratio* 1).

From the perspective of faith, reason is a gift from God. He gave us intellects, and he expects us to use them. There is thus no opposition between faith and reason. Both have a role to play.

Certain questions in life can be investigated by reason without invoking the tenets of faith—for example, various truths of mathematics and science.

However, no human is capable of personally verifying everything within the sphere of human knowledge. It exceeds the capacity of anyone to do this, and so every person must rely on others for some of the things he knows. He exhibits a form of faith in what others have learned (ibid., 31).

Further, even when one does personally verify something, an element of faith is present. This is why the findings of the sciences are always provisional. Although the hypothesis that electrons exist may explain many observations and may be accepted as a certainty by scientists who study the structure of the atom, there is always a gap between the observational evidence and the hypothesis proposed to explain it. Scientists make a leap of faith when they accept a particular hypothesis as the likely explanation of the data.

Thus even in the fields most associated with reason, we see a form of faith in play—we see faith and reason collaborating together in a fruitful manner.

The Christian claim is that the same dynamic applies to the field of religion. Reason is capable of establishing certain foundational matters, such as the existence of God. It also is capable of discovering and evaluating evidence of his activity in the world. When these evidences are examined, they point to the proposition that God has revealed himself to man in the person of Jesus Christ. Reason provides evidence supporting the Christian faith like it supplies evidence for scientific proposals.

There is no opposition between faith and reason; they work together to enhance the scope of human knowledge.

TIP

For a thorough discussion of this topic, see *Fides et Ratio* by John Paul II.

The Real Presence and Scripture

CHALLENGE

"Jesus was clearly speaking symbolically when he said, 'This is my body' and 'This is my blood.' His body and blood are not literally present in the Eucharist."

DEFENSE

Other passages make it clear that Jesus was speaking literally.

We live in an age that is biased against miracles. It's easy for us to interpret things as symbols rather than miracles. When faced with this decision, we need to check our instincts by making a careful reading of the text. Sometimes it will indicate what we are reading is symbolic, but sometimes it will indicate what we are reading is miraculous.

It is helpful to remember that Jesus instituted the Eucharist in a culture more ready to accept miracles than ours. Indeed, the apostles had seen Jesus perform many miracles, and he had empowered them to perform miracles, too (Matt. 10:1, 8; Mark 6:7; 13; Luke 9:1). They would have been more inclined to interpret his words as indicating a miracle than we are.

Other passages confirm that they took his words in this way. Paul states that the eucharistic elements are a participation in, not just a representation of, Christ's body and blood (1 Cor. 10:16). He warns that those who profane the Eucharist "will be guilty of profaning the body and blood of the Lord" (1 Cor. 11:27). He says that "any one who eats and drinks without discerning the body eats and drinks judgment upon himself" (1 Cor. 11:29), and that the consequence of this can even be death (1 Cor. 11:30).

Similarly, in John 6, Jesus repeatedly stresses the need to eat his flesh and drink his blood. When challenged on how this can happen (6:52), Jesus becomes more emphatic, stating: "unless you eat the flesh of the Son of man and drink his blood, you have no life in you" (6:53) and "my flesh is food indeed, and my blood is drink indeed" (6:55). After this teaching, "many of his disciples drew back and no longer went about with him" (6:66). Rather than clarifying the matter privately for the core disciples, as elsewhere (Matt. 16:6, 11–12, 17:19, 24:3; Mark 4:34; Luke 10:23), he asked if they, too, will leave (John 6:67). Jesus was willing to lose core disciples rather than weaken this teaching or explain it as symbolic.

The Real Presence and the Church Fathers

CHALLENGE

"The early Christians did not take Jesus' words 'This is my body' and 'This is my blood literally.' They saw them as symbols."

DEFENSE

The record shows that the Church Fathers interpreted these passages literally.

On the Fathers of the first and second centuries, Protestant patristics expert J.N.D. Kelly writes:

> Ignatius roundly declares that . . . the bread is the flesh of Jesus, the cup his blood. Clearly he intends this realism to be taken strictly, for he makes it the basis of his argument against the Docetists' denial of the reality of Christ's body. . . . Irenaeus teaches that the bread and wine are really the Lord's body and blood. His witness is, indeed, all the more impressive because he produces it quite incidentally while refuting the Gnostic and Docetic rejection of the Lord's real humanity (*Early Christian Doctrines,* 197–198).

Concerning the Fathers of the third century, he writes:

> Hippolytus speaks of "the body and the blood" through which the Church is saved, and Tertullian regularly describes the bread as "the Lord's body." The converted pagan, he remarks, "feeds on the richness of the Lord's body, that is, on the Eucharist." The realism of his theology comes to light in the argument, based on the intimate relation of body and soul, that just as in baptism the body is washed with water so that the soul may be cleansed, so in the Eucharist "the flesh feeds upon Christ's body and blood so that the soul may be filled with God." Clearly his assumption is that the Savior's body and blood are as real as the baptismal water. Cyprian's attitude is similar. Lapsed Christians who claim communion without doing penance, he declares, "do violence to his body and blood, a sin more heinous against the Lord with their hands and mouths than when they denied him." Later he expatiates on the terrifying consequences of profaning the sacrament, and the stories he tells confirm that he took the Real Presence literally" (211–212).

Kelly concludes:

> Eucharistic teaching, it should be understood at the outset, was in general unquestioningly realist, i.e., the consecrated bread and wine were taken to be, and were treated and designated as, the Savior's body and blood (440).

Private Judgment

CHALLENGE

"Catholic apologists say we must not use 'private judgment,' but we can't avoid it. The point of apologetics is to convince someone to use his private judgment to accept a position."

DEFENSE

This misunderstands the role that our exercise of reason plays.

It should be pointed out that, whatever happens in apologetic discussions, the theme of "private judgment" is remarkably rare in Church documents. The phrase does not appear at all in the *Catechism of the Catholic Church*, and when it does appear in Church documents, it does not reject the role of the intellect in theology.

That would scarcely be likely given the rich intellectual tradition of Catholic theology, which has always celebrated the contributions of theologians like Augustine, Aquinas, and others as gifts from God. Indeed, God has granted every individual an intellect, and he expects them to use this gift "that they should seek God, in the hope that they might feel after him and find him" (Acts 17:27; cf. CCC 31–38).

Apologetics thus has an important role providing evidence so that people can understand the reasons for embracing the Faith—whether it is understood as the Christian faith broadly or the Catholic Faith specifically.

When understanding and appreciating this evidence, the individual exercise of reason is indispensible. However, once one has come to the point of faith, the situation changes, because we no longer rely on reason alone but on God's revelation.

Jesus did not start a philosophy club but a religion. He "taught them as one who had authority" (Mark 1:22), proclaiming God's definitive word to man (John 1:4; Heb. 1:1–2; Jude 3). Consequently, when one embraces faith in Christ, one must accept certain things as authoritative that one did not accept before the point of faith. It is here that the individual exercise of reason can become problematic.

It is praiseworthy to exercise one's intellect *in accord with* the authorities established by Christ, as the great theologians have done. However, it is problematic to exercise one's intellect *contrary to* them. This was the origin of the heresies that have arisen in Christian history.

Both Protestants and Catholics agree that it is a mistake to prefer one's "private judgment" to the authorities established by Christ. The question is what the authorities are and how we are to understand them.

The Exceptive Clauses and Remarriage

CHALLENGE

"Matthew contains passages where Jesus indicates that it's possible to get remarried after a divorce for reasons of 'unchastity.'"

DEFENSE

Jesus nowhere says that you can remarry after such a divorce. The exceptive clauses do not imply this.

In Matthew 5:32, Jesus says: "Every one who divorces his wife, except on the ground of unchastity, makes her an adulteress; and whoever marries a divorced woman commits adultery" (cf. Matt. 19:9).

The phrase "except on the ground of unchastity" is not found anywhere else that the New Testament treats this subject. All other instances are exceptionless (see Mark 10:11–12; Luke 16:18; Rom. 7:2–3; 1 Cor. 7:12). This is significant because unchastity was common in the ancient world. If it allowed a person to divorce and remarry, it would have been pastorally irresponsible in the extreme for the other New Testament authors not to mention this.

Many of their readers had spouses who *had* committed one or another form of unchastity (particularly in Corinth and Rome—where the four writings mentioned above were written or directed). Many readers thus could have remarried on this theory, but—under the inspiration of the Holy Spirit (2 Tim. 3:16)—the authors of these books indicated that they could not.

Whatever the exceptive clauses mean, they don't mean that a couple can get divorced and remarried if one party commits unchastity (whether understood as adultery or other sexual sin).

If that were what was meant then, as John P. Meier points out, "Obviously, the only thing to do for a faithful Christian couple who wanted a divorce would be to commit adultery, after which a dissolution of the marriage would be allowed. What we wind up with is divorce on demand, with a technical proviso of committing adultery" (*The Vision of Matthew*, 253).

This does not fit the disciples' reaction to Jesus teaching on divorce and remarriage in Matthew, as they say: "If such is the case of a man with his wife, it is not expedient to marry" (Matt. 19:10). Nobody would think it is expedient not to marry if unchastity would allow you to divorce and remarry. Unchastity was far too common. Their reaction is only intelligible if they understood him as *not* allowing remarriage following divorce.

For more on the meaning of the exceptive clauses, see Day 123.

The Meaning of the Exceptive Clauses

CHALLENGE

"If Matthew's exceptive clauses on divorce don't mean you can get remarried (see Day 122), what do they mean?"

DEFENSE

There are a number of possibilities.

In Matthew 5:32, Jesus states: "Every one who divorces his wife, except on the ground of unchastity, makes her an adulteress; and whoever marries a divorced woman commits adultery."

Social conditions in the ancient world pressured divorced women to remarry, so to divorce a woman was, in effect, to make her an adulteress—*unless she already was one.* Matthew may mean that a husband could divorce an adulterous wife without being guilty of forcing her into adultery, for she had already chosen that path.

Adultery thus might be a valid ground for divorce, but it would not permit remarriage. Note that Jesus says that anyone who marries a divorced woman commits adultery, without making any exceptions (cf. Day 82). This was the classical understanding of the exceptive clauses found in the writings of the Church Fathers.

Another theory points out that the word used in Greek for "unchastity" (*porneia*) and "adultery" (*moicheia*) are different, suggesting that "unchastity" should be taken as a reference to something other than adultery, such as sex with someone else before a marriage had been consummated. If infidelity were discovered before consummation, a person might be able to divorce and remarry, because marriage only becomes indissoluble when it is consummated (CCC 2382).

On either of the above theories, Matthew may have included the exceptive clauses to bring out this aspect of Jesus' teaching because he previously mentioned that Joseph had planned to divorce Mary when, prior to their living together, she was discovered to be with child. Yet he calls Joseph "a just man" (Matt. 1:19). How could he be just if divorce was always wrong? Thus Matthew may have included the exceptive clauses to make it clear how Joseph's intent could be reasonable for a just man to divorce.

Another theory, which has been argued in recent years, is that the word *porneia* here refers to incestuous marriages that were practiced by Gentiles but forbidden by the Jewish Law. Matthew may have wished to make it clear for his Jewish readers that such Gentile marriages were not valid. For a defense of this view, see John P. Meier, *The Vision of Matthew*, 248–57.

Who Did What in the Gospels?

CHALLENGE

"The Gospels contain error since they describe different people performing the same action. Matthew says a centurion approached Jesus about healing his servant, but Luke says Jewish elders did this (Matt. 8:5–13; Luke 7:1–10). Mark says James and John made a request, but Matthew says their mother made it (Mark 10:35–45; Matt. 20:20–28)."

DEFENSE

The biblical authors had liberty to describe events in terms of the principals or their agents.

More than one person can be involved in an action. The person on whose behalf the action is performed is known as the *principal*, while the person who actually does the action is known as the *agent*. Both today and in the ancient world, actions can be described as if the principal or the agent performed them.

During the 1962 Cuban Missile Crisis, newspapers might have reported, "American president Kennedy told Soviet premier Khrushchev to take his missiles out of Cuba." In reality, Kennedy and Khrushchev (the principals) never spoke. Their exchanges were carried on through diplomatic intermediaries (their agents). Because the principals were the main actors, newspapers could speak as if the two directly engaged each other. The diplomatic intermediaries were secondary.

In Scripture, we read that Moses built the tabernacle (2 Chron. 1:3) and Solomon built the temple (1 Kings 6:1–38). In reality, both were leaders too lofty to do the labor themselves. They used workmen who acted on their behalf (Exod. 38:22–23; 1 Kings 7:13–45). Because Moses and Solomon were the principals, they are sometimes mentioned, while the workmen who were their agents may not be mentioned.

The evangelists had the same freedom choosing how to describe an incident. They could describe it in terms of the agents acting (as with Luke's mention of the Jewish elders and Matthew's mention of the apostles' mother) or the principals acting (as with Matthew's mention of the centurion and Mark's mention of James and John).

When the evangelists chose the latter, the action of the agents may be said to be "telescoped" into the principals on whose behalf they acted. This literary technique is used in the Bible in more situations than we use it today, but it is not an error. It is a known literary device.

Arrogance and Truth

CHALLENGE

"How can Christians be so arrogant as to think they alone have the truth?"

DEFENSE

Nobody has a monopoly on the truth. Almost every perspective— religious and otherwise—has elements of truth in it. If it didn't, then nobody would believe it. All human beings possess the gift of reason, and we all use it to discover aspects of the truth.

"The Catholic Church rejects nothing that is true and holy in [other] religions. She regards with sincere reverence those ways of conduct and of life, those precepts and teachings which, though differing in many aspects from the ones she holds and sets forth, nonetheless often reflect a ray of that Truth which enlightens all men" (Vatican II, *Nostra Aetate* 2).

Consequently, we can use the truths that we hold in common as a basis for mutual respect and dialogue: "The missionary task implies a respectful dialogue with those who do not yet accept the Gospel. Believers can profit from this dialogue by learning to appreciate better those elements of truth and grace which are found among peoples, and which are, as it were, a secret presence of God" (CCC 856; cf. CCC 39, 843).

At the same time, Christians recognize that they have been given truth in the Person of Jesus Christ, who is "the way, and the truth, and the life" (John 14:6). This is not arrogance. One is not being arrogant by supposing that he has learned a truth. We do not say that a student of math or science or history is arrogant if his teacher has taught him a truth in one of these fields. The same is true of Christians who have been taught by Jesus.

Indeed, Christians hold that their faith is a gift from God, not something they have earned or deserved. Many of the truths God has revealed exceed the power of human reason to discover, and it is only because of God's grace that we have come to learn them and to have the opportunity to share them with others.

TIP

Sometimes other Christians ask Catholics how they can think they uniquely possess the truth. The same principles above apply when answering this question, and they can help non-Catholic Christians understand the Catholic point of view as well as to examine their own attitude regarding the truth of Christianity in general.

Ex Opere Operato

"The Church has a superstitious understanding of the sacraments, believing that performing them will bring about their effects ex opere operato *('by reason of the work having been performed')."*

DEFENSE

The Church doesn't hold that merely performing the external actions of the sacraments will bring about their effects.

Suppose a group of actors put on a play in which one character is baptized. Though water may be applied with the correct words (Matt. 28:19), the actor playing that character is not truly baptized. The reason is the actor baptizing him is just pretending to do so. He doesn't have the intention to do what the Church does. Therefore, merely performing the external ritual of a sacrament does not bring about its effects.

But when the minister of a sacrament does intend to do what the Church does, God's promise to give his grace is engaged. The teaching that the sacraments work *ex opere operato* mean that their efficacy rests on God's promise, not on the worthiness of the minister.

This is in contrast to the view that the sacraments work *ex opere operantis* ("by reason of the work of the one working"; see *Catholic Encyclopedia,* s.v. "Sacraments"), which means that the minister would need to be personally worthy (not in a state of mortal sin) to be able to perform the sacraments. This view was held in the 400s by the schismatic movement known as Donatism.

Upholding the orthodox view, Augustine argued that the unworthiness of the minister does not affect the validity of the sacrament, and so, for example, baptism could be validly received from a heretic or a schismatic (see his *On Baptism, Against the Donatists*).

The faithful thus need not worry that the sacraments they have received might be invalid because of the unworthiness of the minister. Their efficacy rests on God's promise.

On the other hand, to receive the sacraments fruitfully, the faithful must be open to God's grace. If they are unrepentant of mortal sin then they create a barrier that prevents the sacraments from communicating sanctifying grace. In such cases, they would still be received validly (e.g., an unrepentant person intending to be baptized, confirmed, or married would validly receive the sacrament but would not receive sanctifying grace until he repents).

TIP

For the *Catechism's* summary of this teaching, see CCC 1127–28.

The Star of Bethlehem and Astrology

CHALLENGE

"Doesn't the star of Bethlehem imply the practice of astrology?"

DEFENSE

The fact that the Magi recognized the star's significance implies that *they* practiced astrology, but it doesn't imply we should.

The ancients did not know what the stars really are, and many regarded them as divinities that ruled the fates of men. Thus the sun, moon, and wandering stars (planets) had the names of deities: Sol, Luna, Mercury, Venus, Mars, Jupiter, Saturn. The names varied from culture to culture, but in paganism they were worshipped as deities.

This practice was explicitly condemned in the Old Testament (Deut. 4:19, 17:3; 2 Kings 17:16; Jer. 19:11–13; Amos 5:26–27), and the author of Genesis demythologizes it by describing the heavenly bodies merely as lights created by God (Gen. 1:14–16).

This does not mean God can't use them as signs of major events in his plan. He is omnipotent and can do so if he chooses. Thus in the book of Joel God states: "I will give portents in the heavens. . . . The sun shall be turned to darkness, and the moon to blood" (Joel 2:30–31).

In Acts, Peter interprets this in terms of the dawning of the Christian age (Acts 2:14–21). It is noteworthy that darkness covered the land ("the sun shall be turned to darkness") during the Crucifixion (Matt. 27:45), and—providentially—there was a lunar eclipse that made the moon appear red ("and the moon to blood") on April 3, A.D. 33, the probable date of the Crucifixion.

If God chose to mark the death of his Son with an unusual celestial sign, then he might have done the same to mark his birth, and he may have further allowed the Magi to recognize its significance based on the ideas present in their culture.

However, this would be an exceptional event and not an endorsement of the practice of astrology in general. The stars are not divinities that rule our lives, and they have no power over us. God may providentially use them as markers of certain events in his plan of the ages, but that does not mean we can infer things about the events of our own lives from them. This is what the modern practice of astrology does, however, and so the Church rejects it (CCC 2116).

Objections to the General Resurrection

CHALLENGE

"The resurrection of the dead is absurd. An ancient might believe that God could reanimate dead bodies, but after death our bodies are broken down into their constituent elements. Further, particles from one person's body can end up in another person's body."

DEFENSE

Belief in the afterlife is a human universal. This is a sign that it exists. The question is what form it takes. God has revealed that the afterlife includes an eventual bodily resurrection. He has demonstrated this by raising Jesus from the dead (on the connection between Jesus' Resurrection and ours, see 1 Cor. 15).

The idea that the ancients could believe in the resurrection of the dead because they were unsophisticated is chronological snobbery. They were as aware as we that the body decomposes into tiny particles. In the first book of the Bible, God proclaims to man: "You are dust, and to dust you shall return" (Gen. 3:19).

In Jesus' day it was customary to entomb a body and then, once the flesh had rotted off the bones, to return, clean the bones, and place them in a container known as an ossuary. People were thus brought into immediate contact with the decay of their loved ones' bodies. Nor were the ancients ignorant of the fact that—through cannibalism or less direct means—matter from one person's body could end up in another's. The medieval philosophers explored this question in detail.

The fundamental part of man that guarantees personal identity over time is the soul, which is the "form" of the body (CCC 365). However, over the course of our lives, the matter that makes up our bodies changes dramatically.

The International Theological Commission notes: "The Church has never taught that the very same matter is required for the body to be said to be the same. But the cult of relics, whereby Christians profess that the bodies of the saints who were living members of Christ and the temple of the Holy Spirit must be raised and glorified by Christ, shows that the resurrection cannot be explained independently of the body that once lived" (*Some Current Questions in Eschatology* 1.2.5).

Christian theology thus holds that the resurrected body is connected with the one that previously lived but not that it contains all the matter that was ever part of it in life.

Mary as Mother of God

CHALLENGE

"Catholics shouldn't say Mary is the mother of God. God is eternal and so can't have a mother. Mary merely gave birth to Jesus' human nature."

DEFENSE

This misunderstands the title "mother of God." You can't have a correct view of Christ and still deny this title.

A person's mother contributes genetic matter to him, carries him in her womb, or both.

Normally, a mother is older than her child, but Mary is an exceptional case, as the Virgin Birth shows.

Mary did not exist before the Second Person of the Trinity, who has always existed in the eternal now outside of time, but she did become his mother by contributing genetic matter to him (cf. Rom. 1:3) and by carrying him in her womb (Matt. 1:18; Luke 1:35).

Mary was Jesus' mother in the true sense. As the Second Person of the Trinity, Jesus is God, and so Mary is the mother of God. Mary did not merely give birth to Jesus' human nature. Mothers do not give birth to natures. They give birth to persons, and Jesus was a divine person. To deny that Mary gave birth to the Second Person of the Trinity would be to commit the heresy Nestorianism.

In the fifth century, Nestorius—the patriarch of Constantinople— objected to the title "mother of God" (Greek, *theotokos*, "God-bearer"). His position was rejected by the Council of Ephesus (A.D. 431) because the council fathers recognized that the true understanding of the person of Christ was at stake. If Mary can't be said to give birth to the Second Person of the Trinity, then a wedge is driven between Christ's humanity and his divinity, so he is no longer one person.

This is recognized by many theologians, including Protestants. Martin Luther wrote: "Mary, the mother, does not carry, give birth to, suckle, and nourish only the man, only flesh and blood—for that would be dividing the Person—but she carries and nourishes a son who is God's Son. Therefore she is rightly called not only the mother of the man but also the Mother of God" (*Luther's Works* 24:107).

TIP

Although Scripture does not use the phrase "mother of God," it uses an equivalent when Mary's cousin Elizabeth asks: "Why is this granted me, that *the mother of my Lord* should come to me" (Luke 1:43).

The Nature of Saints

"The Catholic Church shouldn't refer just to people in heaven as saints. All believers are saints."

DEFENSE

The term "saint" is used in multiple senses, even in Scripture.

The term "saint" (Hebrew, *qadosh*; Aramaic, *qaddish*; Greek, *hagios*; Latin, *sanctus*) means "holy one." Anyone who is in some sense holy or sanctified is in that sense a saint. This leads to many uses of the term in Scripture, though this is partially masked because English translators sometimes render the word as "saint" and sometimes as "holy one."

The Israelites were a people holy to God (Lev. 20:26), so the Old Testament describes them as saints (Ps. 34:9; Dan. 7:18, 8:24). Thus, Paul tells Gentile Christians that they have become fellow citizens "with the saints" (Eph. 2:19).

Christians are also holy to God (1 Peter 1:16), so the New Testament often refers to them as saints (2 Cor. 1:1, Eph. 1:1, Phil. 1:1). The Catholic Church acknowledges this usage. After reviewing various passages in the New Testament that refer to Christians as saints, John Paul II noted, "All these cases refer to Christians, or to the faithful, that is, to the brethren who have received the Holy Spirit" (*General Audience*, August 16, 1989).

Jewish people were sanctified by their participation in the Mosaic Covenant, and Christians are sanctified by their participation in the New Covenant of Christ, so this represents two different forms of sanctification or sainthood. There are others.

Thus the holy angels are also referred to as saints (Ps. 89:6, 8; Dan. 4:13, 17, 23, 8:13). In popular speech, a person of notable holiness is often referred to as a saint, and we find this usage in the Bible as well (cf. Isa. 4:3–4, Matt. 27:52–53). Very surprisingly for English speakers, Jesus is described as the Saint or Holy One of God (Mark 1:24; Luke 4:34; John 6:67–69), and God is described as the Saint or Holy One of Israel (Ps. 71:22, 78:41, 89:18; Is. 1:4; Jer. 50:29).

Since there is no single, privileged definition of the term, it is reasonable to use "saint" to refer to those who have their sanctification—or "saintification"—completed by dwelling with God in heaven. This is thus one way the Church uses the term, both for those in heaven who have been canonized and those who have not.

Peter and James the Just

CHALLENGE

"Peter wasn't the first pope because James the Just (aka "the Lord's brother") was the leader; he was the one who decided the results of the Acts 15 council, referring to 'my judgment' (Acts 15:19)."

DEFENSE

Jesus appointed Peter as leader of the Church (Matt. 16:18). Although James did come to have a leadership role, Jesus never made him superior to Peter.

Initially, the brethren of the Lord (see Day 135) did not have leadership roles, as they did not believe in him during his earthly ministry (John 7:5). They only later believed (cf. 1 Cor. 15:7) and became leaders. James eventually became bishop of Jerusalem.

The second-century author Clement of Alexandria records an earlier tradition that James the Just had the office of bishop conferred on him by the apostles: "Peter and James and John after the Ascension of our Saviour, as if also preferred by our Lord, strove not after honor, but chose James the Just bishop of Jerusalem" (Eusebius, *Ecclesiastical History* 2:1:3). If this tradition is accurate, he likely would have become bishop shortly before James son of Zebedee was executed (Acts 12:2) and Peter fled Jerusalem (Acts 12:17—note the reference to James).

In Acts 15, the question is whether Gentiles must keep the Law of Moses. James does not decide this issue. Peter points out that the decision has already been made by God and announced when God chose Peter to preach the gospel to the Gentiles (Acts 15:7–11; cf. 10:1–11:18).

James appeals to what Peter has recounted (Acts 15:14) and provides scriptural support for it (15:16–18). He then expresses his opinion that the Gentiles should not be required to keep the law (15:19). The Greek word sometimes translated "judgment" in this passage (*krinō*) means "to hold a view or have an opinion with regard to something—'to hold a view, to have an opinion, to consider, to regard'" (Johannes Louw and Eugene Nida, *Greek-English Lexicon of the New Testament*, 2nd ed., 31.1). James then proposes pastoral provisions (15:20) to help Jewish and Gentile Christians live harmoniously (15:21).

The fact that he did not decide the results of the council is shown by the letter the council sent, which was addressed in the name of all the apostles and elders and which speaks of the decision being collective, without naming any individuals as the deciders (15:23–29).

Church Teaching on Divorce

"The Catholic Church is too uptight about divorce. People ought to be able to freely divorce and remarry if they choose."

The Church's teaching on divorce is humane, just, and rooted in the teaching of Jesus.

The Church's teaching is humane, for it recognizes that there can be legitimate reasons to obtain a divorce under civil (secular) law: "If civil divorce remains the only possible way of ensuring certain legal rights, the care of the children, or the protection of inheritance, it can be tolerated and does not constitute a moral offense" (CCC 2383). Thus nobody is required to live in an intolerable or unsafe situation, such as with a physically or emotionally abusive spouse.

The Church's teaching is just, for it recognizes that the spouses have made a serious commitment to each other in marriage. There must be grave reason to justify civil divorce, because divorce "introduces disorder into the family and into society. This disorder brings grave harm to the deserted spouse, to children traumatized by the separation of their parents and often torn between them, and because of its contagious effect which makes it truly a plague on society" (CCC 2385).

The Church's teaching is rooted in the teaching of Jesus, who took a strong stand against the permissive attitude toward divorce in the ancient world. Stressing that marriage was instituted by God, so that husband and wife are joined together in a divine institution, Jesus famously stated: "What therefore God has joined together, let not man put asunder" (Matt. 19:6).

He also warned that—because they are united together in this way—they are not free to marry other people if they do divorce: "Whoever divorces his wife and marries another, commits adultery against her; and if she divorces her husband and marries another, she commits adultery" (Mark 10:11–12; cf. Luke 16:18).

This same teaching is reflected in the writings of Paul, who specifically tells his readers that the teaching comes from "the Lord"—i.e., the Lord Jesus (cf. 1 Cor. 1:2–3). He writes: "To the married I give charge, not I but the Lord, that the wife should not separate from her husband (but if she does, let her remain single or else be reconciled to her husband)—and that the husband should not divorce his wife" (1 Cor. 7:10–11).

Miracles and Divine Perfection

CHALLENGE

*"A perfect God could create a world he didn't have to keep fixing.
It would be able to run without periodic miracles."*

DEFENSE

This misunderstands the natures of the universe, of miracles, and of God.

The only reason the universe exists at a particular moment in time is that God sustains it. "What comes forth from nothing would return to nothing if it were left to itself and not conserved in being by the Creator. Having created the cosmos, God continues to create it, by maintaining it in existence. Conservation is a continuous creation" (John Paul II, *General Audience*, May 7, 1986; CCC 301). Ongoing divine intervention is therefore a given. The question is what form the intervention takes.

God could arrange the universe so that his interventions (direct or through secondary causes) always operate according to the regular patterns that humans refer to as the "laws" of nature. Or he could arrange it so some of his interventions deviate from these regular patterns, so that humans regard them with wonder (Latin, *miraculum*).

This is what miracles are. They are not efforts to fix a universe that has broken down like a machine. They are simply divine interventions that depart from the regular patterns we see in the world. "The word 'miracle' indicates . . . the extraordinary aspect of those events in the eyes of those who saw them" (John Paul II, *General Audience*, Nov. 11, 1987).

How God performs his interventions is up to him. We should not think of the universe as if it were a labor-saving device that God should interact with as little as possible. Humans value labor-saving devices because we have limited resources. God does not have limited resources, and so he has no need to save labor. For an omnipotent God, every action is equally easy. No action can deplete the infinite (unlimited) power he has. It is thus a matter of God's choice if he wants to interact with the world in ways that are obvious or non-obvious.

Even humans create devices that require overt intervention on our part (e.g., video games). If we do this for our purposes, God can do the same for his. One of those purposes is helping us realize that God both exists and interacts with the world. Miracles make that clear.

Jesus the One Mediator

CHALLENGE

"Catholics shouldn't ask Mary and the saints for intercession. Scripture says, 'For there is one God, and there is one mediator between God and men, the man Christ Jesus' (1 Tim. 2:5)."

DEFENSE

Christ has a unique role as mediator, but this does not mean that he alone intercedes with God.

The term "mediator" (Greek, *mesitēs*) began as a business term referring to an intermediary who helped two parties do business. In Judaism and other ancient religions, it came to refer to one who served a similar role securing good relations between God and man, reconciling them.

In several senses, Jesus is uniquely the Mediator. First, by virtue of the Incarnation, he alone is the God-man, who shares the natures of God and man (CCC 618). Second, because he is God incarnate, he became the Mediator of the New Covenant (Heb. 8:6, 9:15, 12:24), just as Moses was the mediator of the Old Covenant (Gal. 3:19).

Jesus' status as the "one mediator" does not mean he is the only person with a role between God and men. Paul's apostleship meant he had such a role, and he appealed to his apostleship in the same passage he refers to Jesus as the one Mediator (1 Tim. 2:7). Other ministers have similar roles (2 Cor. 5:20; cf. 1 Thess. 5:12, Heb. 13:17), as do all Christians (2 Cor. 3:2–3; 1 Pet. 3:15).

Although Jesus intercedes for us (Rom. 8:34; Heb. 7:25; 1 John 2:1), he is not the only one to do so. The Holy Spirit does (Rom. 8:26–27), and all Christians are called to as well. Thus Jesus instructs us how to pray for ourselves and others (Matt. 6:5–13), and tells us to pray even for our enemies (Matt. 5:44).

Paul asks for prayer for himself and for others (Rom. 15:30; 2 Cor. 1:11; 2 Thess. 3:1–2), and he introduces the very passage in which he refers to Christ as the one Mediator by exhorting his readers to pray for others: "First of all, then, I urge that supplications, prayers, intercessions, and thanksgivings be made for all men" (1 Tim. 2:1).

TIP

If this objection worked, it would prove too much: If Jesus' status as the one Mediator meant only he could intercede for us, then it would contradict his teaching that we should pray for others.

Jesus' Brothers

CHALLENGE

"Scripture mentions that Jesus had at least four brothers: James, Joses, Judas, and Simon (Mark 6:3). Therefore, there's no way Mary could have remained a virgin after the birth of Christ."

DEFENSE

Just because someone is described as a brother does not mean he had the same mother. The word is used more than one way.

The most common use of "brother" is for a male sibling who has the same mother and father (i.e., a full brother). However, Jesus had no full brothers, for Joseph was not his biological father (Matt. 1:18; Luke 1:26–35). This means that, when Scripture refers to the brothers of Jesus, it is not using the term in its most common sense.

The term can also refer to a brother who has one parent in common (a half brother). This option is preferred by those who hold that Mary did not remain a virgin. However, it is not the only option. The word can refer to a brother by marriage (a stepbrother) or to a brother by adoption (an adopted brother). And there are other uses still.

It can be used for close relations. Genesis 12:5 and 14:12 make it clear that Lot was the son of Abraham's brother (i.e., his nephew), but Genesis 14:14 and 14:16 describe Lot as Abraham's "brother" (Hebrew, *'akh*), and Abraham describes himself and Lot as "brothers" (*'akhim*) in Genesis 13:8.

Thus the fact that *brother* is used does not show that Mary had other children.

If we had no evidence for the Virgin Birth, then the most natural understanding of Jesus' brothers would be full brothers—children of both Joseph and Mary. But we do have evidence of the Virgin Birth, so we must seek another understanding.

In the same way, if we had no evidence that Mary remained a virgin, then it would be reasonable to think Jesus' brothers were half brothers—fellow sons of Mary. But we do have evidence that Mary remained a virgin, meaning we must look to another sense (see Day 188).

TIP

The earliest reference we have to who the brothers were is in the second-century document called the *Protoevangelium of James*. It says they were stepbrothers (children of Joseph—who had been a widower—by a former marriage). Later, the idea the "brothers" were close relations such as cousins also became popular.

Justification "By Faith Alone"

CHALLENGE

"Catholicism rejects justification by faith alone and thus the biblical truth about salvation."

DEFENSE

While the "faith alone" formula is not commonly used in Catholic circles, it can be given an acceptable meaning.

The Catholic Church agrees that you do not have to do good works to enter a state of justification. It teaches that "none of those things that precede justification, whether faith or works, merit the grace of justification" (Council of Trent, *Decree on Justification* 8).

When we repent and are justified, God puts the virtue of charity (supernatural love of God and neighbor) into our hearts (CCC 1991). This virtue makes supernaturally good works possible, so these flow *from* justification. "Good works—a Christian life lived in faith, hope and love—follow justification and are its fruits. When the justified live in Christ and act in the grace they receive, they bring forth, in biblical terms, good fruit" (JD 37).

Thus Paul refers to "faith working through love" (Gal. 5:6). Catholic theologians have held that if this is how faith is understood, then the formula "by faith alone" has an acceptable meaning. Benedict XVI said: "Luther's phrase 'faith alone' is true, if it is not opposed to faith in charity, in love. . . . So it is that in the Letter to the Galatians, in which he primarily developed his teaching on justification, St. Paul speaks of faith that works through love" (General Audience, Nov. 19, 2008).

While the formula *can* have an acceptable meaning, this doesn't mean it's a good or natural expression of the Bible's teaching. It is not the language of Scripture. Paul never uses this phrase. The only time it does appear in Scripture, it is rejected ("a man is justified by works and *not by faith alone*"; James 2:24).

Faith separated from charity is not enough to save: "Faith without works is dead" (James 2:26). Demons have purely intellectual faith, or agreement with the truths of theology: "Even the demons believe— *and shudder*" (James 2:19, emphasis added).

The fact that "faith" is often used to mean intellectual assent rather than "faith working through love," and the fact that the "faith alone" formula is rejected the one time that it is used in Scripture, means we need to be careful, because the formula is very easy to misunderstand.

The Divinity of Jesus

CHALLENGE

"Jesus is not God. He only claimed to be the Son of God."

DEFENSE

By claiming to be God's Son, Jesus claims to be God. His divinity is also indicated by other passages in Scripture.

By nature, Sons are equal to their fathers. When Jesus asserts that he is God's Son, he indicates his equality to God the Father. The son of a man is a man, and the Son of God is God.

The New Testament explicitly acknowledges this. Jesus opponents tried to kill him "because he not only broke the Sabbath but also called God his Father, making himself equal with God" (John 5:18). Note that John—the inspired author—does not say that Jesus' opponents *thought* he made himself equal to God. He says Jesus *did* this.

In light of this, other texts that speak of Jesus' divinity also indicate that he was equal with God, not a lesser, created "god." This is the case when we read: "In the beginning was the Word, and the Word was with God, and the Word was God" (John 1:1). It also sheds light on Jesus' acceptance of Thomas's worship when the latter declares him "My Lord and my God!" (John 20:28).

Paul says that in Jesus "the whole fulness of deity dwells bodily" (Col. 2:9), and he quotes from an early Christian hymn that says, though the preincarnate Jesus "was in the form of God, [he] did not count equality with God a thing to be grasped, but emptied himself, taking the form of a servant, being born in the likeness of men" (Phil. 2:6–7).

Paul directly calls Jesus God when he writes that from the Jewish race, "according to the flesh, is the Christ, who is God over all" (Rom. 9:5), and when he discusses how we should live while awaiting "the appearing of the glory of our great God and Savior Jesus Christ" (Titus 2:13). Peter also declares Jesus God when he speaks of "the righteousness of our God and Savior Jesus Christ" (2 Pet. 1:1).

TIP

For a thorough, book-length defense of Jesus' divinity, see Richard Bauckham's *Jesus and the God of Israel: God Crucified and Other Studies on the New Testament's Christology of Divine Identity.*

Non-canonical Gospels

CHALLENGE

"There is no reason we should trust Matthew, Mark, Luke, and John. They were selected because they supported a particular agenda, and there were dozens of other gospels in existence at the time."

DEFENSE

The canonical Gospels were selected because they are the earliest and most reliable accounts of Jesus' life.

Even skeptical scholars acknowledge the four canonical Gospels were written in the first century, while others are from the second and third centuries or later.

The four Gospels were authored either by eyewitnesses of Jesus (Matthew and John) or close associates of apostles (Mark was a companion of Peter, and Luke was a companion of Paul). They were thus in a good position to know what Jesus said and did, and their Gospels were read at Christian worship services from the beginning.

Other alleged gospels were written much later, and their authors were not in as good of a position to record the story of Jesus accurately. Because they were written later, there was no history of them being read in worship services. This helped early Christians spot them as fakes. If a proposed gospel was authentically from the first followers of Jesus, why hadn't it been used in the Church's worship all this time?

The later gospels are frequently based on the four canonical ones. They often don't attempt to tell the story of Jesus' ministry, but assume the reader already knows it. For example, some "gospels" tell stories about Jesus' parents or about his childhood; they consist of isolated sayings attributed to him; or they claim to record speeches he gave after his Resurrection. They thus try to "fill in" things that the canonical Gospels don't include—and they therefore testify to the unique value of Matthew, Mark, Luke, and John for learning the basic story of Jesus.

The actual teachings of Jesus were transmitted by the canonical Gospels—and through the preaching of the Church—which also made it possible to spot later ones as fakes. Many later "gospels" contain teachings contrary to those in the originals. In particular, many were influenced by the Gnostic heresy of the second and third centuries.

The canonical Gospels thus weren't included because they supported a particular viewpoint; the later ones were excluded because they contradicted what had been passed down from the beginning.

The Real Presence and Cannibalism

CHALLENGE

"The Real Presence can't be true—Jesus would be commanding cannibalism! The Bible also tells us that we are not allowed to consume blood (Gen. 9:4; Lev. 17:14; Deut. 12:23)."

DEFENSE

The Real Presence does not imply cannibalism.

Cannibalism involves chewing another person's flesh, swallowing it, and extracting nutrients from it by digestion. None of that happens to Jesus' flesh when a person receives the Eucharist. Jesus' body and blood remain whole and undigested under the appearances of bread and wine.

Only the appearances are altered by consumption, and when they cease to have the appearance of bread and wine, the Real Presence ceases. God may make "the body and blood of Christ enthroned gloriously in heaven" (Paul VI, *Credo of the People of God*) simultaneously present in the Eucharist, but they are in no way damaged. Therefore, no cannibalism occurs.

The Old Testament prohibition on consuming blood forbade its normal consumption—where blood was eaten and digested as a food. Christ's blood is not digested, and so the Eucharist does not violate the Old Testament prohibition on blood consumption.

This prohibition was part of the dietary regulations that kept Jews culturally and religiously distinct from their pagan neighbors. Globally, many cultures use blood in cooking (e.g., blood sausages like the "black pudding" eaten today in England), and Jesus removed these dietary restrictions when he "declared all foods clean" (Mark 7:19).

The reason the Israelites were prohibited from consuming blood was ritual: The blood represented the life of the animal, and so it belonged to God, the giver of life. Such ritual requirements are gone today, and now God gives us spiritual life through Jesus and the reception of his blood. Jesus declared: "Unless you eat the flesh of the Son of man and drink his blood, you have no life in you" (John 6:53).

If consuming the Eucharist were cannibalism, then saying the elements are merely symbolic would not solve the problem. In that case, Jesus would be commanding us to *symbolically* cannibalize him. This would be as problematic as making the symbolic commission of any intrinsically evil act (e.g., sodomy, rape) part of a sacrament.

The Consecrated Life

CHALLENGE

"Monks and nuns are unbiblical. We don't see them in Scripture."

DEFENSE

Yes, we do. In both testaments we see people who take vows to specially consecrate themselves to God.

In the Old Testament, we read about Nazirites. The Hebrew term *nazir* means "consecrated" or "separated," and the Nazirites were those consecrated to God by a special vow (Num. 6:2). As a result, they were not to drink wine or use any grape products (6:3–4), they were not to cut their hair but let it grow long (6:5), and they were to abstain from contact with dead bodies, even of their own relatives (6:6–12). There were also ceremonies to be performed upon the completion of the vow, which included cutting the hair (6:13–21). Many Nazirites made temporary vows, but some had perpetual ones. These included Samson and Samuel, who were Nazirites from the womb (Judg. 13:5, 1 Sam. 1:11).

Like modern monks and nuns, Nazirites were vowed to live lives of special consecration to God. The parallel is so clear that in modern (twenty-first century) Hebrew, the word for monk is *nazir* and the word for nun is *nazirah* (the feminine form of *nazir*). Monks and nuns thus are the Christian equivalent of Jewish Nazirites.

In the New Testament, Paul appears to have taken temporary Nazirite vows more than once (Acts 18:18, 21:23–27).

He also describes a first-century order that took a perpetual vow of celibacy: "Let a widow be enrolled if she is not less than sixty years of age, having been the wife of one husband; and she must be well attested for her good deeds, as one who has brought up children, shown hospitality, washed the feet of the saints, relieved the afflicted, and devoted herself to doing good in every way. But refuse to enrol younger widows; for when they grow wanton against Christ they desire to marry, and so they incur condemnation for having violated their first pledge" (1 Tim. 5:9–12). Paul is concerned that younger widows will be tempted to remarry and thus break the vow of celibacy the order required, bringing judgment upon themselves. He thus says younger widows should remarry and have children rather than join the order (vv. 14–15).

Both testaments thus affirm the principle of some taking vows of special consecration to God.

"All Have Sinned"

CHALLENGE

"How can Catholics say Mary was sinless when Scripture teaches clearly that 'all have sinned' (Rom. 3:23)?"

DEFENSE

The passage doesn't prove that Mary sinned.

Romans 3:23 occurs in a section where Paul is arguing that both Jews and Gentiles need salvation through Jesus Christ and that this is not achieved through the Law of Moses. This is the major thrust of Romans 1–4.

Thus he writes: "For there is no distinction; since all have sinned and fall short of the glory of God, they are justified by his grace as a gift, through the redemption which is in Christ Jesus. . . . Or is God the God of Jews only? Is he not the God of Gentiles also? Yes, of Gentiles also, since God is one; and he will justify the circumcised on the ground of their faith and the uncircumcised through their faith" (Rom. 3:22–24, 29–30).

When Paul says that "there is no distinction," he means that there is no distinction between Jews and Gentiles. When he explains this statement by saying "for all have sinned," he means sin characterizes both Jews and Gentiles.

However, his use of the term "all" is hyperbole, for Paul does not believe that this is an exceptionless norm. Thus later in Romans, where Paul appeals to the case of Jacob and Esau and speaks of the time when "they were not yet born and had done nothing either good or bad" (Rom. 9:11). Paul therefore recognizes that unborn children have not yet committed personal sin, making them an exception to the "all have sinned" norm he spoke of earlier.

Further, Paul would certainly have acknowledged the sinlessness in adult life of at least one man—Jesus! Paul elsewhere says that Jesus "knew no sin" (2 Cor. 5:21), and belief in Jesus' sinlessness is attested in multiple passages in the New Testament (Heb. 4:15, 7:26, 9:14; 1 Peter 2:22; 1 John 3:5).

If Jesus, as the "Second Adam" (cf. Rom. 5:12–19, 1 Cor. 15:21–22, 45–49), is an exception to what Paul says in Romans 3:23, there may also be an exception for Mary as the "Second Eve" (CCC 411).

Romans 3:23 thus does not disprove that Mary remained sinless through a special application of God's grace.

The Teachings of Jesus

CHALLENGE

"The Gospels don't reliably convey the teachings of Jesus. The evangelists invented material based on their own views and the needs of their communities."

DEFENSE

The evidence shows the Gospels are reliable.

Perhaps the greatest controversy in the early Church was whether Gentiles had to be circumcized and become Jews to be saved. This controversy is mentioned multiple times in Acts (10:1–11:18, 15:1–31, 21:25), and it dominates Paul's epistles of Romans and Galatians. If there was ever a controversy to tempt people to make up a saying of Jesus to settle the matter, it would be this. Yet the circumcision controversy isn't mentioned anywhere in the Gospels. That is a sign the evangelists did not feel free to make up teachings and put them on Jesus' lips.

This is also indicated by the way Mark handles the related question of whether kosher laws were still binding. In his account of a controversy in Jesus' day about why the disciples did not ritually wash their hands before eating, we read of Jesus saying: "'Do you not see that whatever goes into a man from outside cannot defile him, since it enters, not his heart but his stomach, and so passes on?' (Thus he declared all foods clean.) And he said, 'What comes out of a man is what defiles a man. For from within, out of the heart of man, come evil thoughts, fornication, theft, murder, adultery'" (Mark 7:18–21).

In a traditional Jewish view, unclean hands would defile food and make the eater ceremonially unclean. Jesus indicates this isn't true, for any dirt contaminating the food would pass out of the body without bringing about true, spiritual uncleanliness. The comment "thus he declared all foods clean" is Mark's *application* of Jesus' teaching to the different question of kosher foods. This shows Mark did not feel free to invent a teaching of Jesus.

A final point is the fact that Paul's teachings are nowhere quoted in the Gospels. Besides Peter, Paul was the most influential apostle. His letters were among the earliest New Testament writings, and if the evangelists felt free to simply attribute things to Jesus, we would expect some of the things Paul wrote to end up on Jesus' lips. Yet we don't, not even in Luke, which was written by one of Paul's traveling companions.

Genocide in the Bible (1)

CHALLENGE

"How can you believe the Bible when it contains passages in which God commands the extermination of whole peoples (Deut. 7:1–2, 20:16–17)?"

DEFENSE

The answer depends on whether or not those passages are meant to be taken literally.

Tomorrow we will consider the view that the commands are non-literal. Here we will consider the view that they are meant literally.

According to this view, God expected the Israelites to kill certain peoples for two reasons.

First, "according to what is attested in the Bible, the Canaanites are seen by God as guilty of very serious crimes (Gen. 15:16; Lev. 18:3, 24–30, 20:23; Deut. 9:4–5, etc.), among which is the killing of their own children in perverted rituals (Deut. 12:31, 18:10–12). The narrative, then, holds out the prospect of the execution of divine justice in history" (Pontifical Biblical Commission, *The Inspiration and Truth of Sacred Scripture* 127).

Second, the text indicates if these cultures survived, they would corrupt the Israelites with these immoral practices (Deut. 7:4, 20:18). This danger was seen as so severe that, given the conditions in the ancient world, the only effective way to prevent it was extermination. And, in fact, the Israelites were so corrupted.

If the literal view is accurate, how could God issue these commands?

It is worth pointing out that all life is a gift from God. We do not have a right to it. God has a right to determine how much of that gift we receive and when and how it ends. Thus St. Thomas Aquinas writes, "All men alike, both guilty and innocent, die the death of nature: which death of nature is inflicted by the power of God on account of original sin, according to 1 Samuel 2:6: 'The Lord killeth and maketh alive.' Consequently, by the command of God, death can be inflicted on any man, guilty or innocent, without any injustice whatever" (ST I–II:94:5 reply to obj. 2).

Further, death is not the end. Whatever the circumstances of a particular death, it is a finite evil. Eternity lies before us, and God is capable of more than compensating the innocent who have suffered or died (see Day 38).

The actions commanded in these verses are not for our day but, according to this view, they do not involve injustice.

Genocide in the Bible (2)

"The Bible can't be the word of God. It has passages where God commands the Israelites to exterminate whole populations when they entered the promised land (Deut. 7:1–2, 20:16–17)."

DEFENSE

The response still depends on whether the passages are meant literally.

Yesterday we considered the view that they are literal. Here we consider the view that they are non-literal. According to this view, God did not literally expect the Israelites to exterminate certain peoples.

Moses is conventionally referred to as the Pentateuch's author because he is the principal leader it discusses. The Pentateuch does not say Moses is its author, and it contains material he could not have authored, such as the account of his death (Deut. 34).

Although the Pentateuch may contain material that dates to the time of Moses, it was not put in its final form until later. Consequently, the passages concerning the extermination of the Canaanites may not have been written until later. If they are post-Mosaic then they were not intended to be carried out literally, for Israel was already living in the land. In that case, they would have been meant to communicate a spiritual lesson.

Though not a body of the Church's Magisterium, the Pontifical Biblical Commission expresses a common view when it writes:

> As the best interpreters of the patristic tradition [i.e., the Church Fathers] had already suggested, the narration of the conquest epic should be seen as a sort of parable presenting characters of symbolic value; the law of extermination, for its part, requires a non-literal interpretation, as in the case of the command of the Lord to cut off one's hand or pluck out one's eye, if they are a cause of scandal (Matt 5:29; 18:9) (*The Inspiration and Truth of Sacred Scripture* 127).

The portrait given of the Canaanites in the Pentateuch is one of great depravity that even involved child sacrifice (Deut. 12:31, 18:10–12). By contrast, the Israelites are called to holiness, for they are "a people holy to the Lord" (Deut. 7:6, 14:2; cf. Lev. 11:44, 20:26).

The extermination commands may thus be a way of signifying the radical incompatibility of paganism and serving God: Paganism is to be entirely avoided, though this does not mean literal extermination any more than Christ meant we should literally cut off our hand to avoid sin.

Bad Popes

"Some popes in history have been very bad. They could not be the leaders of God's people, therefore the papacy is false."

All Church leaders are sinful to one degree or another, but the sinfulness of a particular leader says nothing about whether or not the office he occupies was instituted by God.

This argument runs the risk of proving too much. If being a sinner prevented you from being a leader, then every Christian community would be leaderless. Yet God insituted leaders in the Church (1 Cor. 12:28; Eph. 4:11–12; 1 Thess. 5:12–13; Heb. 13:17).

Sinfulness doesn't mean a man does not occupy a divinely instituted office. A striking illustration is the high priest Caiaphas. John records that, when the authorities were plotting the death of Jesus, some were concerned that if Jesus were not stopped, he would lead a revolt and the Romans would then destroy the Jewish temple and nation.

John then reports: "But one of them, Caiaphas, who was high priest that year, said to them, 'You know nothing at all; you do not understand that it is expedient for you that one man should die for the people, and that the whole nation should not perish.'"

Then John says: "He did not say this of his own accord, but being high priest that year he prophesied that Jesus should die for the nation, and not for the nation only, but to gather into one the children of God who are scattered abroad" (John 11:47–52).

He thus recognizes Caiaphas as unwittingly prophesying about the death of the Messiah because he was "high priest that year." It's even more remarkable that Caiaphas did this *in the act* of plotting the Messiah's death, which is about as wicked as you can get.

Caiaphas's sin did not mean that he wasn't high priest or that the high priesthood wasn't established by God. It just meant he was a sinner. Similarly, the sins of popes and other Christian leaders do not mean that they don't legitimately hold their offices or that their offices weren't established by God.

Peter even denied the Faith—saying that he wasn't a disciple of Jesus (John 18:17, 25)—yet Jesus confirmed him in his office (John 21: 15–17), and he went on to pen two inspired epistles: 1 and 2 Peter.

Names of the Evangelists

"Matthew, Mark, Luke, and John are made-up names."

DEFENSE
The names themselves provide evidence they are authentic.

Ancient writers sometimes attributed their works to long-dead authors to increase the prestige of their works, but that wouldn't have applied to the Gospels. Not only were their names being used in the first century (see Day 109), when the authors lived, they also weren't the people you'd pick to add prestige to the documents. Their names may be prestigious today, but that is *because* of their Gospels. At the time, things were different.

Mark and Luke weren't even apostles but junior associates. Mark was initially a companion of Paul and Barnabas and later served as Peter's interpreter, and Luke was one of Paul's traveling companions.

Both are mentioned only a handful of times in the New Testament, and the mentions aren't all good. Mark abandoned his first mission trip (Acts 13:13), and Paul refused to take him on a second mission. This led to such a sharp argument between Paul and Barnabas that the two dissolved their partnership (Acts 15:37–40). Mark eventually redeemed himself (2 Tim. 4:11), but his early failure remained a black mark.

Although Luke's reputation was unblemished, he is named only three times (Col. 4:14; 2 Tim. 4:11; Philem. 24), making him far less prominent than other Pauline companions, such as Timothy (twenty-five mentions), Titus (thirteen mentions), and Silas (twelve mentions).

Matthew's Gospel is the most Jewish, which makes Matthew the last person whose name would give it prestige. Not only was Matthew only a midlevel apostle (note his placement when the names of the Twelve are given; Matt. 10:2–4, Mark 3:16–19, Luke 6:14–16, Acts 1:13), he was also a tax collector (Matt. 9:9), and tax collectors were hated by Jews, who saw them as collaborators with the Romans and sinners (Matt. 9:11, 18:17).

The only major name attached to a Gospel is John, and while John son of Zebedee was prominent (note his placement in the lists of the Twelve), there is a question whether the fourth Gospel was written by him or another, lesser-known disciple named John (see Richard Bauckham, *Jesus and the Eyewitnesses*, chapters 14–17). Thus, with the possible exception of John, the evangelists' names are not what one would pick to lend authority to the Gospels.

Non-Christian Sources on Jesus

CHALLENGE

"If Jesus existed, why isn't he mentioned by non-Christian sources?"

DEFENSE

Jesus was mentioned by multiple non-Christian
historians within a century of his ministry.

The Roman historian Suetonius (died c. 122) appears to refer to Jesus when he records that the Emperor Claudius expelled the Jews from Rome in A.D. 49 "since the Jews constantly made disturbances at the instigation of Chrestus" (*The Twelve Caesars*, "Claudius" 25). "Chrestus" is just one vowel different than the Latin word for "Christ"—*Christus*. Many scholars think this refers to the disturbances that occurred in Jewish communities when the Christian message was first preached, as in the book of Acts.

Suetonius also records that during the reign of Nero, "Punishment was inflicted on the Christians, a class of men given to a new and mischievous superstition" (ibid., "Nero" 16).

The Roman historian Tacitus (died c. 117) goes into more detail and describes how Nero tried to deflect the blame for the Great Fire of Rome in A.D. 64 onto the Christians. He explains: "Christ, from whom the name had its origin, suffered the extreme penalty during the reign of Tiberius at the hands of one of our procurators, Pontius Pilate," and he records that Nero's harsh persecution moved many to have sympathy for the Christians (*Annals* 15:44).

Around A.D. 110, the Roman official Pliny the Younger and the Emperor Hadrian had an exchange of letters discussing Christians and how they were to be prosecuted. Pliny records that, in their worship services, Christians "sing responsively a hymn to Christ as to a god" and that true Christians cannot be compelled to "curse Christ" (*Letter* 96).

In his *Antiquities of the Jews*, written around A.D. 93, the Jewish historian Josephus mentions Jesus twice. The first passage focuses on Jesus (*Antiquities* 18:3:3). Unfortunately, this passage was later edited by a Christian scribe, forcing scholars to try to reconstruct what Josephus originally said about Jesus.

The second passage occurs when Josephus recounts that James the Just, the "brother" of Jesus, was put to death in A.D. 62. There is no doubt about this passage, in which Josephus refers to "the brother of Jesus, who was called Christ, whose name was James" (*Antiquities* 20:9:1). This indicates Jesus was more famous than James, for it mentions him first and identifies James with respect to him.

Dependent Historical Sources?

CHALLENGE

"The historical sources that mention Jesus are all dependent on what they've heard from Christians. Why should we believe what they say?"

DEFENSE

The extent to which they are dependent on Christians for their information is questionable, and even if they derived *all* of it from Christian sources that would not make them unreliable.

The sources we cited probably have different degrees of dependence on Christian sources for their information about Jesus:

- Suetonius is not known to have interviewed any Christians. He did have access to the official Roman archives when writing *The Lives of the Caesars*. He also had contact with various learned Romans. The fact that he seems to mistake the word *Christus* as *Chrestus* is a sign that he was getting his information from non-Christian sources.
- Tacitus also is not known to have interviewed any Christians. He did, however, use official Roman records in writing the *Annals*, and it is likely he took his information about Jesus from them.
- Pliny the Younger interviewed Christians about their practices, and it may be that, in writing his *Letters,* he was largely dependent on these interviews and what was commonly said about Christians in Roman society.
- Josephus probably encountered Christians, but he also had access to Jewish records that he used in *Antiquities of the Jews*. He also was born in Palestine in A.D. 37, and there were many non-Christian Jews living there who had independent knowledge of Jesus.

The assertion that these authors derived their knowledge of Jesus exclusively from Christian sources is implausible. While they may have gained information from Christian sources (especially Pliny the Younger), they also had independent information.

Even if they did not, it would not deprive their writings of value. Information is not to be dismissed if it can be traced to a Christian source. Historians do not systematically reject what is said by Christians and treat such sources as "guilty until proven innocent." To do so would simply be anti-Christian bias.

Even if everything these authors wrote was derived from Christian sources—which is very unlikely—it still reveals what was being said in their day about Christ and Christianity, and this itself provides a powerful argument for the existence of Jesus (see Day 8).

The Nature of Luke's Enrollment

CHALLENGE

"Luke says Jesus was born during a census (Luke 2:1–5), but he is wrong about its nature. It wouldn't have been empire-wide, Joseph wouldn't have gone to Bethlehem, and Mary wouldn't have accompanied him."

DEFENSE

There are solutions to each challenge.

Augustus was emperor from 27 B.C. to A.D. 14, and he began the practice of empirewide census taking: "Every five years, the Romans enumerated citizens and their property to determine their liabilities. *This practice was extended to include the entire Roman Empire in 5 B.C.*" ("Census," *Encyclopedia Britannica*, 2016 ed., emphasis added).

Because of the size of the empire, census taking was done in stages, taking place in different countries in different years. The decree of 5 B.C. thus likely wasn't implemented in Palestine for a few years.

If the census was being done for tax purposes—as was normal—it would explain why Joseph returned to Bethlehem: He was from there and still had property there.

However, the enrollment may not have been a census. It may have been an event that took place in 3–2 B.C. when the people of the empire swore allegiance to Augustus (see Day 182 and 138). In this case, Joseph may have returned to Bethlehem because Israel was organized tribally, and the Romans may have used the tribal structure to ensure that the locals took the oath. Since Bethlehem was the ancestral home of Joseph's clan, that is where he went.

Mary went with Joseph because she was his wife and she could be better cared for by him and other relatives in Bethlehem than if she were left at home. Contrary to popular depictions in art, we need not suppose that she made the journey to Bethlehem in the last stages of pregnancy. Luke merely says that "while they were there, the time came for her to be delivered" (Luke 2:6).

There are unanswered questions about this event, but Luke and his readers were familiar with the way such enrollments worked. They had taken part in such events themselves. Even skeptical scholar Raymond Brown notes: "It is dangerous to assume that [Luke] described a process of registration that would have been patently opposed to everything that he and his readers knew" (*The Birth of the Messiah*, 549).

Intercession of the Saints and Necromancy

CHALLENGE

"The Catholic practice of asking dead saints for their intercession is wrong. The Bible forbids necromancy."

DEFENSE

Asking the saints for intercession is not necromancy.

Necromancy is an attempt to gain information by conjuring the dead. The term is derived from the Greek words *nekros* ("dead person") and *manteia* ("oracle, divination"). This practice, which was common in the ancient world, is forbidden in the Old Testament: "There shall not be found among you . . . a medium, or a wizard, or a necromancer" (Deut. 18:10–11).

The fact that necromancy was for purposes of gaining information is made clear by the Hebrew terms for "medium" (*sho'el 'ob*, "a spirit inquirer"), "wizard" (*yidde'oni*, "a spiritist"), and "necromancer" (*doresh 'el-ha-metim*, "an inquirer of the dead"). The focus on gaining information is also made clear by the context in Deuteronomy, which specifies that God will send his people prophets instead of allowing them to use mediums, wizards, and necromancers (Deut. 18:15).

Necromancy is forbidden today, as well. The *Catechism of the Catholic Church* states: "All forms of divination are to be rejected: recourse to Satan or demons, conjuring up the dead or other practices falsely supposed to 'unveil' the future" (CCC 2116).

Both Scripture and the Catholic Church agree that necromancy is forbidden. However, asking the saints for their intercession is a fundamentally different practice. In necromancy, people attempt to contact the dead to obtain information from them—either about the future or about other matters that are hidden from the inquirer. The flow of information is supposed to be from the dead to the living.

When people ask the saints for their intercession, however, they are not seeking information. They are asking the saints to partner with them in prayer to God. If anything, the flow of information is from the living to the dead—that is, a living person is making his prayer request known to a departed saint.

The biblical injunction against necromancy is thus a condemnation of something else. It is not talking about the same thing. This means that the practice of asking the saints for their intercession must be judged on its own merits, and as we cover elsewhere (see Day 36), there are good reasons for the practice.

Moral Evil and Free Will

CHALLENGE

*"An all-good, all-powerful God would not tolerate evil;
thus, God either is not all-good or not all-powerful."*

DEFENSE

This presupposes that God cannot have good reasons to
tolerate evil, but he does. One is that he values free will.

The abuse of free will is the definition of moral evil. Nobody sins except by misusing his free will. Sin, in turn, can produce suffering, as when one person unjustly harms another. Moral evil thus can cause physical evil, and free will can produce both. This is important because we have a good idea why God allows free will: to allow love.

The two greatest commandments are to love God and to love your neighbor (Matt. 22:36–40). Love is the fundamental thing God wants from us.

But if we had no free will, we would not be capable of freely choosing love. We might be able to simulate love, but it would be the programmed "love" of a robot, not the real thing.

It would be like Ira Levin's book *The Stepford Wives*, in which a group of husbands replace their wives with robots programmed to be the perfect homemakers. The robots are always attractive, always submissive, always ready to do whatever their husbands want. But there is no love in the town of Stepford. The husbands do not love their "wives"; they treat them merely as instruments for their own pleasure. And the "wives" don't love their husbands; they are robots with no free will.

For love to be real, it must be freely chosen, and so God has given us free will, knowing that—precisely because it *is* free—we may choose not to love. We may choose to act unlovingly, to sin against him and our neighbors.

God thus allows moral evil in the world to make it possible for us to choose love. By creating room for free will, he must also create room for its misuse and the consequences that follow from that. When we act unlovingly, we harm others, and this causes some of the suffering in the world.

TIP

This answer explains part of the mystery of evil, but not all of it. It
doesn't, for example, deal with evils that are part of the natural order
and that aren't caused by free will (see Days 7 and 38).

The Slaughter of the Innocents

CHALLENGE

"Herod's slaughter of Bethlehem's baby boys (Matt. 2:16) is a myth. We have no historical record of this actually happening."

DEFENSE

We do have a record of it, and the act is entirely in keeping with the character of Herod the Great.

The Gospel of Matthew is *itself* a record. It cannot simply be set aside on a "false until proven true" principle. Scholars do not reflexively reject what ancient sources say, particularly when it fits with known facts.

Although we don't have a *non-Christian* record of this event, we would not expect to. Bethlehem was small (Micah 5:2), and in Jesus' day its population was between 300 and 1,000. The number of males under two was likely no more than 25 to 30; perhaps no more than 6 or 7 (Paul Maier, "Herod and the Infants of Bethlehem," 177–178, in Jerry Vardaman, ed., *Chronos, Kairos, Christos II*). Given the small scale of the event, most people outside of Bethlehem wouldn't have been aware of it.

We don't have any of Herod's court records, and what knowledge we have of his acts is spotty, being principally derived from Josephus, who was born decades after Herod died. Although Josephus does briefly mention Jesus in a couple of passages, it is unlikely that he would have mentioned a small event like the slaughter of the innocents, if he was even aware of it.

Despite this, the story fits with what was known about Herod. During the latter part of his reign he became paranoid and obsessed with keeping power. He saw plots everywhere and consequently executed his favorite wife and three of his sons. Thus Caesar Augustus allegedly quipped, "It is better to be Herod's pig than son" (Macrobius, *Saturnalia* 2:4:2)—the joke being that, as a Jew, Herod wouldn't eat pork and his pig would be safe.

Herod is known to have ordered mass executions. As his own death approached, he had a large number of prominent men confined in a stadium and ordered that they be killed so every family would grieve upon his death (Josephus, *Antiquities of the Jews* 17:6:5–6).

Fortunately, this order was disobeyed when he died, but he was still alive when the slaughter of the innocents occurred, and that order was carried out. It is precisely what we would expect of Herod upon learning a baby was born who had a rival claim to the Jewish throne.

God and "the Gods"

CHALLENGE

"Why should we reject the gods and goddesses that are worshipped by many cultures? Why should the Christian God be the only one?"

DEFENSE

Divine revelation makes clear there is a single God who created the world.

God is infinite and uncreated, but there are also finite, created spirits known as angels (CCC 328–29). They are God's servants and messengers (the word "angel"—Hebrew, *mal'akh*, Greek, *angelos*—means "messenger"). Some serve God but others have fallen and oppose him (CCC 391–93).

The Christian faith thus envisions a heavenly hierarchy with the infinite, uncreated God at the top and created, finite spirits under him—some of whom have become evil. The good angels may be venerated as such, but they are merely servants of God and so are not to be given the worship owed to God (Col. 2:18; Rev. 19:10, 22:8–9).

By contrast, many in the Greco-Roman world acknowledged the existence of a single, supreme God but did not worship him. Instead, they worshipped lesser, created beings, such as Zeus (Jupiter) and Apollo. They also acknowledged the existence of inferior spirits, which could be good or evil and which were not worshipped (Ramsay MacMullen, *Christianizing the Roman Empire*, 12–13). In Greek, the term "god" (*theos*) applied to both the great God and the created ones, while the term "demon" (*daimonion*) applied to the inferior, potentially evil spirits.

Christians agreed there is a great God and that there are lesser spirits who could be called demons. The main issue was how to treat the middle category of finite "gods."

Divine revelation made it clear only the true God is to be worshipped (Exod. 20:2–6; Deut. 5:6–10), and there are no other beings equal to him (Isa. 43:10, 44:6, 8). Therefore, Christians reasoned, the term "god" (*theos*) should not be applied to the pagan deities. To the extent they even exist, they would be inferior spirits or "demons" (*daimoniōn*; cf. 1 Cor. 10:20, MacMullen, 17–19).

The Christian critique of pagan deities thus is not that there aren't finite, created spirits, but that they are fundamentally different from and inferior to God and not worthy of worship.

"The Sun Will Be Darkened"

CHALLENGE

"In his discourse about the destruction of the temple, Jesus said, 'The sun will be darkened, and the moon will not give its light, and the stars will be falling from heaven, and the powers in the heavens will be shaken' (Mark 13:24–25). Those things never happened, so Jesus prophesied falsely."

DEFENSE

The imagery Jesus used does not imply the end of the world.

Some understand the imagery as familiar phenomena: a solar eclipse (sun darkening), a lunar eclipse (moon not giving light), a meteor shower (stars falling). If Jesus merely meant these would occur before the temple's destruction in A.D. 70, he was not predicting that the world would end.

However, there is another understanding. The prophets often used "cosmic cataclysm" language to announce God's judgment on a people (see, e.g., Isa. 13:10; 24:18–23; 34:4; Ezek. 32:7; Amos 8:9; Joel 2:10, 31; Hag. 2:22).

Thus Isaiah 13 contains an oracle against Babylon that says, "The stars of the heavens and their constellations will not give their light; the sun will be dark at its rising and the moon will not shed its light" (v. 10), and God "will make the heavens tremble, and the earth will be shaken out of its place" (v. 13). The oracle also makes clear how the judgment on the Babylonians will be accomplished: "I am stirring up the Medes against them" (v. 17).

This conflict and others the prophets predicted using similar language were long over by Jesus' day, and none involved a literal cosmic cataclysm. Thus the language was seen for what it was: a poetic expression of what the experience of living through judgment would be like. For those experiencing it, it would be *as if* the sun and moon darkened and the stars fell from the sky. Further, some saw the celestial bodies as symbols of the rulers of the people, who would quake and lose their positions in the turmoil.

It is no surprise to find Jesus using the same language describing the coming judgment on Jerusalem at the hands of the Romans.

TIP

The prophets' language has been understood this way for a long time. See the work of the twelfth-century Jewish scholar Moses Maimonides (*Guide for the Perplexed* 2:29).

Why Is John's Gospel Different?

CHALLENGE

"If John's Gospel is reliable, why is it different from the others?"

DEFENSE

Every author has his own style, and John
was supplementing the other Gospels.

Differences between John and the synoptic Gospels (Matthew, Mark, and Luke) are often exaggerated. They tell the same basic story, referring to many of the same incidents in Jesus' life (the Baptism by John, early preaching in Galilee, feeding the 5,000, later ministry in Judaea, the triumphal entry, the Last Supper, the Crucifixion and Resurrection).

The differences are principally of two types: (1) matters of style and (2) incidents John mentions that the synoptics omit or vice versa.

In terms of style, John presents Jesus' teachings in extended speeches rather than pithy sayings. Before tape recorders, long speeches in historical documents involved reconstruction, which the audience knew. The claim was not that a historical speech was a word-for-word transcript, but that it accurately conveyed the thought of the speaker. John was an eyewitness of Jesus' ministry (21:24) and was thus in a position to accurately express Jesus' thought in his own literary style (see Benedict XVI, *Jesus of Nazareth*, 1:229).

That John includes incidents the synoptic Gospels omit and vice versa is primarily because he is writing to *supplement* the synoptics. Early sources indicate he was urged to supplement what they had written (see Eusebius, *Church History* 6:14:7) and that he initially expressed some reluctance to do so (see Muratorian Canon 9-16). This may explain his statement that, were all of Jesus' deeds to be recorded, "I suppose that the world itself could not contain the books that would be written" (21:25)."

John expects his readers to know the synoptic tradition. In 3:24 he mentions John the Baptist "had not yet been put in prison"—the imprisonment being mentioned in the synoptics but not elsewhere in John.

Comparing John and Mark reveals John's outline is structured so its events fit around those recorded in Mark (see Jimmy Akin, "Did John Use Mark as a Template?" online at JimmyAkin.com; Richard Bauckham, "John for Readers of Mark" in *The Gospels for All Christians*). This reveals John intended to supplement the synoptic tradition.

Mustard Seeds

CHALLENGE

"Scripture is inaccurate when it says the mustard seed is the smallest seed. It is larger than a poppy seed, for example. Also, it does not grow into a tree."

DEFENSE

This objection presses the text beyond its intended limits.

Jesus tells this parable: "The kingdom of heaven is like a grain of mustard seed which a man took and sowed in his field; it is the smallest of all seeds, but when it has grown it is the greatest of shrubs and becomes a tree, so that the birds of the air come and make nests in its branches" (Matt. 13:31–32; cf. Mark 4:30–32, Luke 13:18–19).

The cultivated mustard plant of this parable (*brassica nigra*, or black mustard) is native to the Middle East. Though there are plants with smaller seeds, it is disputed whether first-century Jews cultivated any. "No one yet has proved that ancient Palestinians planted anything that bore a smaller seed than that of the black mustard, and that was the framework within which Jesus was speaking" (Gleason Archer, *New International Encyclopedia of Bible Difficulties,* 329).

If Jesus was speaking of plants commonly cultivated at the time—if that was his universe of discourse—he was not referring to other plants. However, if his universe of discourse was broader, it would be natural to understand him as using hyperbole. In ancient literature, the mustard seed was proverbial for its smallness (cf. *Mishnah Tohorot* 8:8H, *Niddah* 5:2D), and Jesus would have been drawing on this mode of speech without implying there was literally nothing smaller.

Regarding the size to which the mustard plant grows, the parable notes it is a "shrub" (Greek, *lachanōn*, "herb, vegetable, garden plant"), and thus not literally at tree. It does, however, grow to a prodigious size. The *Encyclopedia of Life* notes that, "The black mustard plant grows up to 2 m (a little over 6 ft), with many branches" (s.v. *Brassica nigra*; online at eol.org).

Fundamentally, Jesus is not making a point about botany. He is using the growth of mustard as an analogy of how the kingdom of God will grow from his small band of followers to a worldwide communion. To try to get precise, literal statements about botany from the parable presses the text beyond its intended limits.

Consciousness after Death Questioned

CHALLENGE

"The Bible says people aren't conscious after death. It describes the dead as being asleep (Ps. 13:3; Dan. 12:2; Matt. 9:24; John 11:11) and says that 'the dead know nothing' (Eccles. 9:5; cf. Ps. 6:5, 88:10–12, 115:17)."

DEFENSE

These passages are explained by several factors.

One factor is *euphemism*—substituting a more pleasant term for an unpleasant reality. Describing death as sleep is euphemism. People refer to death by many euphemisms ("passing on," "going home," "no longer with us"), and even those who believe in a conscious afterlife use sleep as a euphemism ("Grandma fell asleep"). This is because the dead look asleep. They don't stand up or move, and their eyes are frequently closed. People even close their eyes to make them look more like they are asleep and thus less disturbing.

The sleep euphemism is an example of *phenomenological language*, where something is described by how it appears rather than how it actually is (death is not literally sleep; otherwise, corpses would come back to life every morning). Phenomenological language shapes biblical descriptions of death in other ways. Since corpses do not talk, Scripture notes that dead people don't praise God. Thus the psalmist indicates that, as long as he is alive, he will praise God for delivering him, but if he becomes a corpse, he won't. This fits a common Old Testament pattern of asking for God's blessings so his praise can be declared.

Phenomenological language stems from an *earthly perspective*—one without access to the invisible world. This is particularly the case in Ecclesiastes, where the author deliberately assumes an earthly perspective as a tool of analysis, as stressed by the book's repeated emphasis on what happens "under the sun" (1:3, 9, 14, etc.). From the earthly perspective, he argues that life is better than death, for "he who is joined with all the living has hope" (9:4) and "the living know that they will die, but the dead know nothing" (9:5), for they no longer have "any share in all that is done under the sun" (9:6). This is the expression of a man trying to make sense out of death from an earthly perspective, apart from divine revelation—not a theological assertion about the afterlife.

TIP

Other verses show that the dead are conscious (see Day 158).

Consciousness after Death Established

CHALLENGE

"Perhaps it doesn't disprove consciousness after death, but Scripture does not provide a basis for believing it, either."

DEFENSE

There are Bible verses that demonstrate consciousness after death.

The prophet Samuel is conscious when summoned by the witch of Endor (1 Sam. 28; note the text does not challenge the idea that it is Samuel who is summoned). This is an exceptional incident since a medium is involved (Deut. 18:11–12), but it indicates the possibility of and belief in consciousness after death.

1 Peter 3:19–20 refers to Christ preaching, after death, to spirits who disobeyed in the time of Noah. They were conscious, though some have questioned whether they are human or angelic spirits.

In the Transfiguration, Moses and Elijah are shown interacting with Jesus (Matt. 17:1–9). However, Elijah never died (2 Kings 2:1–12), and although Moses did die (Deut. 34:5), Jude refers to an angelic dispute over his body (Jude 9). According to early Christian writings, this was a reference to an event in *The Assumption of Moses*, whose ending is now lost. Because of ambiguity about what happened to Moses after death (was he assumed? raised from the dead?) and because of the exceptional nature of the Transfiguration, this text is of limited value.

In the account of Lazarus and the rich man (Luke 16:19–31), Jesus describes Lazarus, the rich man, and Abraham as conscious in the intermediate state (i.e., between death and resurrection). It has been objected that this is a parable. However, Jesus' parables are informed by real things (kings, fathers, sons, banquets, vineyards, and so on). If this is a parable, it suggests conscious individuals in the afterlife are also real.

More definitely, Paul expects to be conscious in the intermediate state when he says he "would prefer to be away from the body and at home with the Lord" (2 Cor. 5:8; cf. Phil. 1:21–24).

The clearest passages indicating consciousness in the intermediate state are in Revelation, where the souls of the martyred are depicted praying and worshipping God (Rev. 6:9–11, 7:13–15). These are decisive since they are not exceptional and refer to the souls of many unnamed Christians continuing to be conscious.

The Year Jesus Was Born

CHALLENGE

"Our calendars are mistaken. Jesus wasn't born in 1 B.C. but around 7–6 B.C."

DEFENSE

The year of the calendar is not a matter of faith.

The *Anno Domini* (Latin, "Year of the Lord") system of reckoning was created in A.D. 525 by a monk named Dionysius Exiguus (Dennis "the Short" or "the Humble"). It later came into international use. Made centuries after Christ, this calculation is in no way essential to the Faith. The Church does not teach Christ was born in any particular year, and it is universally recognized that Dionysius's calculations are probably slightly off (Benedict XVI, *Jesus of Nazareth,* vol. 3: *The Infancy Narratives,* 61–62).

The estimate that Christ was born in 7–6 B.C. is based on the view that Herod the Great died in 4 B.C. Matthew records that, attempting to kill Jesus, Herod slaughtered the male infants two years old and under in Bethlehem (Matt. 2:16). This suggests that Jesus' birth took place two or more years before Herod's death, leading many to propose a date of 7 or 6 B.C.

The view that Herod died in 4 B.C. has been popular for some time, but recent studies indicate that this view is probably wrong and that the traditional date of Herod's death, 1 B.C., is correct. This would put the birth of Jesus in the 3–2 B.C. time frame, which is when the Church Fathers say it was. A large majority of early Christian sources place Jesus' birth at this time (see Jack Finegan, *Handbook of Biblical Chronology,* 2nd ed, 291).

Confirmation is found in the Gospel of Luke. It records that John the Baptist began his ministry in the fifteenth year of Tiberius Caesar, or A.D. 29 (Luke 3:1). Shortly afterward, Jesus began his own ministry and Luke reports that he was about thirty years old at the time (Luke 3:23). Deducting thirty years from A.D. 29, and taking into account the fact that there is no "Year 0" (instead, there is a jump from 1 B.C. to A.D. 1), that would indicate Jesus was born around 3–2 B.C, when the Church Fathers say he was. Thus Dionysius Exiguus was probably only a year off.

TIP

On the problems with dating of Herod's death to 4 B.C., see Finegan's book as well as Andrew E. Steinmann, *From Abraham to Paul.*

Salvation and Predestination

CHALLENGE

"Scripture indicates that God has predestined certain people to go to heaven (Rom. 8:28–30), so I'm either one of them or I'm not. Either way, I don't need to do anything with respect to my salvation. I can simply await my fate."

DEFENSE

This misunderstands the nature of predestination and the role of free will.

First, predestination involves both the end and the means by which the end is accomplished. Heaven may be the *end*—the destination—but the *means* of getting there is accepting God's offer of salvation. God doesn't predestine people to go to heaven regardless of what they do. Heaven may be where they are going, but God has also ordained that they arrive there *because* they respond to his grace.

Therefore, if you are predestined to go to heaven, you *will* respond to God's grace. At some point before death, you will accept his offer of salvation, and so you cannot just await your fate. Whether you go to heaven or hell is dependent on your response to God's initiative of grace. Your actions *do* count.

Second, predestination includes free will. From his vantage point in eternity, outside of time, God is aware of all the free-will decisions that are made by creatures in time. Consequently, he is aware whether you will freely choose to accept or reject his offer of salvation, and he includes this in establishing predestination.

The Catechism of the Catholic Church states: "To God, all moments of time are present in their immediacy. When therefore he establishes his eternal plan of 'predestination,' he includes in it each person's free response to his grace" (CCC 600).

Because your free choice determines whether you go to heaven or hell, we can therefore say: "God predestines no one to go to hell; for this, a willful turning away from God (a mortal sin) is necessary, and persistence in it until the end" (CCC 1037).

Predestination thus does not involve a denial of free will. Neither does it provide an excuse to sit back and neglect our salvation. On the contrary, man's freedom is included within the scope of God's plan of predestination, and if we wish to be with him in eternity, we must respond to his initiative of grace and accept his offer of salvation.

The Number and Nature of the Sacraments

CHALLENGE

"The Catholic Church is wrong to say there are seven sacraments. It's even inconsistent with its own history. Historically, some Catholic authorities have listed as many as thirty sacraments."

DEFENSE

How many sacraments there are depends on how you use the term.

The Latin term *sacramentum* comes from *sacrare*, which means "to make sacred" or "to consecrate." At one point, *sacramentum* referred to a sacred oath, but it came to refer to sacred rites in any religion.

St. Augustine wrote: "There can be no religious society, whether the religion be true or false, without some sacrament or visible symbol to serve as a bond of union" (*Reply to Faustus* 19:11). Thus Catholic authors have historically referred to Jewish rites such as the Passover lamb and various blessings as "sacraments of the Old Law" (ST III:60:2 reply to obj. 2, 6; reply to obj. 3, III:61:3, 4).

In the Christian context, "sacrament" came to refer to many Christian rituals. Thus Hugh of St. Victor (1096–1141) listed thirty sacraments (*On the Sacraments of the Christian Faith*). Other authors in the Middle Ages gave different numbers (frequently between five and twelve), showing there was no fixed definition at the time. The term was flexible.

Eventually, a standard definition came into use. This definition recognized sacraments as rites instituted by Christ to impart grace. The *Catechism* states: "The sacraments are efficacious signs of grace, instituted by Christ and entrusted to the Church, by which divine life is dispensed to us" (CCC 1131).

When this definition is applied, the number of sacraments becomes clearer. Some rites—like baptism—were established by Christ to efficaciously convey grace or divine life (Matt. 28:19; 1 Pet. 3:21), and so they count as sacraments. Other rites—like foot washing—may have been established by Christ (John 13:1–17), but they don't convey grace and so are not sacraments. Still others were instituted after the time of Christ and so are not sacraments. Many in the last category have come to be called "sacramentals" (CCC 1667–79).

The Church thus came to recognize that there are seven sacraments according to this definition: baptism, confirmation, the Eucharist, penance, anointing of the sick, holy orders, and matrimony (CCC 1113).

His Father Was *Who*?

CHALLENGE

"Matthew's genealogy of Jesus contradicts Luke's. Matthew says Shealtiel's father was Jeconiah, while Luke says it was Neri (Matt. 1:12; Luke 3:27). Similarly, Matthew says Joseph's father was Jacob, while Luke says it was Heli (Matt. 1:16; Luke 3:23)."

DEFENSE

There are multiple explanations, given how Israelite genealogies worked.

Hebrew and Aramaic didn't distinguish between fathers, grandfathers, and so on. All male ancestors were called "fathers" (see Day 106). Consequently, since one person can be descended from another by more than one line (see Day 85), *both* Jeconiah *and* Neri could have been Shealtiel's "father" (male ancestor) if one genealogy skipped a generation. The same is true of Jacob and Heli with respect to Joseph.

Alternately, adoption (legal rather than biological descent) may have been involved. Shealtiel may have had a legal and a biological father. The same is true of Joseph. This is particularly relevant because of the levirite marriage custom, which required that if a man died childless, his brother was to marry the widow and father a son who was legally attributed to the line of the dead man (Deut. 25:5–6). The *levir* (Latin, "brother-in-law") thus supplied a son for his deceased brother. Given the ancient mortality rate, this situation was common. It is not surprising if it occurred more than once in the millennium between David and Jesus in their family tree.

It may have happened with respect to Shealtiel, and we have early testimony that it did happen with respect to Joseph. Early Christian writer Julius Africanus (c. A.D. 160–240) reported a tradition from Jesus' surviving relatives in his day regarding the fatherhood of Joseph.

According to Jesus' family, Joseph's grandfather Matthan (mentioned in Matthew) married a woman named Estha, who bore him a son named Jacob. After Matthan died, Estha married his close relative Melchi (mentioned in Luke) and bore him a son named Heli. Jacob (mentioned in Matthew) and Heli (mentioned in Luke) were thus half brothers. When Heli died childless, Jacob married his widow and fathered Joseph, who was biologically the son of Jacob but legally the son of Heli (see Eusebius, *Ecclesiastical History* 1:6:7).

Regardless of which explanation is true, the fact that multiple explanations exist indicates that no contradiction has been shown.

Religion and Control

CHALLENGE

"Religion was invented to give some people control over others."

DEFENSE

This is an easy claim to make if you don't look at the evidence.

Religions propose moral values and rules of conduct (don't lie, don't steal, don't murder), but so do other institutions—like philosophy and government. Yet no one would say that philosophy or government were invented merely to control people. Like religion, philosophy seeks to answer profound questions (where did we come from, where are we going, what is ultimately real). Also like religion, government seeks to promote human well-being.

Leaders in every field can be manipulative and self-serving, but it would be false to claim that controlling others is their exclusive motivation.

This is particularly the case with philosophers and religious leaders. Whatever flaws they may have, any realistic appraisal of these individuals shows that most are not power-hungry psychopaths but sincere believers in what they proclaim. This means religion is not just a manipulative game. It is something its leaders believe.

The same is true historically. Most religions do not have specific founders but grew organically. Their leaders, whether village priests or tribal shamans, have always shared the beliefs of those around them. They didn't invent those beliefs to suit themselves but inherited them from previous generations.

When we look at religions that do have founders, we see a mixed picture. Although some religions had founders who benefited materially (e.g., Muhammad, Joseph Smith), other religions had founders who renounced wealth and power (e.g., Gautama Buddha) or who refused political power and suffered greatly, up to and including martyrdom (e.g., Jesus Christ; cf. John 6:15, Matt. 27–28).

Whatever the motives of some founders may have been, we do not have a basis for saying religion is a phenomenon invented to give some people control of others. This is particularly the case when we consider that religion is a human universal. It appears in every society, both today and in history. This indicates religion corresponds to a fundamental part of human nature; it is not something simply invented by a select group of people.

Finally, the behavior-affecting aspects of religion aren't its primary characteristic. Otherwise religions would just be codes of behavior, and they aren't. They are systems of belief about the divine and the afterlife.

Evidence and Belief

CHALLENGE

"Even if a person only has the burden of proof when trying to convince someone else of a belief (see Day 86), he still should have evidence for his own beliefs. We shouldn't adopt beliefs for no reason."

DEFENSE

We should have reasons for our beliefs, but this does not allow us to dismiss religious beliefs.

First, we sometimes have practical reasons to make decisions on religious matters, even when we do not have evidential reasons (see Day 336).

Second, though it is not ideal, we must sometimes make decisions regarding beliefs using partial, inconclusive evidence. As long as the matter isn't urgent, we may have the luxury of not deciding, but sometimes we must, and the rational thing to do is to make the best choice one can, given the evidence available. For example, a dying person may be unsure whether the Christian faith is true and may not have time left to research the question thoroughly. Consequently, he may have to make the best decision he can with the evidence at hand.

Third, it would be false to characterize religious faith, and the Christian faith in particular, as beliefs adopted without reason. Faith and reason work together (see Day 118), and Christianity in particular has developed a robust study of apologetics to offer evidence for the Faith. Christian thinkers have developed multiple lines of argument for the existence of God, the Resurrection of Jesus, the immortality of the soul, and so on. Consequently, it would be a caricature to claim that Christian faith is meant to be held without any reasons being offered for it.

Fourth, although the ideal is for a person to study and be personally familiar with the evidence for a position, this is not necessary, and often it is not possible, for we cannot personally verify all the things we know. The sociology of knowledge is such that we all know many things we have not verified for ourselves but have learned from someone we trust (see Day 78). Thus a person may rationally believe in the existence of electrons or extrasolar planets or God without personally having gone through the details of the proofs. In many situations, it can be enough to know that trustworthy experts have.

Hiding the Commandment Against Idolatry?

CHALLENGE

"The Catholic Church hid God's commandment against idolatry by removing it from the Ten Commandments."

DEFENSE

The Church didn't try to hide the commandment against idolatry. In fact, it condemns idolatry.

The Ten Commandments are in Exodus 20 and Deuteronomy 5. If you look in a Catholic Bible, the prohibition is right there: "You shall not make for yourself a graven image, or any likeness of anything that is in heaven above, or that is in the earth beneath, or that is in the water under the earth; you shall not bow down to them or serve them; for I the Lord your God am a jealous God" (Exod. 20:4–5; Deut. 5:8–9).

The *Catechism* also forcefully condemns idolatry (CCC 2112–2114).

What the Church does—like every Christian community—is provide short summaries of the commandments for memorization. The full text of the Ten Commandments is between 300 and 400 words long (varying by translation), so every group uses a brief, memorizable list instead.

In Catholic and Lutheran lists, the prohibition of idolatry is subsumed under the broader commandment "You shall have no other gods before me" (Exod. 20:3; Deut. 5:7). Some communities treat these as separate commandments, but this is a matter of choice. We are told that there are "Ten Commandments" (Exod. 34:28), but the text contains more than ten requirements and prohibitions. Interpreters must group some of them together to make the total come out to ten, but there is no single way to do this.

"The division and numbering of the Commandments have varied in the course of history. The present catechism follows the division of the Commandments established by St. Augustine, which has become traditional in the Catholic Church. It is also that of the Lutheran confessions. The Greek Fathers worked out a slightly different division, which is found in the Orthodox Churches and Reformed communities" (CCC 2066).

In the ancient world, having other gods meant worshipping idols, so it makes sense to see the prohibitions on both as bringing out different aspects of the same commandment.

The common way of numbering the Ten Commandments in Jewish circles agrees and groups the prohibitions on polytheism and idolatry together in a single commandment.

God as an Exalted Man

CHALLENGE

"God is simply an exalted man. The Bible says we are made in the image of God (Gen. 1:26–27), and it refers to the strong right arm of God (Deut. 4:34), his all-seeing eyes (Prov. 15:3), and so on."

DEFENSE

Scripture is clear that God and man are fundamentally different.

Mormonism is known for teaching that God and man are the same species. Mormons frequently use the couplet, "As man is, God once was; as God is, man may become."

By contrast, Scripture states: "God is not a man" (Num. 23:19), "he is not a man" (1 Sam. 15:29).

God has always been God; he was never a man: "Before the mountains were brought forth, or ever thou hadst formed the earth and the world, from everlasting to everlasting thou art God" (Ps. 90:2).

There are no other gods. In Isaiah, God declares: "I am the first and I am the last; besides me there is no god" (Isa. 44:6). He also states: "Is there a God besides me? . . . I know not any" (Isa. 44:8).

Similarly, men do not become gods. In Isaiah, God states: "Before me no god was formed, nor shall there be any after me" (Isa. 43:10).

The "image" of God that Genesis 1 says we bear is an aspect of our rational soul, which separates us from the animals, which God created in the same chapter.

References to God's strong arm, his eyes, and such, are metaphors referring to God's power and knowledge. They are not to be taken literally any more than Scripture's references to God having feathers and wings ("He will cover you with his feathers, and under his wings you will find refuge," Ps. 91:4).

Other verses make the immaterial nature of God clear. In John 4:24 Jesus teaches, "God is spirit, and those who worship him must worship in spirit and truth." Elsewhere he notes, "a spirit has not flesh and bones" (Luke 24:39).

There is a difference between being a spirit and having a spirit. Jesus indicates that the Father is a spirit, not that he merely has one. This means that the Father lacks a body and is entirely spiritual.

Some Who Will Not Taste Death

CHALLENGE

"Jesus said, 'There are some standing here who will not taste death before they see that the kingdom of God has come with power' (Mark 9:1; cf. Matt. 16:28, Luke 9:27). But that generation died long ago and the world hasn't ended. So Jesus' prediction was false."

DEFENSE

Jesus was not referring to the end of the world.

There is a sense in which the kingdom of God comes at the end of the world (1 Cor. 15:24), but the kingdom is a complex reality that includes God's activity before that time (1 Cor. 15:25). Jesus recognized this. Asked when the kingdom would come, he replied: "Behold, the kingdom of God is in the midst of you" (Luke 17:21).

Thus we must ask if the passages above refer to something in his day. Luke's version merely speaks of some not dying before seeing the kingdom, but Mark refers to them seeing it "come with power" and Matthew refers to them seeing "the Son of man coming in his kingdom."

This suggests we should look for an event where Jesus was manifest in a powerful, miraculous way. And there was one: the Transfiguration.

In each of the synoptic Gospels, the Transfiguration *immediately* follows Jesus' announcement (Matt. 17:1–9; Mark 9:2–10; Luke 9:28–36). Jesus takes three of the disciples—Peter, James, and John—up a mountain. His clothing becomes dazzlingly bright, Moses and Elijah appear beside him, everyone is enveloped in a cloud, and God the Father speaks from heaven, identifying Jesus as his Son/his Chosen, and declaring, "Hear him!"

This manifestation is likely the coming of the kingdom "with power" Jesus referred to, and the text of each Gospel suggests this is the way the evangelists understood it. Not only does the Transfiguration happen right after the announcement, but each Gospel says it was about a week later (Matt. 17:1, Mark 9:1, Luke 9:28; the slight difference in the number of days may reflect reckoning parts of days as wholes and counting days as beginning at sunset, midnight, or dawn).

Peter, James, and John thus were the three who did not taste death before they saw the kingdom coming with power.

TIP

Benedict XVI discusses this in chapter 9 of *Jesus of Nazareth*, vol. 1.

The Contingency Argument

"How would you argue for the existence of God?"

One argument proceeds from the existence of contingent things (i.e., things that could be different than they are).

1. Some things are contingent.
2. All contingent things require a current cause for why they are the way they are.
3. There cannot be an infinite regress of current causes.
4. Therefore, there must be a first, necessary (non-contingent) cause.
5. The first, necessary cause is God.
6. Therefore, God exists.

The premises of this argument are lines 1, 2, 3, and 5. The conclusions (lines 4 and 6) follow from them.

Line 1 is true by experience. Many things could be different than they are. A person may be standing or sitting. A table may be painted red or green. A pyramid may be built or taken apart.

Line 2 is verified by experience. At any moment, there is a reason why a thing is the way it is. For example, if a person is standing, the atoms in his body are arranged a certain way and he is related to something else (e.g., the ground) so that he is standing on it. If a table is painted red, the atoms in its surface are arranged a certain way and will reflect certain frequencies of light.

Line 3 acknowledges that there can be a hierarchy of current causes. For example, the atoms in a standing person's body may be held in place by the four fundamental forces known to physics (electromagnetism, the strong force, the weak force, and gravity). It is possible that these forces may, in turn, be based on a deeper set of presently unknown forces. However, this chain cannot go on forever in this way because in that case there would be no ultimate explanation for why the person is standing. If there is to be an ultimate explanation for why the person is standing, it must be based on something that is not, in turn, based on something else. Therefore, there must be a first cause, which is also necessary (not contingent). Proposing an infinite regress of causes for which we have no evidence also violates Occam's Razor.

Line 5 is based on the standard understanding of God as the First Cause and as a necessary Being.

Objections to the Contingency Argument

CHALLENGE

"The argument from contingency is flawed: (1) Everything could be fated, so nothing would be contingent; (2) we can explain how things are by their history, which could be infinite; (3) there could be multiple ultimate causes; (4) you could call the first, necessary cause something other than God; and (5) if everything needs a cause, then God also must have a cause."

DEFENSE

None of these objections overturn the contingency argument.

First, the argument from fate simply proposes a single, ultimate cause—fate itself—for contingent things. It doesn't show they aren't contingent. It is not necessary for a person to be standing the way it is necessary for a square to have four sides. People can stand or sit, but squares *must* have four sides. If a person is fated to stand, he could also be fated to sit, and his posture is contingent.

Second, history (and whether history might be infinite) is not part of this argument. We are asking why things are the way they are *now*, not what history preceded this.

Third, one could trace the chain of causes for each of the many contingent things up to higher causes, but these would not end in a multiplicity of ultimate explanations, for explanations converge as we go higher. An example is the four fundamental fources of physics (electromagnetism, the strong force, the weak force, and gravity), which explain the state of innumerable contingent physical things. An important goal of science is to find ways to unify these forces and any others that exist.

There cannot be a multiplicity of ultimate explanations. If one proposed a certain set of explanations as ultimate, then they would have to exist within some kind of framework that would allow them to relate to one another. Otherwise, they would not be able to interact to produce the contingent states of affairs we see. However, the framework would then be more fundamental than the proposed explanations, so they would not be ultimate.

Fourth, one can always reject the term "God," but this argument shows that there is a First Cause that is a necessary Being. This does not prove the full Christian understanding of God, but it can be supplemented by other arguments.

Fifth, God would not need a cause because, per the argument, God is necessary rather than contingent.

How Judas Iscariot Died

CHALLENGE

"Matthew and Luke contradict each other. Matthew says that Judas hanged himself (Matt. 27:5), but Luke says that "falling headlong he burst open in the middle and all his bowels gushed out" (Acts 1:18)."

DEFENSE

The accounts preserve different aspects of the event, but they do not contradict each other.

Both agree Judas died shortly after the Crucifixion. Matthew says Judas hanged himself after returning the thirty pieces of silver to the chief priests, while Luke has Peter speaking of the event during the period between the Ascension and Pentecost (between forty and fifty days after the Crucifixion). The fact that they agree on the timing, but describe the death differently, shows independent traditions in circulation that affirmed Judas' death very shortly after the Crucifixion. That indicates Judas did die at this early date.

Judas probably began accompanying Jesus while in his twenties (Jesus began his ministry when about thirty; Luke 3:23). This suggests Judas died a sudden and remarkable death (i.e., not an ordinary death due to old age). Matthew's report of his suicidal hanging accounts for this, leaving us to explain Luke's reference to him falling and bursting open.

The earliest explanation is found in the second-century historian Papias, who wrote around A.D. 120. His works are lost but partially preserved in other writers. According to the fourth-century writer Apollinarius of Laodicea, Judas survived the hanging by being cut down before he choked to death, but he quotes Papias as saying Judas suffered severe swelling (edema) of the head and body, eventually causing him to burst open (see Monte Shanks, *Papias and the New Testament*, chapter 4, fragment 6). We now know that edema of the neck and body can be a consequence of strangulation, so Papias's account may be based in fact.

Others have proposed that Judas remained hanging on a tree branch until his body began to decompose and swell due to the gases decomposition produces. The rope then broke or slipped, causing his body to burst from the force of impact.

Some have noted that the traditional site of Judas's death features trees along a high ridge where strong winds occur. The winds may have caused the rope to slip, and the height of the ridge may have added to the force of impact, causing the body to burst.

Easter and Paganism

CHALLENGE

"Easter is a pagan holiday. Its timing is based on the full moon and the spring equinox, and it's named after the goddess Ishtar."

DEFENSE

Easter's origins are Jewish. It is the Christian equivalent of Passover.

The word "Easter" is of English origin. Ishtar was worshiped in Mesopotamia (modern Iraq), not England, which is thousands of miles away. Despite sounding similar, the two words are unrelated.

The eighth-century British historian Bede claimed the word "Easter" came from the name of the month in which it occurred (basically, April). He said this month used to be called "Eostur," though this was no longer true in his day. He also thought the month was named after a Germanic goddess who was no longer worshiped (*The Reckoning of Time* 15).

Bede is the only source who mentions this goddess, so he may be incorrect. Regardless, this applies only to the origin of the English word—not the origin of the feast. Its origin is revealed by its name in other languages. In Italian, it's *Pasqua*; in Spanish, *Pascha*; in Portuguese, *Páscoa*; in French, *Pâques*; in Danish, *Paaske*; in Dutch, *Pasen*; in Swedish, *Påsk*; and so on. All of these derive from the Latin *Pascha* or Greek *Paskha*, both of which are words for the Jewish feast of Passover (Hebrew, *Pesakh*).

The event Easter celebrates is the Resurrection of Jesus, and it is celebrated in conjunction with Passover because Jesus was crucified at Passover and rose the following Sunday (John 19:14–18, 20:1–20).

The reason Easter's timing is based on the full moon after the spring equinox is because that was the timing of Passover on the Jewish calendar. The Law of Moses requires Passover to be celebrated on the fourteenth of the month of Nisan (Lev. 23:5). This is a spring month that contains the equinox, and because the Jewish months begin on the new moon, the fourteenth fell on the full moon. The timing of the feast thus is Jewish, not pagan.

What is ultimately important is what Easter signifies today—the Resurrection of Jesus—not where it came from.

TIP

The mistake of judging something based on where it came from rather than what it is has been called "the genetic fallacy."

The Will to Believe

CHALLENGE

"I would love to believe. I see the benefits religious faith brings people, and I wish I could embrace it. Yet I find myself unable to do so."

DEFENSE

This problem is common because it's based on our psychological makeup, but it is not insurmountable.

The possibility of overcoming it is indicated by the fact that the vast majority of people have some form of religious faith. It is not contrary to human nature. Indeed, religion is a human universal found in all cultures, both historical and present.

Similarly, choosing one religion over another is not impossible. This is illustrated by the growth of Christianity. As the Christian message spread, evangelists urged people to believe it, and many did. Otherwise, no growth would have occurred. This shows that people are capable of choosing to adopt it, regardless of their prior belief.

Difficulties a particular person feels in this regard are due to circumstance rather than human nature itself. William James's essay "The Will to Believe" (available online) contains a helpful discussion. He describes views as either "live" or "dead." Live views are those that one feels it possible to accept, while dead ones are those that seem impossible to accept.

Which views are live depends on circumstances. Some today feel that being an agnostic is a live option, but being a Christian is not. They have a psychological impediment—which others do not have— against being a Christian. While this impediment remains, it will be hard for them to choose to embrace the Faith.

Having identified Christian faith as desirable (evidentially or otherwise), the solution is to work on the psychological impediment so that it becomes a live option. This can be accomplished more than one way.

One way is by studying Christian apologetics and seeing the evidences that support the Christian faith and answer opposing views. Another is by choosing to live as a Christian. This is discussed by Blaise Pascal: "Follow the way by which [believers] began; by acting as if they believed, taking the holy water, having masses said, etc. Even this will naturally make you believe, and deaden your acuteness" (*Pensées* 233).

Choosing to act on the premise that the Faith is true will gradually lead to it becoming psychologically acceptable and thus make it a live option.

Purgatory and the Bible

CHALLENGE

"The word 'purgatory' doesn't appear in Scripture, which tells of only two destinies for man—heaven and hell. It doesn't say anything about a third destiny or a second chance after death."

DEFENSE

Something can be biblical even if the word isn't used. Purgatory is not a third destiny or a second chance.

Many terms—like *Trinity*, *original sin*, and even *Bible*—were coined after the Bible was written but still express biblical realities.

Purgatory is the final purification God performs for those who died in his friendship but who are still impure. Thus it is not a third destiny besides heaven and hell. Everyone who goes to purgatory goes to heaven. It's simply a stage preparing people so that they have the purity needed for heaven (cf. Heb. 12:14).

Neither is purgatory a "second chance" after death. "It is appointed for men to die once, and after that comes judgment" (Heb. 9:27). There are no second chances. You either die in God's friendship or you don't.

One biblical passage that alludes to purgatory is 2 Maccabees 12:38–46, in which Judah Maccabee discovers the bodies of men who fell in battle while fighting for the Lord, yet while also wearing pagan amulets. He then turns to prayer, asking that this sin might be blotted out, and he takes up a collection so that a sacrifice may be offered for them in Jerusalem. This reflects an awareness that by prayer the living can help those in need of purification after death.

This passage is not found in the Protestant Bible, but 1 Corinthians 3:11–15 is. In the latter passage, Paul speaks of how our works will be tested "with fire." He says that if a person's work survives, he will receive a reward, but "if any man's work is burned up, he will suffer loss, though he himself will be saved, but only as through fire." The person's salvation is not in question, but Paul compares his experience to escaping through flames as he is purified from the impure works he performed in life.

TIP

Though the term "purgatory" is not always used, prayer for the dead so that they might be freed from the consequences of their sins is found in both Judaism and the different branches of Christianity. It is only in the Protestant community that the practice has been rejected.

"God of the Bible" versus "God of the Philosophers"

CHALLENGE

"In Scripture, God has a physical form, doesn't know things, learns new things, changes his mind, and so on, but modern philosophers and theologians portray God as immaterial, changeless, and perfect."

DEFENSE

The early portions of Scripture describe God using anthropomorphic language accommodated to the original audience.

Divine revelation was given to mankind over a period of more than a thousand years. When God began to guide the Israelites, he initiated a "divine pedagogy" in which he "communicates himself to man gradually. He prepares him to welcome by stages the supernatural revelation that is to culminate in the person and mission of the incarnate Word, Jesus Christ" (CCC 53).

This is similar to helping children learn a subject. At an early stage, children are only able to grasp the rudiments of a field—whether theology or anything else. We thus must accommodate our explanations to what children are capable of understanding. But as they develop intellectually, we can give them a more sophisticated presentation of the topic.

The original Israelites were not culturally and intellectually prepared to understand God in the sophisticated way that the history of thought later made possible. They would have no more been able to understand the details of modern theology than they would have been able to understand the technical aspects of modern science. The needed concepts had not yet been developed.

Thus, particularly in Genesis, we find anthropomorphic images used to communicate things about God to the Israelites. He is described as walking in the garden (Gen. 3:8), asking questions (Gen. 3:9–13), "learning" things (Gen. 22:12–13), changing his mind (Gen. 6:6–7), and so on.

This mode of language involves symbols, but it conveys real truths about God (cf. CCC 42, 390). It therefore points beyond itself to the more refined understanding that God led his people to discover, ultimately giving them his definitive word in the person of Jesus Christ (Heb. 1:1–2; Jude 3). We see this process unfolding in Scripture itself, which elsewhere makes clear that God is immaterial (John 4:24; cf. Luke 24:39), all-knowing (Ps. 147:5; 1 John 3:20), and changeless (Num. 23:19; James 1:17).

In the 2,000 years since public revelation ended, further reflection has led to an ever-more refined understanding of the deposit of faith (John 14:26, 16:13).

666 and the Pope

CHALLENGE

"The pope's title "Vicar of the Son of God" in Latin is Vicarius Filii Dei. *When you add up the Roman numerals in this title, you get 666. Therefore, the pope is the Antichrist mentioned in Revelation 13."*

DEFENSE

Vicarius Filii Dei *is not one of the pope's titles, and this method of calculation is unreliable.*

Some have referred to the pope as "vicar of the Son of God," but this is not one of his official titles. These are listed in the *Annuario Pontificio* ("Pontifical Yearbook"), published annually by the Vatican press. They are:

> Bishop of Rome, Vicar of Jesus Christ, Successor of the Prince of the Apostles, Supreme Pontiff of the Universal Church, Primate of Italy, Archbishop and Metropolitan of the Roman Province, Sovereign of the Vatican City State, Servant of the servants of God.

The closest title is "Vicar of Jesus Christ" (Latin, *Vicarius Iesu Christi*), but this does not add up to 666.

Some claim that the phrase *Vicarius Filii Dei* is printed on the papal tiara (a special kind of crown worn by past popes). These reports are false. None of the tiaras had this phrase, and popes today do not use tiaras.

One might argue the pope can still be *described as* the vicar of the Son of God, even if it isn't one of his titles, but this produces an unreliable methodology. All kinds of people and things can be described in ways that add up to 666. The children's TV character Barney may be a cute purple dinosaur, but that doesn't mean he's the Antichrist (CVte pVrpLe DInosaVr = C+V+V+L+D+I+V = 100+5+5+50+500+1+5 = 666).

Ironically, this argument is often made by Seventh-day Adventists, whose founding prophetess was Ellen Gould White (ELLen GoVLD VVhIte = 50+50+5+50+500+5+5+1 = 666).

Finally, while you can get 666 by taking each Roman numeral as an individual digit, out of its immediate context (VICarIVs fILII DeI = V+I+C+I+V+I+L+I+I+D+I = 5+1+100+1+5+1+50+1+1+500+1 = 666), Roman numerals need to be read in context. Placing a smaller number to the left of a larger one results in it being *subtracted*, not added. Thus "IV" means 4, not 6. In the same way, "IC" and "IL" mean 99 and 49, not 101 and 51. Read this way, *Vicarius Filii Dei* is 660, not 666.

Scientific Foreknowledge and the Bible

CHALLENGE

"The Bible would be more credible if it contained scientific knowledge that wasn't known when it was written (e.g., if it said, 'There are no rivers longer than the Amazon,' 'The atomic theory of matter is true,' or 'Epidemics are caused by germs')."

DEFENSE

God could do this if he chose, but it doesn't appear he has. Scripture is a religious rather than scientific text, and God has given us other evidence for our faith.

Some think Scripture contains scientific foreknowledge. For example, Isaiah 40:22 says God "sits above the circle of the earth," which some think refers to earth's spherical shape. This isn't convincing (the passage is poetry—God doesn't literally "sit" anywhere—and a circle is not a sphere; "the circle of the earth" might be envisioned as the horizon or as a flat disk).

Putting scientific foreknowledge in Scripture would be of limited use. It wouldn't help the original audience—only people living after the relevant science was discovered, perhaps thousands of years later. It would even be an apologetic distraction if the science of one age disagreed with it. If Scripture said, "Epidemics are caused by germs," people living after Galen, who thought epidemics were caused by bad air, would have their confidence in Scripture weakened rather than strengthened. Even once the correct science was discovered, this wouldn't guarantee people would see it as foreknowledge.

There's a limit to how advanced the science in Scripture could be since the biblical languages lacked technical scientific terms. Without these, only basic concepts could be described, but basic concepts could be attributed to ancient knowledge rather than foreknowledge.

Suppose the Bible said, "The longest river is in a southern land on the other side of the world" (the Israelites had no knowledge of or name for the Amazon, so a definite description would be needed). After the Amazon's discovery, would that convince people Scripture contained supernatural information or would they conclude there must have been ancient contact between the Old and New Worlds?

Similarly, if the Bible endorsed the atomic theory of matter, people would simply conclude there were ancient Hebrew atomists, just as there were ancient Greek atomists (e.g., the philosophers Leucippus and Democritus).

Finally, we don't know that Scripture *doesn't* contain such foreknowledge. Maybe the relevant science hasn't been discovered yet.

Sola Scriptura and 2 Timothy 3:16–17

CHALLENGE

"The Bible teaches sola scriptura. For example, it says: "All scripture (Greek, pasa graphē) is inspired by God and profitable for teaching, for reproof, for correction, and for training in righteousness, that the man of God may be complete, equipped for every good work" (2 Tim. 3:16–17)."

DEFENSE
There are multiple problems with this challenge.

First, *pasa graphē* ordinarily would be translated "every scripture" (*pasa* generally means "every" rather than "all" before a singular noun like *graphē*). "Every scripture" would be a reference to each individual book of Scripture. Further, in the Bible the word "scripture" (singular) refers to an individual book or passage. The inspired books as a whole are "the scriptures" (plural), not "scripture." But Paul couldn't mean each individual book is sufficient for doctrine. Otherwise, you could do theology by "Genesis alone," "Isaiah alone," and so forth.

Second, Paul says the books are useful toward certain goals, including teaching. But being useful merely means that something makes a contribution—not that it is uniquely and exclusively sufficient.

Third, although the scriptures contribute to the goal of making the man of God "complete, equipped for every good work," they aren't the only things he needs. He also needs holiness, the charisms of the Holy Spirit, the correct understanding of the texts, and so on. The texts are not sufficient by themselves.

Fourth, *sola scriptura* would only have been applicable after the apostles' deaths (see Day 5), but Paul is not telling Timothy something new and meant to apply only after his death. He is saying something that was true then and had been true all along. He articulates this principle immediately after reminding Timothy that he had known the sacred scriptures (plural) from his youth (v. 15). This referred to the Old Testament, and Paul's principle was true when only the Old Testament existed, before any New Testament books were written.

Christians living before any New Testament book was penned were still obliged to accept the elements of the Christian faith not found in the Old Testament. They didn't only become obligatory upon being written (2 Tim. 2:15).

It is likely 2 Timothy was not the last New Testament book written, yet Paul expected Timothy to apply the principle immediately—not wait until after Paul and all the other apostles were dead.

The Fine-Tuning Argument

CHALLENGE

"Modern cosmology gives us no reason to believe in God."

DEFENSE

Elsewhere we cover the support the Big Bang gives to God's existence (see Day 46), but there is also the fact that the universe appears to be finely tuned to allow the possibility of life.

This argument may be phrased as follows:

1. The universe has a significant number of physical constants that fall within narrow ranges that allow life to develop.
2. These values are either the product of design or chance.
3. It is highly unlikely that they are the product of chance.
4. Therefore, the physical constants of the universe are designed to allow intelligent life to develop.
5. Design requires a designer.
6. Therefore, the universe has a designer.
7. The designer of the universe is God.
8. Therefore, modern cosmology gives us reason to believe in God.

The premises of this argument are lines 1, 2, 3, 5, and 7. The conclusions (lines 4, 6, and 8) follow from them.

Line 1 is widely admitted by astronomers and physicists. Cosmologist Stephen Hawking writes: "The laws of science, as we know them at present, contain many fundamental numbers, like the size of the electric charge of the electron and the ratio of the masses of the proton and the electron. . . . The remarkable fact is that the values of these numbers seem to have been very finely adjusted to make possible the development of life" (*A Brief History of Time*, chapter 8).

Line 2 is true by definition, understanding chance to be anything not designed.

Line 3 is supported by the fact that, if we imagine all the possible alternative values the universe's constants might have, it is very improbable that they would all fall within the ranges needed for intelligent life by chance.

Line 5 is required by the concept of design, which presupposes a designer, just as the concept of art presupposes an artist.

Line 7 is based on one of the most common ways of conceptualizing God—i.e., as the Creator of the universe.

TIP

This is an adaptation of the design argument presented by St. Thomas Aquinas as his "fifth way" of demonstrating God's existence (ST I:2:3).

Objections to the Fine-Tuning Argument

CHALLENGE

"The fine-tuning argument is flawed: (1) The fact that our universe's constants appear finely tuned to allow for the existence of life could be due to chance if there are a vast number of universes, each of which has slightly different constants; (2) perhaps there is some law we haven't yet discovered why the universe must have the constants it does; and (3) even if the universe is designed, that doesn't mean the designer is God."

DEFENSE

None of these objections overturn the fine-tuning argument.

First, if it were true that there were a sufficiently vast number of universes, each of which had different constants, then it might be likely that one with our constants would exist. However, we have no evidence that even one other universe exists, much less the vast multitude that would be needed.

Second, the idea there is a hidden law requiring that the constants must be set as they are is pure speculation. Based on the evidence we have at present, the constants appear to be independent. Further, even if we were to discover such a law, it would only raise the question of why *that* law exists.

Third, although some have speculated our universe could be the product of a technologically advanced civilization from a prior universe, and that they designed its constants, we have no evidence this is the case. We don't even have proof it is possible for a technologically advanced civilization to create a new, designer universe.

Further, this technologically advanced civilization would itself need to be made of life-forms or (if robotic) to be the product of previous life-forms. Thus the universe *they* came from would need to have its constants similarly fine-tuned, and the problem would only be kicked back a step.

Each of the above proposals also potentially runs afoul of Occam's Razor, which urges us to seek the simplest solution that fits the evidence. For example, postulating vast numbers of other universes to explain away the fact that ours looks designed may be seen as an egregious violation of the principle.

At a minimum, none of these explanations fit the data better than the proposition that God designed our universe, and thus it is rational to believe in God based on modern cosmology.

Repetitious Prayer

CHALLENGE

"Catholics are wrong to pray the rosary. Jesus condemned 'vain repetitions.'"

DEFENSE

Jesus did not condemn prayer that involves repetition—he endorsed it.

In the King James Version, Jesus says, "But when ye pray, use not vain repetitions, as the heathen do: for they think that they shall be heard for their much speaking" (Matt. 6:7). Even in this translation, he does not condemn repetition but *vain* (useless) repetition.

But there is a problem with this translation. In Greek, Jesus says we should not *battalogēsēte*. This is a rare word not found elsewhere in the New Testament. It's meaning is unclear, so we shouldn't draw dogmatic conclusions about what he meant.

The word appears to come from *battos* (Greek, "a stammerer"). Gentiles did not literally stammer when they prayed, but they could ramble in prayer, thinking that they needed to wear down their gods using many words. This is the attitude Jesus rejects, saying "they think they shall be heard for their much speaking."

It's not repeating words that he's concerned about. It's thinking the efficacy of prayer depends on saying a lot. He points out God knows what we need before we ask him (Matt. 6:8). Jesus makes it clear he doesn't have a problem with repeating things because the next thing he does is teach the Lord's Prayer—a prayer he intends to be repeated (Matt. 6:9–13).

Repetition is essential to corporate worship. It's not possible for people to pray aloud, in unison, unless they know the prayer they're going to use. That's why prayers in the synagogue and the temple of Jesus' day were memorized and repeated.

A striking example is the Psalms—ancient hymns, or prayers set to music. The book of Psalms was Israel's hymn book. In fact, Psalms is one of the most frequently quoted books in the New Testament (Luke 20:42, 24:44; Acts 1:20, 13:33, 35, etc.). Yet the Psalms, by their nature, are meant to be repeated.

The Psalms even involve repetition within themselves. Psalm 136 has a refrain that occurs over and over. In the King James Version, the refrain is translated "for his mercy endureth for ever," and it occurs so frequently that it even interrupts and appears in the middle of sentences. Yet Psalm 136 is a beautiful and spiritually meaningful prayer that was inspired by the Holy Spirit.

The Book of Judith and History

CHALLENGE

"The book of Judith cannot be true. It says in its very first verse that Nebuchadnezzar was king of the Assyrians, but we know from history that he was really the king of the Babylonians."

DEFENSE

The alleged error is itself a cue to the audience, telling them what kind of book they are reading.

The book is about a devout woman named Judith, which means "Lady Jew." She battles a general sent by Nebuchadnezzar—the greatest single *individual* enemy of Israel. He is depicted as the leader of the Assyrians—the *other* great enemy of Israel.

Let's transpose this into a modern context: In the twentieth century, Adolf Hitler was regarded as the greatest individual enemy of America, while the Soviet Union was the other great enemy of America. Beginning in the 1940s, there were also comic book superheroines such as Miss America and Liberty Belle, who were personifications of America's fighting spirit.

Suppose you read a story about Miss America battling a general sent to conquer America by Adolf Hitler, leader of the Soviet Union. You would know immediately that what you were reading was not intended as a historical account but as some kind of parable.

Similarly, Jews in the ancient world would recognize that Judith is a parabolic rather than a historical work. People then knew Nebuchadnezzar was the king of the Babylonians, not the Assyrians, just as people today know Adolf Hitler was the leader of Germany, not the Soviet Union. This is why Nebuchadnezzar is pictured as king of the Assyrians right at the beginning—so the reader will know he is reading a parable. The book shouts "Parable!" from its first verse.

People today may not recognize this because they are less familiar with the ancient world and the sophistication of ancient literature, but it would have been clear to the original audience.

Thus John Paul II stated: "The Books of Tobit, Judith, and Esther, although dealing with the history of the Chosen People, have the character of allegorical and moral narrative rather than history properly so called" (General Audience, May 8, 1985).

The Year of Luke's Enrollment

CHALLENGE

"Luke is mistaken when he says Jesus was born during 'the first enrollment, when Quirinius was governor of Syria' (Luke 2:2). That census happened in A.D. 6–7, long after Jesus' birth."

DEFENSE

There are multiple solutions, some of which are presented here.

First, the word for "first" (Greek, *prōtē*) can mean "before." Taken thus, Luke would be saying this was a census *before* the famous one in A.D. 6–7.

Second, if *prōtē* is translated "first," this implies there was a *second* census under Quirinius. The second census would need to be famous for Luke to point out that Jesus was born during the first one, and the second census may have been the famous one of A.D. 6–7.

Third, the event may not have been a census. Luke says it was an "enrollment" or "registration" (Greek, *apographē*). This may refer to an event in 3–2 B.C. (the year of Christ's birth; see Day 159) when the people of the Roman Empire acknowledged their allegiance to Augustus Caesar (except a few thousand Pharisees who Josephus records refused the oath; *Antiquities of the Jews* 17:2:4). Augustus himself mentions this in an inscription, stating: "In my thirteenth consulship [i.e., 2 B.C.] the senate, the equestrian order, and *the whole people of Rome* gave me the title of Father of my Country" (*Res Gestae Divi Augusti* 35, emphasis added).

Fourth, if the event was a census, the basis for dating it to A.D. 6–7 is based on Josephus's statement that the event occurred in "the thirty-seventh year of [Augustus] Caesar's victory over Antony at Actium," or A.D. 6–7 (*Antiquities of the Jews* 18:2:1). However, internal indications in Josephus's text suggest he was confused regarding when this event happened (see Steinmann, below).

Luke, writing around A.D. 59 (see Day 79) was closer in time to the events than Josephus, who was writing around A.D. 94. The events were more important to Luke than to Josephus, indicating a greater likelihood that his date was correct.

Finally, Quirinius's career is uncertain. Luke says he was "governing" (Greek, *hēgemoneuontos*) Syria, not that he had the formal title "governor." This event could have fit different places in his career.

TIP

See Jack Finegan, *Handbook of Biblical Chronology*, 2nd ed., and Andrew E. Steinmann, *From Abraham to Paul*.

Horrible Things in Scripture

CHALLENGE

"How can you believe the Bible is the true word of God? It contains numerous accounts of people saying and doing horrible things."

DEFENSE

So does a typical newspaper.

A newspaper's job is to report significant things that happened. That doesn't mean it approves. Newspapers report rapes, murders, and crimes the paper does not approve of. They also report people saying things that the paper's reporters and editors completely disagree with.

Similarly, just because Scripture records something doesn't mean it endorses it. It does mean the biblical author thought the event was significant for his audience to know, but it doesn't mean that he—or God—approved. Scripture records the words and actions of the devil, but the devil's activities are strongly disapproved of.

Similarly, when Jephthah makes a rash vow that apparently leads to his daughter being sacrificed as a burnt offering (Judg. 11:30–40), the audience is meant to understand his action was barbarous and horrific. Jephthah is only one example of Scripture's brutal honesty about the leaders of Israel, who were often deeply flawed. Even respected figures like David and Solomon have their blackest sins reported (cf. 2 Sam. 11, 1 Kings 11:1–13).

Consequently, one cannot simply note that Scripture *reports* someone saying or doing something abominable and conclude that it *teaches* something abominable. When evaluating such charges, one must ask whether the proposed evil is condemned.

Sometimes, there will be an explicit condemnation (thus the biblical author condemns Solomon's idolatry; 1 Kings 11:9–10). Other times, the condemnation will be implicit, but clues in the text reveal the disapproval (as when the daughters of Israel mourn what Jephthah did; Judges 11:39b–40). Or disapproval can be inferred because the action is condemned elsewhere in Scripture (e.g., even if David's adultery wasn't explicitly condemned in 2 Sam. 12, we would know his act was wrong because it violates the Ten Commandments; Exod. 20:14, Deut. 5:18).

Finally, our native moral sense can be a clue to the biblical author's disapproval (e.g., even though David didn't personally kill Uriah the Hittite, he engineered the man's death, and even without the explicit condemnation in 2 Sam. 12, the audience would sense he violated the moral prohibition on killing). In general, when our moral sense tells us that something Scripture reports is problematic, it is a clue that Scripture may disapprove too.

Faith and Contrary Evidence

CHALLENGE

*"Religion is irrational. It requires us to maintain
faith even in the face of contrary evidence."*

DEFENSE

No one instantly abandons his convictions upon encountering
the slightest bit of contrary data. This is not true in religion,
and it is not true in other areas.

We encounter vast amounts of data in our lives, some of which will contradict things we believe. When this happens, we have three basic choices: (1) ignore the new data, (2) revise our belief to fit the new data, or (3) abandon our belief.

Each choice can be rational in different situations. If we have strong evidence for our belief and the contrary data is minimal, we may assume it is a fluke and our existing belief is sound. If the new evidence has significant weight, it may be rational to revisit our belief to see if it needs to be tweaked. And if the new data is overwhelming, it may be rational to abandon the belief.

Each decision also can be irrational. For example, a scientist would be foolish to dismiss a well-supported theory based on the first tiny bit of evidence pointing in the other direction. That's not what scientists do. When only small points of contrary data emerge, scientists typically dismiss them, assuming the current theory will be supported by future evidence. As additional contrary evidence mounts, they may tweak the current theory, and they abandon it only when decisive contrary evidence has been accumulated.

It is rational for scientists to proceed in this way, and it is rational for religious believers to do the same. They can have the courage of their convictions and should not be, as Paul says, "tossed to and fro and carried about with every wind of doctrine" (Eph. 4:14).

In religion and other fields, being willing to instantly abandon one's beliefs based on the slightest bit of contrary data is not rational and will result in a person being someone "who will listen to anybody and can never arrive at a knowledge of the truth" (2 Tim. 3:7).

TIP

For a discussion of this topic from a religious viewpoint, see C.S. Lewis's essay, "On Obstinacy in Belief" in *The World's Last Night*. For a discussion from a scientific point of view, see Thomas Kuhn's book *The Structure of Scientific Revolutions*.

The Humanity of the Unborn

CHALLENGE

"There is no proof that the unborn are human beings."

DEFENSE

There is proof, and it is obvious regardless of one's faith perspective.

Objectively speaking, a human being is a living human organism. For the unborn to qualify as human beings, they must meet three criteria:

1. They must be alive.
2. They must be human.
3. They must be organisms.

They meet the first criteria—life. We observed elsewhere that they are alive (see Day 191). This is illustrated by the fact that the unborn have biological processes occuring in their cells, which are multiplying and specializing throughout pregnancy. The simple truth is that dead embryos don't grow, making it unmistakable that the unborn are alive.

They meet the second criteria—humanity—for each has a human genetic code, not that of a cow or a chimpanzee or a carrot. They belong to our species, not some other one, as their genetic codes make clear.

They also meet the third criteria—being organisms. An organism is an entity that is whole in and of itself. That is, it is not part of another, larger organism.

Sometimes abortion advocates claim that the unborn are part of their mothers' bodies, but this is false. The unborn have their own unique genetic code, which is distinct from the mother's.

The fact that there is a stage in which the unborn are single cells also is not contrary to this. There are many single-celled organisms in the world, and at one point in their development, humans pass through this stage.

Fundamentally, the unborn are organisms because they are organic wholes with their own, in-built principles of growth and development. Unless interfered with, they will mature and be born in just a few months, then continue their development toward adulthood.

Since the unborn are living human organisms, they are—objectively speaking—human beings. Any attempt to deny this is a rationalization that violates the known facts.

The unborn also are innocent human beings (see Day 202), and it follows that they must be accorded the same right to life as other innocent human beings. To claim otherwise is to adopt a fundamentally inhuman and immoral position.

Peter and the Church's Foundations

CHALLENGE

"Peter isn't the rock because Paul says, 'For no other foundation can any one lay than that which is laid, which is Jesus Christ' (1 Cor. 3:11)."

DEFENSE

Scripture describes the Church's foundation in at least *five* ways. You can't pick one and ignore the others.

Paul was not speaking of the universal Church's foundation. He was referring to how he started the local church at Corinth, of which Christ is the irreplaceable foundation. One can extend this concept to the universal Church, but not without taking into account other things the New Testament has to say.

In 1 Peter 2:6, Isaiah 28:16 is applied to Christ: "Behold, I am laying in Zion a stone, a cornerstone chosen and precious, and he who believes in him will not be put to shame." Here the word for "stone" isn't *petros* (the name Jesus gave Peter) but *lithos*. Further, 1 Peter 2:6 says Jesus is the Church's "cornerstone" (Greek, *akrogōniaios*). A cornerstone is only one part of a foundation—the *corner* part of it.

Ephesians 2:20 says the household of God is "built upon the foundation of the apostles and prophets, Christ Jesus himself being the cornerstone." The prophets here are likely prophets of the New Testament age, as made clear by the other two references to them in the epistle (Eph. 3:5, 4:11). Together with the apostles, they form the Church's foundation in this passage, with Christ as the cornerstone. The fact that Paul wrote this passage and 1 Corinthians, shows there is no contradiction in his mind between Christ being the foundation in one sense and others being the foundation in another.

In Revelation 21:14, the New Jerusalem is said to have twelve foundations with the names of the twelve apostles written on them. Note that the Twelve were a select group who had followed Jesus during his ministry (Acts 1:21–26); not even Paul and Barnabas, who also were apostles (Acts 14:14), were members of the Twelve.

Finally, in Matthew 16:18 Jesus says: "And I tell you, you are Peter, and on this rock I will build my Church, and the gates of hades shall not prevail against it."

We thus see that Scripture does not depict the foundation of the Church just one way, and what Jesus says to Peter must be given its due.

Details in the Gospels

CHALLENGE

"The Gospels were written long after the fact. They aren't historically reliable."

DEFENSE

On the contrary, the details in the Gospels show they are very reliable.

In John, when Jesus is about to miraculously feed the five thousand, he asks Philip where it would be possible to buy bread (John 6:5–6). This is surprising since Philip was not a major apostle.

However, John also records that Philip was from Bethsaida—the town from which Peter and Andrew originally hailed (John 1:44, 12:21). The feeding of the five thousand occurred in a desolate place near the town of Bethsaida (Luke 9:10–13). That would explain why Jesus might ask Philip where bread could be bought, but since Peter and Andrew also came from Bethsaida, and since they were among the most prominent apostles, we would expect him to ask them.

The matter is clarified in Mark, which indicates Peter and Andrew were now living in the village of Capernaum (Mark 1:21–29). They no longer lived in Bethsaida and would not have up-to-date knowledge of where bread could be bought. Jesus thus asked Philip.

It is striking that each fact is mentioned in only one of the Gospels:

- Only John mentions that Jesus asked Philip where to buy bread.
- Only John mentions that Philip was from Bethsaida.
- Only Luke mentions that the feeding of the five thousand took place near Bethsaida.
- Only Mark mentions that Peter and Andrew were now living in Capernaum.

Yet when careful attention is paid to the details of each Gospel, a coherent picture emerges of why Jesus asked a lesser apostle like Philip where bread could be bought.

This is not the kind of situation that would arise if the evangelists were making up details at random. The Gospels are all too short for chance to explain the matter. Neither does the situation reflect a collusion of authors, for the relevant details are mentioned only in passing and nothing is ever made of them.

This indicates that the evangelists are accurately recording historical details, whose integrity is shown when their accounts are compared.

TIP

See John James Blunt, *Undesigned Coincidences in the Writings Both of the Old and New Testament—An Argument of Their Veracity.*

Biblical Evidence for Mary's Perpetual Virginity

CHALLENGE

"We don't have evidence Mary remained a virgin after the birth of Jesus."

DEFENSE

The New Testament indicates that Mary did remain a virgin.

One passage that suggests this occurs during the Crucifixion, where we read, "When Jesus saw his mother, and the disciple whom he loved standing near, he said to his mother, 'Woman, behold, your son!' Then he said to the disciple, 'Behold, your mother!' And from that hour the disciple took her to his own home" (John 19:26–27).

If Mary had other children, then Jesus would never have entrusted her care to an outsider. It would have been insulting to her children. Jesus' action is best explained by Mary remaining a virgin and having no other children.

Even more strikingly, when the Angel Gabriel announces to Mary that she will give birth, she asks a very significant question: "How can this be, since I have no relations with a man?" (Luke 1:34, NABRE).

The passage can also be literally translated from Greek as "How will this be, for I know not man." This relies on the biblical idiom of "knowing" as being sexually intimate with (as in, "Adam knew Eve his wife, and she conceived and bore Cain"; Gen. 4:1).

The fact that Mary asks the question indicates that she knows that, in the ordinary course of nature, sexual intercourse is required for a woman to have a baby. Yet she asks the angel how she will become pregnant in spite of this.

Further, Luke has already established that Mary was a virgin betrothed to Joseph (Luke 1:27). If Mary were planning a normal marriage with Joseph, it would have been immediately clear how she would become pregnant: After they began cohabiting, they would have marital relations, and she would become pregnant with the son the angel spoke of. The fact that she asks this question suggests that she is *not* planning on a normal marriage. Instead, she is planning a marriage that does not involve sexual intercourse.

TIP

The second-century *Protoevangelium of James* states that Mary was consecrated as a virgin as a child and that she was then married to Joseph, an elderly widower who already had a family and thus could be a suitable guardian for a consecrated virgin.

Jesus and the Herd of Pigs

CHALLENGE

"Jesus purposelessly destroyed another man's property by allowing demons to enter a herd of pigs, causing it to drown in the Sea of Galilee."

DEFENSE

Jesus had reasons for this act; it was not a purposeless destruction of property.

First, Jesus did not destroy the pigs. In freeing a man from demonic possession, he allowed the demons to enter a herd of pigs. These demons had caused self-destructive behavior in the possessed man (Mark 5:5), and they apparently began tormenting the pigs, which tried to flee and unintentionally stampeded downhill into the sea (Mark 5:13).

This may have been a foreseeable result, but foreseeing something is not the same as causing it. Jesus granted the demons' request to enter the pigs, and the demons thwarted their own plan to live in the pigs by tormenting them so that they stampeded and died, revealing the self-destructive nature of evil.

Second, foreseeable events that have negative consequences can be morally justified for an adequate reason. That was the case here, because the event taught multiple valuable lessons.

The owners of the pigs, and the people in the region where this occurred, were Gentiles. Although the pigs' owners suffered economic loss, they stood to gain vastly more in terms of spiritual wealth. The death of the pigs provided a vivid demonstration of Jesus' spiritual authority and his role in God's plan. By allowing the demons to go into the pigs, the exorcism was accompanied by a forceful and memorable demonstration of God's power and of his compassion for the demoniac. The fact that the demons seized control of a herd of 2,000 pigs showed just what kind of spiritual oppression the man was suffering, and yet Jesus was able to free him.

This revealed the power and love of the true God to the Gentile natives. It showed them that the true God could free them from even the most powerful manifestations of evil. It also showed them that the God of the Jews loves and has compassion for Gentiles.

The spiritual value of these lessons—which could bring souls to God—greatly exceeded the economic value of the pigs. Had Jesus not granted the demons' request, the lessons would not be underlined in the unforgettable way they are.

TIP

For more on this event, see Jimmy Akin, *Mark: A Commentary.*

The Whore of Babylon

"The Catholic Church is the whore of Babylon."

DEFENSE

The whore of Babylon is described in detail in Revelation 16:19–19:4.

Babylon was a city in ancient Mesopotamia (modern Iraq), but scholars recognize the use of "Babylon" in Revelation as a symbolic designation of another city (cf. 11:8; also cf. 1 Peter 5:13, where Peter, who is known to have been in Rome, refers to being in "Babylon"):

- The whore is depicted persecuting Christians (cf. 17:6, 14).
- She is seated on a beast with seven heads, which are identified as seven hills (17:9) and seven kings (17:10).
- The beast also has ten horns, which hate the whore, attack her, and burn her with fire (17:16).
- The whore is said to be "the great city which has dominion over the kings of the earth" (17:18).

Most scholars see these as pointing to the ancient, pagan city of Rome, which persecuted Christians, which was built on seven hills, which had a line of emperors plausibly identified with the beast (see Day 203), and which was the capitol of the major empire of the day.

Some scholars have seen the clues as pointing to another city—Jerusalem—which also persecuted Christians in the first century, whose authorities were allied with and supported by the Roman empire (and thus "seated" on the beast), and which was attacked and burned by an alliance of Roman and other troops in A.D. 70, as Jesus predicted (Mark 13). Further, Revelation 11:8 speaks of "the great city" where the "Lord was crucified," the Old Testament speaks of Jerusalem as a whore (Isa. 1:21; Ezek. 16:1, 15–35), and the whore is the antithesis of the bride of Christ, the "New Jerusalem" (Rev. 21:2–22:5), suggesting the old Jerusalem.

Both identifications are possible, but neither fits the Catholic Church. Indeed, according to the standard anti-Catholic theory, the Catholic Church did not exist in the first century and thus could not persecute the apostles, as the whore did (Rev. 18:20).

More fundamentally, Revelation was meant to be understood by the original audience as describing what would happen soon (Rev. 1:1). The audience would have no way of understanding the whore as a future Church rather than one of the persecuting cities of their own day.

When Life Begins

CHALLENGE

"Catholics shouldn't oppose abortion. Nobody really knows when life begins."

DEFENSE

We know exactly when life begins, but this isn't the real question.

First, if it were ambiguous whether the unborn are alive, that would not make it permissible to kill them. You can't kill something just because you don't *know* it is a living human being. If a hunter sees something moving in the woods, he can't shoot it unless he is *sure* it is not a human. He must err on the side of caution, and the same principle would apply if the status of the unborn were unclear.

Second, their status *isn't* unclear. Scientifically speaking, there is no question that unborn children are alive from conception onward. At no point in their development are unborn children dead. If they ever become dead then a miscarriage has occurred.

There is no point in pregnancy at which inanimate matter suddenly becomes animate. Even the sperm and the egg that unite to give the child his genetic code are already alive, with cellular, biological processes going on inside them. From the moment of conception, therefore, life is present. Even at the single-cell stage, unborn children have metabolisms that consume energy, maintain cellular function, and enable them to grow.

Third, "When does life begin?" is the wrong question. Just because something is alive does not mean that it can't be killed. We kill living things all the time. We cannot eat without other living things dying. Even vegetarians must consume and digest the cells of plants. There is simply no other way for us to survive.

The question is not whether the unborn are alive. They *are*. The question is not whether abortion kills them. It *does*. The question is whether they are the *kind* of thing that it is okay to kill.

The pro-life claim is that unborn children are innocent human beings, and the logic of the pro-life position is straightforward:

1. Deliberately killing an innocent human being is wrong.
2. Abortion deliberately kills an innocent human being.
3. Therefore, abortion is wrong.

The argument is so simple that even a child can understand it. If the two premises are true then the conclusion that follows from them is also true (see Days 185 and 202).

Eucharist as Symbol in the Fathers

CHALLENGE

"The Church Fathers sometimes used language implying the Eucharist was symbolic, so they couldn't have believed in the Real Presence."

DEFENSE

The concept of a symbol means something different today from what it did in the time of the early Church.

We have already seen that the Church Fathers were realists in their understanding of Christ's presence in the Eucharist (see Day 120). However, Protestant historian J.N.D. Kelly writes: "Occasionally these writers use language which has been held to imply that, for all its realist sound, their use of the terms 'body' and 'blood' may after all be merely symbolical. Tertullian, for example, refers to the bread as 'a figure' (*figura*) of Christ's body, and once speaks of 'the bread by which he represents (*repraesentat*) his very body'" (*Early Christian Doctrines*, 212).

However, Kelly warns: "Yet we should be cautious about interpreting such expressions in a modern fashion. According to ancient modes of thought a mysterious relationship existed between the thing symbolized and its symbol, figure or type; the symbol in some sense *was* the thing symbolized" (ibid.).

Thus Tertullian's statement that the Eucharist "represents" Christ's body must be understood in its ancient context:

Again, the verb *repraesentare*, in Tertullian's vocabulary, retained its original significance of "to make present." All that his language really suggests is that, while accepting the equation of the elements with the body and blood, he remains conscious of the sacramental distinction between them. In fact, he is trying, with the aid of the concept of *figura*, to rationalize to himself the apparent contradiction between (a) the dogma that the elements are now Christ's body and blood, and (b) the empirical fact that for sensation they remain bread and wine (ibid.).

Given the shift in how the concept of symbol is understood, one should not take language suggesting symbolism as precluding a realist understanding in the Fathers of Christ's presence. Indeed, the Church today uses the language of signs in connection with the Eucharist, though it firmly teaches the Real Presence. Thus the *Catechism* states: "The essential signs of the Eucharistic sacrament are wheat bread and grape wine, on which the blessing of the Holy Spirit is invoked and the priest pronounces the words of consecration spoken by Jesus during the Last Supper" (CCC 1412).

Jesus Calling His Mother "Woman"

CHALLENGE

"Mary should not be given special honors. Jesus certainly didn't show her any. In fact, he abruptly called her 'woman.'"

DEFENSE

At the time, "woman" was a respectful form of address, like "ma'am."

Jesus refers to his mother as "woman" (Greek, *gunai*) in two passages—the wedding at Cana (John 2:4) and the Crucifixion (John 19:26–27).

In the first, Mary informs him their hosts have run out of wine and (translating literally from the Greek), he says, "What (is that) to me and to you, woman?" Notice he puts Mary in the same category as himself—asking how their hosts' concern affects the two of them. This is not a sign of disrespect.

In the second, John says: "When Jesus saw his mother, and the disciple whom he loved standing near, he said to his mother, 'Woman, behold, your son!' Then he said to the disciple, 'Behold, your mother!' And from that hour the disciple took her to his own home." Here again, there is no disrespect. Jesus tenderly provides for his mother's care after his death.

Concerning the way the term "woman" is used as an address in the New Testament:

- Jesus uses it to address the Syro-Phoenician woman (Matt. 15:28).
- Jesus uses it to address the woman with a hemorrhage (Luke 13:12).
- Peter uses it to address the high priest's servant girl (Luke 22:57).
- Jesus uses it to address the Samaritan woman at the well (John 4:21).
- Two angels use it to address Mary Magdalene (John 20:13).
- Jesus uses it to address Mary Magdalene (John 20:15).
- Paul uses it to address individual wives among his readers (1 Cor. 7:16).
- Paul uses it to address the wives in his audience (Col. 3:18, using the plural: *gunaikes*).
- Peter uses it to address the wives in his audience (1 Peter 3:1, using the plural: *gunaikes*).

None of these uses are disrespectful, and they reveal that "woman" was a polite form of address.

TIP

The same was true of the term "man" (Greek, *anthropē* or *anēr*) when used as a form of address. It functioned like the English terms "sir" or "mister." Among other examples, see Luke 5:20, where Jesus tells the paralytic: "Man, your sins are forgiven you."

The Divinity of the Holy Spirit

CHALLENGE

"The Bible does not teach that the Holy Spirit is God."

DEFENSE

The Bible may not contain the words "The Holy Spirit is God," but various passages in Scripture do imply this truth.

One of the most important passages in Scripture concerning the doctrine of the Trinity contains the formula that Jesus indicates is to be used in baptism: "Go therefore and make disciples of all nations, baptizing them in the name of the Father and of the Son and of the Holy Spirit" (Matt. 28:19). This passage places the Holy Spirit alongside the Father and the Son.

Other passages also associate the Father, the Son, and the Holy Spirit (Matt. 3:16–17; John 14:16–17, 25–26; 2 Cor. 13:14; 1 Pet. 1:2), but the trinitarian formula used in baptism is particularly clear, as it speaks of them directly, in sequence, in a simple formula.

Such passages indicate that the Father, the Son, and the Holy Spirit have something in common. The question is what.

It is universally acknowledged that the Father is God. Elsewhere we cover the fact that Jesus, the Son, also is God (see Day 137). But if the first two persons in the trinitarian formula are God then this strongly suggests that the Holy Spirit is God.

Further, as we observe elsewhere (see Day 28), the Holy Spirit is not an energy or force but a Person. The trinitarian formula thus indicates that, like the Father and the Son, he is a divine Person and thus God. This is what all three have in common.

The deity of the Holy Spirit is also indicated by the passage in Acts in which Ananias and Sapphira present a partial offering to the apostles and lie about it. Peter first asks Ananias, "Why has Satan filled your heart to lie to the Holy Spirit and to keep back part of the proceeds of the land?" (Acts 5:3). He then tells him, "You have not lied to men but to God" (Acts 5:4). The two statements, made in parallel, identify the Holy Spirit with God.

The divinity of the Holy Spirit is also indicated by the fact that he is said to be "the Spirit of God" (1 Cor. 2:11) and the fact that he is eternal (Heb. 9:14). God's spirit can only be God, and only God is eternal.

Jesus as "Firstborn"

CHALLENGE

"Luke 2:7 says Mary 'gave birth to her firstborn son.' This implies that Joseph and Mary had other sons; therefore she didn't remain a virgin."

DEFENSE

In ancient Jewish culture, the term "firstborn son" did not imply that other sons came later.

The first male child to be born to a woman was regarded as her firstborn, regardless of whether she had other children. The firstborn son had a special role that applied as soon as he was born. It was not a role he assumed when later children were born.

All life was seen as a gift from God. This applied to human children, the offspring of animals, and crops of fruit and grain. To honor God for these gifts, people would offer him the first of each in recognition of him as their source. Thus, after every harvest, the children of Israel offered to God the "first fruits" of their crops (Exod. 23:19).

The firstborn of men and animals were consecrated to God (Exod. 13:1–2). In the case of firstborn male animals, they were either sacrificed to God or—in some cases—redeemed by paying a special price (Exod. 13:12–13a). God rejected child sacrifice, however. For firstborn humans, fathers had to redeem them. The rule was: "Every firstborn of man among your sons you shall redeem" (Ex. 13:13b; cf. vv. 14–15).

After Jesus' birth, Joseph redeemed Jesus as Mary's firstborn (Luke 2:22–23). This was mandatory for every woman that had just had her first male child, even though she had not yet had a "second born" child and might never have one.

Jesus' status as a firstborn thus does not say anything about Mary and Joseph having additional children or Mary's perpetual virginity.

TIP

The *Jewish Encyclopedia* notes: "Every Israelite is obliged to redeem his firstborn son thirty days after the latter's birth. The mother is exempt from this obligation. The son, if the father fails to redeem him, has to redeem himself when he grows up (*Ḳid.* 29b). The sum of redemption as given in the Bible (Num. 18:16) is five shekels, which should be given to the priest" (*Jewish Encyclopedia*, 1906 ed., s.v. "Firstborn, Redemption Of").

The Book of Tobit and History

CHALLENGE

"The book of Tobit contains numerous implausibilities—for example, a woman being married seven times yet each husband dropping dead on the wedding night, how Tobit is presented as the uncle of the legendary figure of Ahiqar, and the phenomenally long life spans of Tobit and his son."

DEFENSE

The alleged errors are clues to the audience telling them what kind of book they are reading.

Like Judith (see Day 181), Tobit is a literary work that functions as an extended parable rather than a historical account, and various aspects of the text signal the audience that this is the case.

For example, the Pontifical Biblical Commission notes: "The death of the seven husbands of the same woman before the consummation of the marriage ([Tob.] 3:8–17) is a fact so unlikely that, this, by itself, suggests that the narrative is a literary fiction. . . . We have here, then, a popular religious fable with a didactic and edifying purpose which, by its nature, places it in the sphere of the wisdom tradition" (*The Inspiration and Truth of Sacred Scripture* 109).

Similarly, in the book's first chapter, the text describes Tobit as the uncle of Ahiqar (Tob. 1:21), a legendary Middle-Eastern sage. Ahiqar then helps Tobit (Tob. 1:22, 2:10), and he attends Tobias's wedding (Tob. 11:18). This is the ancient equivalent of a modern book whose first chapter establishes that the main character is the uncle of a legendary figure like Paul Bunyan, who then goes on to appear in the story.

Thus when the text says that Tobit lived to be 112 (Tob. 14:1) and Tobias to be 117 (Tob. 14:14)—and some manuscripts list higher ages—in a world where most adults died at half of those figures, it is another clue to the literary nature of the text.

This does not mean that Tobit cannot contain a historical nucleus that has been elaborated in literary style, but its primary character is literary rather than historical, as different aspects of the text make clear.

In view of considerations like these, John Paul II concluded: "The Books of Tobit, Judith, and Esther, although dealing with the history of the Chosen People, have the character of allegorical and moral narrative rather than history properly so called" (General Audience, May 8, 1985).

The Bible and *Pi*

CHALLENGE

"Solomon's temple held a metal basin or 'sea' used for ceremonial washings. According to Scripture, it was ten cubits across and 'a line of thirty cubits measured its circumference' (1 Kings 7:23; 2 Chron. 4:2). This implies that the value of π (pi) is 3, but that is incorrect. We know that π is an irrational number slightly greater than 3.14159."

DEFENSE

Thank you, Mr. Spock. This confuses an approximation with an error.

If the sea was exactly ten cubits across then it would have a radius (r) of 5 cubits, and if it were perfectly circular then its circumference (C) would be just over 31.4159 cubits, according to the formula for the circumference of a circle, $C=2\pi r$.

How are we to account for the difference of just over 1.4 cubits between the biblical and predicted values?

Some note that the Bible says the sea had a curved rim (1 Kings 7:26; 2 Chron. 4:5). Second-century mathematician Rabbi Nehemiah proposed the difference is because the sea's circumference was measured around the inside of the rim while the diameter was measured from the outside of the rim (see Petr Beckmann, *A History of Pi*, chapter 7).

This is possible, but there is a simpler solution: We are dealing with approximations.

The cubit (the length from a man's elbow to middle fingertip) is itself an approximation. So were most ancient measurements. If the circumference of the sea were exactly 30 cubits and its diameter thus turned out to be 9.5493 cubits, the ancient writer would have simply rounded to 10. Most likely, both the diameter and circumference are rounded, approximate values.

Then there is the problem of doing the measurement. The reference to a measuring line suggests someone measured it using a line, but did they get the line to fit the rim exactly? If they had men holding the line at points around the rim, it likely would not have fit exactly, resulting in an approximate measurement. Further, we're assuming the sea was perfectly circular, which it may not have been.

Ultimately, since π is an irrational number, everything using it *must* involve an approximation. The biblical author has simply chosen a different level of approximation than the modern critic. The fact that the biblical author's math works within the level of approximation he selects shows he is giving an honest and accurate report.

Images of Hell

"I can't take the idea of hell seriously. The idea that a loving God would confine people to a fiery place deep in the earth where devils poke them with pitchforks in a torture chamber is ridiculous."

The next world transcends our ability to imagine, and, even at their best, the images we use aren't meant to be more than pointers.

Like some popular depictions of heaven, popular depictions of hell owe more to artistic imagination than they do to Scripture. The image of devils poking people with pitchforks—or otherwise torturing them—is not found in Scripture but in art and in cartoons.

Scripture depicts fallen angels in hell *alongside* fallen humans (Jude 6; Rev. 20:10), not torturing them.

Describing hell, the New Testament uses images like fire (Matt. 13:50; Mark 9:43; Rev. 14:10, 21:8) and being excluded from God's presence (Matt. 8:12, 22:13, 25:30; 2 Thess. 1:9). These give us a way of picturing the next world, but because that world transcends our imagination, we must recognize the limits of the images.

John Paul II stated: "The images of hell that Sacred Scripture presents to us must be correctly interpreted. They show the complete frustration and emptiness of life without God. Rather than a place, hell indicates the state of those who freely and definitively separate themselves from God, the source of all life and joy" (General Audience, July 28, 1999).

Consequently, "The thought of hell—and even less the improper use of biblical images—must not create anxiety or despair, but is a necessary and healthy reminder of freedom" (ibid.).

"Hell's principal punishment consists of eternal separation from God in whom alone man can have the life and happiness for which he was created and for which he longs" (CCC 1057).

We therefore must leave the details of precisely how hell works—where and how the suffering takes place—to God. What is important for us is to recognize the need to ensure that we are united with God, the source of ultimate and eternal happiness.

He Knew Her Not *Until*

CHALLENGE

"Matthew states that Joseph 'knew her [Mary] not until she had borne a son.' This implies that he did have sexual relations with her later."

DEFENSE

This overtaxes the meaning of "until."

The term "until" (Greek, *heōs*) commonly indicated a particular state existed to a certain point, as in "John worked at his desk until five o'clock."

The existing state often changes when the point is reached (thus, at five o'clock, John may go home). But change is not always indicated.

In 2 Samuel 6:23, Saul's daughter Michal scoffed at King David's enthusiasm for the Lord, and we read that she had no child "until" the day of her death. The word in the Septuagint Greek translation of the Old Testament is *heōs*. The passage does not mean Michal had a child after the day of her death. It means she never had children.

We see the same in the New Testament. In Matthew 13:33, Jesus tells a parable in which he says, "The kingdom of heaven is like leaven which a woman took and hid in three measures of flour, till it was all leavened." The use of "till" (*heōs*) does not mean that the leaven was later taken out of the flour.

Similarly, in Matthew 14:22, Jesus is at the Sea of Galilee and "he made the disciples get into the boat and go before him to the other side, while [*heōs*] he dismissed the crowds." This does not mean that the disciples turned around and returned to shore as soon as Jesus dismissed the crowds. They continued their journey to the other side, which resulted in their meeting Jesus as he was walking on the water (Matt. 14:25).

Similarly, in Matthew 1:25, the evangelist's point is that Joseph did not have sex with Mary before Jesus was born. His concern is to emphasize the virgin birth, not to address what happened later. This is consistent with the uses of "until" (*heōs*) documented above.

TIP

Around the year A.D. 383, the Church Father Jerome wrote a work known as *Against Helvidius,* in which he defended the perpetual virginity of Mary. In the course of this work, he gave numerous additional examples where the Greek Bible uses *heōs* ("until") without implying a change in the state of affairs.

Baptism and "Works"

"The Catholic Church teaches a false gospel by saying you need to be baptized. We are saved by faith without works."

Baptism is not a "work." The New Testament teaches—and many Protestants agree—that baptism is important for salvation.

Scripture unambiguously teaches that baptism is important for salvation (see Day 20).

If one accuses Catholics of holding a false gospel because they see baptism as a means of salvation, then one must make the same charge against Orthodox, other Eastern Christians, Anglicans, Lutherans, Methodists, and others. Only a comparatively small group—mostly of Evangelicals—denies baptism a role in salvation.

In fact, one would have to accuse Martin Luther—who popularized the "faith alone" formula—of teaching a false gospel. In his *Small Catechism*, Luther wrote:

Q. What does Baptism give? What good is it?
A. It gives the forgiveness of sins, redeems from death and the Devil, gives eternal salvation to all who believe this, just as God's words and promises declare.

Biblically speaking, baptism is not a "work" that would violate Paul's teaching. He said we are not justified by "works of the law" (Rom. 3:28; Gal. 2:16). This refers to acts done from the belief that you need to fulfill the Mosaic Law (see the question for Day 63). Baptism is not commanded by the Mosaic Law, so it is not a "work of the law."

Some have tried to interpret Paul's reference to "works" as referring to anything that you do, but this is false. Not only would it make his reference to the law superfluous, it would contradict other passages. Jesus exhorted people to "repent and believe in the gospel" (Mark 1:15). Repenting and believing are things you *do*. "Works" can't be anything you do or they would include repenting and having faith.

Others have tried to see works as actions done to earn one's place before God, but undergoing baptism doesn't earn anything. It is simply submitting to what God asks. Suppose you had a fatal disease and a doctor offered to cure you free of charge. All you have to do is submit to treatment. Submitting to treatment would not "earn" your cure.

Will Heaven Be Boring?

CHALLENGE

*"I can't imagine being happy for all eternity in heaven.
Sitting on a cloud playing a harp sounds boring."*

DEFENSE

The reality of heaven transcends human imagination,
and popular images of it are only pointers.

The depiction of robed saints sittting on clouds and playing harps is a modern one. It is found in art and on greeting cards, but it mashes images together in a way not found in the Bible.

Scripture uses many images for heaven. The most fundamental is the sky. John Paul II explained: "In biblical language 'heaven,' when it is joined to the 'earth,' indicates part of the universe. Scripture says about creation: 'In the beginning God created the heavens and the earth' (Gen. 1:1)" (General Audience, July 21, 1999).

The sky, in turn, was used as an image of where God dwells: "Metaphorically speaking, heaven is understood as the dwelling-place of God, who is thus distinguished from human beings (cf. Ps. 104:2–3; 115:16; Isa. 66:1). He sees and judges from the heights of heaven (cf. Ps. 113:4–9) and comes down when he is called upon (cf. Ps. 18:9, 10; 144:5). However, the biblical metaphor makes it clear that God does not identify himself with heaven, nor can he be contained in it (cf. 1 Kings 8:27)" (ibid.).

Scripture uses other images of heaven, though we need to be sensitive to their limitations too. The *Catechism* explains: "This mystery of blessed communion with God and all who are in Christ is beyond all understanding and description. Scripture speaks of it in images: life, light, peace, wedding feast, wine of the kingdom, the Father's house, the heavenly Jerusalem, paradise: 'no eye has seen, nor ear heard, nor the heart of man conceived, what God has prepared for those who love him' (1 Cor. 2:9)" (CCC 1027).

We thus shouldn't be confused by modern images depicting saints sitting on clouds with harps. "In the context of revelation, we know that the 'heaven' or 'happiness' in which we will find ourselves is neither an abstraction nor a physical place in the clouds, but a living, personal relationship with the Holy Trinity. It is our meeting with the Father which takes place in the risen Christ through the communion of the Holy Spirit" (John Paul II, op. cit.).

Killing Innocents

CHALLENGE

"Even if we grant that the unborn are living human beings, that doesn't mean abortion is wrong. Why would it be?"

DEFENSE

A fundamental principle of morality is that you can never deliberately kill an innocent human being. It is a human universal that you cannot slay the innocent. If a society failed to recognize this principle—so its ordinary, innocent members could be killed at will—then that society would descend into anarchy and break apart.

The basic moral intuition that killing innocents is wrong is so strong that when genocides have killed large numbers of innocent people, the killers have had to argue one of two things:

- that the people they were slaughtering were not *really* innocent but guilty of some present or historical wrongdoing, or
- that they were not *really* human but somehow subhuman.

Sometimes both have been argued, as when the Nazis killed millions of Jewish people, claiming that they were subverting German society and that they were racially inferior. The fact that they felt the need for such rationalizations pays tribute to the strength of the basic moral intuition that innocent human beings must not be killed.

This is the fundamental insight that lies behind every society's prohibition on murder.

To deny that we must respect the right to life of every innocent person is to violate a universal human moral norm. It is to embrace an inhuman and fundamentally immoral principle.

Of course, not every form of killing is murder. It is not murder to kill a plant or an animal. Similarly, it may not be murder to kill an aggressor in wartime, or someone who is trying to take your own life. Killing an aggressor in self-defense can be morally permissible.

Yet it is always wrong to deliberately take the life of an innocent human being, which raises the *real* question in the abortion debate: Do the unborn count as innocent human beings? It is clear that they are innocent. The unborn do not have the ability to harm anyone. Few things could be more innocent than an unborn baby in a mother's womb.

The question thus comes down to the issue of whether the unborn are human beings. As we show elsewhere, the scientific evidence is unambiguous that they are (see Day 185).

666 and the Roman Emperors

CHALLENGE

"The pope's title Vicarius Filii Dei *('Vicar of the Son of God') adds up to 666, identifying him as the beast of Revelation."*

DEFENSE

Vicarius Filii Dei is not one of the pope's titles (see Day 175), and a careful study of Revelation shows that the number likely refers to a Roman emperor.

Revelation 13:18 says 666 is the "number of a man" (literal translation). Revelation gives several clues about who this was.

He likely was alive in John's day. Revelation 1:1 and 22:6 say the vision John sees "must soon take place."

The beast has seven heads that represent seven hills (Rev. 17:9), suggesting the city of Rome. The heads also represent seven kings, "five of whom have fallen, one is, the other has not yet come, and when he comes he must remain only a little while" (Rev. 17:10). This suggests the line of first-century Roman emperors.

The beast is associated with the whore of Babylon, who John sees "drunk with the blood of the saints and the blood of the martyrs of Jesus" (Rev. 17:6). This suggest the beast persecuted Christians, which the Roman Empire did.

We are told people worshipped the Beast, which had great military might (Rev. 13:4). The Roman Empire was the dominant military power of the day, and people worshipped the emperor by the Roman imperial cult.

It is thus natural to identify the beast with the line of Roman emperors, and, in a special way, with Nero. In Hebrew and Aramaic, the name "Nero Caesar" (NRWN QSR) adds up to 666 (N+R+W+N+Q+S+R = 50+200+6+50+100+60+200 = 666). A variant spelling (NRW QSR) adds up to 616, and this number is found in some ancient manuscripts of Revelation.

Nero was famous for persecuting Christians, again strengthening his identification with the beast (see the Roman historians Tacitus, *Annals* 15:44, and Suetonius, *Lives of the Twelve Caesars*, "Nero" 16).

In A.D. 68, Nero was declared an enemy of the state by the Roman senate and committed suicide. He was likely one of the five fallen kings of Revelation 17:10. Two of Nero's successors in A.D. 69—Otho and Vitellius—emulated and honored Nero (see Suetonius, "Otho" 7, "Vitellius" 11), making them possible fulfillments of the prophecy of the beast's return after being struck down (Rev. 13:3, 17:8–11).

"Not Because of Works"

CHALLENGE

"Catholic teaching on justification is false. Paul says, 'For by grace you have been saved through faith; and this is not your own doing, it is the gift of God—not because of works, lest any man should boast' (Eph. 2:8–9)."

DEFENSE

This passage does not disagree with Catholic teaching.

Catholics agree we are saved through faith and by grace: "Our justification comes from the grace of God. Grace is favor, the free and undeserved help that God gives us to respond to his call to become children of God" (CCC 1996).

Neither salvation nor faith is our own doing. Both are products of God's grace: "The divine initiative in the work of grace precedes, prepares, and elicits the free response of man" (CCC 2022). "Since the initiative belongs to God in the order of grace, no one can merit the initial grace of forgiveness and justification, at the beginning of conversion" (CCC 2010).

The statement that our salvation "is not of works, lest any man should boast" has often been taken to mean we can't earn our salvation. This is true, as the Church acknowledges: "With regard to God, there is no strict right to any merit on the part of man. Between God and us there is an immeasurable inequality, for we have received everything from him, our Creator" (CCC 2007).

Although we can't earn salvation, this probably isn't what Paul is asserting here. Normally when he refers to "works" in a context like this, he means a specific kind of works: those done to obey the Jewish Law (circumcision, keeping kosher, and so on). His repeated statements that salvation isn't by these kind of works was meant to counter the belief of some first-century Christians that you needed to be a Jew in order to be saved (see Day 63).

That is probably what Paul means here. Thus in the next verse he praises "good works" as part of the Christian life, in preference to the "works" he says do not save us (Eph. 2:10). He then discusses how Gentiles are saved together with Jews, in spite of their uncircumcision (Eph. 2:11–12), and how Jesus has abolished the Law and its commandments so both Jews and Gentiles might be united in one body (Eph. 2:13–16).

TIP

See also the answer for Day 278.

The Good Thief and Purgatory

"Purgatory cannot exist because on the cross, Christ told the good thief, 'Truly, I say to you, today you will be with me in Paradise' (Luke 23:43)."

This assumes that purgatory involves being separated from Jesus and that it takes time.

Purgatory may not involve being separated from Jesus but may be an *encounter* with Jesus.

Paul says our works will be tested by fire, and, if a man's works are burned up, "he will suffer loss, though he himself will be saved, but only as through fire" (1 Cor. 3:15). Commenting on this, Benedict XVI stated:

Some recent theologians are of the opinion that the fire which both burns and saves is Christ himself, the Judge and Savior. The encounter with him is the decisive act of judgment. Before his gaze all falsehood melts away. This encounter with him, as it burns us, transforms and frees us, allowing us to become truly ourselves. All that we build during our lives can prove to be mere straw, pure bluster, and it collapses. Yet in the pain of this encounter, when the impurity and sickness of our lives become evident to us, there lies salvation. His gaze, the touch of his heart heals us through an undeniably painful transformation 'as through fire.' But it is a blessed pain, in which the holy power of his love sears through us like a flame, enabling us to become totally ourselves and thus totally of God (*Spe Salvi* 47).

How long would this take? According to Benedict XVI: "It is clear that we cannot calculate the 'duration' of this transforming burning in terms of the chronological measurements of this world. The transforming 'moment' of this encounter eludes earthly time-reckoning—it is the heart's time" (ibid.).

God can transform a person as quickly as he chooses. Paul speaks of those on the last day being transformed "in the twinkling of an eye" (1 Cor. 15:52). The thief could die with Christ, be transformed by him "in the twinkling of an eye," and be with him in paradise—all on Good Friday.

What Jesus meant by "today" is debatable. The punctuation marks are not in the original Greek, and "today" may refer to *when* Jesus gives the thief the assurance ("Truly, I say to you today") rather than when he will be in paradise.

The Resurrection of Jesus

CHALLENGE

"There's no good evidence that Jesus actually rose from the dead."

DEFENSE

The Resurrection explains the evidence we have
better than any alternative hypothesis does.

According to the Christian message, Jesus was crucified, died, and
was buried. He rose from the dead, his tomb was found empty, and
he appeared to his disciples. Finally, he ascended into heaven in their
presence.

The pivotal claims here are that he died, rose from the dead, and
ascended. The latter is often overlooked, but it was a key part of the
Christian message, both for its theological significance and—for our
present purposes—because it explains why Jesus was no longer walking the streets of Jerusalem.

People saw Jesus die and ascend, but nobody saw him resurrect,
since it happened while he was in the tomb. The evidence the apostles
offered for the Resurrection is that the tomb was found empty and
Jesus began appearing—alive—to the disciples.

How else might one explain the above? Some have proposed that
the disciples lied: They were crooks, stole Jesus' body, and lied about
the Resurrection appearances and the Ascension.

If they didn't lie, how could we explain the empty tomb? Some
have proposed the disciples went to the wrong tomb, that someone
other than the disciples stole the body, or that Jesus didn't die—he just
became unconscious on the cross. That could also explain how he later
appeared to the disciples.

Other proposals for how he could have appeared include that it
wasn't really Jesus who was crucified but an identical twin, that an
impostor afterward appeared to the disciples, or that they simply hallucinated. Some have even proposed that the disciples didn't think the
tomb was empty and that they believed Jesus had been "spiritually"
resurrected.

All these hypotheses are fraught with problems. Most explain *either*
the empty tomb *or* the Resurrection appearances, but not both. Most
also ignore Jesus' Ascension into heaven.

To fix the problems, it could be tempting to combine hypotheses (e.g., the disciples went to the wrong tomb, then hallucinated the
Resurrection appearances), but combined hypotheses inherit problems
from both originals.

In the next few days, we will look at the problems with each of the
alternative theories (see Days 207–215), leading to the conclusion that
Jesus was, indeed, raised from the dead.

The Wrong-Tomb Hypothesis

CHALLENGE

"Why can't we explain the Resurrection by saying that the disciples simply went to the wrong tomb—a tomb that was empty?"

DEFENSE

There are multiple problems with this hypothesis.

First, the Gospels indicate the women who visited the tomb were also eyewitnesses of the burial, and even name the women involved (Matt. 27:61; Mark 15:47; cf. Matt. 28:1, Mark 16:1). The women thus knew where Jesus was buried.

Second, the tomb's location was publicly known. It was in the place where Jesus was crucified (John 19:41–42), so the women merely had to return to the site of the Crucifixion.

Third, the owner of the tomb was known. It was Joseph of Arimathea, who had also performed the burial (Matt. 27:57–60; Mark 15:43–46; Luke 23:50–53; John 19:38–42). If there had been any doubt about the matter, it would have been dispelled by consulting with him.

Fourth, Matthew indicates a guard was placed on the tomb (Matt. 27:62–66), who also served to mark the spot.

Fifth, the wrong-tomb hypothesis at most explains how the disciples could have innocently thought Jesus' tomb was empty on the morning of the Resurrection. However, it implies Jesus' body remained in his own tomb, and once the disciples began proclaiming the Resurrection, the Jewish authorities would simply have gone to the correct tomb—performing a search of recent burials if necessary—and produced Jesus' corpse.

Sixth, this hypothesis does not explain why the disciples would have thought Jesus was resurrected. The disciples were not expecting a resurrection to happen in their own time. They viewed the resurrection of the dead as something that was to happen on the last day (John 6:39–40, 11:24).

Seventh, the Gospels record that when the disciples found the tomb empty they did *not* leap to the conclusion that Jesus had been resurrected. The first interpretation was that someone had moved Jesus' body (John 20:2–13), which was how a Jew who believed in a last-day resurrection would interpret the discovery.

Eighth, the wrong-tomb hypothesis does nothing to explain how the apostles could have innocently thought they saw Jesus alive after the Crucifixion. If Jesus' body was still lying in his tomb, why did the disciples claim to see him, hold conversations with him, and physically interact with him?

The Trick Hypothesis

CHALLENGE
"Why can't we explain the Resurrection by saying someone tricked the disciples? Maybe Jesus was drugged on the cross when he was given a drink (Matt. 27:48; Mark 15:36; John 19:28–30), later he revived, and co-conspirators got him out of the tomb and posed as angels (Matt. 28:2–7; Mark 16:5–7; Luke 24:4–7; John 20:12)."

DEFENSE
Anesthesiology was not a developed science in the first century, and it would be extremely risky to administer a drug to a person who had been severely traumatized and was being crucified. The odds of the drug killing him would be too high.

Further, the Romans checked to ensure Jesus was dead. A soldier plunged a spear into his side, causing a flow of blood and what looked like water (John 19:34). The "water" was likely a clear liquid that had built up in the pleural cavity of the lung, the pericardial sac around the heart, or both. That wound itself would have been fatal.

Who would these conspirators have been? If Jesus was entrusting his survival to them, they must have been very close associates, but then why weren't they among the apostles—Jesus' closest associates? (Remember that the point of this hypothesis is that the apostles were innocently tricked, unlike the hypothesis that they lied; see Day 214.)

Even if they weren't apostles, they would have been close enough associates that the women should have recognized them. (And their clothes wouldn't have been bright white, as the Gospels indicate, after rolling back the stone from the tomb, getting a bloodied Jesus out of his grave clothes, and helping or carrying him from the tomb.)

How did they get past the guard on the tomb (Matt. 27:62–66)? Why would they undertake such a risk? Jesus was a poor man, so what did they get out of it? And why bother to fake a resurrection, when this wasn't something Jews expected to happen until the last day (see Day 213)?

Finally, how did they manage to fake Jesus' Ascension into heaven in front of the apostles (Luke 24:50–51; Acts 1:9–11)? Even if we granted all the previous implausibilities, nobody in the first century had the ability to fly.

The trick hypothesis thus does not explain how the apostles could have innocently thought they saw Jesus ascend after the Crucifixion.

The Swoon Hypothesis

CHALLENGE

"Why can't we explain the Resurrection appearances by saying that Jesus swooned on the cross? After all, Pilate was surprised he 'died' so quickly (Mark 15:44). If Jesus actually revived in the tomb, Pilate and the disciples might have thought he rose from the dead."

DEFENSE

There are multiple problems with this hypothesis.

Jesus did die quickly. Other crucifixion victims lingered for days. However, Jesus was subjected to severe stress and trauma in the hours before the Crucifixion.

This included sleeplessness (Matt. 26:42–46), emotional anguish (Matt. 26:38), being taken to multiple locations for various proceedings (Matt. 26:57, 27:2, 27:31; Luke 23:7, 11; John 18:24), and being physically beaten (Matt. 26:67), scourged (Matt. 27:26), and crowned with thorns (Matt. 27:29). By the end, he was so traumatized he could not carry the cross, so it was carried by Simon of Cyrene (Matt. 27:32).

"The severe scourging, with its intense pain and appreciable blood loss, most probably left Jesus in a preshock state. . . . The physical and mental abuse meted out by the Jews and the Romans, as well as the lack of food, water, and sleep, also contributed to his generally weakened state. Therefore, even before the actual Crucifixion, Jesus' physical condition was at least serious and possibly critical" (see Edwards, 1458, below).

Jesus then underwent the trauma of Crucifixion itself. He may have died due to a sudden cardiac event, as suggested by the loud cry he made immediately before dying (Matt. 27:50; Mark 15:37). Afterward, "one of the soldiers pierced his side with a spear, and at once there came out blood and water" (John 18:34)—the "water" being a clear fluid from the pleural cavity of the lung and/or the pericardial sac surrounding the heart.

If Jesus somehow managed to survive all this, he would not have been able to move the stone and escape his tomb (Mark 16:3), nor would he have been able to ascend into heaven in front of the apostles (Luke 24:51; Acts 1:9–11).

The swoon hypothesis thus does not explain how the apostles could have innocently thought they saw Jesus alive after the Crucifixion.

TIP

On the medical aspects of the Crucifixion, see William D. Edwards, MD, et al., "On the Physical Death of Jesus Christ," *Journal of the American Medical Association*, Mar. 21, 1986, 1455–63 (available online).

The Twin Hypothesis

CHALLENGE

"Why can't we explain the Resurrection appearances by saying Jesus had a twin who was crucified, making the disciples innocently think Jesus was raised? An early Christian text called the Acts of Thomas *says Thomas was Jesus' twin brother (Acts of Thomas 11)."*

DEFENSE

The *Acts of Thomas* is a Gnostic document from the third century. It has no historical value for learning about Jesus' life. It also does *not* claim Thomas was crucified in Jesus' place.

The *Acts of Thomas* claimed Thomas was Jesus' twin because certain Gnostics venerated Thomas. They thus seized on the fact that, in Aramaic, *Thomas* means "twin" and claimed he was Jesus' own twin.

Thomas probably *did* have a twin, leading him to be called "the Twin" (John 11:16, 20:24, 21:2), but it was someone other than Jesus.

Only about 3 in 1,000 births involves identical twins, so it is antecedently very unlikely that Jesus had a twin. When we look at the biblical evidence, this is confirmed. Scripture records Jesus' birth (Matt. 2:1; Luke 2:7), but makes no mention of a twin, as it does on occasions when twins were born (Gen. 25:24–26, 38:27–30). Having a twin—especially an identical twin—is highly unusual and noteworthy, and we would expect it to be mentioned in the accounts of Jesus' birth and infancy.

Further, Thomas was one of the apostles during Jesus' ministry, but if he were Jesus' twin, he would have been his brother, and John makes it clear that "even his brethren did not believe in him" during his ministry (John 7:5).

Also, if Jesus and Thomas were twins, the other apostles would have known it, and the question of who was crucified would have immediately arisen.

While the idea that Thomas was crucified could explain how Jesus appeared alive after the Crucifixion, it would not explain how the two could appear alive *together* (John 20:24–29), or why the Jerusalem authorities didn't go to the tomb and produce Thomas's corpse.

Finally, the twin hypothesis would not explain how the apostles saw Jesus ascend to heaven (Luke 24:51; Acts 1:9–11). Having a twin does not enable you to fly.

The twin hypothesis thus does not explain how the apostles could have innocently thought they saw Jesus alive after the Crucifixion.

The Impostor Hypothesis

CHALLENGE

"The Gospels say the disciples had difficulty recognizing Jesus after the Resurrection (Matt. 28:17; Mark 16:12; Luke 24:13–31; John 20:13–16, 21:4–7). So maybe he was actually replaced by an impostor."

DEFENSE

The passages cited do not support the proposal.

Matthew 28:17 states: "When they saw him they worshiped him; but some doubted." We are not told *what* they doubted. Were they doubting it was Jesus? Were they seeing Jesus but thinking he was a ghost (cf. Luke 24:36–43)? Is this just a way of saying they were amazed? (As when we say, "I can't believe it!" meaning "I'm stunned!") Supposing some did doubt it was Jesus, this was likely because they initially saw him at a distance. The next verse says, "and Jesus *came*" and spoke to them (Matt. 28:18).

Recognizing someone at a distance is frequently difficult, and this is the natural explanation of John 21:4–7, where the disciples are fishing on the Sea of Galilee and Jesus calls to them from the shore. When they arrive on shore and see him up close, John records (to clear up any potential confusion): "None of the disciples dared ask him, 'Who are you?' They knew it was the Lord" (21:12).

Distance may also be involved in John 20:13–16, where Mary Magdalen is weeping and doesn't initially recognize Jesus. The text suggests she got only a brief glimpse amid her tears, but when he said her name, "she turned" (v. 16), got a clear look at him, and recognized him.

Mark 16:12 and Luke 24:13–31 refer to an event where Jesus miraculously kept two from recognizing him. Mark says he appeared "in another form" and Luke indicates they spent time together, but suddenly recognized him when he broke bread in their presence and miraculously vanished.

These passages must be set against those where the disciples immediately recognize Jesus without any questions about his identity (Matt. 28:9; Mark 16:9, 14; Luke 23:34, 36–43; John 20:19–20, 26–28).

Further, it is very improbable that an impostor could convince the disciples he was Jesus. Why would they think someone they'd never seen before was the man they'd spent three years with? If there was an impostor, what was his motive? How was Jesus' body removed from the guarded tomb? And how did the impostor ascend into heaven before the disciples?

The Hallucination Hypothesis

CHALLENGE

"Why can't we explain the Resurrection appearances of Jesus by saying that the disciples innocently hallucinated them all?"

DEFENSE

Hallucinations are normally caused by medical or psychological disorders, so they are experienced by individuals, not groups.

We have no evidence of such disorders among the witnesses of the Resurrection, and—although we have indications of private appearances to Mary Magdalen (Mark 16:9; John 20:14–17), Peter (Luke 24:34; 1 Cor. 15:5), and James the Just (1 Cor. 15:7)—most appearances were to groups (Matt. 28:8–10, 16–20; Mark 16:12–18; Luke 24:13–53; John 20:19–21:23; Acts 1:6–11), including a group of as many as 500 (1 Cor. 15:6).

It is disputed whether true hallucinations are even possible for groups. It is possible for a group to experience an *illusion* (i.e., mistaking something real but poorly seen as something else). Thus a group might mistakenly think a person seen at extreme distance was Jesus, but this doesn't fit the Resurrection appearances.

Instead, the reports indicate Jesus was in close proximity to the disciples, held multiple conversations with them, and physically interacted with them—as when he instructed Thomas to touch his wounds (John 20:27), or when he instructed the disciples to handle him, and when he took a piece of broiled fish from them and ate it (Luke 24:39–43).

Illusions are typically preceded by intense expectation and an uncritical attitude toward what is seen (hallucinations commonly are as well), but we do not have evidence for this among the disciples. The women expect to find Jesus' dead body when they arrive at the tomb, and the male disciples are disbelieving and skeptical (Matt. 28:17; Mark 16:11; Luke 24:10–11; John 20:9, 24–25).

Even if multiple people were hallucinating at the same time, they would not hallucinate the same conversation or see Jesus performing the same, up-close actions.

The Resurrection appearances also happened over an extended period (forty days; Acts 1:3) and then suddenly stopped with Jesus' collectively witnessed Ascension into heaven. This is not characteristic of how hallucinations typically work.

Most fundamentally, the hallucination hypothesis fails to explain why, once the disciples began spreading reports of the Resurrection, the Jerusalem authorities didn't simply go to Jesus' tomb and produce his corpse.

The hallucination hypothesis thus does not explain how the apostles could have innocently thought they saw Jesus alive after the Crucifixion.

The Spiritual Resurrection Hypothesis

CHALLENGE

"Why can't we explain the Resurrection appearances in purely spiritual terms? Paul says that at the general resurrection, people will have a 'spiritual body' (1 Cor. 15:44). What if the disciples simply saw visions and concluded from them that Jesus had been spiritually resurrected?"

DEFENSE

The term "spiritual body" (Greek, *sōma pneumatikon*) does not mean an immaterial body but rather a supernaturally transformed body.

That's why Paul compares the body to a seed that is sown in the ground and then becomes an adult plant (1 Cor. 15:35–44). The plant is the direct continuation of the seed, and the "spiritual body" of the resurrection is the direct continuation of the body we have in this life. Consequently, resurrection does not leave a body in the tomb, and all four of the Gospels stress that Jesus' tomb was empty (Matt. 28:6; Mark 16:6; Luke 24:5; John 20:1–6).

Further, the disciples believed consciousness continued beyond death in a disembodied state. When they saw Jesus walking on the water at night, they initially thought it was a ghost (Matt. 14:26; Mark 6:49). Yet they did not regard disembodied existence as the resurrection—a re-embodiment they believed would occur on the last day (John 6:39–40, 11:24).

Jesus' Resurrection was thus unexpected. When the tomb was discovered empty, the disciples' initial interpretation was that someone had moved the body (John 20:2–13). Only with the Resurrection appearances did they realize something miraculous happened.

Even then, when Jesus appeared to them, they fell back on the next plausible hypothesis, given their worldview, that they were seeing a ghost (Luke 24:37). However, Jesus demonstrated that he was bodily alive, telling them: "See my hands and my feet, that it is I myself; handle me, and see; for a spirit has not flesh and bones as you see that I have" (Luke 24:39; cf. 24:41–43, John 20:24–27).

The disciples thus proclaimed Jesus was bodily resurrected. They did not believe in a "spiritual resurrection" that would leave his body in the tomb.

The spiritual resurrection hypothesis thus does not explain how the apostles could have innocently thought they saw Jesus alive after the Crucifixion.

TIP

For a sustained refutation of the idea of Jesus experiencing a merely spiritual resurrection, see N. T. Wright, *The Resurrection of the Son of God.*

The Stolen Body Hypothesis

CHALLENGE

"The disciples stole Jesus' body and lied about the Resurrection appearances."

DEFENSE

This does not fit the data, particularly of the apostles' later careers.

Matthew reports that the tomb was guarded, that the Jewish authorities paid the guards to say the disciples stole the body after they fell asleep, and that this story was circulating in the Jewish community (Matt. 28:11–15). That Matthew responds to the charge indicates it was viewed as the most plausible alternative to the Resurrection.

However, that doesn't mean it was likely. Guards were paid *not* to fall asleep and faced severe disciplinary action if they did (cf. Matt. 28:14), including death (Acts 12:18–19, cf. 16:27). Further, if the guards were asleep, how did they know what the disciples did? Having previously run away when Jesus was arrested (Matt. 26:56), why would the disciples tiptoe around sleeping guards and risk waking them and being caught and executed? Finally, the guards' report indicates their complicity with the Jewish authorities. If the authorities hadn't bribed the guards, why didn't they complain to Pilate about the guards' dereliction of duty? The stolen body hypothesis is not plausible on its face.

Even more serious problems emerge when considering the later careers of the apostles. They experienced serious hardship because of their testimony to Jesus and his Resurrection. The book of Acts alone records they and other Christian leaders faced numerous incidents of arrest and imprisonment (Acts 4:1–3, 5:18, 6:12, 8:3, 9:1–2, 16:19–24, 21:33–34), beating (Acts 5:40, 16:22–23, 21:32, 23:2), torture (Acts 22:24–25), mob violence (Acts 16:22, 17:5–6, 13, 19:23–41, 21:27–30, 23:10), and both attempted an actual martyrdom (Acts 7:58–60, 9:23, 29, 12:1–4, 14:5, 19, 23:12–13, 25:2–3). Other New Testament books confirm these dangers (cf., e.g., 2 Cor. 11:23–27), as do the writings of the Church Fathers.

On repeated occasions, the apostles could have avoided them by denying the message of Jesus—or even just ceasing to preach it—yet the apostles defied orders to stop preaching (Acts 4:18–19, 5:27–32, 40–42) and even remained in Jerusalem when other Christians fled under violent persecution (Acts 8:1).

Their enduring of repeated, extreme hardships and—ultimately—martyrdom for the message of Jesus does not suggest they were a bunch of crooks who stole the body and then lied, but that they were honest and profoundly convinced of what they had witnessed.

Combined Hypotheses

CHALLENGE

"Why can't we explain the Resurrection by combining hypotheses, such as proposing the disciples went to the wrong tomb and then hallucinated?"

DEFENSE

Combined hypotheses avoid some problems but inherit problems from both original hypotheses.

The challenge may explain the empty tomb, Resurrection appearances, and Ascension, but it inherits problems from both the wrong tomb and hallucination hypotheses. From the wrong tomb hypothesis (see Day 207), it inherits the facts that:

- Specific, named women saw where Jesus was buried and returned to find the tomb empty.
- Jesus' burial site was public—it was where he was crucified, so the women merely had to go back to the site of the Crucifixion.
- The owner of the tomb and the man who performed the burial (Joseph of Arimathea) was known and would have cleared up any confusion.
- There were guards marking the place of burial.
- Once the disciples started preaching the Resurrection, the Jewish authorities would have gone to the correct tomb—performing a search of recent burials if necessary—and produced Jesus' corpse.
- Jews did not expect resurrection to occur in their own time but on the last day.
- The latter point is strengthened because the disciples initially *did not* think Jesus was resurrected but that his body had been moved.

From the hallucination hypothesis (see Day 212), it inherits:

- Multiple people would not hallucinate the same conversation or physical interaction with Jesus.
- We have no evidence that the witnesses to Resurrection appearances had the kinds of mental disorders that produce hallucinations.
- It is disputed whether hallucinations are even possible for groups.
- We can't explain the Resurrection appearances as an illusion caused by seeing something unclearly at a distance.
- The Gospels show disciples in the wrong frame of mind to experience illusions and hallucinations.
- We wouldn't expect the hallucinations to occur for forty days and suddenly stop with the collective event of the Ascension.
- The Jewish authorities would have simply produced Jesus' corpse.

Religion and War

CHALLENGE

"Religion is inherently violent, producing countless wars."

DEFENSE

This claim does not withstand scrutiny.

War is not unique to humanity. Other species—including ants, bees, and chimpanzees—wage war, understood as the organized, collective use of lethal violence against external enemies (such as for control of territory). Yet these species do not have religion. War's roots are thus non-religious.

Religion is a human universal, and historically there have been *no* atheist societies. It is thus impossible to argue that non-religious societies were less violent than religious ones. The officially atheist societies that arose in the Communist world in the twentieth century were not more peaceful than others. They warred, exported revolution, and killed tens of millions of people, including their own citizens.

If religion predisposed people to violence, we should see this on the small scale, yet violent criminals don't usually seem to be devout churchgoers.

Like non-religious viewpoints, religions have differing attitudes toward violence, ranging from advocating violence for a variety of causes to advocating it only in self-defense to thoroughgoing pacifism. One cannot tar all religious viewpoints with the same brush. If religion can inspire people to kill, it can also inspire them to refrain from killing ("You shall not kill," Exod. 20:13; "Love your enemies," Matt. 5:44).

Similarly, if lack of religious zealotry deprives one non-religious person of a motive to kill, another non-religious person may go on to slay because he is not constrained by religious values against killing.

Ultimately, religions don't go to war. Governments do, and they usually must convince an ambivalent populace of their decision to do so. In this, they may use religion as a motivating factor (whether or not the religion of the enemies is different), but that doesn't make religion the cause of war.

Often wars are fought when there is no difference in religion. In the bloodiest war in U.S. history—the Civil War—the North and the South had the same religion.

Most wars are not fought over religious goals such as converting, subjugating, or killing people because they have a different religion. Instead, they are fought over secular goals such as control of territory and resources, self-determination, defending national prestige, or seeking revenge for perceived wrongs.

TIP

For more, see the book *The Myth of Religious Violence* by William Cavanaugh.

The Date of Luke

CHALLENGE

*"Luke's Gospel isn't reliable. It was written long
after the events, and Luke was not an eyewitness."*

DEFENSE

Luke's Gospel was written within living memory of the events
that it records, and it is based on eyewitness testimony.

We elsewhere discuss the fact that Luke wasn't an eyewitness (see Day 44). Biographies are commonly written by people who aren't eyewitnesses, and Luke was in an especially good position as a biographer because he consulted eyewitnesses (Luke 1:2).

Raymond Brown proposed a late date for Luke and Acts of "85, give or take five to ten years" (*An Introduction to the New Testament*, 226, 280). If so, Luke would have been written a little more than fifty years after the ministry of Jesus, which was within living memory.

However, Luke was probably written earlier. The key to identifying when is its relationship with the book of Acts. Luke and Acts were written as a two-volume set, the first of which covered Jesus' life and ministry and the second of which covered the history of the Church up to the time Acts was written.

The fact that they are meant as companion works is indicated by several factors: (1) Acts picks up exactly where Luke leaves off (compare Acts 1:1–2 with Luke 24:44–52). (2) Both are dedicated to the same man—Theophilus—who was apparently Luke's patron (Luke 1:1–4, Acts 1:1). (3) Acts refers to the Gospel of Luke as "the first book" (Acts 1:1), implying that Acts is the second in the set.

This indicates that Luke was written earlier than Acts, and we have a very good idea of when Acts was written. Luke apparently completed it during the second year of Paul's first imprisonment in Rome (see Day 79). Most hold that Paul's imprisonment began in A.D. 60, though a careful reading of the evidence suggests it was in A.D. 58 (see Jack Finegan, *Handbook of Biblical Chronology*, 2nd ed., and Andrew Steinmann, *From Abraham to Paul*). Acts would then be written in A.D. 60, and Luke's Gospel was written before that.

It is probable, given their dedication to the same man and the fact that the end of Luke seems to envision the beginning of Acts, that Luke was written only shortly before Acts, in A.D. 59, less than thirty years after Jesus' ministry.

Christian Hypocrisy

"Christians are a bunch of hypocrites."

DEFENSE

Yes. And?

Consciousness of the fact that we don't think and act the way we should is a human universal. So is the desire for others to think well of us. Everyone wishes to save face and, at one time or another, either shades the truth or flat out lies to appear better than he is. This makes hypocrisy another human universal, and it applies to Christians and everyone else.

When confronted with the fact that we don't live up to our moral standards, we have several options. One—which is not good at all—is to abandon our standards. Reviewing them to make sure they are correct is one thing, but tossing them aside so we can indulge in immoral behavior is another. It also will not work in the long run, for we cannot escape the moral law written on our hearts. We can only temporarily suppress it.

A second choice—also not good—is to pretend we are better than we are. This is the option of hypocrisy. It is not good because it's an offense against the truth. Hypocrisy is a form of lying—specifically, lying about our own behavior, using either words or deceptive actions (CCC 2483). Hypocrisy is also risky, because in the long run the truth tends to be found out, and people will see you for the hypocrite you are. For Christians, hypocrisy takes on added gravity because it can push people away from God (Rom. 2:23–24).

The third choice—and the only good one—is the hardest. It means maintaining our moral standards, being honest about the fact that we don't live up to them and seeking God's grace to do better in the future. This doesn't mean telling everyone everything we've done wrong (CCC 2489). Frequently, it is none of their concern, and in some situations knowing could even hurt them (e.g., marriages can be harmed by a naive and imprudent sharing of information about one's sexual failings). However, it does mean being humble and willing to admit the fact that we are sinners.

Christians may share the universal inclination to hypocrisy, but that doesn't mean Christianity is false. Christianity teaches that we are all sinners. The good news is that there is mercy, even for hypocrites like us.

"Our God and Savior, Jesus Christ"

CHALLENGE

"Passages like Titus 2:13 and 2 Peter 1:1, which refer to 'Our God and Savior, Jesus Christ,' do not prove the divinity of Christ. The authors are referring to God and Jesus separately."

DEFENSE

That's not how New Testament Greek grammar works.

In 1798, the Englishman Granville Sharp published a book in which he identified a rule of Greek grammar that has since become known as Granville Sharp's rule. It has a direct bearing on the interpretation of Titus 2:13 and 2 Peter 1:1.

The rule focuses on New Testament Greek phrases like the one translated "Our God and Savior," and it shows that the two nouns in these phrases *always* refer to the same person when certain conditions are met. The conditions are:

1. In Greek, the phrase begins with the definite article (i.e., the Greek equivalent of "the").
2. The nouns are joined by the Greek equivalent of "and" (*kai*).
3. The nouns are personal, singular, and not proper names.

There are more than eighty instances of this construction in the New Testament, and they *all* obey Granville Sharp's rule. Examples include:

- "Is not this the carpenter, *the son* of Mary *and brother* of James" (Mark 6:13).
- "I am ascending to my *Father and* your *Father*" (John 20:17).
- "Tychicus *the* beloved *brother and* faithful *minister*" (Eph. 6:21).
- "Jesus, *the apostle and high priest* of our confession" (Heb. 3:1).
- "Blessed be *the God and Father* of our Lord Jesus Christ" (1 Pet. 1:3).

Not all of these contain "the" in the English translation (Greek uses the definite article more than English does, so it is not always translated), but it is there in the Greek. The same is true of the phrases found in Titus 2:13 and 2 Peter 1:1. They are:

- *Tou* megalou *theou kai sotēros* hēmōn Iēsou Christou ("Our great *God and Savior*, Jesus Christ"; Titus 2:13)
- *Tou theou* hēmōn *kai sotēros* Iēsou Christou ("Our *God and Savior*, Jesus Christ"; 2 Pet. 1:1)

Both these passages thus directly affirm the divinity of Christ.

"Give Us Barabbas!"

CHALLENGE

"The Gospels' claim that Pilate customarily released a criminal at Passover is fiction. We have no records of this ever happening."

DEFENSE

We do have records: the four Gospels.

We don't have an extrabiblical record that says, "Pilate customarily released a prisoner at Passover," but that's hardly surprising. Releasing a prisoner at the Jewish capital on a Jewish feast would be a purely local custom, and we don't have detailed records of the Roman administration in Judaea. The surviving sources are too patchy for that.

However, leaders often pardon popular prisoners to curry favor with their subjects. That happens today, even with political prisoners considered a danger to the established regime (e.g., Gandhi, Nelson Mandela, Martin Luther King Jr.).

Further, we have records of ancient rulers in Judaea releasing prisoners to win favor. Both Herod Archelaus (4 B.C.–A.D. 6) and the Roman governor Albinus (A.D. 62–64) did so (Josephus, *Antiquities* 17:8:4[204–205], 20:9:5[215]).

Also, the Jewish Mishnah contains provisions for slaughtering the Passover lamb for prisoners to be released at Passover (*m. Pesahim* 8:6).

Passover was a time when Jewish religious and national feeling ran high, and riots were known to break out in Jerusalem then (*Antiquities* 17:9:3[213–218], 20:5:3[106–112]), so releasing a prisoner to pacify the populace could be quite reasonable. (In fact, Matthew records a riot began to break out when Pilate dithered about releasing Barabbas; Matt. 27:24).

Even if we didn't know all that, the Gospels are historical records in their own right, and if even one of them mentioned the custom, it would need to be taken seriously. But the custom is mentioned in *all four* Gospels (Matt. 27:15; Mark 15:6; Luke 23:18; John 18:39), which adds weight in several ways:

- If, as many think, John wrote independently of the synoptics (not my view), we would have a second and clearly independent source attesting the custom.
- Even if John knew the synoptics (my view), he was an eyewitness, as was Matthew, meaning we have two eyewitnesses reporting it.
- If the custom didn't exist, this would subject the evangelists to criticism. The first evangelist to write wouldn't be inclined to invent the custom, and later evangelists wouldn't be inclined to repeat it. The fact that it appears in all four makes the report especially credible.

Born Atheists?

*"Babies don't believe in God. They are born atheists.
So atheism is the natural condition of mankind."*

This claim is based on a misunderstanding of what atheism is.

People can have a number of attitudes toward any proposition:

- They may never have considered the proposition.
- They may have considered it but neither affirm nor deny it.
- They may affirm the proposition.
- They may deny the proposition.

More specific attitudes are also possible based on how strongly one affirms or denies a proposition (e.g., holding that it is certain, all but certain, very likely, likely, somewhat likely, equiprobable, somewhat unlikely, unlikely, and so on), but these four general attitudes are sufficient for our present purposes.

If we relate them to the proposition "God exists," the following positions emerge:

1. Those who have never considered whether God exists (alogism)
2. Those who don't know whether God exists (agnosticism)
3. Those who affirm that God exists (theism)
4. Those who deny that God exists (atheism)

When these distinctions are made, it's clear to which category babies belong. They have never considered whether God exists—a position we may call *alogism* (Greek, *a,* "not" and *logizomai,* "consider"). Indeed, they belong to the category of alogists by necessity, for they don't have the conceptual apparatus needed to understand the proposition "God exists." Even if someone explained the concept of God's existence to them, they wouldn't understand what was being said.

Atheism involves the denial of God's existence. Therefore, it is a category mistake to claim that babies are atheists. They aren't even agnostics but "alogists."

The claim that atheism is mankind's natural state is also undermined by the fact that religion is a human universal (see Day 313). Historically, there have been *no* non-religious societies. Indeed, recent research indicates that, as children's cognitive powers develop, they are predisposed toward religious faith.

"Justification by Faith and Works"

CHALLENGE

"The Catholic Church is wrong to say we're justified by faith and works."

DEFENSE

The Church doesn't use "by faith and works"
as an overall summary of how we are justified.

It's not to be denied that some individual Catholics do this, but that's not the same thing as the Magisterium of the Church doing it:

- The Church's most authoritative and key historical document on justification is the Council of Trent's Decree on Justification, and the phrase "justified by faith and works" never appears in it.
- The Church's most important and authoritative presentation of the faith as a whole is the *Catechism of the Catholic Church*, and the relevant phrase doesn't appear in it either.
- The Church's most important and detailed contemporary discussion of justification is the Joint Declaration on the Doctrine of Justification, together with the Church's official response and the annex (all available online), and the phrase appears in none of these.
- The phrase appears nowhere on the Vatican website (Vatican.va).

That the Church does not use the phrase "justified by faith and works" is indication that the discussion has been misframed by both individual Catholics and individual Protestants. The reported phrases simply *aren't used* in the Church's official documents.

So what does the Church say? How does it handle the famous passage saying "man is justified by works and not by faith alone" (James 2:24)?

It's dealt with in chapter 10 of Trent's Decree on Justification, which discusses the increase in righteousness Christians experience after their initial justification. According to Trent, after we first come to God and are forgiven, we continue to grow in righteousness (justification) by cooperating with God's grace and performing good works (Eph. 2:10). It's with respect to this *ongoing justification* that the Church holds good works have a role to play (see also Days 312 and 354).

With respect to initial justification, "none of those things that precede justification, whether faith or works, merit the grace of justification" (Decree on Justification 8). Good works therefore flow from, but do not cause, our initial justification.

It's misleading for Catholics to say we're justified by "faith and works," because to Protestant ears this will mean we need good works to be forgiven, which we don't.

Purgatory and the Work of Christ

CHALLENGE

"Purgatory contradicts the finished work of Christ. If Christ paid for all our sins on the cross, there is nothing left to be done."

DEFENSE

Christ's work is finished, but it's not applied all at once.

Christ died on the cross "once for all" (Heb. 10:10), but the resulting grace is applied to us over the course of the Christian life.

Sometimes, a grace is given to us instantaneously. When we first come to God to be forgiven and justified, we receive these graces instantaneously.

But even after being forgiven and justified, we still struggle with sin and its consequences. Although it is God's will that the eternal consequences of our sins be forgiven, Christian experience shows that it is not his will that we be made perfect all in a flash.

Throughout the Christian life, we continue to struggle with sin and, by God's grace, to grow in holiness. This happens through the process known as *sanctification*. Thus Paul prays, "May the God of peace himself sanctify you wholly; and may your spirit and soul and body be kept sound and blameless at the coming of our Lord Jesus Christ" (1 Thess. 5:23).

Many people die in God's friendship rather than in mortal sin, but few of us have been fully freed from sin and its consequences. Consequently, we need to be purified before we enter heaven—for Scripture tells us that "nothing unclean shall enter it" (Rev. 21:27).

Heaven is being fully united with God, and since he is infinitely holy, nothing that is still impure can be fully united with him. Consequently, Scripture exhorts us to seek "the holiness without which no one will see the Lord" (Heb. 12:14).

If nothing impure enters heaven then, between death and heaven, there must be a purification. As the final purification of the elect, purgatory can be thought of as simply the final stage of sanctification, where we are fully freed and liberated from sin and its consequences.

Rather than conflicting with the finished work of Christ, the process of sanctification—and its final stage, purgatory—is an outgrowth of Christ's work. It is one of the ways his grace is applied to us.

Mary's Savior

CHALLENGE

"Mary says, 'My spirit rejoices in God my Savior' (Luke 1:47). This means that she was a sinner and couldn't have been immaculately conceived."

DEFENSE

God can save a person in multiple ways, and Mary was saved by God in more than one sense.

Salvation from the eternal consequences of sin only comes into focus with the ministry of Jesus. Prior to this, the Bible is overwhelmingly concerned with salvation from temporal calamities (war, disease, famine, death, and so on). We may refer to this as temporal salvation.

This seems to be what Mary has in mind. She says she rejoices in God her Savior, *"for* he has regarded the low estate of his handmaiden—for behold, henceforth all generations will call me blessed; for he who is mighty has done great things for me." God has thus saved her from a low estate and given her an exalted one to be remembered and honored forever.

This is reinforced as Mary then lists multiple kinds of temporal salvation ("He has scattered the proud in the imagination of their hearts, he has put down the mighty from their thrones, and exalted those of low degree; he has filled the hungry with good things, and the rich he has sent empty away. He has helped his servant Israel" Luke 1:51–54). It is also suggested by the parallel canticle in which Zechariah proclaims the praise of God as temporal Savior (Luke 1:68–75).

There is also a sense in which God saves Mary from sin: He saved her *from ever contracting it.* Theologians sometimes compare the way God rescued Mary from sin to stopping a person from falling into a pit as opposed to pulling him out of a pit. Both can be described as saving a person from a pit, but which would you prefer?

Being saved from ever committing sin is a more excellent form of salvation than rescuing a person from sin *after* he has fallen into it. Thus Mary was redeemed, in view of what Christ would do on the cross, in a way that prevented her from falling into sin, and so the *Catechism* refers to her as "the most excellent fruit of redemption" (CCC 508).

TIP

See Jimmy Akin, *The Drama of Salvation,* for more on temporal salvation.

The Time and Place of the Ascension

CHALLENGE

"The Gospel of Luke contradicts Acts on the Ascension. Luke says it happened at Bethany on the same day as the Resurrection; Acts says it happened on the Mount of Olives forty days after."

DEFENSE

Neither is a contradiction.

First, let's look at the texts involved in the place of the Ascension:

> Then he led them out as far as Bethany . . . and was carried up into heaven (Luke 24:50–51).
>   He was lifted up, and a cloud took him out of their sight. . . . Then they returned to Jerusalem from the mount called Olivet (Acts 1:9, 12).

This solution simply requires a little knowledge of the geography around Jerusalem: Bethany was *on* the Mount of Olives (*aka* Mount Olivet). The "most frequently mentioned town of this name [is] located on the [East] slopes of the Mount of Olives" (*Anchor Yale Bible Dictionary*, s.v., "Bethany (Place)").

You can tell this simply by reading Luke. Just before the Triumphal Entry, we read: "When he drew near to Bethphage and *Bethany, at the mount that is called Olivet*, he sent two of the disciples (Luke 19:29, emphasis added)."

Second, regarding the time of the Ascension, Luke's Gospel records events taking place on the day of the Resurrection (Luke 24:1ff) and then advances to the Ascension without mentioning the gap of time between them.

Luke merely says "Then he led them out as far as Bethany," without specifying how much time transpired before the word "then"—a term that merely means the Ascension took place at some point after the events that preceded it. This is the kind of chronological approximation expected in ancient literature (see Day 258).

It so happens that in Acts Luke clarifies the matter and indicates how long after the Resurrection the Ascension took place (Acts 1:3). He also expected his Gospel to be read in light of Acts. That's why he referred Theophilus back to the Gospel, calling it "the first book" (Acts 1:1). The fact that both books were written by the same author and intended as companion works means they should be read in light of each other.

There is no contradiction here. The objection simply expects more chronological detail than the ancient audience did.

Peter's Denials

CHALLENGE

"The Gospels contradict one another regarding Peter's three denials: (1) Mark has the cock crowing twice, but the other Gospels only once; (2) the dialogue used by Peter and his accusers differs; and (3) the people making the accusations are different."

DEFENSE

None of these involve contradictions.

First, roosters crow multiple times at every dawn. Mark 14:72 mentions the second crowing specifically, and the others streamline the account for simplicity (see Day 37).

Second, no transcriptionist was present, and the dialogue is based on Peter and John's memories (they being the only disciples present). It involves normal paraphrase and reconstruction within the limits of verbal approximation in ancient documents (see Day 258).

Third, although an ancient author would have been within his rights to simply reconstruct the accusations prompting the three denials—which are what would have been principally remembered—the Gospels recount details indicating eyewitnesses' memories.

Thus all four Gospels state Peter's first denial occurred after he was accused by a female servant, and John indicates it was the one who kept the door (Matt. 26:69; Mark 14:66–67; Luke 22:56; John 18:17).

Peter's second denial was prompted by a group accusation. John says "they" made it (John 18:25), while Mark mentions that "the maid" (apparently the first maid) identified Peter "to the bystanders" (Mark 14:69) and Matthew mentions "another maid" spoke "to the bystanders" (Matt. 26:71), one of whom—a man—accused Peter more directly (Luke 22:58).

Peter's third denial was also prompted by a group, which Matthew and Mark describe as "the bystanders" (Matt. 26:73; Mark 14:70). Luke indicates another person—again a man—accused Peter more directly (Luke 22:59–60), and John indicates it was "one of the servants of the high priest, a kinsman of the man whose ear Peter had cut off" (John 18:26).

Only the first denial is preceded by an accusation by a single person (the door maid), and as the idea begins to spread through the group, the latter two denials are preceded by accusations that at least two of the Gospels say involved groups (Matthew, Mark, and John in the case of the second denial and Matthew and Mark in the case of the third).

We thus see evidence that a real historical event is being recounted in keeping with the literary conventions of the time.

'Elohim and the Gods

CHALLENGE

"The Old Testament teaches polytheism. Genesis says that 'elohim (Hebrew for 'gods') created the world."

DEFENSE

Context makes it clear this refers to a single God.

Hebrew has different words for "God/god." These include *'el, 'eloah,* and *'elohim.* The first two have a singular grammatical form, while *'elohim* has a plural grammatical form (indicated by the *–im* ending).

However, grammatical form doesn't determine meaning. Usage does. Consequently, many languages have words used differently than their grammatical form would suggest.

Thus the English word "species" has a plural grammatical form (note the *–ies* ending, found on plural words like *babies, cities,* and *parties*). But species can refer either to several types of animals (e.g., types of lions, tigers, and bears) or just one (e.g., a type of lion). Despite its plural form, species can be *used* in either a singular or a plural fashion, as in sentences like:

1. This species is carnivorous, which means it eats meat.
2. These species are mammalian, so they have warm blood.

The way to tell whether species is being used in a singular or plural fashion is to examine the context—specifically, the pronouns and verbs used with it. In the first sentence, the singular pronouns (this, it) and verbs (is, eats) show it is referring to just one species. In the second sentence, the plural pronouns (these, they) and verbs (are, have) show it's referring to more than one.

This is how *'elohim* works in Hebrew: It has a plural grammatical form, but it can be used to refer either to the one true God or to multiple gods, and context tells you which. In Genesis 1:1 ("In the beginning God created the heavens and the earth") the verb for "created" (Hebrew, *bara'*) is singular, indicating that here *'elohim* is being used to mean God, not gods. This understanding is confirmed by the verbs in the verses that follow. In 1:3, where God says "Let there be light," the verb for "says" (*yo'mer*) is singular. In 1:4, when God sees the light is good, the verb for "saw" (*yar'*) is also singular, and so on. Similarly, in 1:27, when God creates man in his image, the pronoun for "his" (*hu'*) is singular.

Consequently, Genesis 1 teaches that a single Creator God, not a pantheon of gods, made the world.

Justification Past, Present, and Future

CHALLENGE

"The idea we can be justified at different points in our lives makes no sense."

DEFENSE

Scripture unambiguously teaches that justification has past, present, and future dimensions.

The term "justify" (Greek, *dikaoō*) means to declare or make someone righteous. In the Protestant community, it is normal to think of justification only as an event at the beginning of the Christian life. And Scripture does sometimes speak of justification as a past event: "You *were justified* in the name of the Lord Jesus Christ" (1 Cor. 6:11b).

But Scripture also speaks of justification as a future event when we stand before God:

- "It is not the hearers of the law who are righteous before God, but the doers of the law who *will be justified*" (Rom. 2:13).
- "No human being *will be justified* in his sight by works of the law" (Rom. 3:20).
- "We *wait for* the hope of righteousness" (Greek, *elipida dikaiosunēs*, "the hope of righteousness/justification"; Gal. 5:5).

We also see multiple dimensions of justification in how the New Testament authors discuss Abraham, who must have been justified in at least three ways:

- Abraham pleased God (Heb. 11:2) and thus was justified when he followed God's command and left his homeland (Heb. 11:8–9); this was in the early stages of his career, corresponding to Genesis 12.
- Abraham was justified or reckoned righteous when he believed God that he would have descendants (Rom. 4:1–4, James 2:23), corresponding to Genesis 15:6.
- Abraham was also justified when he offered Isaac on the altar (James 2:21), corresponding to Genesis 22.

Scripture thus indicates that Abraham was justified at different stages of his walk with God, including Genesis 12, 15, and 22. This means that we can't conceive of justification simply as an event that occurs at the beginning of the Christian life. It is an event that has an initial dimension that is then furthered as we grow with God and that will finally be complete when we stand before God on the last day (see Days 257 and 274).

Self-Authenticating Scriptures?

CHALLENGE

"We don't need the Church to help us identify Scripture. God's word is self-authenticating."

DEFENSE

This makes for good rhetoric but does not stand up to examination.

The word of God is powerful (Ps. 33:6; Eph. 6:17; Heb. 4:12), but this does not mean it is self-authenticating. Scripture records that even prophets could be mistaken about whether a word they heard came from God (1 Sam. 3:2–9).

Taken literally, the claim that Scripture is self-authenticating would mean that the text of Scripture has certain qualities that prove it to be (that is, authenticate it as) the word of God. What might these be?

According to the Westminster Confession of Faith, "the heavenliness of the matter [in the Bible], the efficacy of the doctrine, the majesty of the style, the consent of all the parts, the scope of the whole (which is to give all glory to God), the full discovery it makes of the only way of man's salvation, the many other incomparable excellencies, and the entire perfection thereof, are arguments whereby it doth abundantly evidence itself to be the Word of God" (1:5). This is stirring rhetoric, but it can't be cashed out in practical terms:

- It is impossible to state a list of objective literary qualities that characterize *all* the books of the Bible and *only* the books of the Bible.
- Even if one did so, one would need to argue *why* this collection of qualities shows it to be the word of God.
- And why couldn't someone write new literature that *also* displayed those qualities? If so, such writings would also self-authenticate as the word of God and would be new scriptures.

For a closed canon, one thus would need to specify a set of literary qualities that not only marked out the Bible as unique and as the word of God but that would also be impossible to duplicate.

This is not possible, as shown by the fact that nobody really applies this test. Those who claim Scripture is self-authenticating (including the authors of the Westminster Confession; see Day 236) end up appealing to factors *other than* the text, such as the witness of the Holy Spirit, meaning that the text is not *self*-authenticating.

A Quantum Mechanical Argument

CHALLENGE
"Modern physics undermines belief in the existence of God."

DEFENSE
On the contrary, modern physics supports the existence of God.

Quantum mechanics is a branch of physics that studies very small phenomena like the behavior of subatomic particles. According to some interpretations of quantum mechanics, an argument supporting God's existence may be constructed as follows:

1. The universe contains phenomena that appear to require a conscious observer to achieve a definite state.
2. These phenomena achieve definite states.
3. Therefore, there are conscious observers.
4. There cannot be an infinite regress of physical observers.
5. Therefore, there was a first physical observer.
6. The first physical observer cannot have actualized its own existence.
7. Therefore, a non-physical observer actualized it.
8. That non-physical observer is God.
9. Therefore, God exists.

The premises of this argument are lines 1, 2, 4, 6, and 8. The conclusions (lines 3, 5, 7, and 9) follow from them.

Line 1 is a finding of quantum mechanics. Nobel Prize-winning physicist Eugene Wigner wrote: "It was not possible to formulate the laws of quantum mechanics in a fully consistent way without reference to consciousness" (*Symmetries and Reflections*, 172). A famous non-technical illustration is Schrödinger's cat (a thought experiment in which a cat is not definitely alive or dead until it is observed).

Line 2 is established by experiment. Line 4 is supported by the fact that the known history of the universe would not allow life, and thus conscious physical observers, to exist before a certain point.

Line 6 is based on the fact that the first conscious physical observer would need to be in a definite state—actually alive—in order to observe things in the world. It is also based on the metaphysical principle that nothing that could be otherwise (such as a physical observer who did not previously exist) is its own cause. This is also verified by experience. We do not see things causing themselves in the world.

Line 8 is based on the conception of God as the Supreme Being who is ultimately responsible for life. This fits with the idea of a non-physical observer being responsible for the first physical observer being actually alive.

Objections to the Quantum Mechanical Argument

CHALLENGE

"The quantum mechanical argument is flawed: (1) There are other interpretations of quantum mechanics; (2) there could be more than one initial physical observer; (3) the first physical observer could be actualized by a physical observer from another universe; (4) a non-physical observer other than God could actualize the first physical observer; and (5) God doesn't observe things the way we do."

DEFENSE

None of these objections overturn the quantum mechanical argument.

First, there are different interpretations of quantum mechanics, but this is a legitimate interpretation that cannot be eliminated on scientific grounds.

Second, the odds of two or more initial conscious physical observers becoming actual at the same moment is very improbable. Even if it happened, some observer would still have to make them actually alive. Saying they simultaneously observed one another at the first moment of their existence—a causal loop—would be improbable and wouldn't explain why the loop exists rather than not.

Third, physical observers from another universe only kicks the problem back a step. How did physical observers become actually *there*? Without an infinite regress of such universes (for which we have no evidence and which would create its own problems), we would still need a non-physical observer to start the process.

Fourth, non-divine observers not made of physical matter/energy would—in human terms—be angels. That would itself establish a plank in the Christian worldview, and it would raise questions of how the angels came to exist, again leading in the direction of God.

Fifth, God *doesn't* observe things the way we do, through physical senses. He has a direct, immediate knowledge of what he creates, and his act of knowing created things is not distinct from his act of creating them. Therefore, his knowledge of created things actualizes them on the most fundamental level.

This suggests possible ways of expanding the argument. Here we have focused on what actualized the first physical observer. However, if (as common sense would suggest) there were definite events before this in this history of the universe (e.g., at the Big Bang), a non-physical observer like God would be needed to actualize those. The same would be true of definite events occurring today that are not seen by physical observers (e.g., a rock falling off a cliff on Mars).

The Women at the Tomb

CHALLENGE

"The Gospels contradict each other about which women went to Jesus' tomb."

DEFENSE

The Gospels simply record different details.

The following women are mentioned as going to the tomb:

- Mary Magdalen and the "other Mary," who is identified as "the mother of James and Joseph" (Matt. 28:1; cf. Matt. 27:56, 61)
- Mary Magdalen, Mary the mother of James, and Salome (Mark 16:1)
- Mary Magdalene, Joanna, Mary the mother of James, and the other women with them (Luke 24:10)
- Mary Magdalen (John 20:1)

For a contradiction to exist, one Gospel would have to *assert* a particular woman was there and another would have to *deny* she was, but this is not what happens. No Gospel asserts any of the women *wasn't* there. This means different evangelists merely chose to record different details, in keeping with the choices every author must make (see Day 258's discussion of descriptive approximation).

Based on Luke's list, which is the most extensive, there were a minimum of five women who went to the tomb and possibly more, so it's not surprising the evangelists chose not to name everyone.

We may be able to determine why they made some of the choices they did. Mary Magdalen is always mentioned first, indicating a special prominence. It's likely she went on to be the most well-known female witness to the empty tomb in the first-century Church.

The other named women may be mentioned because the evangelist who names them was personally familiar with their testimony. Named individuals in the Gospels sometimes appear to be the key tradents (tradition-bearers) for the sections where they appear (see Richard Bauckham, *Jesus and the Eyewitnesses*, chapter 3). It's also possible they were mentioned because they were known to the audiences of the individual Gospels (compare the way Mark 15:21 mentions Alexander and Rufus, who were apparently known to his audience). It's even possible the named women were *among* the Gospels' intended audiences.

The reason John mentions only Mary Magdalen is likely because he intended to supplement the synoptic Gospels (see Bauckham, "John for Readers of Mark" in *The Gospels for All Christians*), because she was involved in his own eyewitness experience (John 20:1–10), and because he had information about her encounter not recorded in the other Gospels (John 20:11–18).

Josephus on Jesus

CHALLENGE

"Jesus never existed. The passage where Josephus refers to him is fake."

DEFENSE

The passage in question is not a fake.

Most manuscripts of Josephus's *Antiquities of the Jews*, written around A.D. 93, contain this passage:

> Now, there was about this time Jesus, a wise man, if it be lawful to call him a man, for he was a doer of wonderful works—a teacher of such men as receive the truth with pleasure. He drew over to him both many of the Jews, and many of the Gentiles. He was Christ; and when Pilate, at the suggestion of the principal men amongst us, had condemned him to the cross, those that loved him at the first did not forsake him, for he appeared to them alive again the third day, as the divine prophets had foretold these and ten thousand other wonderful things concerning him; and the tribe of Christians, so named from him, are not extinct at this day (18:3:3).

This speaks of Jesus the way a Christian might, but Josephus was not a Christian, so scholars have concluded the passage did not appear in this form in his original writings. However, that doesn't mean it's fake. It means it was edited by a later Christian.

There is a broad consensus among scholars that *Antiquities* originally contained a version of this passage, but certain phrases were added by a Christian editor. When the phrases indicating a Christian editor are removed, the original passage may be reconstructed along these lines:

> At that time there appeared Jesus, a wise man. For he was a doer of startling deeds, a teacher of people who receive the truth with pleasure. And he gained a following both among many Jews and among many of Greek origin. And when Pilate, because of an accusation made by the leading men among us, condemned him to the cross, those who had loved him previously did not cease to do so. And up until this very day the tribe of Christians (named after him) has not died out (John Meier, *A Marginal Jew*, 1:61).

In addition, there is a later passage (*Antiquities* 20:9:1) that refers back to Jesus, further indicating that Josephus originally included a version of this passage (see Day 147).

TIP

For further discussion, see Michael Licona, *The Resurrection of Jesus*, 235–42.

Entering or Leaving Jericho?

CHALLENGE

"The Gospels contradict each other about whether Jesus healed the blind beggar Bartimaeus when he was entering or leaving Jericho."

DEFENSE

There are several responses to this challenge.

To begin, let's look at the texts describing where Jesus was when the event took place:

- *"As they went out of Jericho*, a great crowd followed him" (Matt. 20:29).
- "And they came to Jericho; and *as he was leaving Jericho* with his disciples and a great multitude, Bartimaeus, a blind beggar, the son of Timaeus, was sitting by the roadside" (Mark 10:46).
- *"As he drew near to Jericho*, a blind man was sitting by the roadside begging" (Luke 18:35)

Matthew and Mark have Jesus leaving Jericho, whereas Luke has him approaching it.

It would be possible to explain this in an excessively artificial manner, either by saying Jesus was leaving Jericho but turned around and started to go back, or by saying he was heading toward Jericho but turned around and started to leave. These explanations are logically possible but not plausible. Fortunately, there are better explanations.

One involves the fact that there were two sites for Jericho: an ancient and a recent one. Thus, Jesus could have passed through the older site (mentioned by Matthew and Mark) and been approaching the newer settlement (mentioned by Luke), which had been built by the Hasmoneans and recently renovated and expanded by Herod the Great. The newer settlement is sometimes called "Herodian" or "New Testament" Jericho (*Anchor Yale Bible Dictionary*, s.v. "Jericho [Place]").

This is possible, but given the freedom the evangelists had in presenting events in a non–chronological order (see Day 89), it's possible Luke set the encounter with Bartimaeus before Jesus arrives in Jericho because he wants next to relate an event that occurred *in* Jericho (the dinner with Zacchaeus; Luke 19:1–10).

Tradition preserved the fact that the encounter with Bartimaeus occurred just outside Jericho and that the encounter with Zacchaeus occurred in it. But it is an open question whether Luke grouped these two together because of their chronological order or because of their association with Jericho. Either way, the Gospels agree the healing occurred just outside Jericho. Jesus' direction of travel falls below the level of precision that the Gospel authors were expected to track.

Born with Temptations

"Why would a good God allow people to be born with temptations to sin?"

This is a subcase of the problem of evil. It's mysterious, but we can still discern the outlines of the solution.

Elsewhere we have covered other aspects of the problem of evil (see Days 7, 38, and 151). Here we look at the specific question of why God allows people to be born with temptations to sin.

One way of putting the answer is: God created mankind in a state of original justice or holiness. However, when our first parents turned away from God and committed original sin, they lost this holiness and human nature was corrupted in a way that made us prone to sin (CCC 375, 379, 405).

Although the causes were on the spiritual rather than the purely physical level, the situation is similar to that of a person with a healthy genetic code who, by recklessly exposing himself to radioactive material, damages his genes in a way that causes his offspring to be born with birth defects. In other words: We are born with temptations because we inherit the damage done to human nature by sin.

Although this answers the question on one level, it leaves the question of why God would allow this to happen. Here there is an element of mystery, because God could have prevented us from inheriting temptations. However, we can say the following:

1. God takes our inborn weaknesses into account in assessing how culpable we are. Our culpability for sin is diminished when we are under strong internal pressures. "The promptings of feelings and passions can also diminish the voluntary and free character of the offense, as can external pressures or pathological disorders" (CCC 1860).

2. God will not allow us to be separated from him except by a truly free choice of the kind involved in mortal sin (CCC 1037).

3. God gives us his grace to deal with temptations (1 Cor. 10:13).

4. God subjects himself to our weakness. In the person of Jesus, he subjected himself to conditions like those we experience. "For we do not have a high priest [i.e., Jesus] who is unable to sympathize with our weaknesses, but one who has similarly been tested in every way, yet without sin" (Heb. 4:15, NABRE).

The Witness of the Holy Spirit and Scripture

CHALLENGE

*"We don't need the Church to identify Scripture.
The Holy Spirit witnesses to it."*

DEFENSE

The Holy Spirit does witness to Scripture, but it does
this through the instrumentality of the Church.

Although some have argued that Scripture is "self-authenticating" (see
Day 229), they don't usually mean this and instead appeal to another
form of authentication.

Thus, after proposing the Bible's literary qualities as evidence of
divine authorship, the Westminster Confession of Faith goes on to
say, "notwithstanding, our full persuasion and assurance of the infallible truth, and divine authority thereof, is from the inward work of
the Holy Spirit, bearing witness by and with the Word in our hearts"
(1:5). It is true that the Holy Spirit provides guidance about the canon
of Scripture. The question is how this guidance is manifest—to individuals or through the Church?

If we had a promise that the Holy Spirit would enable individuals
to recognize the canon, then Mormons would be correct when they
invite people to pray about whether the Book of Mormon is Scripture,
promising them a "burning in the bosom" or similar "witness of the
Holy Ghost" that it is true.

Most in the Protestant community have recognized that this is an
unacceptably subjective and spiritually dangerous practice. It can easily
cause a person to be led by his emotions rather than the Holy Spirit and
invites the possibility of self-deception (cf. Jer. 17:9). The reason it is
dangerous is that the Holy Spirit has not promised to guide individuals
in this way.

Mormons may appeal to James 1:5 ("If any of you lack wisdom, let
him ask of God, that giveth to all men liberally, and upbraideth not;
and it shall be given him," KJV), but this is a general promise that God
will help people gain wisdom, not a promise to give them a private
revelation concerning the canon of Scripture.

Thus Protestants do not typically encourage people to seek such a
revelation but to rely on the Holy Spirit's guidance of the Church in
recognizing the canon of Scripture.

TIP

The fact that Scripture does not promise us this kind of personal revelation
is a theological claim, which makes it a problem for the view that we
should get all of our theology from Scripture alone (*sola scriptura*).

Constantine and the Catholic Church

CHALLENGE

*"The Catholic Church was created by the Emperor Constantine when
he made Christianity the official religion of the Roman Empire."*

DEFENSE

Both of these claims are historically false.

Although Constantine is often credited with being the first Christian emperor, he didn't make Christianity the official religion. What he did, together with his colleague and rival, Licinius, was issue the Edict of Milan in A.D. 313, which proclaimed religious toleration for Christianity among the other religions in the empire.

He also didn't create the Catholic Church, which already existed in his day. Indeed, it had already been known by that name for more than 200 years. Thus, writing around A.D. 110, St. Ignatius of Antioch stated: "Wherever the bishop shall appear, there let the multitude also be; even as, wherever Jesus Christ is, there is the Catholic Church" (*Letter to the Smyrneans* 8).

The fact that Ignatius introduces the phrase "Catholic Church" without stopping to explain it indicates it was already in use, and he could expect people in the distant church of Smyrna to understand what it meant. This wide circulation therefore must have begun in the second half of the first century.

The meaning of the Greek term for "Catholic" (*katholikos*) is "universal" (from *kata holos*, "according to the whole"). It was introduced as a way of identifying the universal Church established by Christ (Matt. 16:18), as distinct from local congregations. "Very quickly, however, in the latter half of the second century at latest, we find it conveying the suggestion that the Catholic is the true Church as distinct from the heretical congregations" (J.N.D. Kelly, *Early Christian Doctrines*, 5th ed., 190).

"The Catholic Church" was thus simply the common way of referring to the original Church established by Christ, not Constantine.

Those who make this objection frequently claim that, at the time of Constantine, various doctrinal changes were introduced that are characteristic of the Catholic Church and that separate it from apostolic Christianity. However, no doctrinal changes were introduced. Even the definition of the divinity of Christ, which occurred during Constantine's reign at the First Council of Nicaea (A.D. 325), was an affirmation of previous Church teaching.

TIP

On the doctrinal continuity of the Catholic Church from the first century onward, see Jimmy Akin, *The Fathers Know Best*.

The Timing of the Fig Tree

CHALLENGE

"Matthew and Mark contradict each other on when Jesus cursed the fig tree."

DEFENSE

The challenge involves the sequencing of three key events (in italics, below).

Here is the sequence of events in Matthew:

- Jesus visits the temple (21:12a)
- *Jesus clears the temple* (21:12b–16)
- Jesus stays in Bethany that night (21:17)
- *Returning, Jesus curses the fig tree* (21:18–19a)
- *The disciples see the fig tree withered* (21:19b–22)

And here is the sequence in Mark:

- Jesus visits the temple (11:11a)
- Jesus stays in Bethany that night (11:11b)
- *Returning, Jesus curses the fig tree* (11:12–14)
- *Jesus clears the temple* (11:15–19)
- *The disciples see the fig tree withered* (11:20–23)

It has been obvious to scholars throughout Church history that the evangelists don't always arrange material in chronological order (see Day 89). This may have been commented on as early as the first century, when John the Presbyter stated: "Mark, having become the interpreter of Peter, wrote down accurately, though not in order, whatsoever he remembered of the things said or done by Christ" (Eusebius, *Church History* 3:39:15).

Sometimes the evangelists use chronology to organize material (e.g., the Crucifixion is always at the end of the Gospels), but other times they use other considerations.

This can be seen from how Matthew handles the material in Jesus' major ethical and prophetic discourses (Matt. 5–7, 24–25). Much of the same material is in Luke, but it is scattered in different places. Matthew is not contradicting Luke; he's simply grouping material together by topic.

With the fig tree, Matthew arranges material topically, so he keeps events involving the temple together (Jesus' visit and clearing of it) and events involving the fig tree together (its cursing and withering).

Mark, by contrast, often arranges material in what scholars have called "Markan sandwiches," where one event is placed between two others as a way of commenting on it. Thus Mark has the clearing of the temple between the two halves of the fig tree account to show the spiritual barrenness of the temple (see Day 93).

God in the Old and New Testaments

CHALLENGE

"The God of the Old Testament is depicted as angry and jealous, but the God of the New Testament is depicted as loving and kind."

DEFENSE

This claim has elements of both truth and falsehood.

It has an element of falsehood because God is depicted as both just and merciful in both Testaments. Anyone who reads the Old Testament encounters many descriptions of God as loving and kind: "The Lord [is] a God merciful and gracious, slow to anger, and abounding in steadfast love and faithfulness" (Exod. 34:6; cf. Num. 14:18, Deut. 4:31, 2 Chron. 30:9, Neh. 9:17, Ps. 86:5). And anyone who reads the New Testament encounters many mentions of God's wrath: "It is a fearful thing to fall into the hands of the living God" (Heb. 10:31; cf. Matt. 25:41, Rom. 1:18, 2 Thess. 1:8–9, Rev. 20:11–15).

Both the Old and New Testaments thus depict God as stern and as kind, and the passages in question illustrate two of his attributes—justice and mercy—which he possesses and displays eternally. Therefore, there aren't two different Gods in the Bible, but one God who displays both attributes.

This is not to say that there are not differences in emphasis. There are, and they have to do with the different stages of God's plan, by which he progressively reveals himself to man (CCC 69).

The earlier portions of Scripture were written in a very violent period, and they reflect the character of the time. In the Old Testament, polytheism was a real threat to the Israelites, and there was constant oppression and exploitation of the poor and the weak. God thus used the image of himself as a powerful, heavenly king to warn the Israelites against polytheism and oppression—the sins that are regularly singled out for the strongest condemnation in the Old Testament.

When Jesus came, a new phase in God's plan dawned—a phase in which God made himself vulnerable and offered himself on the cross, underscoring in the most dramatic way his love for mankind (John 3:16). The impact of this event naturally colored the way God is revealed in the New Testament and balances the emphases found in the Old.

The Church's "Obsession" with Sex

CHALLENGE

"The Church is obsessed with sex—premarital sex, divorce, contraception, homosexuality. Why can't it shut up about this subject?"

DEFENSE

The Church isn't obsessed with sex. Our culture is.

The Church has remained constant in its teachings on sexuality. It proposes the simple and beautiful understanding that God designed humans to express their sexuality in marriage—the lifelong partnership of man and woman, oriented to the good of the spouses and the procreation and education of children.

But our culture has undergone dramatic changes. The last hundred years have seen a huge rise in divorces and unwed motherhood, the "sexual revolution" of the 1960s, widespread use of contraception and abortion, the explosive growth of pornography due to the Internet, and homosexual "marriage."

What changed was not the Church, but society, which became obsessed with sex and sexual license.

This would be a good reason for the Church to ramp up its discussion of sex—to speak about the problems of the day and help society find the healing it needs. Yet anyone who attends Catholic services knows one only rarely hears sex discussed from the pulpit. At most, there are only occasional brief comments and allusions.

This suggests the charge of the Church being "obsessed" is due to something else: the uneasy conscience of those taking sexual license. Proverbs says the guilty "flee when no one pursues" (Prov. 28:1), and that is happening here. Those who engage in sexual sin know they are violating the Christian vision of human sexuality and suppose that in church there must be constant, thunderous condemnations of what they are doing. This is not the case. The Church's message is far broader, but this one area can seem disproportionately emphasized if it is where a person is in conflict with the Christian vision.

This creates a risk of missing the Church's message altogether. The Church is not interested in telling people "no," but in helping them find happiness. The truth is that living according to God's design for human sexuality will let us find long-term happiness in a way that living for momentary pleasures will not. It is from love and concern that the Church proclaims the truth about sexuality.

TIP

For a positive articulation of the Church's vision, see John Paul II, *The Theology of the Body.*

Jerome and the Deuterocanonicals

CHALLENGE

"St. Jerome (c. 347–420), the foremost Scripture scholar of his day, didn't accept the deuterocanonical books as Scripture."

DEFENSE

Jerome's attitude is ambiguous and may have changed over time. Furthermore, no one Church Father can settle the canon.

While learning to translate Hebrew, Jerome was in contact with non-Christian Jews who were intellectual descendants of the Pharisees and therefore rejected the deuterocanonicals (see Days 255 and 257). Under this influence, he at least for a time rejected their canonicity.

This is indicated in the prologues to the Vulgate, where he says certain books are non-canonical (e.g., he says this of Wisdom, Sirach, Judith, and Tobit in the prologue to Kings). In other cases, he says a book is not read among Hebrew-speaking Jews but does not clearly state his own view (e.g., he says this of Baruch in the prologue to Jeremiah).

Nevertheless, Jerome shows deference to the judgment of the Church. In the prologue to Judith, he tells his patron that "because this book is found by the Nicene Council [of A.D. 325] to have been counted among the number of the Sacred Scriptures, I have acquiesced to your request" to translate it. This is interesting because we have only partial records of First Nicaea, and we don't otherwise know what this ecumenical council said concerning the canon.

Jerome's deference to Church authority was also illustrated when he later defended the deuterocanonical portions of Daniel, writing: "What sin have I committed in following the judgment of the churches?" (*Against Rufinus* 2:33). In the same place he stated that what he said concerning Daniel in his prologues was what non-Christian Jews said but was not his own view. This may indicate Jerome changed his mind or that his reporting of Jewish views may not indicate his own view.

Jerome's deference to the Church is correct. The guidance of the Holy Spirit is given to the Church as a whole. No one Church Father, however prominent, can settle the canon of Scripture, and on this subject Jerome was in the minority (see Day 273).

TIP

Appealing to Jerome on this subject is often a matter of convenience. Despite his status as a Scripture scholar, people making this challenge pay little attention to his widespread support of Catholic doctrines using Scripture (see Jimmy Akin, *The Fathers Know Best*).

Nothing but Science?

"We shouldn't believe anything that can't be verified by science."

Authentic science does not maintain this.

Science involves the use of a particular method (i.e., "scientific method"), the principal steps of which are:

1. Observing some aspect of the world
2. Formulating hypotheses to explain the observed data
3. Making predictions about further observations based on the hypotheses
4. Performing experiments to test the predictions (particularly by trying to falsify them).

This general method has proved useful for investigating many subjects, but, as we cover elsewhere (see Day 333), there are limits to what can be investigated by science.

Sometimes the reason is practical, as when an experiment cannot be performed without affecting the behavior of the phenomenon to be observed. This situation is frequently encountered in studying the behavior of subatomic particles, leading to Heisenberg's Uncertainty Principle (according to which we cannot measure both the position and the momentum of a particle).

Other times the limit is due to a matter of principle. Science—like every other field—cannot get off the ground without using truths of logic that are fundamental to all reasoning. Yet these principles cannot be verified by the scientific method. Instead, they are assumed.

Science also presupposes other principles that it cannot demonstrate, such as the lawlike behavior of natural phenomena and the extension of those laws into the past and future. It also must assume that the data that has been observed is representative of the way things are and not just a misleading set of fluke observations. Repeating experiments to gain more data is good, but the new experiments also could involve fluke observations, so there must remain an assumption that the observed data is representative of the way things really are.

Most fundamentally, the claim that we should not accept anything that cannot be verified by science does not meet its own test. In view of the limits of science we have covered, the hypothesis proposed in the challenge does not fit the observed data. It is a bad hypothesis and therefore something that authentic science does not support. Authentic science recognizes its own limits and does not claim to be the single tool needed to prove every type of proposition.

"The Firstborn of All Creation"

CHALLENGE

"Jesus is a created being. Paul describes him as the 'firstborn of all creation' (Col. 1:15)."

DEFENSE

Without knowledge of the relevant context, the phrase "firstborn of all creation" could suggest Jesus was the first created being. However, context makes it clear this isn't the case.

The term "firstborn" had a special meaning in Jewish society. A firstborn male was sacred to God (Exod. 13:1, 11–15) and had special rights (Deut. 21:15–17).

With time, "firstborn" became a title of privilege that didn't necessarily indicate a literal firstborn male. Thus God says he will make David his firstborn (Ps. 89:20, 27), though David was the last son in his family (1 Sam. 16:10–11). In context, the reference to David as God's firstborn is clarified as "the highest of the kings of the earth," indicating a position of preeminence, not of age. Similarly, God describes Israel as his firstborn (Exod. 4:22), though Israel was not chronologically the first nation. God also describes Ephraim as his firstborn (Jer. 31:9), though Ephraim was not the chronologically first tribe.

It is as a title of preeminence that the term "firstborn" is used for Jesus in the first-century hymn to Christ that Paul records in Colossians 1:15–20. In the ancient world, hymns were sung to deities, and this hymn puts Christ in that class. He is the firstborn "of" creation in that he is preeminent *over* creation, the same way David was king "of" Israel—i.e., king *over* Israel.

That Jesus is not a created being is indicated by what the hymn says next: "For in him all things were created, in heaven and on earth, visible and invisible, whether thrones or dominions or principalities or authorities—all things were created through him and for him. He is before all things. . . . He is the beginning . . . that in everything he might be preeminent. For in him all the fulness of God was pleased to dwell" (Col. 1:16–19).

If all things were created through Christ, if he existed before all things, then he is not a created being. (Jehovah's Witnesses put the word "other" between "all" and "things" to avoid the implication Christ isn't a created being, but that's not what the Greek says.) Jesus possessed "the fulness of God" and thus had equality with God (John 5:18, Phil. 2:6).

The Infancy Narratives

"The infancy narratives in Matthew and Luke contradict each other. For example, Luke has Mary living in Nazareth before going to Bethlehem, while in Matthew they don't go to Nazareth until later."

DEFENSE

The infancy narratives don't contradict each other. In fact, they fit together very well. Here we provide an interwoven narrative.

Initially, Gabriel appears to Zechariah to announce the birth of John the Baptist (Luke 1:5–25). A few months later, Gabriel appears to Mary in Nazareth to announce the birth of Jesus (Luke 1:26–38), and Mary goes to visit Elizabeth before returning to Nazareth (Luke 1:39–56). Then John the Baptist is born (Luke 1:57–80).

Around this time, Joseph is informed that Mary is pregnant. He plans to divorce her, but an angel tells him to continue the marriage (Matt. 1:18–23). The two begin cohabiting (Matt. 1:24). This would be in Nazareth, per Luke's account.

Because of the enrollment announced by Caesar Augustus, the Holy Family travels to Bethlehem (Luke 2:1–5), where Jesus is born (Luke 2:7, Matt. 1:24a). That night, the shepherds visit them (Luke 2:8–20). Around the same time, the Magi observe the star in their homeland (cf. Matt. 2:2, 16).

Eight days after birth, Jesus is circumcised and named (Luke 2:21; Matt. 1:24b), and after forty days he is presented at the temple (Luke 2:22–38).

At this point, the Holy Family either returns to Nazareth or remains in Bethlehem (which is not clear). If they returned to Nazareth, they continued to visit Jerusalem and their relatives in Bethlehem multiple times every year for the three annual pilgrimage feasts (Exod. 23:14–17; cf. Luke 2:41).

Between one and two years after the birth (cf. Matt. 2:16), the Magi arrive and are directed to Bethlehem, where they find the Holy Family (Matt. 2:1–11). They are warned in a dream to return to their country by a different route (Matt. 2:12). Also warned in a dream, the Holy Family flees to Egypt (Matt. 2:13–15) to avoid the slaughter of the innocent (Matt. 2:16–18).

When Herod the Great dies, the Holy Family then returns to Israel (Matt. 2:19–21), but Joseph learns Herod Archelaus is ruling in Judea and so takes the family to Nazareth (Matt. 2:22–23).

TIP

For further discussion, see Jimmy Akin, "How the Accounts of Jesus' Childhood Fit Together," at JimmyAkin.com.

Men Becoming Gods

CHALLENGE

"The Catechism *states that men can become gods (CCC 460), but this is false."*

DEFENSE

The Church's teaching is biblically grounded and doesn't mean we become equal to God.

The Church emphatically teaches there is only one God (CCC 200–202, 2112). There is a single, uncreated Creator, but the term "god" can be used more than one way. In addition to being used of pagan deities, it is used to refer to angels and some humans (see Day 263).

Thus Jesus quotes the statement "You are gods" (Ps. 82:6), which he interprets as a reference to those "to whom the word of God came" (John 10:34). It is thus possible for men to be linked to the divine or divinized in a way they can be called "gods" from contact with the word of God.

This theme is mentioned by Peter, who says Christians "become partakers of the divine nature" (2 Pet. 1:4). This means that, by God's grace, we come to share in certain of his attributes to the extent a creature can. Theologians sometimes call these God's "communicable attributes," and they include things like immortality, glory, and holiness.

We have begun to share in these, for in Christ we are new creations (2 Cor. 5:17) and we have tasted "the powers of the age to come" (Heb. 6:5). The process will be complete at the Second Coming, when "we shall be like him, for we shall see him as he is" (1 John 3:2). This process, known in the East as *theosis* and in the West as *divinization*, is discussed by Church Fathers such as St. Irenaeus and St. Athanasius, and theologians like St. Thomas Aquinas (see CCC 460).

Theosis or *divinization* means we become godlike (like God), but we will never be equal to God. That's impossible, for we are finite and created and can never become infinite and uncreated.

TIP

The English edition of CCC 460 mistranslates a quote from Athanasius as saying Jesus became man "that we might become God." The authoritative Latin edition of the *Catechism* has *"ut nos dii efficeremur,"* meaning "that we might be made gods" (see Tim Staples, "Does the Catholic Church Teach We Are Gods?" at TimStaples.com). The Church thus does not teach that we become God but "gods" in the sense discussed above.

The God of the Gaps

CHALLENGE

"Christians use God to explain what currently can't be explained by science (i.e. 'the gaps'). But as scientific knowledge grows, what's left for God shrinks to nothing."

DEFENSE

Christians understand God as the ultimate explanation for everything, not just things science can't presently explain.

God causes some things directly and some indirectly, using created things as secondary causes. "The truth that God is at work in all the actions of his creatures is inseparable from faith in God the Creator. God is the first cause who operates in and through secondary causes" (CCC 308).

Scripture often attributes "actions to God without mentioning any secondary causes. This is not a 'primitive mode of speech,' but a profound way of recalling God's primacy and absolute Lordship over history and the world" (CCC 304).

Science is a valuable tool for understanding secondary causation. By studying the visible, created world, we have gained a better understanding of it, and that continues to grow.

When confronted with a scientifically unexplained phenomenon in the natural world, it would be a mistake to reflexively say, "God must have done it; it's a miracle." It may be that further investigation will produce a scientific explanation. If so, science will have increased our understanding of how secondary causation works in God's plan.

However, some events are genuine miracles that resist scientific explanation. These are examples of God using primary causation.

We cannot assume, without investigation or reflection, which category a phenomenon falls into. Neither can we assume that either category is empty: We must open-mindedly allow for the possibility of both the scientifically explainable and the miraculous. To assume *all* events must be scientifically explainable would be just as prejudiced as assuming *none* are.

Regardless of whether an event is produced by primary or secondary causation, God is its ultimate explanation, at least in the sense that he created the world and allowed the event to occur as part of his providential plan.

This is not "God of the gaps" thinking because it does not see God as explaining *only* those things that science can't presently explain. Neither does it assume that something *must* be miraculous just because there is no known scientific explanation. It allows the open-minded exploration of both primary and secondary causation.

Tradition and the Canon of Scripture

CHALLENGE

"Tradition may be valuable in some ways, but it can't be allowed to play a determinative role with respect to Scripture."

DEFENSE

It is precisely by Tradition that Scripture itself is determined.

How do we know what belongs in Scripture? Various criteria have been proposed, the most fundamental of which is inspiration, for Paul says, "All scripture is inspired by God" (2 Tim. 3:16). It's true that if a book is inspired then it is Scripture, but this is not a practical test, for inspiration is not an objectively verifiable literary property (see Day 229).

Another test is "apostolicity"—that a book was written by an apostle or approved as Scripture by the apostles. The difficulty is that, like inspiration, apostolicity isn't a detectable literary quality. It must be known by means apart from the text.

The way the early Church determined inspiration when the canon was being recognized was whether a book had been handed down to and read in the churches as apostolic. As Evangelical scholar C.E. Hill notes:

> Christian writers often spoke of their Gospels (and other books) as handed down to them. Christian writers of the second century do not speak of choosing the Gospels, or of the criteria they might have created for making such choices. This is not the way they thought. When speaking of the church's part in the process they instead use words like "receive," "recognize," "confess," "acknowledge," and their opposites. Just like the faith itself, which had been "received from the apostles and transmitted to its children" (Irenaeus, *Against Heresies* 3:1:praef.; cf. 1:10:1), so the Gospels themselves were "handed down to the church by the same apostles (*Against Heresies* 3:1:praef.; 3:1:1, 2) (*Who Chose the Gospels?*, 231–32).

The act of handing something down is what tradition *is*. The Latin verb *tradere*, from which "tradition" is derived, means "to hand down." Tradition is thus the means by which we know which books are Scripture, giving it a determinative role.

The teachings handed down from the apostles also were used to identify false scriptures that disagreed with this teaching (see Day 138). Tradition—in the form of apostolic doctrine—thus also played a determinitive role in establishing the canon.

Truth versus Precision

"The Bible contains many passages that say something close to the truth but are still not quite accurate."

This confuses truth with precision.

Perhaps you've seen the *Star Trek* episode "Errand of Mercy," where the following exchange occurs:

> KIRK: What would you say the odds are on our getting out of here?
>
> SPOCK: Difficult to be precise, Captain. I should say, approximately 7,824.7 to 1.
>
> KIRK: Difficult to be precise? 7,824 to 1?
>
> SPOCK: 7,824.7 to 1.
>
> KIRK: That's a pretty close approximation.
>
> SPOCK: I endeavor to be accurate.

This illustrates the different levels of precision expected by humans and vulcans. Something similar occurs when modern audiences read ancient texts. We live in an age in which things are rigorously measured and recorded. But the ancient world was very different. There were few and imprecise measuring tools, no audio or video recorders, and most people could not read or write.

Consequently, the ancients expected a lesser degree of precision than we do. They would have rolled their eyes at us the way we roll our eyes at Mr. Spock and his absurd overprecision.

This has implications for how we read the Bible. We can't hold its authors to a higher level of precision than they used. They expressed truths according to the level of precision expected in *their* day, not *ours*.

Statements of truth regularly involve approximation. When we say the speed of light is 186,000 miles per second or that *pi* is 3.14, we are expressing truths, but in an approximate manner. Approximation is so common that scientists even speak of the different "orders of approximation" they use in their work. At some point, it becomes foolish to try to be more precise, and this judgment must be made based on the situation in which we find ourselves.

We must thus respect the circumstances in which the biblical authors wrote and not expect more precision of them than their situation allowed. If we want to charge them with error, then we need to show that they weren't using the degree of precision expected in the ancient world.

Paul's Conversion

"Accounts of Paul's conversion in the New Testament contradict each other."

The passages are easily harmonized.

At the time of his conversion, Paul (aka Saul) was traveling to Damascus when a great light from heaven shone around him and Jesus spoke to him. A contradiction is alleged between two verses describing the reaction of the men who were with Paul:

> The men who were traveling with him stood speechless, hearing (*akouontes*) the voice (*phōnēs*) but seeing no one (Acts 9:7).
>
> Now those who were with me saw the light but did not hear (*ēkousan*) the voice (*phōnēn*) of the one who was speaking to me (Acts 22:9).

Both verses have forms of the Greek verb *akouō* for "hear" and the noun *phōnē* for "voice." One seems to say the men with Paul heard the voice and the other that they didn't.

However, both texts were written by the same author (Luke), who got the information from the same source (Paul). Luke was Paul's traveling companion (see Day 26; cf. Col. 4:14, 2 Tim. 4:11, Philem. 24), and both accounts are based on Paul's reminiscences to Luke. Consequently, if the passages can be read in harmony with each other, they should be. And, although it is not obvious from the above English translation, they can.

The verb *akouō* doesn't just mean "hear." It can also mean "understand." Further, the noun *phōnē* doesn't just mean "voice." It also means "sound." These are not controversial translations. They are found in any standard Greek lexicon.

Since the texts were written by the same author, relying on the same source, it is natural and straightforward to read the passages as saying that the men with Paul heard the sound but did not understand what the voice was saying to him.

This would be similar to John 12:28–29—when God speaks from heaven and some bystanders perceive it as thunder—indicating an objective experience only incompletely perceived by those who were not its primary recipients. There is thus no contradiction.

Some apologists try to answer this challenge with an argument that cites the grammatical case of the noun following *akouō*. This argument is unnecessary and shaky. It is better avoided.

Is Christmas Pagan?

"Christmas is based on a pagan holiday."

There are multiple responses to this challenge.

First, which pagan holiday are we talking about? Sometimes Saturnalia—a Roman festival honoring the god Saturn—is proposed. But Saturnalia was held on December 17 (and later extended through December 23). It wasn't December 25.

Another proposal is *Dies Natalis Solis Invicti* (Latin, "The Birthday of the Unconquerable Sun"), but the evidence this was the basis of the dating of Christmas is problematic. The Christian *Chronography of A.D. 354* records the "Birthday of the Unconquerable" was celebrated on that date in 354, but the identity of "the Unconquerable" is unclear. Since it's a Christian document that elsewhere (twice) lists Jesus' birthday as December 25, it could be the Unconquerable Christ—not the sun—whose birth was celebrated.

Second, correlation is not causation. Even if Christmas and Sol Invictus were both on December 25, Christmas might have been the basis of Sol Invictus, or the reverse, or it might just be a coincidence. If you want to claim the date of Sol Invictus is the basis for the date of Christmas, you need evidence.

Third, that evidence is hard to come by. Even if the *Chronology of A.D. 354* refers to Sol Invictus being celebrated on December 25, this is the first reference to the fact, and we know some Christians held that Jesus was born on that date long before 354.

For example, St. Hippolytus of Rome (c. 170–c. 240) stated in his commentary on Daniel that Jesus was born on December 25, and he wrote around a century and a half before 354 (see Jack Finegan, *Handbook of Biblical Chronology*, 2nd ed., §562). Further, Sol Invictus wasn't even an official Roman cult until 274, when the Emperor Aurelian made it one.

Fourth, if Christians were subverting Sol Invictus, we should find the Church Fathers saying, "Let's subvert Sol Invictus by celebrating Christmas instead." But we don't. The Fathers who celebrate December 25 sincerely think that's when Jesus was born (ibid., §§562–567).

Finally, even if Christmas was timed to subvert a pagan holiday, so what? Christmas is the celebration of the birth of Jesus Christ, and celebrating the birth of Christ is a good thing. So is subverting paganism. If the early Christians were doing both, big deal!

Assurance of Salvation

CHALLENGE

"Belief in mortal sin denies Catholics assurance of salvation, but God wants us to have it: 'I write this to you who believe in the name of the Son of God, that you may know that you have eternal life' (1 John 5:13, emphasis added)."

DEFENSE

We can have assurance of salvation if we fulfill God's conditions for it, but self-deception and mortal sin are real possibilities.

We must be careful about the term "know." Knowledge can mean different things. "I know physics," "I know it's raining," "I know John," and "Adam knew his wife" involve different senses of knowing.

We often say we know something without implying there is no possibility of being wrong. If you ask someone, "Do you know what you had for dinner last night?" he might say, "Yes." But if you ask, "Do you have an infallible memory so there is absolutely no possibility you are misremembering?" he would likely say, "No."

Scripture sets forth the conditions for salvation. In fact, 1 John sets out multiple conditions, including keeping the commandments (2:3–5, 5:1–3) and believing in Jesus and loving one another (3:23–24, 4:20–21). If we have fulfilled these conditions then, per 1 John 5:13, we may know that we have salvation in the ordinary sense of the term "know," but that doesn't mean there is absolutely no possibility of being wrong.

Paul says: "I am not aware of anything against myself, but I am not thereby acquitted [Greek, *dedikaiōmai,* "justified"]. It is the Lord who judges me" (1 Cor. 4:4). If even a figure like Paul refused to pronounce definitively on his own spiritual state, so must we.

The possibility of self-deception is real. "The heart is deceitful above all things, and desperately corrupt; who can understand it?" (Jer. 17:9). Thus the New Testament repeatedly warns Christians against self-deception, particularly with regard to sin and its consequences (1 Cor. 6:9–10, 15:33–34; Gal. 6:7–8; Eph. 5:5–6; James 1:22, 26; 1 John 1:8, 3:6–7).

If we fulfill the conditions Scripture lays out for salvation, then we may be assured of and know that we have salvation. But we cannot claim infallible certitude as if there were no possibility of self-deception.

Further, mortal sin is a real possibility, and John goes on to warn against it right after the verse this challenge is based on (1 John 5:16–17; cf. Day 302).

Three Gods?

*"The doctrine of the Trinity is polytheistic;
it teaches that there are three gods."*

DEFENSE

This is a fundamental misunderstanding of the doctrine.

There is another word for belief in three gods: *tritheism*. The fact that *trinitarianism* has a different name indicates it is something different.

Of course, the concept of threeness is involved. The word "Trinity" is derived from the Latin root *trinus* ("threefold, triple") and the suffix *–itas*, indicating a state or condition. "Trinity" thus indicates that God is threefold, but the question must be asked: Three of what?

The answer is not three gods but three Persons. Trinitarians are very clear on the fact that there is only one God. Thus the *Catechism* states: "If God is not one, he is not God" (CCC 228), and "the Trinity is One. We do not confess three Gods, but one God in three Persons" (CCC 253).

The phrase "one God in three Persons" is a classic expression of the doctrine of the Trinity, used by Christians all over the world, and both parts of the expression must be taken seriously. One cannot ignore the "one God" part and then rewrite the "three Persons" part to make it "three gods." That would falsify the concept of the Trinity and replace it with something else—something Christians do *not* believe.

Indeed, for a Christian to hold that the Father, the Son, and the Holy Spirit are three gods would be such an extreme falsification of Christian doctrine that it would constitute heresy. For a Catholic to maintain it obstinately would be the canonical crime of heresy and would result in an automatic excommunication (*Code of Canon Law*, canons 751, 1364 §1). That's how serious the Church is about the subject.

In response, a non-trinitarian might say he doesn't understand how one God can be three Persons, but an informed non-trinitarian can't in good faith say Christians believe in three gods.

Ultimately, you have to take someone at his word when he says, "That's *not* what I believe." You may not understand what he believes, you may even think it involves a contradiction (which the Trinity doesn't; see Day 39), but it displays bad faith to continue to assert that someone believes something when he explicitly denies it.

The Prophecy of Immanuel

CHALLENGE

"Matthew misunderstands Isaiah's prophecy of Immanuel (Isa. 7:14). It doesn't point to Jesus."

DEFENSE

Matthew understands the prophecy better than you think.

The biblical authors recognized Scripture as operating on multiple levels. For example, Matthew interprets the Holy Family's flight to Egypt as a fulfillment of the prophetic statement, "Out of Egypt I have called my son." In its original context, it is *obvious* the "son" of God being discussed is Israel: "When Israel was a child, I loved him, and out of Egypt, I called my son" (Hos. 11:1).

Matthew understood this. He had read the first half of the verse and knew that, on the primary, literal level, the statement applied to the nation of Israel. But he recognized that on another level it applied to Christ as the divine Son who recapitulates and fulfills the aspirations of Israel.

In the same way, it is obvious in Isaiah that on the primary, literal level the prophecy of Immanuel applied to the time of King Ahaz (732–716 B.C.). At this point, Syria had forged a military alliance with the northern kingdom of Israel that threatened to conquer Jerusalem (Isa. 7:1–2). God sent Isaiah to reassure Ahaz the alliance would not succeed (Isa. 7:3–9) and told him to name a sign that God would give him as proof (Isa. 7:10–11).

Ahaz balked and refused to name a sign (Isa. 7:12), so God declared one: "Therefore the Lord himself will give you a sign. Behold, a young woman shall conceive and bear a son, and shall call his name Immanuel. . . . For before the child knows how to refuse the evil and choose the good, the land before whose two kings you are in dread will be deserted" (Isa. 7:14–16).

For this sign to be meaningful to Ahaz, it would have to be fulfilled in his own day—indeed, very quickly. It therefore points, on the primary, literal level, to a child conceived at that time (perhaps Ahaz's son, the future King Hezekiah).

This was as obvious to Matthew as it is to us, but—like the other New Testament authors—he recognized the biblical text as having multiple dimensions, so the prophecy was not only fulfilled in Ahaz's day but also pointed to Christ as "Immanuel" (Hebrew, "God with us").

"A Virgin Shall Conceive"

CHALLENGE

"Isaiah's prophecy of Immanuel (Isa. 7:14) doesn't apply to Jesus. It doesn't say 'a virgin shall conceive.' The Hebrew word 'almāh doesn't mean 'virgin,' but 'young woman.'"

DEFENSE

Actually, *'almāh* can mean either.

Its basic meaning is a young woman of marriageable age. In Hebrew society, such women were expected to be and normally were virgins. The term thus was sometimes used to indicate virginity, though not always. After reviewing how the term is used in the Old Testament, John Watts concludes: "It is difficult to find a word in English that is capable of the same range of meaning. 'Virgin' is too narrow, while 'young woman' is too broad (*Word Biblical Commentary, vol. 24: Isaiah 1–33* (rev. ed.), 136).

Translators therefore have to choose how to render it in particular cases. Watts points out (ibid.) that the translators of the Greek Septuagint rendered it *parthenos* ("virgin"), while other Greek translators used *neanis* ("young woman").

We elsewhere discuss the fact that, on the primary, literal level, the Immanuel prophecy was fulfilled in the time of King Ahaz (732–716 B.C.) and that the child was, perhaps, his son Hezekiah (see Day 253). If so, the *'almāh* in question would have been Hezekiah's mother, Abijah (2 Chron. 29:1). Either way, some young woman known to Ahaz conceived the child.

This young woman may still have been a virgin at the time the prophecy was given, in which case the Greek translation *parthenos* would have applied to her in a precise way. Even if she was not a virgin, prophetic texts operate on more than one level, and this one had a greater fulfillment that occurred long after Ahaz's time.

When that fulfillment occurred, God chose a woman—Mary—who was not only a virgin but who conceived while remaining a virgin (Matt. 1:18–25; Luke 1:26–35). Also, the child she bore was not simply called "Immanuel" (as Hezekiah may have been called early in life, as a second name; cf. 2 Sam. 12:24–25). Instead, the child was *literally* "God with us."

In view of this, the first Christians looked back on Isaiah's prophecy and naturally saw it fulfilled in Jesus. The connection would have been obvious from the Hebrew text alone, and the fact that, by divine providence, the Septuagint translators had used the term *parthenos* only underscored the point.

The Old Testament Canon in Jesus' Day

CHALLENGE

"There were two Old Testament canons in Jesus' day—the Palestinian canon and the Alexandrian canon. As Palestinian Jews, Jesus and his disciples would've accepted the Palestinian canon, which excluded the deuterocanonical books. Therefore, they are not Scripture."

DEFENSE

This claim is based on outdated scholarship and is false.

In Jesus' day different groups of Jews held that different collections of books were canonical, and some of these collections had fuzzy boundaries. It is more accurate to speak of there being different canonical *traditions* rather than different canons. There were four prominent traditions:

1. *The Sadducee/Samaritan tradition*: This included the Torah or Pentateuch (Gen.-Deut.) and only those books. Thus the Sadducees rejected doctrines like the resurrection of the dead (Matt. 22:23; Acts 23:8), which are clearly attested outside the Torah (Dan. 12:2; 2 Macc. 12:43–45). This is why Jesus only quoted from the Torah when refuting them (Matt. 22:31–32; cf. Exod. 3:6). The Samaritan tradition was identical except for using the Samaritan edition of the Torah.

2. *The Pharisee tradition*: This canonical tradition was still being formed in Jesus' day. It was broadly similar to the canon later adopted by rabbinic Judaism (used in Protestant Old Testaments), but precisely which books belonged to it was debated until at least the third century.

3. *The Septuagint tradition*: This tradition also was still being formed in Jesus' day. It was broadly similar to the canon later used in the Christian church (including the deuterocanonical books), though precisely which books belong to it was also debated. (Note: We may refer to this tradition by the name of the major Greek translation of the Old Testament, but virtually all its books were written in Hebrew or Aramaic; see Day 27).

4. *The Qumran tradition*: This tradition was used by the Qumran sect (commonly identified as the Essenes). We do not know whether it was closed. It was similar to the Pharisee tradition but also included certain other books, including 1 Enoch, Jubilees, and the Temple Scroll (James VanderKam, *The Dead Sea Scrolls Today*, 149–57).

All four traditions were used in first-century Palestine, and many individuals undoubtedly held to further variations that are no longer identifiable. The New Testament reveals that Jesus and his followers used the Septuagint tradition, which they passed on to the Church (see Days 273 and 305).

Peter the Rock

CHALLENGE

"Peter is not the rock Jesus is referring to in Matthew 16:18."

DEFENSE

The structure of the passage clearly indicates that he is.

In Matthew 16:15–16, Jesus asks the disciples who they say he is, and Peter replies, "You are the Christ, the Son of the living God." In answer, Jesus gives a threefold response (Matt. 16:17–19), which may be diagrammed as follows:

1. Blessed are you, Simon Bar-Jona!

    1a. For flesh and blood has not revealed this to you,

    1b. But my Father who is in heaven.

2. And I tell you, you are Peter,

    2a. And on this rock I will build my Church,

    2b. And the gates of hades shall not prevail against it.

3. I will give you the keys of the kingdom of heaven,

    3a. And whatever you bind on earth shall be bound in heaven,

    3b. And whatever you loose on earth shall be loosed in heaven.

The parallelism among these statements indicates that Peter is the rock that Jesus is discussing.

First, there are the root statements: (1) "Blessed are you, Simon Bar-Jona!" (2) "And I tell you, you are Peter," (3) "I will give you the keys of the kingdom of heaven." Each of these is a blessing pronounced on Peter. They would make no sense if the middle statement was read as a way of diminishing Peter as an insignificant stone (see Day 282) in contrast to the much greater rock on which Jesus would build his Church. In that case, the passage would scan as, "Blessed are you Simon Bar-Jona! You are very insignificant. Here are the keys to the kingdom of heaven!"

Second, each of the root statements is explained by a pair of follow-up statements (labeled *a* and *b*). Thus statement (1) is explained by statements (1a) and (1b), and statement (3) is explained by statements (3a) and (3b). Similarly, statement (2) is explained by statements (2a) and (2b). Thus, the *meaning* of "You are Peter" is explained by "On this rock I will build my Church" and "the gates of hades shall not prevail against it."

This means that Peter is the rock on which Jesus will build his Church, and it is indicated by the parallelism displayed even in the English translation.

Justification: Quality and Quantity

CHALLENGE

"The Catholic idea that there is more than one form of justification doesn't make any sense. You are either righteous before God or you're not."

DEFENSE

This view doesn't reflect the biblical data (see Day 228).

The key to understanding this issue involves the difference between the quality and the quantity of righteousness.

Along the axis of quality, people hypothetically could range from totally unrighteous (purely evil) to totally righteous (purely good). Viewed in these terms, justification (being declared, reckoned, or made righteous by God) would involve having one's unrighteousness removed and being instead given a pure righteousness before God.

This corresponds to how justification is commonly understood in Protestant circles. It also corresponds to how *initial* justification is understood in Catholic circles. Thus the Church acknowledges that, when people first come to God and are forgiven, they "are made innocent, immaculate, pure, guiltless and beloved of God, heirs indeed of God, joint heirs with Christ; so that there is nothing whatever to hinder their entrance into heaven" (Trent, Decree on Original Sin 5).

If justification only operated on a single axis—quality—then from this state, no further improvement would be possible. However, justification also works along another axis—quantity.

Along this axis, there would be the possibility of further improvement in righteousness. The situation may be compared to light. Even if a light is pure white, it may be either dim or bright. One could thus take a lamp that is emitting pure white light and turn up the intensity so that it shines more brightly. In the same way, after God has given a person a pure righteousness before him, he may by his grace lead that person to grow in the quantity of righteousness he has.

This is the understanding the Catholic Church has of *ongoing* justification. Having been initially justified, people "increase in that justice received through the grace of Christ and are further justified, as it is written: . . . 'Do you see that by works a man is justified, and not by faith only?'" (Trent, Decree on Justification 10, citing James 2:24).

Note that it is only in regard to ongoing growth in righteousness, not initial justification, that the Church cites James 2:24 (see Day 222).

Approximation in the Bible

CHALLENGE

"Why do you claim that the biblical authors used a different level of precision than we do?"

DEFENSE

Approximations were more common because of the inability in the ancient world to accurately measure and record things (see Day 248).

We can show Scripture uses many forms of approximation, including:

1. *Numerical approximations*: For example, a basin in Solomon's temple is said to have a diameter of ten cubits and a circumference of thirty cubits (1 Kings 7:23; 2 Chron. 4:2), indicating the approximate value of π (*pi*) as 3 (see Day 197). Numerical approximations are also involved when we encounter stock numbers in Scripture (40, 120, 1,000, etc).

2. *Verbal approximations*: Because the ancient world had no recording devices and few stenographers, ancient audiences didn't expect written dialogue to be a verbatim transcript but an approximation of what was said. Reconstruction and paraphrase were normal. We see examples when Scripture presents parallel accounts of the same events and the biblical authors give dialogue in somewhat different forms (e.g., in the Gospels).

3. *Descriptive approximations*: Every time we describe an event, we must decide which details to include and omit. There is an inescapable element of approximation in every event description, and this applied to the biblical authors too. Consequently, one evangelist may mention that Jesus healed two men on an occasion, while another may streamline the account by mentioning only one (see Day 37). Similarly, one author may give a more detailed account by mentioning both the principals in an encounter and the agents they employed, while another may mention only the principals (see Day 124).

4. *Chronological approximations*: Usually, the ancients did not keep detailed chronological records, and they had the liberty to record events either chronologically or non-chronologically, within the same general time frame (e.g., within the ministry of Christ; see Day 89).

5. *Literary approximations*: We often convey truth using literary devices not meant to be taken literally ("We should roll out the red carpet for this visitor"), and so did the ancients (see Day 31). Symbolism and figures of speech like hyperbole are common in Scripture.

Approximations are intrinsic to human speech; we can't avoid using them, and we use the same kinds as the ancients. We just use them differently.

The Causes of Homosexuality

CHALLENGE

"Some people are born homosexual, so it's in accord with their nature for them to engage in homosexual behavior. God made them that way."

DEFENSE

The premise of this challenge is shaky, and the conclusions drawn from it are erroneous.

First, the claim that some people are born homosexual is problematic. The origins of same-sex attraction are not well understood.

It may be true that most people with same-sex attraction do not recall a moment where they chose to have this condition, but humans are a highly cognitive species for whom training is important. It would be very surprising if our sexual desires were not in some degree conditioned by our life history and the sexual training we have experienced (e.g., what we choose to fantasize about). This applies both to people with same-sex attraction and those without it.

At the same time, we also have innate tendencies, which may be based on a variety of factors, including the hormones our bodies produce, our individual genetics, and so on.

The Catholic Church does not claim that the cause or causes of same-sex attraction have been established. The *Catechism* states: "Its psychological genesis remains largely unexplained" (CCC 2357).

Second, just because people are born with temptations does not mean that we can simply say "God made them that way" (see Day 235).

Third, even if same-sex attraction were purely innate, this would not lead to the conclusion that it is moral to engage in homosexual behavior. Everyone has temptations, and sometimes these are due to factors we have no control over.

It is commonly thought that some people have a genetic predisposition to alcohol abuse. Other people have suffered traumatic brain injuries that increase the risk of their engaging in violent and criminal behavior. However, these predispositions do not justify giving in to one's impulses.

A person with a genetic predisposition to alcohol abuse is not justified in becoming an alcoholic, and a person with traumatic brain injury is not justified in committing violent crime. We all have immoral impulses—temptations—and we are called not to give in to them but to resist and overcome them.

Compassion for Those with Same-Sex Attraction

CHALLENGE

"The Catholic Faith is homophobic. It hates and fears gay people."

DEFENSE

The Church recognizes everyone, including those with same-sex attraction, as people God loves and for whom Christ died.

Sometimes homosexual activists accuse those who disagree with them of "hate." Or they may accuse others of irrational fear—of being "homophobic." Although some individuals may hate or fear homosexuals, these allegations are used indiscriminately to attack those who disagree and to shut down rational discussion. However, merely disagreeing with homosexuality does not involve either hate or fear.

Homosexual behavior is a distortion of the way human sexuality is meant to work, but it is far from alone. There are many other distortions, including pornography, prostitution, and adultery. People with same-sex attraction are suffering a particular form of temptation, but everyone suffers temptation. We are all tempted to do things we should not, and we must all be clear-eyed about this fact and resist temptation.

People who have same-sex attraction have the same inherent dignity as other human beings, and they must be treated with respect—so much respect that we offer them both the truth about human sin and the hope for dealing with it that is found in Jesus Christ.

For people with same-sex attraction, as for people with every other temptation, we must be "speaking the truth in love" (Eph. 4:15). The *Catechism* states:

> The number of men and women who have deep-seated homosexual tendencies is not negligible. This inclination, which is objectively disordered, constitutes for most of them a trial. They must be accepted with respect, compassion, and sensitivity. Every sign of unjust discrimination in their regard should be avoided. These persons are called to fulfill God's will in their lives and, if they are Christians, to unite to the sacrifice of the Lord's Cross the difficulties they may encounter from their condition.
>
> Homosexual persons are called to chastity. By the virtues of self-mastery that teach them inner freedom, at times by the support of disinterested friendship, by prayer and sacramental grace, they can and should gradually and resolutely approach Christian perfection (CCC 2358–59).

TIP

For assistance dealing with same-sex attraction, see the support group Courage International (www.CourageRC.org).

Infallibility and Convenience

CHALLENGE

"Infallibility is a matter of convenience. When it suits Catholic apologists, they declare a teaching infallible, but when it's embarrassing, they say it's not. There aren't objective criteria for when a teaching is infallible."

DEFENSE

This challenge is false on a number of levels.

First, there are objective criteria for when a teaching is infallible (see *Code of Canon Law* 749 §§1–2; Vatican I, *Pastor Aeternus* 4; Vatican II, *Lumen Gentium* 25).

Second, Catholic apologists are frequently in situations where it would be easier if they did *not* have to defend infallible teachings, particularly ones that are difficult for human reason to grasp (e.g., God is a Trinity of Persons, transubstantiation occurs in the Eucharist) or that are supported primarily by Tradition rather than Scripture (e.g., Mary was immaculately conceived and bodily assumed into heaven). The fact that competent apologists *don't* claim that these teachings aren't infallible reveals infallibility isn't a matter of convenience for them.

Third, a certain expertise in Catholic theology and how the Magisterium uses language is needed to evaluate whether the criteria for infallibility have been fulfilled. This leads to misunderstandings in this area.

Sometimes Catholic apologists may make mistakes in thinking that a particular teaching is infallible when it is not (or vice versa). However, they naturally tend to have more expertise in reading Church documents than critics of the Church do. Consequently, critics are more prone to misunderstand the status of a teaching.

This tendency is reinforced by the history of Protestant/Catholic polemics and tension between the two groups. It is a natural human tendency, which all must guard against, to commit the straw man fallacy by attacking a caricature of another's position rather than his real position. As a result, there has been a tendency among anti-Catholics to assume that statements made in historical sources are infallible, when they were not, for purposes of having an easier target to attack. Thus critics have had more of a hermeneutic of convenience when it comes to infallibility than Catholic apologists have.

Fourth, the Church indicates that in cases of doubt a teaching is to be regarded as *non*-infallible: "No doctrine is understood as defined infallibly unless this is manifestly evident" (can. 749 §3). Canonically, the burden of proof is on the one who would claim that a particular teaching is infallible.

Internal Biblical References and the Canon

CHALLENGE

"Your claim that Tradition determines the canon of Scripture (see Day 247) is false. The books of the Bible witness to one another as Scripture."

DEFENSE

There are several problems with this view.

Various biblical books do refer to other books as Scripture. For example, Matthew 21:42 quotes Psalm 118:22–23 as being among "the scriptures." Other passages in Matthew use the formula "it is written," which commonly introduces Scripture quotations, to refer to Micah 5:2 (Matt. 2:5), Deuteronomy 8:3 (Matt. 4:4), Isaiah 56:7 (Matt. 21:13), and Zechariah 13:7 (Matt. 26:31). From this one may build a case that Matthew acknowledged the Psalms, Micah, Deuteronomy, Isaiah, and Zechariah as Scripture.

This is actually a useful technique for determining what the biblical authors regarded as Scripture. However, it has several major limitations that create problems.

First, it won't give you the complete Old Testament, for there are multiple books that the New Testament either never quotes or never quotes as Scripture (see Day 288).

Second, the test is of very little help with the New Testament canon. There are only two places where the New Testament refers to other New Testament books as Scripture. One is 1 Timothy 5:17, which appears to refer to Luke 10:7 as Scripture, and 1 Peter 3:16, where Peter refers in a general way to Paul's letters as Scripture. The trouble is: He doesn't *name* the letters, so we don't know which ones he's acknowledging.

Third, although one can use internal references to build a partial knowledge of which books the biblical authors considered Scripture, there is an even more fundamental problem: You must know some books are apostolic to get the process off the ground.

For example, it does no good to know that Matthew's Gospel treats Deuteronomy, the Psalms, Isaiah, and so on, as Scripture unless you *first* know the Gospel of Matthew is apostolic in the sense needed to make it part of the canon. Without that knowledge, you can't begin applying the technique.

Consequently, we must still appeal to Tradition to know which books are apostolic and thus Scripture. Internal biblical references can play a clarifying and supporting role, but Tradition is still fundamental for identifying Scripture.

"You Are Gods."

CHALLENGE

*"Scripture teaches men can become gods.
Jesus said, 'You are gods' (John 10:34)."*

DEFENSE

Men do not become gods the way Jesus is God.

The Hebrew word *'elohim* normally refers to either the one true God or pagan gods (see Day 227). However, it has other, lesser-known meanings.

Thus it can refer to angels. Psalm 8:5 says God made man lower than *'elohim*, and the Septuagint translated this as *angelous* (a plural form of the Greek word *angelos*, "angel"). This understanding was endorsed by the New Testament (see Heb. 8:7).

Similarly, some Aramaic translations of Old Testament passages rendered *'elohim* using the word for "judges" (*dayyān*).

In John, when Jesus asks why a group is about to stone him, they reply, "Because you, being a man, make yourself God" (John 10:33). We then read:

> Jesus answered them, "Is it not written in your law, 'I said, you are gods'? If he called them gods to whom the word of God came . . . do you say of him whom the Father consecrated and sent into the world, 'You are blaspheming,' because I said, 'I am the Son of God'?" (John 10:34–36).

Here Jesus quotes Psalm 82:6, which is part of a psalm where God condemns "gods" for judging unjustly, showing partiality to the wicked, denying justice to the weak and fatherless, and so on. Scholars have often taken this psalm as using *'elohim* in the sense of "judges," and Jesus may have this in mind.

It is clear, though, he identifies these "gods" as those "to whom the word of God came." They are thus men linked to the divine or divinized by contact with God's word. However, the structure of Jesus' argument indicates he is God in a unique sense.

Jesus uses an *a fortiori* argument, according to which if one thing is true then another thing is even more true: Thus, if Scripture can apply the term "gods" even to men who have come into contact with God's word, Jesus has a much greater claim for he's the one who "the Father consecrated and sent into the world." Jesus is thus God in a unique sense that transcends the way men can be (see Day 245).

TIP

For more on how John's Gospel teaches Jesus' divinity, see Day 12.

The Perspicuity of Scripture

"We don't need Tradition or the Magisterium to help us understand Scripture. It is perspicuous—i.e., clear and readily understandable."

DEFENSE

This claim can be understood more than one way.

It may be understood in a strong sense, according to which Scripture is sufficiently clear that every point of theology can be settled by Scripture alone. However, Scripture contains many passages that are very difficult to understand. Anyone with minimal exposure to the Bible knows it is far from perspicuous. If it were, the diverse interpretations and debates about its meaning would not exist.

Scripture comments on the difficulty people experience reading it. When Philip encounters the Ethiopian eunuch, who is reading Isaiah 53 (perhaps the single most significant messianic prophecy), Philip asks: "'Do you understand what you are reading?' And he said, 'How can I, unless some one guides me?'" (Acts 8:30–31).

Scripture contains many passages, including prophecies and parables, which are intended *not* to be perspicuous. God apparently wants us to wrestle with the meaning of Scripture, and the claim that it is so clear every point of theology can be settled by Scripture alone is not credible.

Consequently, many have proposed a weakened version of the claim, according to which Scripture is only perspicuous enough that its main doctrines are clear. It is sometimes said, "The main things are the plain things, and the plain things are the main things." The weakened claim is more defensible. There are certain, central doctrines that Scripture clearly teaches (e.g., God exists, God created the world, there is only one God, Jesus is the Messiah).

However, it wrongly conveys the idea that only the clear things in Scripture are important. This is not true. Peter comments on Paul's letters: "There are some things in them hard to understand, which the ignorant and unstable twist to their own destruction, as they do the other scriptures" (2 Pet. 3:16). If Paul's writings contain things hard enough to understand that the unlearned destroy themselves, not all the important things are clear and salvation is on the line.

More fundamentally, weakening the claim so it does not cover all points of theology makes it too weak to support the doctrine of *sola scriptura*. There will still be points of theology one needs Tradition or the Magisterium to make clear.

Natural Disasters

"Why would a good God allow natural disasters? It doesn't seem to be because of original sin, because our telescopes and probes show that floods and quakes have occurred on other planets and moons."

Destructive events in nature are morally neutral in themselves.

A flood is just a wave of water passing over dry land. An earthquake is a shaking of the ground, typically caused by the motion of tectonic plates. Other "natural disasters"—volcanic eruptions, heat waves, cold waves, storms, and so on—fit the same pattern. They are changes in an environment caused by natural, physical forces.

We think of them as destructive disasters because of the impact they have on humans and other life-forms. However, considered in themselves they are morally neutral. If a flood, quake, or volcanic eruption occurs on a lifeless planet or moon then there is no harm. Such events are only physical evils when they impact life. Otherwise, they just involve natural forces moving matter around.

Even from the viewpoint of life, they are not always bad. For example, the elements necessary for life are released when stars collapse into white dwarfs or explode as supernovas. Sometimes an event is good for some life-forms and bad for others. The cataclysm that killed the dinosaurs made the rise of mammals and man possible. If an earthquake causes a fox's den to collapse, killing the fox, it allows all the rabbits the fox would have eaten to live.

God allows such events to occur because of the way the universe is presently configured. The *Catechism* says:

> With infinite wisdom and goodness God freely willed to create a world "in a state of journeying" towards its ultimate perfection. In God's plan this process of becoming involves the appearance of certain beings and the disappearance of others, the existence of the more perfect alongside the less perfect, both constructive and destructive forces of nature. With physical good there exists also physical evil as long as creation has not reached perfection (CCC 310).

In some cases, the suffering caused by such events may have beneficial effects that give it purpose (see Day 7). Other times, it may have no apparent purpose, but God can still make it up to us when we innocently suffer the effects of a natural disaster (see Day 38).

Religion Hostile to Science?

CHALLENGE

"Religion is intrinsically hostile to science."

DEFENSE

This is a gross caricature that itself exhibits hostility to religion.

There have been conflicts involving science and religion (e.g., the Galileo affair, the Scopes Monkey Trial). There are religious individuals who are hostile to science, but there also are scientifically oriented individuals who are hostile to religion. Looking down on something as "unscientific" displays hostility in the same way dismissing it as "irreligious" does.

The supporters of both religion and science are flawed human beings who are sometimes unjustly hostile, but this does not make the two fields intrinsically hostile to each other.

Religion is a diverse phenomenon. When one thinks of all the different religions in the world, all the diversity of viewpoint and attitude that can exist within a single religion, and all of the *scientists* who belong to different religions, it is a gross caricature to assert that religion is somehow fundamentally opposed to science.

Christianity, in particular, understands God as a divine lawgiver who embedded certain laws in nature. These laws can be investigated by humans, and it has been argued that this understanding has played an important role in the rise of modern science, in which many Christian scientists were prominent.

Religion, science, and philosophy each ask fundamental questions about the world, and sometimes the areas investigated by the three disciplines overlap. However, this does not make the three disciplines intrinsically hostile to each other.

From a Christian point of view, all truth is God's truth, and he is glorified when humans use their divinely given intellects to discover what God has done, regardless of which field makes the discovery.

The Catholic attitude toward science is expressed in the *Catechism*:

The question about the origins of the world and of man has been the object of many scientific studies which have splendidly enriched our knowledge of the age and dimensions of the cosmos, the development of life-forms and the appearance of man. These discoveries invite us to even greater admiration for the greatness of the Creator, prompting us to give him thanks for all his works and for the understanding and wisdom he gives to scholars and researchers (CCC 283).

Immersion Only?

CHALLENGE

"People should be baptized only by immersion: (1) In Greek the word for "baptize" (baptizein) means 'to dip'; (2) immersion better fits the symbolism of Jesus' burial (Rom. 6:1–4; Col. 2:12); and (3) when Jesus was baptized, he 'came up out of the water' (Mark 1:10) and the Ethiopian eunuch 'went down into the water' (Acts 8:38)."

DEFENSE

These arguments do not show immersion is the only means of baptizing.

First, *baptizein* doesn't simply mean dip: "The word that invariably means 'to dip' is not *baptizein* but *baptein*; *baptizein* has a wider signification; and its use to denote the Jewish ceremonial of pouring water on the hands (Luke 11:38; Mark 7:4) . . . shows that it is impossible to conclude from the word itself that immersion is the only valid method of performing the rite" (*International Standard Bible Encyclopedia* 1:419).

Second, although we are familiar with graves dug down into the ground, Jews were commonly buried in tombs cut sideways into cliffs. Jesus was buried this way (Matt. 27:60; John 20:4–8). The downward motion of immersion, therefore, does not perfectly correspond to how Jesus was buried. Also, the Holy Spirit descended at Jesus' baptism (Matt. 3:16), and when baptism is administered by pouring water on the head, this corresponds to the Holy Spirit being "poured out" on the disciples (Acts 2:33, 10:45).

Third, the statements about Jesus and the Ethiopian eunuch coming up out of and going down into the water only show where they were standing when the baptism occurred. They don't describe how it was performed.

When Jesus is said to come up out of the water, it means he climbed out of the Jordan River, not that he broke the surface of the water after being immersed. Similarly, we read that the eunuch "commanded the chariot to stop, and they both went down into the water, Philip and the eunuch, and he baptized him." *Both* Philip and the eunuch "went down into the water," meaning that they were standing there when Philip baptized him.

The fact that people were standing in water when the baptisms were performed doesn't prove immersion. Christian art from the early centuries commonly depicts those being baptized standing in water and having water poured on their heads. This understanding may also be indicated by the *Didache* (see Day 308).

Praying to the Saints

CHALLENGE

"Catholics shouldn't pray to the saints. Prayer is an act of worship, which is due only to God."

DEFENSE

This involves a confusion of terms based on how the English language developed.

In contemporary American English, "pray" indicates an act of worshipping God. However, Catholics do not give divine worship to the saints.

The root of the confusion lies in the fact that the English word "pray" is derived from the Latin word *precare*, which meant "to ask/implore/entreat."

By the 1300s, the English phrase "I pray thee" was used as a way to make a polite request—i.e., "I ask you" (equivalent to "please" or "if you will"). "I pray thee" was later contracted to the single word "prithee," which is rare in American English but more familiar in British English. Because of the Protestant influence on American English, the word "pray" was eventually restricted to acts of worshipping God. However, this was not its original meaning.

The original sense of the term is preserved in settings like law courts (where the phrase "My client prays that the court . . ." still means "My client asks that the court . . .") or in Catholic circles (where it indicates *asking* the saints for their prayers).

If you read the *Catechism* (or other official Catholic documents), you won't commonly find the phrases "praying to the saints" or "prayer to the saints." What the Church normally uses instead is the phrase "intercession of the saints" (cf. CCC 956, 1434), which expresses more precisely what Catholics are asking when they "pray to the saints." They are asking the saints for their intercession—i.e., they are asking them to ask God to grant their prayer requests.

In other words, they are asking the saints to be prayer partners with them.

They are *not* giving the saints the worship that is due to God alone. No matter what respect a created being may be due (cf. Exod. 20:12, Rom. 13:7, 1 Pet. 2:17), God is an infinite, uncreated being who is due the supreme form of worship. Catholics do not violate this when they ask the saints to be their prayer partners.

Judging Others

CHALLENGE

"Christians shouldn't criticize others' lifestyles or actions. Didn't Jesus say not to judge?"

DEFENSE

Jesus didn't tell us that we should close our eyes to moral evil in the world.

The exhortation not to judge is found in Jesus' major ethical discourse (Matt. 5:1–7:29, Luke 6:17–49). The *point* of the discourse is to give moral instruction. In it, Jesus discusses what conduct counts as good and bad, and he expects his followers to acknowledge the difference.

Not only does he expect them to distinguish between good and evil in their own behavior, he also expects them to do so with others' conduct, telling them, "You will know them by their fruits" (Matt. 7:20). Thus, whatever Jesus meant, it was not that we should pretend that nobody does evil.

What he did mean is not difficult to discern if we read the statement itself: "Judge not, that you be not judged. For with the judgment you pronounce you will be judged, and the measure you give will be the measure you get" (Matt. 7:1–2); "Judge not, and you will not be judged; condemn not, and you will not be condemned; forgive, and you will be forgiven" (Luke 6:37).

Jesus is saying we should take a generous, forgiving attitude with others so God will take a generous, forgiving attitude with us. We should treat others as we want to be treated. This is a prominent theme in his teaching (cf. Matt. 5:43–48, 6:12–15, 7:12, 18:21–35).

Although we are to be forgiving and merciful to others, this does not mean ignoring, much less approving, immoral behavior. Neither does it mean we should not try to help others. Admonishing the sinner is a spiritual work of mercy. Scripture elsewhere says: "Let him know that whoever brings back a sinner from the error of his way will save his soul from death and will cover a multitude of sins" (James 5:20).

Often the exhortation not to judge is used as a conversation stopper to shut down discussions of immoral behavior. Sometimes it carries the insinuation that the one "judging" is doing something morally wrong. When this is the case, the person making the accusation is himself judging, and thus risks being a hypocrite (cf. Matt. 7:3–5).

The Concept of *Sola Scriptura*

CHALLENGE

"Catholic apologists misrepresent the Protestant doctrine of sola scriptura *('Scripture alone'). It merely means that Scripture contains everything necessary for salvation."*

DEFENSE

This is not how the teaching is understood by most Protestants, who apply it to all Christian doctrine.

Salvation-based explanations of *sola scriptura* are sometimes found in popular-level writings of Protestant apologetics, but they are also found elsewhere. For example, the Anglican Articles of Religion state: "Holy Scripture containeth all things necessary to salvation: so that whatsoever is not read therein, nor may be proved thereby, is not to be required of any man, that it should be believed as an article of the Faith, or be thought requisite or necessary to salvation" (art. 6).

Those who define *sola scriptura* in terms of what is needed for salvation presumably mean Scripture contains all truths of soteriology (the doctrine of salvation), which is a subset of theology in general. Saying we should be able to prove all truths of soteriology by Scripture alone is a more modest claim than that we should be able to prove all theology this way. It is thus a more defensible claim, and one with which Catholics could potentially agree.

However, this is not how *sola scriptura* is generally understood or applied. Even the Articles of Religion indicate a broader application, for they say that nothing that can't be proved by Scripture is an article of faith—the faith as a whole being broader than the subject of salvation.

A more typical formulation is found in the Westminster Confession of Faith: "The whole counsel of God concerning all things necessary for His own glory, man's salvation, faith, and life, is either expressly set down in Scripture, or by good and necessary consequence may be deduced from Scripture" (1:6).

Here *sola scriptura* is said to cover everything necessary for "salvation, faith, and life"—with *faith* and *life* including doctrinal and moral theology.

The broader use of the concept is also confirmed by experience, which shows Protestants regularly ask the question "Where is that in the Bible?" on theological subjects in general, not just on soteriological ones.

This broader understanding, however, is a more expansive and thus less defensible claim (see Days 5 and 16).

Jesus the Rock

CHALLENGE

"Peter can't be the rock in Matthew 16:18 because Scripture says God *is the rock (Isa. 51:1). Further, Peter describes Jesus as a stone (1 Pet. 2:4–8). Therefore, Jesus must be the rock."*

DEFENSE

This challenge does not understand the way metaphors work.

Although Isaiah does refer to God as "the rock from which you were hewn," there is nothing about this passage indicating that *only* God can be described as a rock.

If *only* God could be described as a rock then Jesus could not have given Simon bar-Jonah the nickname Cephas/Peter/Rock (John 1:42; Matt. 16:18). The fact that Jesus bestows this nickname means that the metaphor of a rock can be used to refer to non-divine individuals, so we must ask what metaphor is being used in any given passage.

When Peter refers to Jesus as a living stone, he uses the normal Greek word for stone: *lithos*. The fact that he uses this rather than *petra* or *petros* (see Day 282) indicates a different metaphor is being used than when he gave Peter his nickname.

Metaphors are not just used in a single way. Protestant scholar D.A. Carson notes:

> The objection that Peter considers Jesus the rock is insubstantial because metaphors are commonly used variously, till they become stereotyped, and sometimes even then. Here [in Matt. 16:18] Jesus builds his church; in 1 Corinthians 3:10, Paul is "an expert builder." In 1 Corinthians 3:11, Jesus is the church's foundation; in Ephesians 2:19–20, the apostles and prophets are the foundation (cf. also Rev 21:14), and Jesus is the "cornerstone." Here Peter has the keys; in Revelation 1:18; 3:7, Jesus has the keys. In John 9:5, Jesus is "the light of the world"; in Matthew 5:14, his disciples are. None of these pairs threatens Jesus' uniqueness. They simply show how metaphors must be interpreted primarily with reference to their immediate contexts (*The Expositor's Bible Commentary* on Matt. 16:18).

Carson also notes: "In this passage Jesus is the builder of the church and it would be a strange mixture of metaphors that also sees him within the same clauses as its foundation" (ibid.).

The challenge thus uses a simplistic understanding of how metaphors work and forces metaphors used elsewhere in Scripture into the text of Matthew 16:18.

The Use of Religious Images

CHALLENGE

"Catholics use statues and pictures, but the Ten Commandments prohibit such religious images (Exod. 20:4–6; Deut. 5:8–10)."

DEFENSE

The Ten Commandments prohibit making idols, not religious images.

Idols are manufactured objects that people falsely believe to be deities. Their use was commonplace in paganism, and God rightly prohibited the Israelites from making them. However, not all religious use of images is idolatry, and God commanded the religious use of images in the Old Testament.

At one point the Israelites are being bitten by serpents, and God had Moses make a bronze serpent "and set it on a pole; and if a serpent bit any man, he would look at the bronze serpent and live" (Num. 21:9). Looking at the bronze serpent to be healed was a religious act God authorized. (Nevertheless, when the bronze serpent began to be worshipped as a god itself, it was destroyed; 2 Kings 18:4).

Similarly, God commanded statues of golden cherubim be made at each end of the mercy seat on the Ark of the Covenant (Exod. 25:18–22). He similarly commanded images of cherubim be woven into the curtains of the tabernacle (Exod. 26:1). When the tabernacle was replaced by the temple, images of cherubim were fashioned on the temple's walls, its doors, and its veil (2 King. 6:29–35; 2 Chron. 3:7, 14). And there were two giant (15–feet tall) statues of cherubim in the holy of holies (2 Kings 6:23–28; 2 Chron. 3:10–13).

The inclusion of these images on the ark, in the tabernacle, and in the temple indicates their religious function. They represent the inhabitants of heaven, the angels who surround God. In our age, now that humans have been admitted to heaven (Rev. 6:9, 7:14–17), it is natural for statues of human saints also to be placed in churches.

Most significantly, by virtue of the Incarnation, Jesus inaugurated a new age in which God took on visible form. It has been natural since then for Christians to depict Jesus in religious art. This includes the Protestant community, where two-dimensional images of Jesus are common. Adding a third dimension to make a carving or statue does not fundamentally change the situation.

All today recognize that images of Christ and the saints are merely symbols of the individuals they represent (a precursor of modern photographs). They are not idols (see Day 307).

The Canonicity of the Deuterocanonicals

CHALLENGE

"Why should we think the deuterocanonicals are Scripture?"

DEFENSE

Multiple lines of evidence support this conclusion.

The deuterocanonicals are seven books (Tobit, Judith, Baruch, Sirach, Wisdom, 1–2 Maccabees) and parts of two others (Daniel, Esther) considered canonical in the Catholic Church and many Eastern Orthodox and other Eastern Christian Churches but not in the Protestant community.

They were included in the canonical tradition represented by the Septuagint, the major Greek translation of the Old Testament. Where the Septuagint was translated is unclear. The traditional account links it to Alexandria; another possibility is Palestine, "because only a Palestinian origin could have generated sufficient prestige for the new translation" (*Yale Anchor Bible Dictionary*, s.v., "Septuagint").

It was so prestigious that it was the version of the Old Testament overwhelmingly quoted by the authors of the New Testament. Although they could have translated from Hebrew or Aramaic versions, they used the Septuagint. According to figures provided by Gleason Archer and G.C. Chirichigno, there are 340 times when the New Testament authors appear to quote from the Septuagint, but only thirty-three times they clearly translate from the Hebrew text (*Old Testament Quotations in the New Testament: A Complete Survey*, xxv–xxviii).

The New Testament authors overwhelmingly used the Septuagint, which contained the deuterocanonicals. They also alluded to these books (see Day 305), and they *never warned* their audience against the deuterocanonical books. Consequently, it was natural for the first Christians to regard them as Scripture.

Protestant Church historian J.N.D. Kelly writes that, although some early writers had different views on these books, "for the great majority, however, the deuterocanonical writings ranked as Scripture in the fullest sense" (*Early Christian Doctrines*, 5th ed., 55). We thus find the use of the deuterocanonicals widely attested among the Fathers.

The reception of these books as canonical was affirmed at various councils, including Rome (382), Hippo (393), the Council of Carthage of 397, and the Council of Carthage of 419. These were local councils, but the canonicity of the books was also affirmed at the ecumenical council of Florence (1442) and infallibly defined at the Council of Trent (1546).

The canonicity of the deuterocanonicals is thus supported by Scripture, Tradition, and the Magisterium.

Justification in James 2

"Catholics misunderstand James 2. When James talks about faith, he's referring to dead faith, and when he talks about justification, he's referring to justification before men."

DEFENSE

This isn't supported by a careful reading of James 2.

James says "faith apart from works is dead" (James 2:26), but it does not follow from this that he is talking about "dead faith." Read the passage and substitute the phrase "dead faith" where James says "faith." This will result in absurdities. Thus James 2:18b would read, "I by my works will show you my dead faith," and 2:22a would read, "You see that dead faith was active along with his works."

James doesn't see anything wrong with the faith he is discussing. It's just limited to intellectual assent (the kind of belief in God even demons have; see below). What makes that intellectual assent alive or dead, he says, is whether it is accompanied by works.

Further, James isn't referring to "justification before men." This phrase is understood to mean an outward demonstration of justification before God, the thought being that if you are right with God, it will manifest in actions men can see and know of your justification before God.

It's true that those who are justified before God will naturally perform visible good works (Eph. 2:10), but we can't limit the justification James is talking about to "justification before men." This phrase doesn't appear in the text, which indicates James has justification before God in mind. Thus he begins by asking, "What does it profit, my brethren, if a man says he has faith but has not works? Can his faith save him?" (James 2:14).

The reference to salvation indicates he's concerned with justification before God. That's the context in which he says, "So faith by itself, if it has no works, is dead" (James 2:17), meaning *dead before God*, not merely before men.

James similarly raises the issue of eternal salvation when he notes, "Even the demons believe—and shudder" at the prospect of God's wrath (James 2:19). By implication, if the audience has only the intellectual belief that demons do, then they, too, will not be saved. James thus once more indicates justification before God is under discussion.

TIP

For more on the interpretation of this passage, see Day 222.

Between Two Robbers?

CHALLENGE

"The Gospels say that Jesus was crucified between two robbers (Matt. 27:38; Mark 15:27), but this is inaccurate. We know that the ancient Romans only crucified people who committed acts of rebellion."

DEFENSE

Romans did crucify robbers, but these two were likely rebels.

Robbery isn't the same as theft. Theft is taking someone's property, but robbery is taking it by force. There's an inherent element of violence in robbery that differentiates it from theft.

When robbery is committed on water, it's called piracy. Pirates are robbers who travel by water, and we know the Romans sometimes crucified pirates. For example, as a young man and before he was a political leader, Julius Caesar was kidnapped by pirates and held for ransom on an island. "But after his ransom had come from Miletus and he had paid it and was set free, he immediately manned vessels and put to sea from the harbour of Miletus against the robbers. He caught them . . . and crucified them all, just as he had often warned them on the island that he would do, when they thought he was joking" (Plutarch, *Life of Julius Caesar* 2:5–7).

Because of the violence inherent in robbery, it often blended into rebellion. Gangs of robbers would hide in the countryside, taking valuables from both locals and travelers by force, and the political authorities would send men to battle them. Alternately, political revolutionaries would hide out in the countryside, taking what they needed from others by force, and the political authorities would pursue them.

Either way, robbery was associated with battling the political authorities, and thus there was a single Greek word to describe a person who did these things: *lēstēs*. It can be translated either "robber, highwayman, bandit" or "revolutionary, insurrectionist, guerrilla" (Bauer, Arndt, Gingrich, and Danker, *A Greek-English Lexicon of the New Testament and Early Christian Literature*, s.v. *lēstēs*).

This is the word used for the two "robbers" crucified with Jesus. It's also used to describe Barabbas (John 18:40), "who had been thrown into prison for an insurrection started in the city, and for murder" (Luke 23:19; cf. Mark 15:7).

Scholars have suggested that, as a "notorious prisoner" (Matt. 27:16), Barabbas led the insurrection and the two "robbers" were his followers. Originally, Barabbas their leader would have been crucified between them, but Jesus took his place.

Who Is the Greatest?

CHALLENGE

"During the Last Supper the apostles argued over who was the greatest (Luke 22:24). Jesus shamed them, indicating that none of them was the greatest—not even Peter."

DEFENSE

This misreads the text. Jesus gives a threefold response indicating that Peter was the disciples' leader.

Responding to the dispute, Jesus says three things. These form a single, continuous quotation of Jesus (they aren't even interrupted by breaks like "then he said"). It's all one block, indicating all three parts form his answer to the dispute about greatness.

First, he tells them the principle of servant leadership, which they are all to employ: "The kings of the Gentiles exercise lordship over them; and those in authority over them are called benefactors. But not so with you; rather let the greatest among you become as the youngest, and the leader as one who serves. For which is the greater, one who sits at table, or one who serves? Is it not the one who sits at table? But I am among you as one who serves" (Luke 22:25–27).

Second, he assures them they will all have a prominent place in his kingdom: "You are those who have continued with me in my trials; and I assign to you, as my Father assigned to me, a kingdom, that you may eat and drink at my table in my kingdom, and sit on thrones judging the twelve tribes of Israel" (Luke 22:28–30).

Third, he singles out Peter and charges him with a special pastoral task with respect to the other disciples: "Simon, Simon, behold, Satan demanded to have you, that he might sift you like wheat, but I have prayed for you that your faith may not fail; and when you have turned again, strengthen your brethren" (Luke 22:31–32).

Jesus' reply begins with a general principle and is progressively more specific. It indicates the disciples have been thinking about the question the wrong way around. Leadership is not about personal greatness but serving others. And there is still a leader—Peter—but he is told "strengthen your brethren," not "exercise lordship over them."

TIP

This passage is the background to the pope's title *servus servorum Dei* (Latin, "servant of the servants of God").

The Jewish People and the Old Testament Canon

CHALLENGE

"Scripture says that the Jews were 'entrusted with the oracles of God' (Rom. 3:2), so we should look to them for the Old Testament canon. They reject the deuterocanonicals, and so should we."

DEFENSE

There are multiple problems with this argument.

First, not all Jewish people have the same canon. Falashas (Ethiopian Jews) have a canon including deuterocanonical books. It was rabbinic Jews that Protestants were familiar with in the 1500s, and their canon that the Reformers borrowed.

Second, as we cover elsewhere (see Day 255), there were multiple canonical traditions in the first century. The Pharisee tradition, which gave rise to the canon used by rabbinic Judaism, was only one tradition.

Third, first-century Christians did not use the Pharisee canonical tradition. They used the Septuagint tradition, which they passed on to the early Church (see Day 273).

Fourth, the Pharisee canonical tradition continued to be debated after the split with Christianity.

According to now outdated scholarship, the Pharisee/rabbinical canon was settled around A.D. 90 at the "Council of Jamnia" ("Jabneh," "Yavneh"). However, there was no such council. Christians held councils to settle issues; Jews did not. This "council" was actually a Jewish school set up in Yavneh after the destruction of the temple in A.D. 70, and it did not settle the canon of Scripture.

The so-called Council of Jamnia was more in the nature of a school or an academy that sat in Jamnia between the years 75 and 117. There is no evidence of a decision drawing up a list of books. It seems that the canon of the Jewish Scriptures was not definitively fixed before the end of the second century. Scholarly discussion on the status of certain books continued into the third century (Pontifical Biblical Commission, "The Jewish People and Their Sacred Scriptures," fn. 33).

Although the Jewish people were "entrusted with the oracles of God," they had not reached a conclusion in Jesus' day on what books counted as Scripture, and Christians should look to the decision of the Church on this matter—not that of a particular Jewish school, whose canon only solidified later in the Christian age.

TIP

For a good discussion of this from a Protestant perspective, see Lee McDonald, *The Biblical Canon: Its Origin, Transmission, and Authority.*

"Lest Any Man Should Boast"

CHALLENGE

"Doesn't Paul's statement that we are saved 'not because of works, lest any man should boast' (Eph. 2:9) show he teaches justification by 'faith alone'?"

DEFENSE

This misunderstands the kind of boasting in question.

Paul never uses the phrase "faith alone," and we elsewhere cover how the context of this passage shows it's about the Jewish-Gentile question found elsewhere in Paul's writings, meaning the "works" are actions done to obey the Law of Moses (see Days 63, 136, and 204).

This is also indicated when, in the next verse, Paul praises "good works" as part of the Christian life, in contrast to the "works" he says don't save us. It would be awkward to pivot from the non-necessity of "works" to the importance of "good works" if they were the same thing. (Indeed, Paul stresses their importance greatly, saying we are "created in Christ Jesus for good works, which God prepared beforehand, that we should walk in them"; Eph. 2:10.) It is more natural to take "works" and "good works" as different things, with "works" being works of the Mosaic Law, as elsewhere in Paul.

The reference to boasting doesn't show the "works" belong to the moral sphere. The word translated "boast" (Greek, *kauchaomai*) also means "glory," "rejoice," and Paul frequently uses it to refer to things other than boasting about one's own accomplishments.

Specifically: He speaks of both Jews and Christians "boasting" in an evangelistic sense before non-believers. Thus he speaks of Jews boasting "in God" (Rom. 2:17) and "in the Law" (Rom. 2:23). Using the same Greek word, he also speaks of Christians boasting "in our hope" (Rom. 5:2) and "in God through our Lord Jesus Christ" (Rom. 5:11).

Non-Christian Jews thus aren't boasting of their moral accomplishments, but telling pagan Gentiles of God and how they have a special relationship with him through the Law. Christians, similarly, aren't boasting of their moral accomplishments, but telling unbelievers of God and how they have a special relationship with him through Christ.

Read in context, Paul's saying salvation is "not because of works, lest any man should boast" means neither Jew nor Gentile can boast of having a special, saving relationship with God in preference to the other: Both are saved through faith in Christ.

TIP

See Jimmy Akin, *The Drama of Salvation*, chapter 6.

Does Mary's Perpetual Virginity Matter?

CHALLENGE

"What difference does it make if Mary remained a virgin? Couldn't God have continued Jesus' mission if she had other children?"

DEFENSE

God is omnipotent and can do anything he chooses, but this doesn't mean his choices are arbitrary.

This objection is a subcase of a broader one: Why should Mary be a virgin in the first place? Couldn't God's Son be born of a woman who *wasn't* a virgin?

He could have. Being omnipotent, God could do that. He even could have had his Son born of a prostitute if he chose.

It isn't intrinsically required that Mary be any special kind of woman to be Jesus' mother—just that she be a woman. However, this doesn't mean it wasn't appropriate for God to give Mary certain qualities to make her a more fitting mother for his Son.

This applies, in the first place, to the virginal conception itself. The fact that Jesus was conceived without a human father is striking, arresting. It naturally raises the question: "What does this mean?"

One could say, "It makes a difference because God had prophesied in advance that his Son would be born of a virgin" (see Days 253 and 254). But this only raises the question: "Why did God prophesy that? What difference did it make that his Son be virgin-born?"

The answer is that, if Jesus doesn't have a human father, his father must be looked for outside of the human realm. Jesus' Father is not on earth but in heaven: His Father is God. This is the fundamental point underscored by the Virgin Birth.

It is also the fundamental reason for Mary's perpetual virginity (see Day 188). Consider: If Joseph and Mary later had children, it would raise doubts about the Virgin Birth itself.

Jesus was conceived when Mary was already legally married to Joseph, but before their time of cohabitation began (Matt. 1:18; Luke 1:26–34). If the two had gone on to have other children, it would have been all the easier to say, "Jesus wasn't literally the Son of God. His parents just had sex sooner than they let on."

The fact that Mary remained a virgin even after Jesus' birth thus underscores the fact that he is God's Son, the same way the Virgin Birth itself does.

The Role of the Church Fathers

"Why should I care about the Church Fathers? They aren't inspired like the New Testament authors."

The Church Fathers were writers in the early centuries who were notable for their holiness and soundness of teaching. They are important for a number of reasons.

First, they were closer in time and in culture to the New Testament authors, and their writings provide context needed to understand aspects of the New Testament. The writings of the Church Fathers—together with ancient Jewish sources—are the two most important groups of writings for this purpose. Ancient Jewish sources shed light on the ideas that flowed into the writing of Scripture, and the Church Fathers shed light on the teachings that flowed from Christ and the apostles. Indeed, the earliest Fathers were taught directly by apostles and eyewitnesses of Christ's ministry.

Second, from the perspective of faith, Jesus said he would be with his Church forever (Matt. 28:20). He promised to send his Church the Holy Spirit "to be with you for ever," to "teach you all things," and to "guide you into all the truth" (John 14:16, 26, 16:13). The Holy Spirit's ministry began in a special way on Pentecost (Acts 2) and has continued throughout the Church age. The New Testament indicates that the Church is "the pillar and bulwark of the truth" (1 Tim. 3:15) and "the gates of hades shall not prevail against it" (Matt. 16:18).

All this indicates providential care and guidance extending throughout the Christian age and including the age of the Church Fathers. Consequently, we would be foolish to ignore the writings of this period.

Third, the age of the Fathers was one in which supremely important questions were worked out, including the divinity of Christ and the doctrine of the Trinity.

Fourth, the Fathers were the bearers of the apostolic Tradition that allowed the canon of Scripture to be discerned (see Day 247). Without them, we wouldn't even know the canon.

Although no one Father, individually, may be relied upon the way the inspired authors of the New Testament can be, the Fathers as a group represent an indispensible witness to the Christian faith.

For information on the teachings of the Church Fathers, see Jimmy Akin, *The Fathers Know Best.*

Cafeteria Christianity

CHALLENGE

"Why can't I, as a Christian, simply choose the beliefs I think are right? Why should anybody else tell me what I should believe?"

DEFENSE

This may be an attractive proposition in our individualistic age, but it wasn't Jesus' view.

If you're going to be a Christian, that means listening to Jesus Christ, and he set up a Church, not a cafeteria. We aren't allowed to pick and choose our beliefs like we pick and choose dishes in a serving line.

This is evident from the way Jesus teaches. In the Sermon on the Mount, he repeatedly takes on common interpretations of Jewish law and corrects them by his own authority, using the formula, "You have heard . . . but *I* say . . ." (Matt. 5:21–22, 27–28, 31–32, 33–34, 38–39, 43–44). The authority with which he taught was remarkable even in his own day: "The crowds were astonished at his teaching, for he taught them as one who had authority, and not as their scribes" (Matt. 7:28–29; cf. Mark 1:22, Luke 4:32).

Jesus is the Messiah and the Son of God. His teaching is backed by divine authority—"My teaching is not mine, but his who sent me" (John 7:16)—and one is not a faithful Christian if one rejects what Christ taught. That has implications, because Christ did not keep this authority to himself. He gave teaching authority to the ministers he put in charge of his Church, telling them: "He who hears you hears me, and he who rejects you rejects me, and he who rejects me rejects him who sent me" (Luke 10:16).

He further promised them, "When the Spirit of truth comes, he will guide you into all the truth" (John 16:13), and he declared: "All authority in heaven and on earth has been given to me. Go therefore and make disciples of all nations, baptizing them in the name of the Father and of the Son and of the Holy Spirit, teaching them to observe all that I have commanded you; and lo, I am with you always, to the close of the age" (Matt. 28:18–20).

Jesus thus invested his Church with the authority to teach until the end of the world, and if we want to be Jesus' followers, we cannot simply pick and choose our own beliefs.

Petros versus *Petra*

CHALLENGE

"Peter can't be the rock that Jesus refers to in Matthew 16:18. He uses the word petros *(small stone) for 'Peter' but* petra *(large rock) for 'rock.' Why would he change the word if he was referring to Peter both times?"*

DEFENSE

This challenge has several problems and does not prove its case.

Protestant scholar D.A. Carson notes:

> Although it is true that *petros* and *petra* can mean "[small] stone" and "[large] rock" respectively in earlier Greek, the distinction is largely confined to poetry. Moreover the underlying Aramaic is in this case unquestionable; and most probably *kêphā'* was used in both clauses ("you are *kêphā'* and on this *kêphā'*"), since the word was used both for a name and for a "rock." The Peshitta (written in Syriac, a language cognate with Aramaic) makes no distinction between the words in the two clauses. The Greek makes the distinction between *petros* and *petra* simply because it is trying to preserve the pun, and in Greek the feminine *petra* could not very well serve as a masculine name (*The Expositor's Bible Commentary* on Matt. 16:18).

He further notes: "Had Matthew wanted to say no more than that Peter was a stone in contrast with Jesus the Rock, the more common word would have been *lithos* ("stone" of almost any size). Then there would have been no pun—and that is just the point!" (ibid.).

Although Jesus' words could have been translated into Greek using *petros* in both cases ("You are *petros* and on this *petros*"), *petra* may appear in the second instance simply to avoid using the same word too closely in quick succession. Avoiding repetition by using a synonym is often an important element of style (so much so that it is the reason pronouns exist).

Even if we were to grant that *petros* and *petra* referred to small and large stones respectively, this would not show Peter isn't the rock. That interpretation assumes *antithetic* parallelism, where the two are contrasted ("You are a small stone, but on this *other* big rock . . . "). However, it could just as well be *synthetic* parallelism, where the second idea builds on the first ("You may appear to be a small stone, but on the big rock you really are . . . ").

The Benefits of Religion

"Religion is a destructive force that harms people."

This is not supported by the evidence.

Every institution—churches, hospitals, schools, governments—makes mistakes and harms people on occasion. However, to claim an institution is fundamentally harmful, one needs to provide evidence it does more harm than good.

Further, one would need to show not just that individual examples of an institution do more harm than good (individual churches, hospitals, schools, or governments may, in fact, be destructive). Instead, one would need to show that the institution itself, conceived generally, is, on balance, harmful. This claim is implausible when applied to major, widespread human institutions. People aren't stupid, and if an institution were fundamentally harmful then it would not become a major, widespread one. People would abandon it before it ever got that far.

The reason people support and patronize institutions is they perceive the benefits the institutions bring to their lives. Some are so successful that they have become human universals—institutions that appear in every culture in history. Examples include religion, medicine, education, and government.

In particular historical circumstances, the track record of these institutions is decidedly mixed (paleolithic medicine was nowhere near as good as modern medicine), but they still have provided enough benefit that they achieved universal status.

Indeed, it's hard to see how an institution that did net harm could become a universal, because biological and cultural evolution would select against it (i.e., people who did not practice some form of it would outcompete and outreproduce those who did, and the institution would die out).

In the case of religion, it's easy to see how it provides benefits to people even in this life. These include helping individuals find meaning and purpose, helping groups bond together and share resources, and helping societies promote moral behaviors ("Honor thy father and mother") and discourage immoral ones ("Thou shalt not kill").

Also, statistically speaking, religious individuals live longer on average than non-religious ones.

For a discussion of how religions in many parts of the world promote moral values, see the appendix of C.S. Lewis's *The Abolition of Man*.

Justification in James and Paul

CHALLENGE

"James says we're justified by faith and works (James 2:24), but that contradicts Paul, who says we're justified by faith without works (Rom. 3:28, Gal. 2:16)."

DEFENSE

A careful examination shows the two are using key terms— faith, works, and justification—in different senses.

James uses *faith* to refer to intellectual assent to the truths of faith. Thus he says, "You believe that God is one; you do well. Even the demons believe—and shudder" (James 2:19).

But Paul refers to what theologians call "formed faith" or "faith formed by charity." Thus he says what counts is "faith working through love" (Gal. 5:6).

James uses *works* to refer to positive actions flowing from belief in God—good works—such as giving food and clothing to the needy (James 2:15–16) or the actions performed by Abraham and Rahab in God's service (James 2:23, 25).

But Paul refers to "works of the law"—i.e., works done because they're required by the Law of Moses (see Day 63). He thus sees works of the law as characteristic of Jews but not Gentiles (Rom. 3:28–29; Gal. 2:11–16), and the key work he is concerned with is the Jewish initiation ritual of circumcision (Rom. 2:25–29, 3:30; Gal. 5:6, 6:13–15).

James refers to a different kind of justification than Paul. In addition to the justification that occurs when we first come to God and are forgiven, there is an ongoing growth in righteousness throughout the Christian life. Thus James refers to Abraham as being justified when he offered Isaac on the altar (James 2:21). However, this was in Genesis 22, long after Abraham was initially justified. Indeed, he had been explicitly pronounced righteous as early as Genesis 15:6.

But Paul is principally concerned with initial justification—the kind that occurs when we first come to God. Thus he speaks of justification in the context of Christian conversion (1 Cor. 6:9–11, Gal. 2:16), and he stresses that circumcision does not need to be part of Christian initiation (Gal. 5:4, 6:15).

James thus holds that intellectual faith alone does not save and that our ongoing, postconversion growth in righteousness is furthered by doing good works, while Paul holds that if we have faith working through love, then we have been forgiven and do not need to obey the Jewish law to be justified.

Can Science Eliminate God?

CHALLENGE

"Science has progressively explained more and more of the world, leaving less room for God. Why can't science one day explain everything, eliminating the need for (and possibility of) God?"

DEFENSE

This objection makes several mistakes.

First, it commits the fallacy of "God of the gaps" thinking by supposing that scientific explanations somehow take something away from God. They don't. God is the ultimate explanation for the world, including those things that science is capable of investigating (see Day 246).

Second, it assumes that science will continue to explain more and more, with no barriers to its future growth, but this is not to be taken for granted (see Day 97).

Third, while many physicists have harbored the dream of producing a "Theory of Everything"—a single set of formulas describing the behavior of all physical phenomena—there are serious doubts about whether such a theory is possible.

In 1931, the mathematician Kurt Gödel shocked his colleagues by demonstrating that there will always be mathematical truths that cannot be proved. (He did this using two proofs known as Gödel's Incompleteness Theorems.) Mathematics is closely allied with physics, and some physicists have concluded that the same is true of their field—that there will always be physical truths that cannot be proved. Thus Stephen Hawking wrote:

> Some people will be very disappointed if there is not an ultimate theory that can be formulated as a finite number of principles. I used to belong to that camp, but I have changed my mind. I'm now glad that our search for understanding will never come to an end, and that we will always have the challenge of new discovery ("Gödel and the End of the Universe," available online).

Fourth, even if there was a "Theory of Everything"—a single, master law explaining the behavior of all physical phenomena—it would explain only that and no more. It would not explain *why* that law exists, why there is something rather than nothing, or what may take place outside the realm of nature.

Fifth, we have very good proofs for the existence of God, and the future growth of science will not change that. The scientific method is only capable of dealing with certain types of questions, and it cannot disprove truths that are established by other methods.

Being Born Again in Scripture

"People don't need to be baptized, just born again."

Scripture teaches people are born again in baptism.

The phrase translated "born again" occurs in John 3:3, where Jesus tells Nicodemus, "Except a man be born again, he cannot see the kingdom of God" (KJV). In Greek the phrase involves a pun. The word for "again" is *anōthen*, which can mean either "again" or "from above." The point is one must receive a second birth and this birth must be from God.

Context reveals how the second birth occurs. Clarifying his initial statement, Jesus tells Nicodemus, "unless one is born of water and the Spirit, he cannot enter the kingdom of God" (John 3:5). The reference to water and the action of the Spirit indicates baptism (John 1:33).

Jesus expects Nicodemus to already be familiar with this concept (John 3:10), suggesting an Old Testament background to his teaching. Thus Ezekiel 36:25–27 says that at the restoration of Israel God will sprinkle clean water on people, give them a new heart, and put his Spirit within them so they may keep his commandments, all of which point to Christian baptism.

Further, in the verse immediately after Jesus' discussion with Nicodemus, John tells us: "After this Jesus and his disciples went into the land of Judea; there he remained with them and baptized" (John 3:22). This, in turn, is followed by a controversy sparked by Jesus beginning to baptize (John 3:23–4:3). The conversation with Nicodemus sets up the controversy.

All this indicates being "born again" in baptism. This is confirmed by other passages, which link the reception of new life and regeneration to baptism.

Thus Paul tells the Romans: "Do you not know that all of us who have been baptized into Christ Jesus were baptized into his death? We were buried therefore with him by baptism into death, so that as Christ was raised from the dead by the glory of the Father, we too might walk in newness of life" (Rom. 6:3–4). And Paul tells Titus that "he saved us, not because of deeds done by us in righteousness, but in virtue of his own mercy, by the washing of regeneration and renewal in the Holy Spirit" (Titus 3:5).

This same understanding is confirmed by the Church Fathers (see Day 287).

Being Born Again in the Church Fathers

CHALLENGE

"The idea we're born again or regenerated in baptism is an invention of men that the early Christians would never have heard of."

DEFENSE

The writings of the Church Fathers reveal that they believed in baptismal regeneration.

We elsewhere cover the scriptural basis for this teaching (see Day 286), and the writings of the Church Fathers confirm that they believed it too. In fact, despite searching, I have been unable to discover any Father who denied that Jesus' statements regarding being "born again" and "born of water and Spirit" (John 3:3, 5) referred to baptism.

For example, around A.D. 151, St. Justin Martyr wrote:

As many as are persuaded and believe that what we teach and say is true, and undertake to be able to live accordingly . . . are brought by us where there is water, and are regenerated in the same way we were ourselves regenerated. For, in the name of God, the Father and Lord of the universe, and of our Savior Jesus Christ, and of the Holy Spirit, they receive the washing with water. For Christ also said, "Unless you be born again, you shall not enter into the kingdom of heaven" [John 3:3] (*First Apology* 61).

Around A.D. 190, St. Irenaeus of Lyons wrote:

It was not for nothing that Naaman, when suffering from leprosy, was purified upon being baptized [2 Kings 5:14], but as an indication to us. For as we are lepers in sin, we are made clean of our old transgressions by means of the sacred water and the invocation of the Lord; we are spiritually regenerated as newborn babes, even as the Lord has declared: "Except a man be born again through water and the Spirit, he shall not enter into the kingdom of heaven" [John 3:5] (*Fragment* 34).

And around A.D. 203, Tertullian wrote:

The prescript is laid down that "without baptism, salvation is attainable by none"—chiefly on the ground of that declaration of the Lord, who says, "Unless one be born of water, he has not life" (*Baptism* 12).

These are just three examples among many.

TIP

For more, see Jimmy Akin, *The Fathers Know Best*, chapter 37.

Quoting the Deuterocanonicals

CHALLENGE

"Jesus and the authors of the New Testament never quote from the deuterocanonical books, so they do not belong in the Bible."

DEFENSE

The absence of a quotation does not prove that a book is noncanonical.

Jesus and the authors of the New Testament sometimes introduce quotations in a way that makes it clear they regarded the source as a book of Scripture. This is indicated when they use formulas like "scripture says" (John 19:37; Rom. 9:17, 10:11, 11:2) or "it is written" (Matt. 4:4; Mark 1:2; Luke 7:27, etc.).

When these formulas are not present, it is not always clear they regard the source as Scripture. Indeed, they sometimes quote sources that are not Scripture. Thus Acts 17:28 quotes Epimenides, 1 Corinthians 15:33 quotes Menander, Titus 1:12 quotes Epimenides, Jude 9 quotes *The Assumption of Moses*, and Jude 14–15 quotes 1 Enoch.

If we restricted ourselves to books of the Old Testament that are quoted with formulas like "scripture says" or "it is written," many books would have to be cut out of the canon.

However, even if we allow quotations without such formulas to count, twelve of the thirty-nine protocanonical books of the Old Testament—almost a third of the total—remain without quotations in the New.

These twelve are: Judges, Ruth, 2 Kings, Esther, Ezra, Nehemiah, Song of Songs, Ecclesiastes, Lamentations, Obadiah, Jonah, and Zephaniah (cf. Gleason Archer and C.G. Chirichigno, *Old Testament Quotations in the New Testament: A Complete Survey*, xvii).

In the first century, books of the Bible were combined in ways they are not today. For example, 2 Kings was then part of 1 Kings, and Obadiah, Jonah, and Zephaniah were included with the other minor prophets in a book known as "the Twelve" (Aramaic, *Trey 'Asar*).

Taking this into account, there would still be eight protocanonical books not quoted in the New Testament. Unless we are prepared to excise these books from the Old Testament, then we must acknowledge that the test proposed in this challenge does not work: An Old Testament book does not have to be quoted in the New Testament to be canonical.

The proposed test thus does not exclude the deuterocanonical books, and we must be ready to consider the arguments for their inclusion in the canon (see Days 273, 296, and 305).

Eternal Life

CHALLENGE

"Christians can't lose salvation. Scripture says, 'He who believes in the Son has eternal life' (John 3:36a), and if life is eternal, it can't end."

DEFENSE

This fails to understand both the biblical concept of eternal life and other things Scripture says.

A basic truth of linguistics is that you can't define a term simply by looking at its parts; you must look at how it's used in practice. To violate this principle is to commit the etymological fallacy (e.g., the word *awful* is a combination of *awe* and *full;* it originally meant something full of awe and that thus inspired reverence, but now it means something exceedingly bad).

Similarly, you can't look at the phrase "eternal life" and define it just by looking at its parts. You must look at how it's used in the New Testament. When you do this, it is clear that eternal life does not refer simply to unending bodily life. That is something even the damned will have after the resurrection of the dead, but it is clear the damned don't have eternal life in the sense the New Testament is interested in (see, e.g., John 3:36b). Eternal life thus deals not just with a quantity but a quality or kind of life.

Further, while there are verses that speak of eternal life as a present possession of believers, there are also passages that speak of it as something they have not yet achieved. Thus Paul says that on the last day God "will give eternal life" to believers (Rom. 2:7) and "he who sows to the Spirit will from the Spirit reap eternal life . . . if we do not lose heart" (Gal. 6:8–9; cf. 1 Tim. 6:12, Titus 1:2, 3:7).

Thus we don't yet have eternal life in the final sense. We may have a promise (1 John 2:25) and even a partial experience of it, but we can lose these through mortal sin (see Day 302). Thus John warns his audience: "Any one who hates his brother is a murderer, and you know that no murderer has eternal life abiding in him" (1 John 3:15).

To receive eternal life on the last day, Scripture says to "keep yourselves in the love of God; wait for the mercy of our Lord Jesus Christ unto eternal life" (Jude 21).

The Early Chapters of Genesis

CHALLENGE

"Genesis 1–11 contains many things that don't correspond to the modern, scientific understanding of the world (such as talking snakes, a universal flood, and so on)."

DEFENSE

These chapters pertain to history in a true sense, but they are written according to a set of literary conventions that conveys truth using more symbolism than later passages.

The Magisterium has indicated this for Genesis 1, stating, "Scripture presents the work of the Creator symbolically as a succession of six days of divine 'work,' concluded by the 'rest' of the seventh day" (CCC 337). It has said the same for Genesis 3, stating, "The account of the fall in Genesis 3 uses figurative language, but affirms a primeval event, a deed that took place at the beginning of the history of man" (CCC 390).

The Magisterium has not yet similarly commented on other events in Genesis 1–11 (e.g., the Flood, the Tower of Babel), but it likely would take the same approach. Thus in 1950, Pius XII stated:

> The first eleven chapters of Genesis, although properly speaking not conforming to the historical method used by the best Greek and Latin writers or by competent authors of our time, do nevertheless pertain to history in a true sense, which however must be further studied and determined by exegetes; the same chapters, in simple and metaphorical language adapted to the mentality of a people but little cultured, both state the principal truths which are fundamental for our salvation, and also give a popular description of the origin of the human race and the chosen people (*Humani Generis* 38).

The reason for the greater use of symbolism in these chapters is because of the remoteness of the events in time. This period is before Israel's recorded history began, and truth concerning this period cannot be conveyed the same way it can for the period after detailed historical records began to be kept.

A different set of literary conventions were thus used for describing the period before the arrival of Abraham in Genesis 12. From Abraham to the time of Israel's kings, less symbolism is used. And a more conventional way of recording history begins with the advent of the kings and the keeping of court records.

Appealing to Natural Law

CHALLENGE

"Christian appeals to natural law are futile. In nature we see animals committing all kinds of acts—such as rape, homosexuality, and purposeless killing—that Christianity considers immoral."

DEFENSE

This misunderstands the concept of natural law.

Confusion on this point is understandable. We see many "laws" in operation in nature. Some of these are studied by sciences such as physics and commonly referred to as laws (e.g., the laws of gravitation, optics, or thermodynamics).

The field of ethology studies animal behavior and, though its findings aren't as often referred to as laws, it does frequently report animal behaviors that would be deemed immoral if done by humans.

However, when moral theologians refer to natural law, they are not talking about either of these. The *Catechism* explains: "This law is called 'natural,' not in reference to the nature of irrational beings, but because reason which decrees it properly belongs to human nature" (CCC 1955). In other words, in discussions of moral theology, the natural law refers to the moral laws that we can discern by reason, which is rooted in human nature.

Moral theology thus does not make appeals to the behavior of animals. It does not matter whether ducks rape ducks, whether penguins engage in homosexual behavior with penguins, or whether baboons gratuitously kill baboons. None of these creatures have the human gift of reason.

Appeals to natural law are thus appeals to *human* nature and to what reason tells us about moral behavior:

The natural law is nothing other than the light of understanding placed in us by God; through it we know what we must do and what we must avoid (CCC 1955).

The natural law, present in the heart of each man and established by reason, is universal in its precepts and its authority extends to all men. It expresses the dignity of the person and determines the basis for his fundamental rights and duties (CCC 1956).

Although our reason is disfigured by sin and we find it easy to rationalize immoral behavior, moral reasoning is a human universal, and thus the natural moral law finds expression in all cultures.

TIP

For more, see the International Theological Commission's document, "In Search of a Universal Ethic: A New Look at the Natural Law," available online.

Why Isn't Everything Infallible?

CHALLENGE

"If the Church can teach infallibly, why doesn't it go ahead and teach everything infallibly?"

DEFENSE

Because it is not God's will.

Consider a parallel: The New Testament authors wrote under the charism of inspiration (2 Tim. 3:16), which is greater than and includes infallibility. If it was God's will, he could've had them write a single, systematic theology textbook with every proposition he wished to reveal to man carefully explained, yet he chose not to. We can speculate on why, but it is clear he chose not to or it would have happened. If that was God's will when he was still divinely inspiring authors, it is hardly likely he would wish the Magisterium to attempt a parallel task today. This is confirmed when we consider the challenges the Magisterium would face if it tried to do so.

First, infallibility is a negative protection. It means God won't allow the Magisterium to define something false, but it doesn't mean the Magisterium doesn't have to do its homework. A large amount of work must be done to prepare for a definition. The subject must be carefully considered from all angles in light of the sources of faith, the arguments examined, God's guidance prayerfully sought, and so on. Trying to define every point of theology would be a massive undertaking that would consume the Magisterium's energies and prevent the Church's pastors from fulfilling their duties.

Second, if the Magisterium tried to circumvent this by defining things in a slapdash manner, the result would be slapdash definitions. Infallibility guarantees that a teaching is not *false*, not that it's well phrased or timely in its delivery. The effort to define everything would produce poorly phrased teachings that were not properly introduced to the faithful. The pastoral damage would be enormous.

Third, the Magisterium can't answer questions that haven't been asked, and new questions arise constantly. For example, questions about how original sin works could not be considered until the concept of original sin was formulated from the sources of faith. Theologians prior to that time did not have the ability to pose or answer such questions. In the same way, the Magisterium today can't define the answers to unasked questions (many of which may be prompted by the moral implications of new technologies).

Historical Polytheism

"If monotheism is true, why have most people historically been polytheists?"

Several factors play a role in this.

First, the relationship between monotheism and polytheism is more complex than often assumed. As we cover elsewhere (see Day 153), many classical polytheists acknowledged the existence of an ultimate Creator, who was not typically worshipped. Instead, they worshipped lesser supernatural beings (Zeus, Apollos, Hera, and so on.).

The Judeo-Christian view agrees there is a single Creator *and* a multiplicity of lesser beings (angels). It disagrees where worship should be directed. While angels may be given respect corresponding to their nature as finite creatures (just as we show respect to fellow human beings; Rom. 13:7), the recipient of ultimate worship must be the Creator, not a creature. Consequently, it is harder to set monotheism and polytheism in opposition if polytheists frequently agree with the Judeo-Christian view about what types of supernatural beings exist.

Second, we don't have a good estimate of the number of people in history who would count as "pure polytheists" (i.e., people believing in multiple gods *and* denying the existence of a single, ultimate Creator). Indeed, many people lived before recorded history and, although we can tell by their artifacts and by studies of primitive societies that they may well have been polytheistic in worship, we don't know what they believed about an ultimate Creator.

Third, the tendency to worship created beings rather than the Creator is a product of human sin (cf. Rom. 1:19–25). If there is an infinite, ultimate Creator, then it stands to reason that he should be given respect corresponding to this (i.e., the ultimate form of worship). Respect shown to finite, created beings should not be of the same sort.

Fourth, from a Christian point of view, God has placed the religious instinct in the human heart. He has written his law on the hearts of men (cf. Rom. 2:15), but knowledge of this law has been disfigured by sin. This is why men deprived of knowledge of the true God will manufacture gods of their own, seeking to give expression to their natural religious instinct.

Ultimately, if most people in history have been polytheistic in worship, it is because of the universality of sin—a fact that our consciences testify to, for we each find sin in our own hearts.

Church Councils

"Why should I listen to what a Church council says?"

"Because Scripture supports the role of Church councils."

Jesus did not reserve teaching authority to himself, but assigned it to the leaders he put in charge of his Church (see Day 281). He thus created a Magisterium (Latin, "teaching authority") within his Church.

Usually this Magisterium is exercised personally—by individuals (originally by the apostles and later by the bishops who succeeded them). However, it is also God's will that, when the occasion calls for it, the Magisterium be exercised in a collective fashion.

We see an example of this in Scripture when a dispute arises in the Christian community in Antioch over whether Gentiles need to be circumcized in order to be saved (Acts 15:1).

Paul was involved in this dispute (Acts 15:2), and, as an apostle, was capable of teaching authoritatively on this point. Nevertheless, it was God's will that the matter be dealt with in a collective fashion. Thus the Antiochian church sent a delegation, including Paul, to the church in Jerusalem. Paul states that, on this occasion, "I went up by revelation" (Gal. 2:2), suggesting that the impetus for the consultation came directly from the Holy Spirit.

When the delegation arrived, the apostles and elders held a council to consider the question (Acts 15:6–21). After reviewing the matter, including what God had already revealed through Peter's ministry (Acts 10–11), it was concluded that Gentiles do not need to be circumcized to be saved, and a pastoral plan was devised for how Jews and Gentiles could live harmoniously in the Church.

They then sent a delegation back to Antioch along with a letter announcing the results of the council (Acts 15:22–31). Particularly noteworthy is this phrase from the letter: "It has seemed good to the Holy Spirit and to us to lay upon you no greater burden than these necessary things" (v. 28).

The fathers of the council thus saw the Holy Spirit as working through their deliberations and validating the results of the council, though Luke gives no indication that any revelations were received during it.

Since Scripture reveals it is God's will for the Magisterium of the Church to sometimes be exercised this way, the Jerusalem council became the model for all later Church councils.

The Time of the Crucifixion

CHALLENGE

"The Gospels contradict each other on the time of the Crucifixion. Mark says Jesus was crucified at 'the third hour' (Mark 15:25), and all three synoptics record the darkness from 'the sixth hour' to 'the ninth hour' while he was on the cross (Matt. 27:45; Mark 15:33; Luke 23:44), but John indicates that Jesus wasn't yet crucified at 'the sixth hour' (John 19:14)."

DEFENSE

John uses a different way of reckoning hours than the synoptics.

There are four natural points where one could begin counting hours: midnight, sunrise, noon, and sunset. Each has been used by different cultures. In America, we use midnight and noon (thus "one o'clock" is the first hour to strike after both).

In first-century Judaea, the custom was to count twelve hours from sunrise, as illustrated in Jesus' parable in Matthew 20:1–16, where a man hires workers at the third, sixth, ninth, and eleventh hours. The last group are said to work "only one hour," while those hired earlier bore "the burden of the day and the scorching heat."

The Roman practice, however, was to reckon the day as beginning at midnight (cf. Pliny the Elder, *Natural History* 2:79[77]). We can show that John was using this method in his Gospel and counting the hours from midnight: "For example, in John 1:39 a reckoning from the morning would make the 'tenth hour' four o'clock in the afternoon, but a reckoning from midnight would make it ten o'clock in the morning, the latter being more appropriate to the fact that the two disciples then stayed with Jesus 'that day'" (Jack Finegan, *Handbook of Biblical Chronology*, 2nd ed., §19; Finegan also offers additional examples).

The timing of the Crucifixion is thus described in the synoptics using the Jewish system of counting hours and in John by the Roman system. Thus in John, Pilate brings Jesus out to the crowd at "about the sixth hour" after midnight (around 6 a.m.). According to Mark he is then crucified at "the third hour" after dawn (around 9 a.m.). And according to all three synoptics, darkness covered the land from the sixth to the ninth hours after dawn (from around 12 p.m. to 3 p.m.).

TIP

See also Andrew Steinmann, *From Abraham to Paul*, 10, 293–96.

"Adding" the Deuterocanonicals

CHALLENGE

"Catholics violate the prohibition against adding to Scripture (Rev. 22:18–19) by including the Apocrypha (what Catholics call the deuterocanonicals) in their Bibles."

DEFENSE

The passage in question does not mean what is supposed, and if it did, it would create a problem for Protestants.

The passage in Revelation states: "I warn every one who hears the words of the prophecy of this book: if any one adds to them, God will add to him the plagues described in this book, and if any one takes away from the words of the book of this prophecy, God will take away his share in the tree of life and in the holy city, which are described in this book."

The term "book" (Greek, *biblion*) refers to an individual scroll, which was a work much shorter than the Bible. In the ancient world, it was impossible to fit the entire Bible into a single scroll. Physical constraints limited the size of a scroll to not much longer than an individual Gospel. Therefore, the passage in question refers to deliberately adding or removing words from the book of Revelation, not the Bible as a whole.

Of course, one should not add or subtract books from the Bible, but this is not what the passage is discussing. Even if it was, the Protestant community would have a problem.

The challenge supposes that at an early stage in Christian history the Bible consisted of only the books included in the Protestant canon and that the Apocrypha (i.e., the deuterocanonicals) were added at a later date.

This is false. The early Christians treated the Bible—including the deuterocanonicals—as Scripture, and it was at the time of the Protestant Reformation that a movement began denying their canonicity. Prior to this point, only some individuals did so, but the majority recognized the deuterocanonicals' place in Scripture.

Thus Protestant church historian J.N.D. Kelly writes that, although some early Christian writers had different views regarding the status of these books, "For the great majority, however, the deuterocanonical writings ranked as Scripture in the fullest sense" (*Early Christian Doctrines*, 5th ed., 55).

It would therefore have been Protestants who removed these books from Scripture, violating the prohibition on taking away from God's word.

Peter in Rome

CHALLENGE

"The pope cannot be the successor of Peter as the bishop of Rome. Peter was never even in Rome."

DEFENSE

The evidence indicates that Peter was in Rome at the end of his career, and that he was martyred there, along with Paul, around A.D. 67.

In 1 Peter 5:13, Peter writes, "She who is at Babylon, who is likewise chosen, sends you greetings; and so does my son Mark."

This is commonly understood as a greeting on behalf of the church in Rome to the churches to whom Peter was writing (1 Pet. 1:1). The term "Babylon" is understood as a code word for Rome, based on the fact that Babylon was a great persecutor of God's people in the Old Testament. This usage also may be reflected in Revelation's depiction of the Whore of Babylon (see Day 190).

The Church Fathers make it even clearer that Peter was in Rome. Thus St. Ignatius of Antioch, writing around A.D. 110 (a mere forty-three years after Peter's martyrdom) writes a letter to the church at Rome in which he states: "I do not, as Peter and Paul, issue commandments to you. They were apostles; I am but a condemned man: They were free, while I am, even until now, a servant" (*Letter to the Romans* 4).

Around 170, St. Dionysius of Corinth wrote to Pope Soter and stated: "You have thus by such an admonition bound together the planting of Peter and of Paul at Rome and Corinth. For both of them planted and taught us in Corinth. And they taught together in Italy, and suffered martyrdom at the same time" (cited in Eusebius, *Church History* 2:25:8).

To quote a third source from the second century, St. Irenaeus of Lyons wrote around A.D. 189: "Matthew also issued among the Hebrews a written Gospel in their own language, while Peter and Paul were evangelizing in Rome and laying the foundation of the Church" (*Against Heresies*, 3:1:1).

He also wrote: "The greatest and most ancient church known to all [was] founded and organized at Rome by the two most glorious apostles, Peter and Paul" (ibid., 3:3:2).

TIP

For more, see Jimmy Akin, *The Fathers Know Best*, chapter 28.

Many Religions

"When you look at all the different religions in world history, the odds of yours being the right one are low. We should conclude that religious truth, even if it exists, is unknowable."

DEFENSE

This overlooks both the way religious views are structured and the role that evidence plays.

Consider a parallel: Throughout history there have been many scientific theories about the way the world works, but they contradict one another and can't all be true. The odds of a single theory being correct are thus low and we should conclude that, if scientific truth exists, it is unknowable.

There are two major problems with this argument.

First, it ignores how scientific views are structured. Every field has certain basic questions on which there are a limited number of answers. There may be diversity in the details, but the basic options are limited.

In physics, a basic question is whether matter is made of tiny, discrete particles (the atomic theory) or whether it is an infinitely divisible continuum. Similarly, in religion a basic question is whether there is a single Creator God or not. Adherents of the view that matter is made of particles may differ on the details of how particles work, but they are united on the fundamental nature of matter. Similarly, religions such as Judaism, Christianity, and Islam may differ on how they understand the Creator, but they are agreed on the fundamental question of monotheism.

Whether selecting among scientific or religious views, one is not faced with infinite diversity. Both fields are structured around certain basic questions that, once settled, lead to more specific questions involving detail.

Second, the parallel argument given above ignores the role of evidence. The odds of selecting the correct scientific or religious views would be low if one had no evidence as to which are true, but the fact is that we do have evidence. In science, experiments provide that evidence, and in religion, apologetics does.

Thus the multiplicity of views on science and religion should not lead to despair about finding the truth. What one needs to do is identify the basic questions a field involves, to look at the evidence concerning those questions, and when they are settled to move on to more detailed questions.

The principles are the same, whether one is investigating scientific or religious truth.

The Timing of Christmas

CHALLENGE

"Christians are wrong to celebrate Christmas on December 25. Jesus could not have been born then—it would have been too cold for the shepherds to keep their flocks outdoors (Luke 2:8)."

DEFENSE

There are several problems with this challenge.

First, the Catholic Church celebrates Jesus' birth on December 25, but this is a matter of custom rather than doctrine. It is not Church teaching that this is when Jesus was born (note that the matter isn't even mentioned in the *Catechism*).

Second, although most Christians today celebrate Christ's birth on December 25, this was not the only date proposed. Around A.D. 194, Clement of Alexandria stated Christ was born November 18. Other early proposals included January 10, April 19 or 20, and May 20 (Jack Finegan, *Handbook of Biblical Chronology*, 2nd ed., §488, §553). By far the most common proposals, however, were January 6 (ibid., §§554–61) and December 25 (ibid., §§562–68).

While the last was eventually adopted by the Catholic Church for use in its liturgy, the fact that the Church did not declare alternate proposals heretical shows the matter was not considered essential to the Faith.

Third, the proposals that put Jesus' birth in the colder part of the year (November 18, December 25, January 6, and January 10) are not ruled out by the fact that there were shepherds keeping watch over their flocks at night.

Ancient Jews did not have large indoor spaces for housing sheep. Flocks were kept outdoors during winter in Judaea, as they are elsewhere in the world today, including in places where snow is common (search for "winter sheep care" on the Internet). Sheep are adapted to life outdoors. That's why they have wool, which keeps body heat in and moisture out.

Sheep are kept outdoors in winter in Israel today: "William Hendricksen quotes a letter dated Jan. 16, 1967, received from the New Testament scholar Harry Mulder, then teaching in Beirut, in which the latter tells of being in Shepherd Field at Bethlehem on the just-passed Christmas Eve, and says: 'Right near us a few flocks of sheep were nestled. Even the lambs were not lacking. . . . It is therefore definitely not impossible that the Lord Jesus was born in December'" (ibid., §569).

The Dating of Mark

CHALLENGE

"Mark's Gospel isn't reliable. It was written long after the events, and by a non-eyewitness."

DEFENSE

Mark was written within living memory of the events it records, and it's based on eyewitness testimony.

We elsewhere deal with the fact that Mark wasn't an eyewitness (see Day 44). Biographies are written all the time by people who aren't eyewitnesses, and Mark was in an especially good position as a biographer because he based his Gospel on the testimony of an eyewitness: Peter. Thus the first-century figure John the Presbyter stated:

Mark, having become the interpreter of Peter, wrote down accurately, though not in order, whatsoever he remembered of the things said or done by Christ. For he neither heard the Lord nor followed him, but afterward, as I said, he followed Peter, who adapted his teaching to the needs of his hearers, but with no intention of giving a connected account of the Lord's discourses, so that Mark committed no error while he thus wrote some things as he remembered them. For he was careful of one thing, not to omit any of the things which he had heard, and not to state any of them falsely (Eusebius, *Church History* 3:39:15).

This is the earliest statement about the composition of Mark, dating from only a few decades after it was written.

It helps us pin down when Mark was written, because there is a literary relationship between Mark and Luke. Enough of Mark is found in Luke, often in the same words, that it is highly probable either Mark used Luke or Luke used Mark.

Since Mark is said to be based on his memories of Peter's preaching (not on Luke) and since Luke acknowledges prior written sources (Luke 1:1), almost all scholars conclude that Luke used Mark. (Other factors also point to this conclusion; see Jimmy Akin, "Did Mark Base His Gospel on Matthew and Luke?" at JimmyAkin.com).

Since we have good reason to think that Luke was written in A.D. 59 (see Day 217), Mark would have been written earlier than this.

Mark did not become one of Peter's traveling companions until after he ceased being one of Paul's. The latter event, recorded in Acts 15:36–39, took place in A.D. 49. Therefore, Mark was written some time in the A.D. 50s.

The Church: Visible or Invisible?

CHALLENGE

"Catholics are wrong to believe that Christ's Church is a visible, hierarchical institution; it is the invisible union of all believers."

DEFENSE

This does not fit the scriptural data.

First, if Jesus wished to found an "invisible" Church, he wouldn't have instituted baptism. As the Christian equivalent of circumcision (Col. 2:11–12), baptism is the Christian initiation ritual. It thus gives the Church an identifiable membership.

Second, if Jesus didn't wish to found a hierarchical Church, he wouldn't have established a hierarchy. Yet he did. He appointed leaders, beginning with the apostles, who then appointed other leaders, resulting in the ministry of bishops, priests (presbyters) and deacons.

What's more, entrance into these offices was accomplished by ordination through the laying on of hands (Acts 6:6, 13:3; 1 Tim. 4:14; 2 Tim. 1:6), so membership in the hierarchy was objectively verifiable.

Third, the nature of the Church as a "visible" entity is underscored by the duty of obedience that the members have toward their ordained leaders (1 Cor. 16:16; 1 Thess. 5:12; Heb. 13:7, 17).

Fourth, Jesus speaks of his Church—using that term—in only two passages in the Gospels: Matthew 16 and 18. In both, he indicates the visible nature of the institution.

Thus in Matthew 16:18–19, Jesus says he will build his Church on Peter, indicating that Peter is its leader (see Day 256). He also gives Peter "the keys of the kingdom of heaven" and tells him, "whatever you bind on earth shall be bound in heaven, and whatever you loose on earth shall be loosed in heaven," indicating Peter's authority in the Church (see Days 30 and 349)

Similarly, in Matthew 18:15–18, Jesus shares the power of binding and loosing with the hierarchy more broadly, in the context of Church discipline. He states that if "your brother" (i.e., a fellow Christian) sins against you then the matter may need to be referred to the Church, "and if he refuses to listen even to the church, let him be to you as a Gentile and a tax collector." This indicates the authority of the Church to discipline and exclude members who commit offenses.

Far from instituting an invisible Church that is merely the spiritual union of all believers, Jesus instituted a visible one with a definite membership and an authoritative hierarchy.

Mortal Sin

"There is no such thing as mortal sin."

The concept of mortal sin is clearly taught in Scripture.

First, the language of the doctrine is drawn from Scripture itself: "If any one sees his brother committing what is not a mortal sin, he will ask, and God will give him life for those whose sin is not mortal. There is sin which is mortal; I do not say that one is to pray for that. All wrong-doing is sin, but there is sin which is not mortal" (1 John 5:16–17).

The phrase here translated "mortal" (Greek, *pros thanaton*) literally means "unto death." It can be understood to mean a sin that causes spiritual death, a sin so grave that it causes physical death, or grave sin continued to the point of death. In any case, the text envisions the possibility of a Christian (a "brother") sinning this way.

A full exegesis of this passage is beyond what we can cover, but the New Testament indicates Christians can commit sins costing them salvation. Paul warns: "Now I would remind you, brethren, in what terms I preached to you the gospel, which you received, in which you stand, by which you are saved, if you hold it fast—unless you believed in vain" (1 Cor. 15:1–2). This indicates it is possible for Christians to believe the gospel in vain. Here Paul names one cause for this—failure to adhere to the gospel.

Elsewhere he is more specific, saying: "Do not be deceived; neither the immoral, nor idolaters, nor adulterers, nor sexual perverts, nor thieves, nor the greedy, nor drunkards, nor revilers, nor robbers will inherit the kingdom of God" (1 Cor. 6:9–10). The fact that Paul felt the need to warn his Christian audience against deception on this indicates both that Christians can commit sins costing them salvation and that they could deceive themselves on this point.

Many similar New Testament passages could be cited, but we should note that the need to avoid mortal sin is stressed by our Lord: "If you would enter life, keep the commandments. . . . You shall not kill, You shall not commit adultery, You shall not steal, You shall not bear false witness, Honor your father and mother, and, You shall love your neighbor as yourself" (Matt. 19:17–19).

The Church's Infallibility

CHALLENGE

"Why should I think the Church can teach infallibly?"

DEFENSE

Reflection on Christ's teaching reveals why.

Christ did not reserve teaching authority to himself but established a teaching authority (Latin, *magisterium*) in his Church (see Day 281). This authority was originally vested in Peter and the apostles, and when they passed from the scene it was inherited by their successors, the pope, and the bishops (cf. 1 Tim. 3:2, 2 Tim. 2:2; Irenaeus, *Against Heresies* 3:3:1; CCC 861–62).

Christ willed his Church to endure to the end of the world (Matt. 16:18), and teaching is one of its essential functions (Matt. 28:19; Acts 1:8). Since the pope and the bishops are the highest-ranking teachers the apostles left in the Church, the ultimate exercise of the Church's teaching authority fell to them.

Authority can be exercised in different degrees, placing different levels of obligation on those who are its subjects. This raised the question: What would happen if the Church's Magisterium used its authority in the fullest manner, to oblige the faithful to believe a particular teaching in a definitive way? In that case, could the Church be wrong?

Theological reflection led to the conclusion this would be inconsistent with how Christ constituted "the church of the living God," which is present in the world as "the pillar and bulwark of the truth" (1 Tim. 3:15). He also promised to be with his Church until the end of time (Matt. 28:20); he promised the Holy Spirit would lead its leaders "into all the truth" (John 16:13); and he told his appointed ministers, "He who hears you hears me, and he who rejects you rejects me" (Luke 10:16).

In view of the declarations of Christ and the mission he gave the Church in the world, it would be impossible for his Church's Magisterium to bind the faithful in conscience to believe something false. Consequently, "in order to preserve the Church in the purity of the faith handed on by the apostles, Christ who is the Truth willed to confer on her a share in his own infallibility" (CCC 889).

This infallibility can be exercised in different ways—by the pope or by the bishops (either scattered or gathered in an ecumenical council; CCC 891). But when the Magisterium teaches definitively, it is infallible.

God Hates Shrimp?

CHALLENGE

"The book of Leviticus condemns homosexuality (Lev. 18:22), but it also condemns eating shrimp since they don't have fins and scales (cf. Lev. 11:9–12). If we aren't obliged to follow it when it comes to the latter, why should we follow it when it comes to the former?"

DEFENSE

Homosexuality is contrary to human nature; shrimp-eating is not.

The Law of Moses (Gen.-Deut.) contains a variety of types of laws. Some, such as the prohibitions on murder, are based directly on human nature and apply to all cultures in all of history.

Other laws, such as the observance of the Sabbath, were related to human nature in a less direct way and applied specifically to the people of Israel. For example, although all humans have a need to devote adequate time to rest and worship, there is nothing about human nature that demands this be done on Saturday in particular. God therefore chose Saturday as the day of rest and worship for Israel, though the underlying principles could be fulfilled another way, as with the Christian observance of Sunday.

This is similar to the way some countries today have motorists drive on the left side of the road and others have them drive on the right side of the road. It doesn't matter which choice a country makes as long as it makes a choice, so motorists don't drive in an unsafe manner.

It is widely recognized that the dietary laws found in the Old Testament were of the second category. They were not based directly on human nature the way the prohibition on murder was. Instead, they were given specifically to regulate the common life of Israel.

They had a role in establishing and reinforcing Jewish culture and helping keep Israelites distinct from their pagan neighbors, but they did not apply to other nations nor do they apply to Christians today (Mark 7:19, Acts 10:9–16, Col. 2:16–17).

The prohibitions on homosexuality, however, are directly related to human nature. Even a consideration of the anatomy involved, as well as the ability to conceive new human beings, indicates that men and women are designed to go together. Consequently, the prohibition on homosexual behavior is a moral requirement applicable to all cultures, not just Israel (Rom. 1:26–27).

Referring to the Deuterocanonicals

CHALLENGE

"If Jesus and the New Testament authors thought the deuterocanonical books were part of the canon, why doesn't the Bible refer to them?"

DEFENSE

They do refer to them. The New Testament contains multiple allusions to the deuterocanonicals.

It does not contain clear quotations from them—or from many protocanonical books of the Old Testament (see Day 288)—but it does contain clear allusions.

One of Jesus' most famous teachings is that God's willingness to forgive us is linked to our willingness to forgive others. This is expressed, for example, in the Lord's Prayer: "And forgive us our debts, as we also have forgiven our debtors" (Matt. 6:12).

And, too, in the verses that follow it: "For if you forgive men their trespasses, your heavenly Father also will forgive you; but if you do not forgive men their trespasses, neither will your Father forgive your trespasses" (Matt. 6:14–15).

The Old Testament contains many passages discussing divine forgiveness, but only one where it is linked to our willingness to forgive others. That passage is in the deuterocanonical book of Sirach: "Forgive your neighbor the wrong he has done, and then your sins will be pardoned when you pray" (Sir. 28:2). Jesus thus picks up and develops this teaching from Sirach the same way he picks up and develops other themes from Old Testament scriptures.

Not only does the New Testament allude to teachings found in the deuterocanonicals, it also refers to the historical events they record. Thus the book of Hebrews contains an extensive list of Old Testament figures who pleased God by their faith. In the course of listing them, the inspired author writes: "Some were tortured, refusing to accept release, that they might rise again to a better life" (Heb. 11:35).

This combination of torture and refusal of release to obtain a better resurrection is found in only one place in the Old Testament. It is a reference to the seven brothers who were tortured and martyred by Antiochus Ephiphanes in 2 Maccabees 7. The author of Hebrews thus appears to recognize 2 Maccabees as one of the books of the Old Testament.

TIP

For additional examples, see Gary Michuta, *The Case for the Deuterocanon: Evidence and Arguments*, chapter 1.

Evolution and Faith

CHALLENGE

"Faith and science are fundamentally opposed, as illustrated by Christians' opposition to the theory of evolution."

DEFENSE

The Catholic Church doesn't have a problem with evolution.

Some Christians have read the early chapters of Genesis in a way that would preclude evolution, but the Church recognizes these chapters as using significant symbolism (see Days 90 and 290).

The statement God created man from the dust of the ground is understood as an affirmation that "the human person, created in the image of God, is a being at once corporeal and spiritual. The biblical account expresses this reality in symbolic language when it affirms that 'then the Lord God formed man of dust from the ground, and breathed into his nostrils the breath of life; and man became a living being' (Gen. 2:7)" (CCC 362).

Faith thus allows the view that the way God "formed man of the dust" was through a process of biological evolution, leading to the development of primates and eventually to man, whom God endowed with a soul. "If the origin of the human body comes through living matter which existed previously, the spiritual soul is created directly by God" (John Paul II, Message to the Pontifical Academy of Sciences, October 22, 1996).

Consequently, the Church is able to express appreciation for the "many scientific studies which have splendidly enriched our knowledge of the age and dimensions of the cosmos, the development of life-forms and the appearance of man. These discoveries invite us to even greater admiration for the greatness of the Creator, prompting us to give him thanks for all his works and for the understanding and wisdom he gives to scholars and researchers" (CCC 283).

This doesn't mean every version of the theory of evolution is compatible with the Faith. For example, one must recognize God as the Creator and Ruler of the universe, so the process of evolution would take place only as part of his providential plan.

On the other hand, the Church's appreciation for scientific studies pointing to evolution doesn't mean evolution is a doctrine of the Faith. Although the Church has concluded the biblical texts can be understood in a way compatible with evolution, beyond that the theory must stand or fall on its scientific merits, for it is a matter of science rather than faith.

Devotional Use of Images

CHALLENGE

"God may permit the use of religious images (see Day 179), but we should not kneel before or kiss them. The Bible says, 'you shall not bow down to them' (Exod. 20:5; Deut. 5:9), and it condemns those who have bent their knees to or kissed Ba'al (1 Kings 19:18)."

DEFENSE

These prohibitions apply to idols.

If there is an idol—a statue of a pagan god—then you absolutely should not kneel before or kiss it! However, not all kneeling and kissing falls under this ban. Scripture contains innocent examples of kneeling (Judg. 7:5–6), bowing (Gen. 23:7, 12), prostration (1 Sam. 25:24), and kissing (Gen. 27:6).

These are physical acts that take their meaning from context. They are outward expressions of an attitude of the heart, but they can convey different things. Kissing your father and kissing an idol of Ba'al are different. The outward act may be the same, but they convey different attitudes of heart—one indicating filial affection and the other divine worship.

Even using these acts in divine worship is not wrong. People devotionally knelt (1 Kings 8:54), bowed (2 Chron. 7:3), prostrated themselves in God's presence (Deut. 9:18), and devotionally kissed Jesus (Luke 7:38).

What makes such acts wrong is using them to reverence a god that does not exist, like Ba'al, or using them to reverence something that is not a god, supposing that it is (e.g., worshipping one of the Roman emperors—like Caligula or Nero—as a god).

If one recognizes in one's heart that the thing is not a god, these outward acts are not misdirected divine worship and don't fall under condemnation. In the ancient world, these actions may have been so closely associated with idolatry that they were to be altogether avoided in the devotional use of images, but we don't live in the ancient world.

Today, Catholics who use such devotional practices (which, it should be pointed out, are voluntary, not obligatory) are in no danger of thinking that a statue or icon is a deity. It's universally recognized that statues and icons are mere symbols of Jesus and the saints, and kneeling before or kissing them is a symbolic way of expressing affection, like kissing the photograph of an absent loved one.

Dunking, Pouring, or Sprinkling?

CHALLENGE

"The only legitimate way to baptize is immersion."

DEFENSE

There is more than one mode by which baptism can be performed.

Different groups of Christians have baptized using three methods: immersion (dunking), affusion (pouring), and aspersion (sprinkling).

There is misinformation in some circles about which the Catholic Church uses, with the claim being that it uses sprinkling and not immersion. However, Catholics do not use sprinkling, and they do use immersion. In fact, the Church acknowledges immersion as the most expressive way of administering baptism.

The *Catechism* states: "Baptism is performed in the most expressive way by triple immersion in the baptismal water. However, from ancient times it has also been able to be conferred by pouring the water three times over the candidate's head" (CCC 1239).

The New Testament does not identify any particular mode for baptism. If it did, there would be no controversy. As it is, the New Testament is silent on the question, which is why biblical arguments tend to turn on small details (see Day 267).

The reason the New Testament doesn't discuss the question is that it was written for a Christian audience, and—as Christians—its first readers had already been baptized. There was no need for the sacred authors to spend time explaining how the rite is performed. They expected the audience to look to the practice of the Church on this question.

When we do that, we find that the assumption there must be only one way of administering baptism is false. The first reference we have with any degree of detail about how baptism was performed is found in the *Didache*. Though not part of the New Testament, this was a first-century document. It serves as our earliest witness to the mode of baptism, and it reveals that it was performed in different ways, stating: "Baptize into the name of the Father, and of the Son, and of the Holy Spirit, in living [i.e., running] water. But if you have not living water, baptize in other water; and if you cannot in cold, in warm. But if you have not either, pour out water three times upon the head in the name of the Father and Son and Holy Spirit" (*Didache* 7).

The Day of the Crucifixion

CHALLENGE

"Jesus couldn't have been crucified on a Friday. He rose Sunday morning, and he said he would be in the tomb "three days and three nights" (Matt. 12:40). There aren't three days and nights between Friday and Sunday."

DEFENSE

This fails to understand the modes of speech then used.

In the most literal sense, "three days and three nights" means seventy-two hours. The Gospels agree Jesus died in the afternoon and was buried in the evening, just before the beginning of the Sabbath at sunset (Matt. 27:57; Mark 15:42; Luke 23:54; John 19:42). If he remained buried for seventy-two hours, he also would have had to rise just before sunset.

This is not the picture indicated by the Gospels, which depict the empty tomb being discovered early in the morning on Sunday, the first day of the week (Matt. 28:1; Mark 16:2; Luke 24:1; John 20:1), which then became "the Lord's day," the Christian day of worship (Rev. 1:10; 1 Cor. 16:2), because that was when Jesus rose.

Therefore, "three days and three nights" should not be taken in a fully literal sense. So how should it be taken?

According to the modes of speech then used, parts were often reckoned for wholes, so "three days" could be one full day and parts of two others. This is the picture we get from the Gospels: Jesus died in the afternoon and was buried shortly before sunset on one day, he lay in the tomb on a second day (the Sabbath), and he rose early in the morning on the third day. This corresponds to the repeated biblical affirmation that Jesus was raised "on the third day" (Matt. 16:21, 17:23, 20:19; Luke 9:22, 18:33, 24:7, 46; Acts 10:40; 1 Cor. 15:4).

The "three days" are thus explained, leaving the "three nights." Here is where another ancient mode of speech is relevant: Adding "three nights" to "three days" is a poetic flourish not meant to be taken literally. *"Three days and three nights* was a Jewish idiom appropriate to a period covering only two nights" (R.T. France, *The Gospel According to Matthew*, 213).

Finally, the Gospels are explicit that Jesus was crucified on a Friday, which was referred to as the "day of preparation" when people got ready for the Sabbath (Matt. 27:62; Mark 15:42; Luke 23:54; John 19:14, 31, 42).

Historical Sins

"Catholics have committed grave sins in history, including sins of avarice, intolerance, and persecution."

DEFENSE

Yes, they have! Jesus did not come to make men sinless in this life but to make it possible for sinners to be saved.

Sin is an ongoing reality (James 3:2; 1 John 1:8) against which we must struggle (1 Cor. 10:13). Jesus taught us to pray, on a regular basis, "Forgive us our debts, as we also have forgiven our debtors" (Matt. 6:12).

We must also recognize that sins are not only committed against God; they affect those on earth, and their forgiveness must also be sought.

People alive today did not commit the sins of the past and so are not responsible for them. Nevertheless, the past sins have continuing negative effects in the world, and we must do what we can to remedy them. This applies to all of us, and in the year 2000 John Paul II made a dramatic act of public apology for the sins committed by Catholics in the past, stating: "We cannot fail to recognize the infidelities to the Gospel committed by some of our brethren, especially during the second millennium. Let us ask pardon for the divisions which have occurred among Christians, for the violence some have used in the service of the truth, and for the distrustful and hostile attitudes sometimes taken towards the followers of other religions."

He went on to say: "Let us confess, even more, our responsibilities as Christians for the evils of today. We must ask ourselves what our responsibilities are regarding atheism, religious indifference, secularism, ethical relativism, the violations of the right to life, disregard for the poor in many countries. We humbly ask forgiveness for the part which each of us has had in these evils by our own actions, thus helping to disfigure the face of the Church" (Homily, March 12, 2000).

Having made this act of public apology, it remains to be seen whether others will take a similar attitude regarding their own sins and those of their forebears.

TIP

For an in-depth theological reflection on this issue, see the International Theological Commission's document, "Memory and Reconciliation: The Church and the Faults of the Past" (Vatican.va).

Scripture as Final Authority?

CHALLENGE

"We know that the Bible teaches we should do theology 'by Scripture alone' (sola scriptura) because Jesus and the apostles quote Scripture as their final authority."

DEFENSE

This claim is demonstrably false.

Although Jesus and the apostles quote from Scripture, all this shows is that they considered it an authority capable of settling questions it deals with, not that it was the only authority. Speaking of it as "their final authority" misleadingly assumes there *was* a single, final authority for them, but a person can have Scripture as an authority while also having other authorities.

Thus Catholics, Orthodox, and other Christians who do not accept *sola scriptura* also quote Scripture to settle issues. Just look at other entries in this book. Scripture is regularly cited to prove different points, yet the author clearly does not believe in *sola scriptura*. Therefore, the *sola scriptura* advocate will need to show more than that Jesus and the apostles quoted Scripture to settle issues. He will need to show they recognized no other authorities.

This is not possible. For a start, Jesus and the early Christians lived in an age when public revelation was still being given. Some of these revelations are recorded in Scripture (e.g., Matt. 1:20–21, 2:13; Luke 1:11–20, 28–37, 2:9–14; Acts 9:4–6, 10–17, 10:10–16; Rev. 1:10–11). Regardless of whether a revelation was recorded in Scripture (and many were not until decades after they were given), its message was authoritative. This, of itself, reveals that the early Christians did not believe in *sola scriptura*.

The transmission of revealed material (whether it took the form of a vision or not) is Tradition, and the early Christians passed on Tradition in oral form long before it was written in Scripture (e.g., Matt. 10:7; Luke 10:1–16; Acts 2:14–40; 1 Cor. 11:1–2; 2 Thess. 2:15, 3:6).

They also believed a divine teaching authority (Latin, *magisterium*) had been given to the Church, beginning with Jesus, who "taught them as one who had authority, and not as their scribes" (Matt. 8:29) and pronounced authoritatively on the correct interpretation of prior revelation (Matt. 5:21–48). Similarly, the leaders of the Church recognized that they were divinely guided in a way that allowed them to pronounce authoritatively on the questions of their day (Acts 15:1–29).

We thus see the early Church using Scripture, Tradition, and the Magisterium.

Merit and Reward

CHALLENGE

*"Catholic teaching on merit is unbiblical.
We can't merit anything before God."*

DEFENSE

The term "merit" (Latin, *meritum*) refers to a reward. By extension, it has also come to refer to actions that God chooses to reward. The doctrine of merit is thus the biblical doctrine of rewards under another name.

The Bible is clear that our actions in this life can affect the degree of reward we receive in heaven. Jesus told us: "Lay up for yourselves treasures in heaven, where neither moth nor rust consumes and where thieves do not break in and steal. For where your treasure is, there will your heart be also" (Matt. 6:20–21).

Sometimes people imagine there will be no degrees of reward in heaven—that going to heaven is the only reward God gives. However, Jesus indicates that individual actions we perform are the subject of rewards.

He warns that certain actions will not receive rewards, such as doing good deeds to receive praise from men (Matt. 6:1–2, 5, 16), while other actions will receive rewards, such as doing good deeds to please God (Matt. 6:4, 6, 18, 10:41–42).

Similarly, Paul indicates that some people will enter heaven with greater rewards than others. He speaks of how individuals build on the foundation of Jesus Christ by doing various things, and he says that one day these works will be tested by fire. He then says, "If the work which any man has built on the foundation survives, he will receive a reward. If any man's work is burned up, he will suffer loss, though he himself will be saved, but only as through fire" (1 Cor. 3:14–15). Some individuals, therefore, will both enter heaven and receive rewards in addition to that, but others will simply enter heaven.

Paul also discusses the nature of the rewards that we will receive, writing: "For he [God] will render to every man according to his works: to those who by patience in well-doing seek for glory and honor and immortality, he will give eternal life" (Rom. 2:6–7).

Here he indicates that those who display "patience in well-doing" (literally, "in good work") seek the rewards of "glory and honor and immortality" from God, and this hope does not disappoint, for God gives them "eternal life."

TIP

See also Day 354.

Born Believers

CHALLENGE

"Religion is unnatural. Children are not born as believers but have to be indoctrinated into it."

DEFENSE

On the contrary, children are naturally predisposed to religious belief.

As scientists have shown using tests that measure the amount of attention babies pay to things, they are aware in the first year of life of the difference between beings with mind and intention (agents) and inanimate objects.

Further tests have indicated that small children do not presuppose that agents are human or that they must be visible, and they are prepared to attribute superhuman levels of knowledge and power to agents, as well as the ability to survive death.

Small children are also predisposed to see purpose and design in the world and to attribute its creation, and the creation of the life-forms within it, to non-human agents. This predisposition persists even when their parents offer contrary explanations.

Children of this age also recognize the difference between what is real and what is "make-believe" or pretend. They are aware, for example, that real cats cannot talk, only pretend ones can. Yet they place the kind of non-human agents that we have been describing in the real rather than the make-believe category.

All of this means children are naturally predisposed to believe in religious concepts like souls, the afterlife, angels, gods, and God. It is no wonder, then, that religion is a human universal—something found in every human culture, both historically and today (see Day 353).

The specific way that childen's faith develops depends on the way they are raised (see Day 10), but the predisposition to faith—and not to atheism—remains.

Due to the time it takes for children's cognitive apparatus to develop, it similarly requires time for these religious beliefs to appear, but there is a natural predisposition toward them. Children thus are not "indoctrinated" into religion. Religious belief is a condition that is natural to them, and its emergence is a normal, natural part of childhood development.

If any position is unnatural or one that involves "indoctrination," it is the attempt to prevent religious belief from emerging in children.

TIP

For a book on this subject, see Justin Barrett's
Born Believers: The Science of Children's Religious Belief.

Omitting Doubted Books

"If the deuterocanonical books were doubted by some early on, shouldn't we err on the side of caution and omit them rather than risk adding to the word of God?"

DEFENSE

This is based on a faulty premise that would lead to dramatic consequences.

First, the deuterocanonicals weren't the only doubted books of the Old Testament. At least five additional books were disputed in the Pharisee tradition but later included in the canon of modern rabbinic Judaism (see Day 255). These books—Esther, Proverbs, Ecclesiastes, Song of Solomon, and Ezekiel—are sometimes referred to as the Old Testament *antilegomena* (Greek, "spoken against"). Applying the above principle would result in their also being taken out of the Bible.

Second, some Jews (the Sadducees), only accepted the Torah as Scripture, meaning the other protocanonical books were disputed by some Jewish authorities. Thus the principle could lead to the truncation of the Old Testament to just its first five books.

Third, the New Testament would not remain untouched, for some New Testament books were also disputed in the early Christian community. Eusebius famously labeled James, 2 Peter, 2–3 John, Jude, and potentially Revelation as *antilegomena* (*Church History* 3:25). We also know from other sources that Hebrews was also doubted. The principle under consideration would thus truncate the New Testament canon.

Fourth, the principle is faulty, and not just because it would truncate the canon. It is also faulty because omitting a doubted book is not "erring on the side of caution." In doubtful cases, one would assume risk either way. Including a doubtful book would entail the risk of "adding to the word of God," while excluding it would entail the risk of "subtracting from the word of God." The book of Revelation contains a warning against either adding to or taking away from the words of that book (Rev. 22:18–19), and that principle can be extended to the canon as a whole.

Finally, the principle is faulty because we are not in the position of early Jews or Christians having to decide which books belong in the Bible. Jesus promised that the Holy Spirit would lead us into all truth (John 16:13), and the Spirit has led the Church to recognize the books of Scripture. This is not an individual decision but a divinely guided historical process.

The Limits of Infallibility

CHALLENGE

"The Catholic Church claims a dangerous and sweeping power for itself when it says that it can teach infallibly. That means it can bind Catholics to believe anything."

DEFENSE

There are limits to the Church's ability to teach infallibly, and it is used far less frequently than many suppose.

First, it is limited by topic. Christ didn't give the Church the charism of infallibility so it could pronounce on just any subject. He gave it so the faithful could profess the Christian faith correctly (CCC 890). As a result, the Magisterium can infallibly teach truths that God has given by divine revelation, as well as certain truths of doctrine and morals closely connected with them (CCC 2035).

However, it can't infallibly teach on just *any* subject. It could not, for example, infallibly teach on matters of medicine, chemistry, botany, archaeology, or a host of other subjects, as long as they are not connected with faith and morals.

To give a relevant illustration: The theory of evolution is a scientific theory. The Church has examined the sources of faith to determine whether they preclude this theory, and it has concluded they do not (see Day 90). The sources of faith can be understood in a way consistent with evolution. However, because it is a matter of science rather than faith, evolution must stand or fall on its scientific merits. It is not, itself, a subject of Church teaching.

Second, the Magisterium only teaches infallibly under very specific circumstances—when it attempts to use the fullest measure of its teaching authority. This occurs when it completely ends legitimate dispute on a subject by teaching on that subject definitively (Latin, *de-*, "completely" and *finire,* "to end").

Third, this does not happen very often, and it has happened even less often in recent times. Thus in the twentieth century Vatican II chose not to make any new infallible definitions, and only one pope in the century chose to define a doctrine (i.e., Pius XII, who defined the Assumption of Mary in 1950). So far in the twenty-first century, no doctrines have been infallibly defined.

Fourth, the Church has established that non-infallible teaching is the norm: "No doctrine is understood as defined infallibly unless this is manifestly evident" (*Code of Canon Law,* 749 §3).

Bishops, Priests, and Deacons

CHALLENGE

"In the New Testament, Church leadership wasn't divided up among bishops, priests (aka presbyters/elders), and deacons. In particular, the office of bishop and elder were the same (Titus 1:5–7)."

DEFENSE

The offices of Church leadership developed during the first century under the guidance of the apostles.

Originally, the only office in the Church was apostle. Jesus appointed the Twelve to serve as apostles toward the beginning of his ministry, around A.D. 30 or 31 (Matt. 10:1–4). He appointed others to temporary assignments, but not ongoing offices (Luke 10:1). Thus the apostles are the only leaders of the Church at the beginning of Acts (A.D. 33).

As the Church grew, its pastoral needs exceeded what the apostles themselves could provide, and they appointed additional officers. By the early A.D. 40s, they were being assisted in Jerusalem by a body of elders (Acts 11:30), with elders soon being ordained in other churches, such as by Paul and Barnabas around A.D. 48 (Acts 14:23).

Bishops and deacons are mentioned by name for the first time in the literature of the A.D. 60s (Phil. 1:1; 1 Tim. 3:1–2, 8–13; Titus 5:7).

The terms for these offices originally had non-Christian uses. "Bishop" (Greek, *episkopos*) meant "overseer"; "presbyter/priest" (Greek, *presbuteros*) meant "elder"; and "deacon" (Greek, *diakonos*) meant "minister, servant." Consequently, it took time for them to acquire stable, technical meanings. Thus on occasion even apostles could describe themselves as "elders" (1 Pet. 5:1) or "deacons" (Eph. 3:7). This fluidity is why "elder" and "bishop" are sometimes applied to the same office.

By the end of the apostolic age, a threefold ministry had become universal in the churches, with the loftiest term ("overseer") being attached to the highest office and the humblest term ("servant") being attached to the lowest.

Thus, writing around A.D. 110, St. Ignatius of Antioch stated that apart from the threefold ministry of bishops, priests, and deacons, "there is no church" (Letter to the Trallians 3). He also refers to a threefold ministry operating in the churches of Ephesus, Magnesia, Tralles, Philadelphia, and Smyrna.

For the threefold ministry to be so widespread and considered so essential at the beginning of the second century, its origin must be placed in the second half of the first century, as the final form of the structure bequeathed to the Church by the apostles.

The Last Supper and Passover

CHALLENGE

"The synoptic Gospels say the Last Supper was a Passover meal, but John indicates it wasn't (John 18:28, 19:14)."

DEFENSE

There are multiple resolutions to this challenge.

First, there were disputes about the calendar in first-century Judaism. Some have proposed Jesus used a different calendar than the temple authorities, so he ate the Passover meal a day earlier than the Jewish authorities mentioned in John 18:28.

Second, it's been proposed Jesus simply celebrated the Passover a day early because he knew he was going to die. He made other changes to the meal as well (e.g., instituting the Eucharist), and the disciples—who recognized him as having "the words of eternal life" (John 6:68)—would have gone along with their Lord's celebration a day early.

Third, it's been argued John has been misunderstood.

There are several indications in John that [the Last Supper] was a Passover meal: It was held in Jerusalem, although Jesus was staying in Bethany for the festival (John 12:1). Jesus and his disciples did not return to Bethany that evening—it was required that the Passover night be spent within the ritual limits of the city. Jesus' statement that those who have washed need only their feet cleaned implies that the disciples had washed before the meal (John 13:10). This would have been a ceremonial cleansing to prepare for the Passover meal. The disciples thought that Judas left the meal to buy (additional?) provisions for the feast or to donate money to the poor. It was customary to donate to the poor on Passover night (Andrew Steinmann, *From Abraham to Paul*, 275).

On this view, the passages in John thought to show the Crucifixion occurred before Passover have been similarly misunderstood. John 18:28 says the Jewish authorities had not yet eaten the Passover meal, but they had been busy all night, preparing for Jesus' arrest, taking him into custody, and interrogating him (Steinmann, 278–79). They hadn't had time yet! John 19:14 says the Crucifixion happened on "the day of preparation of the Passover." This wasn't the day before Passover. "The day of preparation" was an idiom referring to Friday, and "Passover" was commonly reckoned as including the weeklong feast of unleavened bread. John means Jesus was crucified on the Friday of Passover week (Steinmann, 275–78).

Pascal's Wager

CHALLENGE

"I am unable to decide between Christianity and skepticism, and it doesn't help to review the evidence. My dilemma seems insoluble."

DEFENSE

In his *Pensées,* the French philosopher Blaise Pascal proposed a practical solution that became known as Pascal's Wager.

He proposed that, if evidential reasoning cannot settle the question for a particular person, then practical reasoning may (see Day 336).

Pascal's Wager can be put different ways (in fact, Pascal himself put it more than one way), but here we will follow his main presentation of it.

He compared the decision of whether to believe, in the absence of convincing evidence one way or the other, to tossing a coin and not knowing whether it will come up heads or tails. Though one does not know which will come up, it can be rational in some situations to bet one way or the other. Indeed, the rules of the game may require one to wager.

This is similar to the situation of a person deciding between Christianity and skepticism (understood as agnosticism or atheism). If these are the two positions a person is torn between, he must either choose one or the other, either Christianity (faith) or skepticism (non-faith). There is no third position, given these options.

If he can't make the decision based on evidence concerning which is true, then it is rational for him to solve the dilemma by asking which wager will benefit him more.

Pascal proposes that, in terms of this life, the rational choice is to accept faith, because faith produces a net benefit in this life. One will incur a cost in that one will live by the Christian moral code and deny oneself certain pleasures, but these will be more than offset by the benefits in this life of believing (see Day 283).

He similarly proposes that, in terms of the next life, the rational choice is also to accept faith. If it turns out that Christianity is true then one will gain the infinite happiness of heaven, while if it turns out that Christianity is not true one will lose nothing as there would be no afterlife.

Therefore, both in terms of this life and the next, the rational choice is to embrace faith rather than skepticism.

TIP

For more, see Day 319.

Objections to Pascal's Wager

CHALLENGE

"Pascal's Wager is open to objections: (1) It isn't based on evidence; (2) Christianity and skepticism aren't the only two options we can choose; and (3) how do you know that God won't perversely decide to put you in hell for placing your faith in him?"

DEFENSE

None of these objections overturn Paschal's Wager.

First, as we observe elsewhere (see Day 318), Pascal's Wager is designed to deal with situations where an individual feels unable to make a decision based on evidence, yet where a decision must be made because not to choose would be to accept one position by default. If an individual has convincing evidence, then the decision can be made on that basis, but if he does not have convincing evidence then—since the decision must be made—it is rational to decide based on practical reason.

Second, as classically formulated, Pascal's Wager is only meant to decide between Christianity and skepticism. There are other religious positions, but for many people in the west, Christianity and skepticism are the two "live" options (i.e., the only options they feel torn between), and the Wager is legitimate and useful for those in that situation.

The Wager can be reformulated for other situations. For example, if a person is torn between Christianity and Hinduism, one could point out that wagering on Christianity is preferable, because on the Christian view one's fate is decided at death (Heb. 9:27), whereas if Hinduism were true, one would receive multiple additional chances through reincarnation.

Third, the idea God would perversely condemn those who place their faith in him to hell is not the Christian view but an evil-deity view. It is a third position, besides Christianity and standard skepticism. We are therefore discussing a different situation than the one the Wager is designed to apply to.

Further, one can always propose that the world is inherently perverse and, despite the evidence, one will suffer horribly for doing what reason suggests. One can suggest that will happen to a Christian who does the reasonable thing and to a skeptic who does the reasonable thing. If the latter is entitled to assume that the world *isn't* inherently perverse, then so is the former.

TIP

For further discussion, see the philosopher William James's essay "The Will to Believe" (available online).

Past, Present, and Future Sins

CHALLENGE

"Once we are saved, we are always saved. We don't need to worry about mortal sins, because when we are justified, God forgives all of our sins—past, present, and future."

DEFENSE

Scripture teaches the opposite.

It is, of course, true that when we come to God and are justified that he forgives all of our past sins. However, this is not true of present and future sins.

One of the requirements for coming to God is repentance. Jesus' own message was, "Repent and believe in the gospel" (Mark 1:15). Repentance involves an actual turning away from sin (see Day 53).

This means that if we are still willfully committing the kind of sins we know will separate us from God—mortal sins—then we have not repented and will not be justified. Justification therefore does not involve the remission of present, unrepented mortal sins.

Neither does it involve the forgiveness of sins that have not yet been committed. This is also something our Lord teaches. In fact, he teaches it in the model Christian prayer he gave us—the Lord's Prayer—in which he taught us to pray: "Forgive us our debts, as we also have forgiven our debtors" (Matt. 6:12; cf. Luke 11:4).

Jesus even singles out this petition for special comment, underscoring its importance and stating: "For if you forgive men their trespasses, your heavenly Father also will forgive you; but if you do not forgive men their trespasses, neither will your Father forgive your trespasses" (Matt. 6:14–15).

Since we are meant to pray the Lord's Prayer on an ongoing basis, Jesus teaches us to pray for forgiveness on an ongoing basis. Therefore, we *need* this forgiveness: As we commit new sins, we need to repent and be forgiven for them.

The claim that when we first come to God, he forgives all our sins "past, present, and future" may be pithy, but it is not what Scripture teaches. This is clear from many passages besides the Lord's Prayer. The fact that we haven't been forgiven for sins we haven't yet committed is indicated by the New Testament's warnings against mortal sin and its implications for our salvation, which would otherwise be meaningless (see Day 302).

An Evolutionary By-Product?

CHALLENGE

"If human nature has a predisposition to religious belief (see Day 313), why can't we explain this as an evolutionary by-product?"

DEFENSE

We can't dismiss our religious disposition so easily.

Religion requires a robust set of cognitive faculties, which is why humans have religion and less intelligent species do not. According to the theory of evolution, the needed faculties would have developed over a long period of time, with different aspects appearing among the different species that led up to the human race.

This is no different than other faculties humans possess, such as those allowing us to use language, do mathematics, or perform scientific reasoning. The cognitive faculties needed for these also would have developed over a long period of time among our ancestors, and we even see traces of these faculties in other species that are alive today.

However, at some point in the history of life, the right set of cognitive faculties appeared in a species—our species, *homo sapiens*—that allowed us to have the robust and complex institutions of religion, language, math, and science that we display today.

A purely evolutionary perspective would say that each of these is just a product of evolution. The needed cognitive faculties developed (evolved) over time, and so today we have the institutions they make possible.

However, that doesn't mean that they can be dismissed as "just an evolutionary by-product." The question is not whether evolution played a role in our being able to have these institutions. That may be granted. The question is what these institutions tell us about the world.

As we cover elsewhere (see Day 353), basic human impulses may be taken as evidence about the world. If our cognitive faculties for mathematical and scientific reasoning developed in a way that allows us to know things about the world, then we must be prepared to acknowledge that the cognitive faculties for religious reasoning are the same.

Put differently, if our mind has the ability to deduce the hypoteneuse of a triangle or the existence of electrons, it may also allow us to deduce the existence of God.

This is all the more true if, as the Judeo-Christian view holds, the creation of man was superintended by divine providence and there is a God who wants us to know him.

Old Testament Laws

CHALLENGE

"Jesus was a Jew. If Christians are really his followers, why don't they keep Old Testament laws like circumcision, eating kosher food, and so on? Jesus said he didn't come to destroy the Law and not a jot or tittle would pass away from it (Matt. 5:17–18)."

DEFENSE

Such prescriptions were only binding on Jewish people before Jesus fulfilled the Law.

Everyone must obey the natural, moral law God has placed in the human heart (Rom. 2:14–16; see Day 291). The Law of Moses includes many aspects of this law (CCC 1961), but it also adds provisions of a non-moral nature.

The reason these added laws aren't binding on non-Jewish people is that the Law of Moses was a covenant God made with Israel. It was not made with other peoples, so it wasn't binding on them (St. Thomas Aquinas, ST I–II:98:5).

Theologians often divide the requirements of the Mosaic Law into three groups: moral precepts, judicial or civil precepts, and ceremonial precepts. The first deal with basic moral requirements (e.g., don't kill, don't steal), the second with the civic life of Israel (e.g., establishing cities of refuge where a person who had accidentally killed someone could flee for protection; cf. Num. 35:9–15), and the third with ritual requirements of being a Jew (e.g., circumcision, food laws).

The moral precepts are binding on all human beings, not because they are contained in the Law of Moses but because they are part of human nature. The judicial and ceremonial precepts were binding only on the Jewish people.

It was established in the first century that one doesn't need to be circumcised and become a Jew to be a Christian (Acts 10–11, 15), so non-Jewish Christians have never been obliged to keep the judicial and ceremonial precepts.

Further, those precepts are no longer binding on Jewish people today. Jesus said he came not to abolish the Law and the prophets "but to fulfill them," and that nothing would pass away from the Law "until all is accomplished" (Matt. 5:17–18). Jesus then fulfilled the Law by his perfect life, allowing it to pass away (CCC 578). Thus "Christ is the end of the Law" (Rom. 10:4; cf. Gal. 3:23–25, Eph. 2:15, Col. 2:16–17), and the non-moral precepts aren't objectively binding even on Jewish people today.

Why Sacraments?

CHALLENGE

"If what is ultimately important is our faith in God, then there is no reason for the Church to have sacraments."

DEFENSE

Interior dispositions like faith are not the only thing that is important. We are also physical beings. The Church has sacraments because they correspond to human nature and thus Christ instituted them.

Every religion has certain rites it regards as sacred. Such rites are a human universal, found in every religion, in every culture, which means they are rooted in human nature. Thus God made use of them in Judaism and Christianity.

In Judaism there were what are sometimes called the "sacraments of the Old Law." These included rites such as eating the Passover Lamb, the sacrifices offered at the temple, circumcision, and various washings for purification (see Exod. 12; Lev. 1–7, 12:3, 14:8–9).

While there are a rich variety of rites used in the Christian faith, certain ones have a special place and are referred to as the "sacraments of the New Law" or the "sacraments of the New Covenant" established by Christ.

Used this way, the word "sacraments" refers to "efficacious signs of grace, instituted by Christ and entrusted to the Church, by which divine life is dispensed to us" (CCC 1131).

In contrast to the rites that were part of the Old Covenant, the sacraments of the New Covenant impart the graces they signify. Each is a visible sign of the invisible grace it imparts. This twofold nature of the sacraments corresponds to the twofold nature of man. We are not simply created spirits, like the angels. By nature, human beings are composed of both body and spirit. Consequently, God imparts spiritual graces to us through visible, bodily signs (see St. Thomas Aquinas, ST III:61:1).

In his ministry, Jesus frequently performed miracles through sensible signs like the spoken word (Mark 4:39; John 11:43–44) and the laying on of hands (Mark 8:23–25; Luke 4:40). This same principle is at work in the sacraments that Jesus established for his Church.

Over the course of time, the Church discerned that there are seven such sacraments: baptism (Matt. 28:19), confirmation (Acts 8:14–17; Heb. 6:2), the Eucharist (1 Cor. 10:16), confession (John 20:21–23), the anointing of the sick (Mark 6:13; James 5:14–15), holy orders (Acts 13:2–3; 2 Tim. 1:6), and matrimony (CCC 1612–17).

Genesis and Ancient Texts

CHALLENGE

"Genesis can't be the word of God because it borrows from pagan texts."

DEFENSE

God can interact with pagan works if he chooses.

Proposed parallels between the Old Testament and pagan sources are often exaggerated. Other times they may be due to independent development. When a parallel is not coincidence, it is possible that both the biblical and the pagan authors are drawing from a common, lost source. In some cases, a pagan author may draw from a biblical one! However, there are cases where biblical authors respond to or borrow from pagan ones.

The Catholic attitude toward such interactions with pagan literature was expressed by Pius XII: "If, however, the ancient sacred writers have taken anything from popular narrations (and this may be conceded), it must never be forgotten that they did so with the help of divine inspiration, through which they were rendered immune from any error in selecting and evaluating those documents" (*Humani Generis* 38).

Ultimately, condemning something just because it had a pagan origin is to commit the genetic fallacy, according to which a thing is judged by its source rather than by its merits.

There is no reason that God—and the inspired authors of Scripture—can't interact with pagan sources. In fact, to protect Israel against polytheism, responding to pagan ideas would be wise. Consequently, we see the author of Genesis doing this. It is not immediately obvious to us, not being familiar with ancient pagan culture, but it leapt out at the original audience.

For example, Genesis 1 describes God making the sun and the moon, but it does not refer to them by their names. It describes them simply as lights: "God made the two great lights, the greater light to rule the day, and the lesser light to rule the night" (Gen. 1:16).

The reason is the sun and the moon were popularly worshipped as deities, and using their names could have conveyed the impression that the supreme God made the solar and lunar deities. By referring to them as lights, the author of Genesis subverts and corrects this. The message is: "The sun and the moon are just lights, not deities; don't worship them!"

The Individual and the Canon of Scripture

CHALLENGE

"Why shouldn't the individual decide for himself what books belong in the Bible?"

DEFENSE

God didn't promise to guide individuals in this way. It's also a dangerous thing to try.

First, how would an individual decide what books are canonical? Some have claimed these books are "self-authenticating" or that the Holy Spirit will provide what amounts to a private revelation to the individual, but neither proposal works (see Days 229 and 236).

An individual might establish that certain books are reliable historical records (e.g., that the Gospels reliably record the ministry of Jesus), but the claim they are Scripture—divinely inspired—is a matter of faith that goes beyond such historical evidence.

There is thus a problem with the evidence an individual would have at his disposal if he set aside the conclusions God guided the Church to reach about the canon and tried to consider the matter afresh.

Second, if he tried to do this, he would very likely end up with a canon that was too large or too small.

Daunted by the difficulties that certain books face, he might truncate the canon by ejecting certain books from it that belong there (as Martin Luther tried to do with James, Hebrews, Jude, and Revelation). Alternately, he might be attracted by the possibility of exotic, esoteric new books of Scripture and wish to include books that do not belong in the canon (as many moderns have done with writings like the Gospel of Thomas, the Gnostic gospels, or the writings of Joseph Smith).

Third, since there is no promise in Scripture that the canon will close (see Days 52 and 110), one would have to remain open to new works. Any book that one had not read and personally evaluated would have to be regarded as a potential book of Scripture.

Fourth, the actual historical practice of the vast majority of Christians has not been to try to settle the matter themselves, but to rely on the guidance of the Church. That God guided them to do this is a sign that it is what they *should* do (though this fact does not fit well with the doctrine of *sola scriptura*). If they were meant to decide the matter individually, God would have made this clear.

Separation from God

"We know we can't lose our salvation by committing mortal sin because Scripture says we can't be separated from God (John 6:37, 39, 10:27–29, Rom. 8:38–39)."

DEFENSE

None of those biblical passages show that we cannot separate *ourselves* from God.

John 6:37 states: "All that the Father gives me will come to me; and him who comes to me I will not cast out." Jesus will not cast us out, but that doesn't mean we can't leave Jesus voluntarily.

John 6:39 states: "this is the will of him who sent me, that I should lose nothing of all that he has given me, but raise it up at the last day."

It is God's will that Christians not be lost, but it's also God's will that they not commit adultery, and some do. Later in John, Jesus refers to the Twelve as those God "hast given me" (17:11) and says, "none of them is lost but the son of perdition [i.e., Judas Iscariot]" (17:12)—indicating it's possible to once be given to Jesus and yet be lost.

John 10:27–29 states: "My sheep hear my voice, and I know them, and they follow me; and I give them eternal life, and they shall never perish, and no one shall snatch them out of my hand. My Father, who has given them to me, is greater than all, and no one is able to snatch them out of the Father's hand."

This doesn't say the sheep can't leave voluntarily. We've already seen Judas was once given to Jesus and then lost. Further, Jesus tells the disciples later in John: "Abide in me. . . . If a man does not abide in me, he is cast forth as a branch and withers; and the branches are gathered, thrown into the fire and burned" (15:4–6). This indicates it's possible for the disciples to fail to abide in Jesus.

Romans 8:38–39 states: "I am sure that neither death, nor life, nor angels, nor principalities, nor things present, nor things to come, nor powers, nor height, nor depth, nor anything else in all creation, will be able to separate us from the love of God in Christ Jesus our Lord."

As with the other passages, this doesn't say we can't separate ourselves from God. Paul elsewhere indicates we can (see Day 302).

The Triumphal Entry

CHALLENGE

"Matthew contradicts the other Gospels when he says that Jesus used two animals during his triumphal entry into Jerusalem. It also, absurdly, says he rode both at once."

DEFENSE

There is no contradiction, and he didn't ride both at once.

When two things are involved in an encounter, the evangelists frequently simplify their recounting of the event by mentioning only one (see Day 37). This is within the level of descriptive approximation one expects (see Day 258).

Here Matthew gives the fuller account by mentioning both animals (Matt. 21:2), while the others simplify by mentioning only one (Mark 11:2; Luke 19:30; John 12:14).

Jesus undertook the triumphal entry to fulfill the prophecy: "Rejoice greatly, O daughter of Zion! . . . Lo, your king comes to you . . . humble and riding on an ass, on a colt the foal of an ass" (Zech. 9:9; cf. Matt. 21:5).

At the time, some understood this prophecy as involving two animals and some as involving one. Because of the first interpretation, it would be reasonable for Jesus to use two animals, even if only one were needed. Matthew wants to make sure those who understood the prophecy in the first sense realize Jesus fulfilled it, so he mentions both animals.

By contrast, John is less concerned about the two-animal interpretation, and he mentions only one. However, to prevent confusion, he further abbreviates the prophecy to remove the part some interpreted as referring to the colt's mother (see John 12:15).

Regarding Matthew's statement, "they brought the ass and the colt, and put their garments on them, and he sat thereon" (Matt. 21:7), it may just mean he sat on the garments. Even if not, the ancient audience would not have understood this as meaning that Jesus rode both simultaneously.

They were more used to riding animals than we and fully knew this was not possible for a person to do, particularly if the animals have no special riding equipment but only some clothing put on them as makeshift saddles.

They would have understood the statement in the natural sense that Jesus rode one animal and then the other to fulfill the prophecy. (Alternately, some have proposed the disciples put the garments on the colt and Jesus rode it, but Matthew uses the plural pronoun "them" because the previously unridden colt was tied to its mother, which was being used to calm and guide it.)

Objections to Papal Infallibility

CHALLENGE

*"The pope is a sinful man who makes mistakes.
Therefore, he can't be infallible."*

DEFENSE

The premise of this challenge is true; the conclusion is false.

The pope is a sinful man, but this does not lead to the conclusion that he can't be infallible. Sinlessness—sometimes called *impeccability*—operates in a different sphere than infallibility does.

Sinlessness is a quality pertaining to the moral order: It means not making a mistake in the sphere of one's own moral behavior. Infallibility is a quality pertaining to the doctrinal order: It deals with not making a mistake when proclaiming a doctrine.

The quality of sinlessness is not required for infallibility. One can do sinful things and yet have an accurate understanding. Solomon was supremely wise (1 Kings 4:29–34), yet he also sinned greatly (1 Kings 11:4–10). The most evil beings there are have an accurate knowledge of God: "Even the demons believe—and shudder" at the prospect of divine judgment (James 2:19).

More to the point, the very first pope—Peter—was a sinful man (see Day 19), but this did not stop him from writing two inspired letters (1 and 2 Peter). Inspiration is a greater charism than infallibility and that includes infallibility, therefore even a sinful man like Peter could teach infallibly by God's grace.

It is also possible for a pope to make mistakes, including of a doctrinal nature—just not when he is teaching under the charism of infallibility.

Again we may look to Peter as an example. His understanding of Christian doctrine was not always perfect. Thus, when Jesus foretold future events, Peter sometimes did not understand or accept the truth of our Lord's statements (Matt. 16:21–23, 26:31–35). However, that did not stop him from later writing the inspired, and thus infallible, letters 1 and 2 Peter.

We therefore see that a pope is capable of making mistakes both of the moral and doctrinal order and yet still exercise the charism of infallibility.

God guides the pope, like every validly ordained minister, in the exercise of his ministry—just as he guided Peter. But this does not mean the pope is continuously infallible. The Church does not claim he is, and it would be attacking a straw man to inflate the doctrine of papal infallibility beyond what the Church claims.

Why Isn't the Bible Clearer?

CHALLENGE

"If God wants us to know him, and if the Bible is his word, why isn't it clearer?"

DEFENSE

Several answers may be given.

First, much of the Bible is quite clear, including many of its main teachings (e.g., there is one God, who created the world, and who loves man enough to send his Son to die on a cross so we might be saved from our sins). So is the main sequence of events it narrates. For the most part, it tends to be the subsidiary points that are less clear.

Second, the Bible was written in a certain period of time and in a certain culture. It therefore reflects modes of speech and thought then in use. If we lived back then, it would be clearer to us. But we live in a different time and culture, so it is less clear, and we have to work harder to understand it fully. For God to give us the Bible, he had to pick some time and place to deliver it, so it is only natural people from other eras and lands would need to work harder to understand it than the original audience.

Third, the Bible is a rich work of literature. It works on many levels and rewards its readers by the amount of effort they spend on it, like a great novel. If even ordinary human authors produce works of literature that reward multiple and attentive readings, we would expect the same of God, who is communicating multiple aspects of his infinite mystery within the cramped confines of human language.

Fourth, God appears to want to reward those who are willing to wrestle with the meaning of his word. Thus some parts of the Bible are written in a symbolic manner (e.g., prophecies, parables). These only yield their meaning to those willing to devote the thought needed to understand them. This both intrigues us and rewards those willing to undertake the effort. They end up learning its lessons better than if they had been given a simple, straightforward statement.

Fifth, Scripture isn't meant to be read alone but in the context of Tradition and the teaching of the Magisterium. Even the simplest person willing to rely on these will learn all he needs to go to heaven.

"The Father Is Greater Than I"

CHALLENGE

"Jesus can't be God if he said, 'The Father is greater than I' (John 14:28)."

DEFENSE

The divinity of Christ is consistent with Jesus' statement.

Jesus has the same nature as his Father: They are both divine, both God. This does not mean that the Son doesn't hold a lesser place in other respects.

To consider a human analogy, both a father and a son are equal in nature, but the father ranks higher in the relationships within the family. Further, if he sends his son on a mission, the son has a lower place with respect to the mission: He is the one sent, not the sender.

Both understandings apply to Jesus. First, he "called God his Father, making himself equal with God" (John 5:18). He is thus equal to the Father in nature. However, because he is Son, he occupies second place to the Father in the divine relationships. Thus he is the Second Person of the Trinity, not the First.

He also is on a mission. "God sent the Son into the world, not to condemn the world, but that the world might be saved through him" (John 3:17). This implies the Son played a subordinate role in that mission, for "a servant is not greater than his master; nor is he who is sent greater than he who sent him" (John 13:16).

At the end of the mission, Jesus prays to the Father, saying, "I glorified thee on earth, having accomplished the work which thou gavest me to do; and now, Father, glorify thou me in thy own presence with the glory which I had with thee before the world was made" (John 17:4–5).

This explains the meaning of Jesus' statement about the Father being greater. In its original context, Jesus was reassuring the disciples about his coming departure, when he said, "If you loved me, you would have rejoiced, because I go to the Father; for the Father is greater than I" (John 14:28). If the disciples love Jesus, they should rejoice because his work is over. He is returning to be again glorified by the Father—who holds the higher rank both as the Father and the one who sent him.

TIP

For more on how John's Gospel teaches Jesus' divinity, see Day 12.

God's Hiddenness

CHALLENGE

"If God really exists and wants us to know him, why doesn't he make his existence more obvious to us?"

DEFENSE

This is a subcase of the problem of evil—specifically, why God would allow us to have less knowledge of him than we would prefer to have. Its solutions fall along the same lines as other aspects of the problem of evil.

God could make it undeniably obvious that he exists, and it is commonly understood he will do so in the next life, paralleling the way he will vanquish evil in the next life in general.

Why God remains partially hidden in this life is a mystery. A common proposal is he does so to avoid overwhelming our free will so we may make a free choice for or against him. It is also proposed he does so to allow us to exercise and grow in virtues such as faith and hope.

Not having the amount of evidence we would like does not mean God is committing an injustice, however. He remains just, even while remaining partially hidden, as long as he ensures that we have *adequate* evidence concerning him. Even if it isn't the amount of evidence we would *prefer,* we have the evidence we need as long as we have the philosophical proofs of God's existence (cf. Rom. 1:18–20).

Also, the difficulty we have in processing this evidence is due in part to the effects of both original and personal sin (cf. Rom. 1:21, Eph. 4:18).

However, God will not hold us accountable for what we are not personally responsible for. Scripture recognizes that one is not accountable for what one innocently does not know (John 9:41, 15:22, 24; James 4:17). Thus Paul tells the Athenians—who had achieved a measure of knowledge of the divine (Acts 17:22–29)—that "the times of [their] ignorance God overlooked" (Acts 17:30). God will therefore not hold people accountable who innocently lacked the evidence they needed (see Day 113).

As with other aspects of the problem of evil, a mystery remains, but "faith gives us the certainty that God would not permit an evil if he did not cause a good to come from that very evil, by ways that we shall fully know only in eternal life" (CCC 324).

The Assumption of Mary

CHALLENGE

"The Assumption of Mary isn't taught anywhere in the Bible."

DEFENSE

From a Catholic perspective, it doesn't have to be.

The idea theology should be done *sola scriptura* (Latin, "by Scripture alone") is a distinctly Protestant idea not shared by most Christians. It also has numerous difficulties (see Days 5, 16, 311, and 352).

In general, it is better to sort out how theology is to be done before engaging in apologetic discussions of issues, like the Assumption of Mary, that depend significantly on apostolic Tradition not recorded in Scripture. If a Protestant dialogue partner is unwilling to consider the question apart from *sola scriptura*, little progress is likely, and the discussion may generate more heat than light. However, if a dialogue partner is willing to consider the question from a Catholic point of view, the following may be helpful.

First, it isn't clear Mary had reached the end of her earthly life when the New Testament was finished. Mary would have been a little more than eighty when the book of Revelation was written, either toward the end of the reign of Nero (d. A.D. 68) or in that of his successor, Galba (A.D. 68–69). (This is based on Revelation 17:10's indication it was written in the reign of the sixth emperor; see Day 68 on the approximate year of Mary's birth). If the Assumption had not yet happened, we wouldn't expect it to be mentioned.

Second, the Assumption may be alluded to in Revelation 12:1–5, where John sees the mother of Jesus depicted in heaven. This woman can be understood other ways and may include references to Eve, Israel, and the Church, but Revelation is known to use symbols to refer to more than one thing (cf. Rev. 17:9–10), and it is natural to see Mary as one of them.

Third, the Church's faith in the Assumption is ultimately based on apostolic Tradition. Thus John Paul II noted: "The first trace of belief in the Virgin's Assumption can be found in the apocryphal accounts entitled *Transitus Mariae,* whose origin dates to the second and third centuries. These are popular and sometimes romanticized depictions, which in this case, however, pick up an intuition of faith on the part of God's People" (General Audience, July 2, 1997).

TIP

For more, see Tim Staples, *Behold Your Mother.*

The Limits of Science

"Why shouldn't science be the ultimate guide to truth in all matters?"

Because some truths are inaccessible to science.

First, there are many subjects in life where it would be foolish to try to apply the scientific method. For example, it would be foolish for a man who desires to know if his wife still loves him to subject her to a series of scientific tests. Even if such tests were well designed, they would be likely to crush her remaining affection for him. This is a case where the attempt to impose scientific method disturbs the very thing being observed (a phenomenon also encountered on the subatomic level with Heisenberg's Uncertainty Principle). This is not to say that it's impossible to determine spousal love, but it is to say that science does not offer the method required.

Second, there are whole fields of knowledge that are inaccessible to science. One is morality. Moral goodness is a non-empirical quality—that is, we cannot detect qualities like good and evil using our senses or through devices that extend the range of our senses (e.g., telescopes, microscopes, spectrometers). Science can investigate the question of what people *regard* as morally good and evil. But since these qualities are scientifically undetectable, it is impossible to perform an experiment showing that a particular act is, objectively, one or the other. Thus science could show that most people regard torturing babies for fun is morally wrong, but there is no experiment capable of proving that it is, in fact, wrong.

Third, science draws heavily on principles from logic and mathematics. But in these fields, a different methodology is used to provide proofs. Instead of being based on prediction and experiment, logical and mathematical truths are proved by being derived from certain foundational principles (axioms) that are not demonstrable. Science does not and cannot use the scientific method to prove logical and mathematical truths it presupposes.

Fourth, science depends on metaphysical assumptions that cannot be verified by scientific method. For example, it assumes that the universe behaves in a lawlike manner that can be extended into the past and future, so that the world did not spring into existence five seconds ago (complete with traces of a fictional history) and will not cease to exist five seconds from now.

Legislating Morality

CHALLENGE

"People should not try to legislate morality."

DEFENSE

Any degree of scrutiny causes this claim to fall apart.

First, law deals with the ordering of human affairs—what people are and are not to do—and this has an inescapably moral dimension. This is obvious with laws prohibiting things like murder and rape, but it is true of legislation in general. Laws that redistribute wealth or raise public funds to be spent on certain projects imply a set of values. Even laws that seem completely arbitrary from one perspective (e.g., drive on the right side of the road rather than the left) imply underlying values (i.e., drive in a way that doesn't endanger others' lives).

Second, what is the alternative to "legislating morality"? Would that mean eliminating all laws dealing with moral subjects? If so, the entire body of law we have would vanish. Suddenly, there would be no laws against murder, no prohibitions on rape, and you could take anyone's property at will. In short, you could do anything you wanted as long as you were strong or swift enough to get away with it. The law of civilization would be replaced with the law of the jungle.

Or perhaps the idea would be not to eliminate laws but to merely make them in an amoral manner, not guided by moral considerations. In that case, we would end up with laws expressing an arbitrary set of values. There might be a law forbidding murder but endorsing rape (or visa versa).

Third, what is meant by saying that people *should* not try to legislate morality? According to what standard? There is no civil law saying that one should not do this. In the absence of a legal prohibition, the use of the term *should* suggests that a moral claim is being made. If so, then the claim is even more incoherent, as it would suggest it is immoral to make moral laws.

Ultimately, the proposal that people should not try to legislate morality is not a serious claim. Instead, it is used as a conversation stopper to shut people up, to shut down rational discussion, and to avoid having to answer others' arguments. It is not a rational claim but an attempt to evade and fake out people with whom one disagrees.

Solo Magisterio

CHALLENGE

"Catholics may claim that they rely on Scripture, Tradition, and the Magisterium, but the Magisterium has the final say. What Catholics really believe in is solo magisterio ("by the Magisterium alone"). It could make up anything, and Catholics would have to believe it."

DEFENSE

This claim does not stand up to analysis.

First, the Magisterium is not itself a source of the Faith. Its function is to proclaim and clarify what is found in Scripture and Tradition, which together "make up a single sacred deposit of the Word of God" (CCC 97). Scripture and Tradition thus represent the source upon which the Magisterium must draw. It can't simply "make up anything."

It could not, for example, say the Faith requires us to hold that a UFO crashed in Roswell, New Mexico, that Lee Harvey Oswald was or wasn't responsible for the assassination of President John F. Kennedy, or that the Great Wall of China is made of marshmallows. Scripture and Tradition say nothing about these matters, and so the Magisterium cannot proclaim them as articles of faith.

Second, the Magisterium is limited by what Scripture and Tradition *do* say. To cite just a few examples, they make it abundantly clear that God created the world, that Jesus is the Messiah, and that the afterlife is real. Consequently, the Magisterium can't teach contrary to these points.

Third, the Magisterium is limited by its own history. Every time it infallibly settles an issue, that teaching is "irreformable" (incapable of being changed). It can be further clarified and supplemented, but it cannot be reversed. Consequently, what the Magisterium is potentially able to teach in the future is limited by what it has infallibly taught in the past.

It may be rhetorically useful for those critical of the Catholic Church to claim that the Magisterium can simply teach anything, but this is not the case. There are practical, real-world limits to what it can and cannot say. Even apart from the perspective of faith, the scope of what the Magisterium can teach has definite limits.

And from the perspective of faith, it is even more limited, for Christ promised that the Holy Spirit would guide his Church "into all the truth" (John 16:13), thus making it "the pillar and bulwark of the truth" (1 Tim. 3:15).

TIP

See also Day 315.

Practical and Evidential Reason

CHALLENGE

"Belief without evidence is irrational. A rational man will proportion his beliefs strictly according to the evidence."

DEFENSE

Actions are irrational if they're done contrary to reason, but not all reasons are evidential. We sometimes have practical rather than evidential reasons.

Suppose you are fleeing danger and the only way to escape certain death is to leap across a chasm. Suppose further that the chasm is wide enough you can't tell whether leaping it is within your ability, but if you lose confidence you will certainly fail. In this situation, you have a practical reason to screw up your nerve and adopt the belief you can leap the chasm. You don't have solid evidence of this, but practical reason dictates that you take a (literal) leap of faith.

This happens more in life than commonly recognized. Often practical reasons urge us to make a decision even though we do not have the kind of evidential reasons we would like. This can happen in unusual, dramatic situations like the one above, and it can happen in simple, daily situations, as when we need to make a decision just so we can move on to something else.

It is easy to see how the approach of death can give practical reasons to make a decision on religious matters, such as whether there is a God, an afterlife, and whether we can affect our state in the afterlife. Due to our survival instinct, human beings naturally fear death and try to avoid it. When it is unavoidable, we can experience intense anxiety. One way of relieving this anxiety would be to put faith in God and ask for his forgiveness. Another would be to conclude that there is no afterlife and so there is nothing to fear. Yet another would be to say, "God, I don't know if you and the afterlife exist, but if you do, please forgive me."

A study of the evidence about God and the afterlife points to the first of these options, but regardless what evidence a person has previously examined, the practical realities of a dying person's situation give him reason to make *some* decision on these topics.

TIP

For a related discussion, see the essay "The Will to Believe" by William James (available online).

Extraordinary Claims, Extraordinary Evidence

CHALLENGE

"Extraordinary claims require extraordinary evidence. Religion makes extraordinary claims, therefore we must have extraordinary evidence for them."

DEFENSE

This depends on what you mean by "extraordinary."

In its original sense, *extraordinary* refers to things outside of or different from the ordinary. It thus refers to anything uncommon. However, the term has acquired an additional sense, according to which *extraordinary* refers to things that are startling, overwhelming, or awe-inspiring. Used this way, the term becomes subjective, because different people find different things startling, overwhelming, or awe-inspiring. These distinctions must be kept in mind when evaluating the claim that extraordinary claims require extraordinary evidence.

For example, if the statement is taken to mean that religion makes claims about things that are outside of the ordinary then this is true, taking the word "ordinary" to refer to the ordinary course of nature. Religion holds that, in addition to the natural world, there is a supernatural realm that sometimes interacts with it, producing non-ordinary events like miracles. To validate these claims, one would need "extraordinary evidence" in the sense of evidence concerning the extraordinary—i.e., evidence that non-ordinary (uncommon, rare) things have happened.

To give a parallel, modern science holds that there are uncommon or rare events in cosmic history—like the Big Bang, which is a unique event so far as we can presently tell. To validate these claims one needs to produce "extraordinary evidence" in the sense of evidence about the extraordinary or evidence that such events have happened.

From a scientific point of view, however, one would not need to produce subjectively startling, overwhelming, or awe-inspiring evidence to validate the Big Bang—merely evidence that the unique event happened. In the same way, to validate the occurrence of a miracle, such as the Resurrection of Jesus, one would not need to produce subjectively overwhelming evidence, but merely evidence that such a rare or unique event occurred.

On the other hand, if the term "extraordinary" is taken in the subjective sense, then it is true that an extraordinary event (a startling, overwhelming one) could require startling, overwhelming evidence to convince a person it happened. However, this only reveals something about the subjective psychological state of the person considering the claim, not what an objective, dispassionate person would conclude.

Unanswered Prayer

CHALLENGE

"Unanswered prayer disproves Christ's teaching on prayer. Jesus said, 'If you have faith as a grain of mustard seed, you will say to this mountain, "Move from here to there," and it will move; and nothing will be impossible to you' (Matt. 17:20b). But experience shows that we can't do such things by prayer."

DEFENSE

Jesus' teaching is more complex than this challenge suggests. It doesn't involve a promise that we'll always get what we ask.

First, Jesus makes the statement when the disciples have just failed to exorcise a demon. When they ask why they were unable to drive it out, he says, "Because of your little faith" (Matt. 17:20a). If the apostles, who were accustomed to working miracles, including driving out demons (Matt. 10:1, 5–8), could have inadequate faith, then we may, too. (Also, in this instance the disciples were trying to cast out a particularly powerful type of demon; Mark 9:29).

Second, the statement that having faith as small as a mustard seed can move mountains does not mean that faith has some magical power of its own. The point is that it is God who performs miracles, and he is omnipotent. The size of the miracle is therefore not dependent on the size of the person's faith but on God.

Third, this means that we do not have a promise that simply anything we pray for will happen. It must be the will of God (cf. Luke 22:42; James 4:13–15; 1 John 5:14).

Fourth, the fact that mountains usually do not move in response to prayer indicates it is usually not God's will for this to happen. That's why Jesus uses this example—because of how striking it is. He is using hyperbole (exaggeration to make a point). The point is that our prayers are dependent on God, not the size of our faith; Jesus is not issuing a promise that simply anything we ask for will be granted.

Fifth, elsewhere Jesus indicates that in some cases we will need to believe without doubting (Matt. 21:21; cf. James 1:6–7).

Sixth, the New Testament indicates that our individual dispositions can affect the outcome of our prayers in other ways, particularly with regard to whether we are living in a way pleasing to God (John 15:7; James. 4:3, 5:16; 1 Pet. 3:12; 1 John 3:22).

The Use of Alcohol

"Catholics are wrong to allow the use of alcohol. Jesus would never have approved of it. In the Bible, there were two types of wine—fermented and unfermented—and only the second, also known as 'new wine,' is ever endorsed."

The Bible contains multiple warnings against drunkenness (Prov. 20:1, Isa. 5:11–12, Luke 21:34, 1 Cor. 6:10, Eph. 5:18). But it does not condemn the moderate use of alcohol.

In the biblical languages, as in English, the term "wine" (Hebrew, *yayin*; Greek, *oinos*) is used to refer to the fermented juice of grapes. Even "new wine" was fermented, as shown by the crowd's accusation on the day of Pentecost that the disciples were "filled with new wine" (Acts 2:13), to which Peter replied, "these men are not drunk, as you suppose, since it is only the third hour of the day" (Acts 2:15).

Jesus certainly approved of drinking alcoholic wine. He produced around 150 gallons of it at the wedding at Cana (John 2:6) to keep a wedding party going when people had already drunk enough to exhaust the original supply of wine.

We know what Jesus produced was alcoholic because, after Jesus turned the water into wine, the steward of the feast complimented the groom, telling him, "Every man serves the good wine first; and when men have drunk freely, then the poor wine; but you have kept the good wine until now" (John 2:10). The steward thus identifies the "good wine" as high-quality wine that will cause people to lose their taste, making lesser quality wine palatable. Unfermented grape juice does not cause people to lose their taste; therefore, the wine Jesus produced was alcoholic.

The Old Testament, similarly, permits the use of alcoholic beverages. Thus, Deuteronomy states that, when fulfilling their obligation under the Mosaic Law to tithe, the Israelites could convert their crops to cash and then "spend the money for whatever you desire, oxen, or sheep, or wine or strong drink, whatever your appetite craves; and you shall eat there before the Lord your God and rejoice, you and your household" (Deut. 14:26). Even if one were to maintain, contrary to the linguistic evidence, that the wine in this passage were unfermented, the "strong drink" would not be.

Reincarnation and the Bible

CHALLENGE

"The Bible originally taught reincarnation, but the relevant passages were struck out by the Council of Nicaea."

DEFENSE

This claim is not credible for numerous reasons.

First, the surviving records of the First Council of Nicaea (A.D. 325) and the Second Council of Nicaea (A.D. 787), as well as the writings of those who took part in them, give no indication the topic of reincarnation was even discussed, much less was anything as dramatic as taking passages out of the Bible contemplated.

Second, the fathers of these councils regarded Scripture as the inspired word of God (cf. 2 Tim. 3:16). They weren't about to cut passages out of it. To do so would court eternal damnation.

Third, even had they wanted to do this, they had no ability. By the time the councils met, there were thousands of copies of Scripture in circulation, and there was no central registry allowing them to go around and snip out the offending passages. It would have been physically impossible to undertake the task.

Fourth, had they tried, it would have caused a tremendous uproar, and we would have records of the attempt. Like the council fathers, ordinary Christians prized Scripture as God's word, and if anyone tried to seize and mutilate it, the outcry would have been deafening.

Fifth, any such attempt would have been preceded and followed by fierce theological debate over reincarnation, with different groups taking different sides. We would thus have a record of this debate the same way we have records of the other theological debates in the period.

Sixth, copies of Scripture were already lost in the sands of Egypt and in monastery libraries, waiting to be rediscovered by modern archaeologists and historians. The council fathers would have had no ability to touch these lost copies, which we now have, and none of them teach reincarnation.

Seventh, this challenge misses the obvious: the Christian vision of the afterlife was resurrection, as demonstrated by the Resurrection of Jesus. Christians understood that his Resurrection set the pattern for us, so we also will be resurrected (1 Cor. 15:1–49), not reincarnated (Heb. 9:27).

TIP

For more on the early Church and reincarnation, see Jimmy Akin, *The Fathers Know Best*, chapter 59.

How Many Good Works?

CHALLENGE

"Catholics can't have assurance of salvation because the Church teaches justification by faith plus works, meaning that they will always have to be wondering whether they have done enough good works to be justified and enter heaven."

DEFENSE

This is not what the Church teaches.

We elsewhere cover the fact that the Church does not use the phrase "justification by faith and works" (see Day 222).

What the Church does teach is that "in those who are born again God hates nothing, because there is no condemnation to those who are truly buried together with Christ by baptism unto death (Rom. 6:4), who walk not according to the flesh (Rom. 8:1), but, putting off the old man and putting on the new one who is created according to God (Eph. 4:22, 24, Col. 3:9–10), are made innocent, immaculate, pure, guiltless and beloved of God, heirs indeed of God, joint heirs with Christ (Rom. 8:17); so that there is nothing whatever to hinder their entrance into heaven" (Trent, Decree on Original Sin 5).

Consequently, at the time a person comes to God and is initially justified, he does not have to do anything to enter heaven. There isn't some magic number of good works he has to perform.

The only way to lose the state of justification is by mortal sin, which requires "full knowledge and deliberate consent" (CCC 1857; see Day 302). As long as people haven't done that, they *can* be assured of their salvation.

If they do commit mortal sin, they need to repent and go to confession to be restored to the state of justification (see Day 45).

This is not to say good works have no role to play in the Christian life. They do. Thus Paul says, "we are his workmanship, created in Christ Jesus for good works, which God prepared beforehand, that we should walk in them" (Eph. 2:10). Good works flow from the love God pours into our hearts (Rom. 5:5) at initial justification, and God will ultimately reward these good works (Rom. 2:6–7; see Day 312).

However, once a person is justified, he has what is needed to enter heaven. He doesn't need to worry about not having done enough good works.

Imprecatory Psalms

CHALLENGE

"Some psalms contain violent and bloodthirsty language that calls down wrath upon (imprecates) one's enemies."

DEFENSE

The key to understanding these is recognizing their genre and the modes of language they employ.

The psalms were written in a world in which people experienced many violent acts that were bound to stir up powerful emotions. Expressing an emotion, however, is not the same thing as literally performing an act, much less does it mean God would approve of literally performing the act. The psalms thus use hyperbolic language to express emotions without implying divine approval of the literal acts described. The Pontifical Biblical Commission writes:

> The literary genre of the lament makes use of exaggerated and exasperated expressions, both in its description of suffering, which is always extreme, . . . and in the request for remedies, which should be swift and definitive. This is motivated by the fact that such a prayer expresses the emotional state of mind of those who find themselves in a dramatic situation. . . .
>
> The images employed should be regarded as metaphors: "break the teeth of the wicked" (Ps. 3:7; 58:7) means to put an end to the lies and greed of the overbearing; "smash their children against the rock" means to annihilate, without the possibility of their reproducing in the future the malignant forces which destroy life; and so on (The Inspiration and Truth of Scripture 129).

It also notes:

> In the imprecatory prayer, no magical action is performed which would have a direct effect on one's enemies; instead the person praying entrusts to God the task of administering that justice which no one on earth can. There is in this the renunciation of personal vengeance (ibid., 130).

It should also be remembered that the psalms were written at a state of Israel's journey before the definitive revelation that came with Jesus Christ. The attitude of turning the other cheek and forgiving and praying for one's enemies had not yet been revealed (Matt. 5:39, 43–44). This is a supernatural attitude that goes beyond a natural response (Matt. 5:45–48). Consequently, at the stage when the psalms were written, the natural human response was the one that found expression.

Non-Christian Miracles

CHALLENGE

"Why should I be Christian when other religions report miracles? Why would God even allow non-Christians to have miracles?"

DEFENSE

There are several explanations for reports of miracles in non-Christian circles, but none undermine the value of Christianity's central miracle, the Resurrection.

There are reports of supernatural phenomena in religions all over the world, but most are minor and are not investigated, and so their actual status is unclear. Some may be misinterpreted natural phenomena, some may be imaginary, and some may be frauds. (This applies to phenomena reported today in Christian circles as well; without investigation, the status of an event is not knowable.) If we eliminate these cases from consideration, there can be several reasons for genuinely supernatural events occurring in non-Christian circles.

First, God is not the only supernatural power active in the world. There are others, who are opposed to God (Eph. 6:12), and they are capable of producing supernatural effects. Thus Paul and his companions encountered a girl who had a spirit of divination that foretold the future (Acts 16:16–18). Because these forces operate in the world, we need to be on our guard against their attempts to mislead people (Matt. 24:24; 2 Thess. 2:9; Rev. 13:13–14, 19:20).

Second, Christianity is the fulfillment of Judaism, and Christians have never had a problem acknowledging that God performed miracles among Jews in the Old Testament. In his own day, Jesus acknowledged Jewish people were performing valid exorcisms (Luke 11:19), and we know that God has an ongoing relationship with the Jewish people (Rom. 11:25–32).

Third, God loves all people. As Jesus says, he "makes his sun rise on the evil and on the good, and sends rain on the just and on the unjust" (Matt. 5:45). If God provides providential care for people through natural causation, even knowing that they might misinterpret this care (e.g., as being produced by a sun god or a rain god), then he might choose to do so directly, through supernatural causation, knowing that this also might be misunderstood.

Ultimately, the miraculous evidence for Christianity is greater than that for any other religion. The Resurrection of Jesus is a major miracle that withstands skeptical scrutiny (see Days 206–215). Other religions have nothing comparable to this. The Resurrection thus provides unique and compelling evidence for Christianity.

Purgatory in 1 Corinthians

CHALLENGE

"1 Corinthians 3 isn't a good text for purgatory: (1) Paul speaks of ministers, not ordinary people; (2) their works are being tested, not them; and (3) this happens at Judgment Day, not the end of life."

DEFENSE

None of these objections deprive the passage of its evidential value.

First, in 1 Corinthians 3:10–17, Paul uses a metaphor comparing the Corinthian church to a temple. He laid its foundation, and others are now building on that. In the surrounding context, Paul refers to other ministers (Apollos and Peter), but he doesn't limit his remarks to ministers.

He says, "Let each man take care how he builds upon" the temple's foundation (v. 10) and warns, "If any one destroys God's temple, God will destroy him" (v. 17). This suggests an application to all church members, for everyone has a role to play in "building up" the church (1 Cor. 8:1, 10:23, 14:12), and all have the potential to "destroy" in the church (1 Cor. 8:11). Even if Paul were thinking exclusively of ministers in this passage, the principle has a broader application that includes everyone, for God "will render to every man according to his works" (Rom. 2:6).

Second, Paul speaks of people building "on the foundation with gold, silver, precious stones, wood, hay, straw" (v. 12) and of these being tested with "fire" (v. 13a). Although the object of the testing is "what sort of work each one has done" (v. 13b), this has existential consequences for the worker: He will "receive a reward" (v. 14) or "suffer loss" (v. 15a). If the latter, "he himself will be saved, but only as through fire" (v. 15b). Paul thus compares that man's situation to a person escaping from a burning temple.

Third, although Paul says, "the Day will disclose" each man's work (v. 13), he was writing at a time when he expected much of his audience to be alive at the Second Coming (cf. 1 Cor. 15:51; 1 Thess. 4:15, 17). If someone is alive at Judgment Day, that's when this will happen. However, for those who die before Judgment Day, it occurs when we stand before the Lord at the particular judgment (CCC 1021–22). Therefore, whenever they stand before the Lord, even the saved can have a testing comparable to escaping through flames.

Religion versus Relationship

CHALLENGE

"God doesn't want us to have religion; he just wants us to have a relationship with him."

DEFENSE

This is not the biblical way of thinking.

Linguists are familiar with a phenomenon that occurs when a new way of talking about a subject is introduced. At first, it may be perceived as innovative and attention-getting. If it becomes popular, however, it loses these connotations and becomes a standard mode of expression. Eventually, it may become so rote that it loses its rhetorical punch and people start looking for a new, more arresting way to express the idea.

We see this happening in the history of evangelization in the English-speaking Protestant world. Over the last few centuries there have been periodic efforts to find new, compelling ways to preach the gospel. This has led to a series of evangelistic modes of speech, each being replaced by another as it becomes shopworn: "Have you been saved?" "Have you accepted Jesus as your personal Lord and Savior?" "Ask Jesus into your heart," and so on. The religion versus relationship meme is simply one of the most recent.

There is nothing wrong with finding new, innovative ways to get people to respond to the gospel, but there is a problem when you become so daring and radical that you end up attacking what you are trying to serve. This is what is happening in the religion versus relationship meme. It is true that we can, should, and do have a relationship with God. However, religion is not a bad thing, as these verses from the New Testament indicate:

Great indeed, we confess, is the mystery of our religion (1 Tim. 3:16).

Women should adorn themselves . . . by good deeds, as befits women who profess religion (1 Tim. 2:9–10).

If any one thinks he is religious, and does not bridle his tongue but deceives his heart, this man's religion is vain. Religion that is pure and undefiled before God and the Father is this: to visit orphans and widows in their affliction, and to keep oneself unstained from the world (James 1:26–27).

God doesn't have a problem with religion, and we don't serve him by stating or implying that he does. He wants us to have the right kind of religion.

Security and Sonship

CHALLENGE

"Believers are eternally secure in their salvation. We cannot lose our salvation because when we come to God and believe, we become his sons (John 1:12–13; Rom. 8:14–23; Gal. 4:3–6; 1 John 3:1). And once you are a son, you can't cease to be a son."

DEFENSE

This presses the concept of sonship beyond its limits and fails to do justice to other things the biblical text indicates.

First, the concept of Christian sonship involves a metaphor. We are not children of God the way we are children of our earthly parents. Furthermore, Scripture uses this metaphor in more than one way, as illustrated by the fact that it uses two different images to describe how we become God's children—being born again (John 3:3; cf. Titus 3:5) and being adopted (Rom. 8:23; Gal. 4:5). Consequently, we must be on our guard against pressing the metaphor beyond its limits by transferring ideas from our earthly understanding of sonship in a way that violates things Scripture says.

Second, even if we press the details of the metaphor, the challenge is based on a false assumption, because it is possible to cease to be someone's son. In real life, fathers do disown and disinherit children. If a child can be adopted, he can also be disowned, and cultures around the world have ways of terminating legal ties between parents and children.

Third, even if the biological relationship between a parent and child cannot be undone, sons can die. This suggests the possibility of us becoming God's spiritual children and then spiritually dying through mortal sin (see Day 302).

Fourth, this understanding is used by our Lord in the parable of the prodigal son (Luke 15:11–32). In this parable, the relevant character begins as a son of his father, experiencing the life of the family. Then he turns his back on the father and leaves the family, falling into a life of grave sin. Later, he repents, returns, and is accepted back by the father, who declares that his son "was dead, and is alive" (v. 32). The parable thus reveals that we can begin as sons of the Father, spiritually die through sin, and then come back to the Father and be restored to spiritual life.

The Dating of Matthew

CHALLENGE

"Matthew's Gospel isn't reliable. It was written long after the events by a non-eyewitness."

DEFENSE

Matthew was written by an eyewitness within living memory of the events it records.

We elsewhere cover that the names of the evangelists were not made up at a later date and that they indicate actual authors of the Gospels (see Days 109 and 146). Matthew's Gospel was already called by that name in the first century, as shown by the testimony of the first-century figure John the Presbyter (Eusebius, *Church History* 3:39:16). The evidence thus points to Matthew the apostle, one of the eyewitnesses, as the author of the Gospel.

There is a literary relationship between Matthew and Mark that can help us determine when Matthew was written. Ninety percent of the material in Mark is paralleled in Matthew, often with the same wording. It is very probable that either Matthew used Mark or Mark used Matthew.

From the second century until the nineteenth century, the standard view was that Matthew wrote first and Mark abridged Matthew. If so, then since Mark was written in the A.D. 50s (see Day 300), Matthew would have written some time between A.D. 33 (the year of the Crucifixion) and the A.D. 50s.

However, today almost all scholars conclude that Mark wrote first and Matthew used Mark in composing his own Gospel. One thing supporting this is the first-century statement from John the Presbyter that Mark's Gospel was based on his memories of Peter's preaching (i.e., not on the Gospel of Matthew). Also, while abridgments were common in the ancient world, the evidence does not fit the hypothesis that Mark is an abridgment of either Matthew or of Matthew and Luke (see Jimmy Akin, "Did Mark Abridge Matthew's Gospel?" and "Did Mark Base His Gospel on Matthew and Luke?" at JimmyAkin.com).

On this view, Matthew would have been written some time after Mark. Raymond Brown proposed a late date for Matthew of "80–90, give or take a decade" (*An Introduction to the New Testament*, 172). However, this is too late.

Each of the Gospels refers to Jesus' prediction that the temple would be destroyed in A.D. 70, but none records its fulfillment, suggesting they were written before this date. This would point to Matthew being written between A.D. 50 and 70.

God Is Unscientific?

"Belief in God is unscientific."

DEFENSE

This challenge can mean different things, but none show that
God does not exist or that it is unreasonable to believe in him.

The statement that something is "unscientific" can mean different
things. Taken in the most charitable sense, it would mean that the
methodology used by science (i.e., scientific method) cannot establish
the existence of God.

Although this view is widely held among both scientists and theologians, it is not clear that this is the case. The scientific method involves
proposing an explanation based on observed data, figuring out what
the explanation would predict, and then seeing if this prediction is
verified or falsified.

To apply the scientific method to God, one would need to specify
what the existence of God would mean, make a prediction, and then
see if the prediction is verified or falsified. It is not clear that this cannot be done. It is true that God cannot be directly observed, but this
is also true of many entities considered established by science. For example, electrons are invisible entities that we have no direct means of
observing, yet they are considered well established by scientific means.

It may be that some traditional arguments for God's existence—or
new arguments—can be framed in a way provable by scientific method. If so, the existence of God would be scientifically verifiable.

However, suppose that this is not the case. This would in no way
rule out proof for the existence of God. It would merely mean that the
scientific method could not be used to do so. His existence could be
proved by other means.

The ideas proposed by mathematics and philosophy are supported
by means other than the scientific method. You don't have to do observational experiments to construct a mathematical proof or to verify
"I think, therefore I am." In the same way, one could use means other
than the scientific method to show that God exists.

Of course, one could be using the term "unscientific" as a slur
against anything not susceptible to proof by the scientific method, but
then the word would simply be an insult and would not stop fields like
mathematics, philosophy, or theology from using their own methods
to prove things—including the existence of God.

Binding and Loosing

CHALLENGE

"Peter didn't have any special authority, because Jesus gave the power of binding and loosing to others. This simply refers to the ability to preach the gospel and admit people to the kingdom, as Peter did with Jews on Pentecost (Acts 2) and Gentiles with the household of Cornelius (Acts 10–11)."

DEFENSE

This interpretation does not fit the text or the context.

First, while Jesus gave the power of binding and loosing both to Peter (Matt. 16:19b) and to others (Matt. 18:18), this wasn't the thing that made Peter unique (cf. CCC 881). In addition to giving him this authority, Jesus gave him the name *Peter* ("Rock") and declared him to be the rock on which he would build his Church (Matt. 16:18). He further gave him "the keys of the kingdom of heaven" (Matt. 16:19a), making him a unique leader in the Church (see Day 30). Thus the interpretation does not fit what the text says about Peter, who was singled out as unique.

Second, the interpretation does not fit the context of other New Testament passages, which also indicate Peter had a special role (e.g., Luke 22:31–32, John 21:15; see Days 19 and 276).

Third, the idea that the power of binding and loosing merely refers to preaching the gospel doesn't fit the text. In Matthew 18, the concept is raised in the context of Church discipline—of disciplining a Christian brother who sins against another Christian (cf. 18:15)—not preaching to the unevangelized.

Fourth, the power to bind and the power to loose are two distinct and opposite abilities. If one were preaching the gospel then the other would be withholding the gospel, and it was not within the purview of the apostles to do that. Peter could not have decided to withhold the gospel from either Jews or Gentiles (Matt. 28:19–20, Acts 1:8).

Fifth, the phrase "bind and loose" was an established Jewish idiom. It referred, among other things, to the ability to forbid and to permit—i.e., to make and abolish rules of conduct (cf. Matt. 23:2–4). Thus Josephus records that during the reign of Queen Alexandra, the Pharisees exercised the power of binding and loosing in Judea (*Jewish War* 1:5:2[110]). It also had reference to the ability to absolve or to refuse to absolve sins (cf. John 20:21–23, CCC 1444).

Objective Righteousness

CHALLENGE

"Catholic teaching on justification is confused. Catholics hold that, when God justifies us, he gives us more than legal righteousness, yet we obviously aren't fully righteous in our behavior."

DEFENSE

This concern is caused by the categories used to look at the question.

In the Protestant community, justification (here meaning the initial justification at the beginning of the Christian life) is usually thought to involve the bestowal of only *legal* righteousness (sometimes called "forensic" righteousness). On this model, God acts like a courtroom judge and declares the sinner innocent, giving him legal righteousness, regardless of his past sins.

The other form of righteousness typically discussed in Protestant circles has to do with our behavior and may be called *behavioral* righteousness. It is understood that God gives us this form of righteousness over time through the process of sanctification, so that we progressively overcome sinful patterns of behavior.

If these are the only two forms of righteousness, then the Catholic claim that justification involves more than legal righteousness would be problematic because we obviously aren't completely behaviorally righteous after initial justification.

However, these two are not the only types of righteousness Catholics envision. There is another, which may be called *objective* or *metaphysical* righteousness. Metaphysics is the study of what is ultimately real, and the idea is that when we sin, it changes the condition of our souls in a real, objective way by depriving them of holiness. This is reflected in the biblical images depicting sin as dirty, unclean, or defiling.

But when God justifies us, he changes this and gives us the objective holiness that we had been deprived of due to our sins. This inward transformation is reflected, for example, in the famous statement, "though your sins are like scarlet, they shall be as white as snow; though they are red like crimson, they shall become like wool" (Isa. 1:18).

On the Catholic view, God's word is efficacious and brings about what he declares (Isa. 55:11). Thus, when he declares a person righteous, that person becomes objectively (metaphysically) righteous. This is what prevents God's declaration of righteousness from simply being a legal fiction.

This objective righteousness is also referred to as "sanctifying grace" (cf. CCC 2023), and it is what grows during the process of ongoing justification (see Days 99 and 257).

The Standard of Goodness

CHALLENGE

"If something is good just because God says it is, then morality is arbitrary. But if there's an independent standard of morality that even God is bound to, that means there exists something besides God that is eternal and that is able to bind God."

DEFENSE

God is the ultimate standard of goodness.

A version of this argument was proposed in Plato's dialogue *Euthyphro* around 400 B.C. In it, Socrates debates whether piety is *whatever* the gods love or whether the gods love something *because* it is pious. In philosophy, this has become known as the "Euthyphro dilemma."

The view that goodness is whatever God (or the gods) command is known as *divine command theory*. There is some truth to this view, for some moral requirements are based on divine commands. An example was the weekly observance of the Sabbath by the Jewish people. There is nothing in the eternal moral law that requires Saturday in particular, rather than some other day, to be set aside for rest and worship.

However, the Sabbath was based on deeper moral principles. Humans *do* need to set aside adequate time for rest and worship. The way in which these were to be fulfilled in Israel may have been determined by divine command, but the command was based on a deeper set of principles that God designed into human nature. Today these principles are fulfilled in a different way (CCC 2175–76).

Consequently, the element of truth in divine command theory is limited, and the important question is where the deeper principles come from.

It would be possible to combine an independent standard of goodness with the idea of the Greek gods since they were held to be finite, created beings and thus not the ultimate standard of reference in the world. However, it does not fit with the Judeo-Christian understanding of God.

According to this view, God and the things he has created are all that exist. Consequently, if the ultimate standard of goodness is not created (as in divine command theory), then it must be God. This is the ultimate solution to the Euthyphro dilemma: The standard of goodness is God's eternal nature, and thus it is neither arbitrary nor independent of God. All particular moral laws are an unfolding of God's own goodness.

A Fallible Canon?

CHALLENGE

"We don't need the Church to infallibly settle the canon of Scripture; we have a fallible collection of infallible books. Further, the Catholic Church didn't even attempt to define the canon for centuries."

DEFENSE

There are several responses to this challenge.

First, if you want to claim we have certain knowledge that all the books included in the canon belong there, then you do need an infallible authority. Although some Protestants have been willing to say our knowledge of the canon is fallible ("a fallible collection of infallible books"), many find this prospect profoundly disturbing.

Second, it is particularly disturbing from a Protestant point of view because of the Protestant claim that theology should be done *sola scriptura* (Latin, "by Scripture alone"). If that is how to do theology, if you have nothing else authoritative to rely on, then the question of what belongs in Scripture takes on special urgency.

If there is the possibility that books have been included in Scripture that shouldn't be there—and multiple books were in doubt in the early centuries (see Day 314)—then the foundations of Protestant theology are uncertain. False elements may have been introduced into data it rests upon, with potentially grave consequences. Similarly, if some inspired books were left out of the Protestant canon, important data would be missing, again with potentially grave consequences. Determining, precisely and with certainty, what belongs in Scripture is thus a critical priority for *sola scriptura*.

Third, we elsewhere cover various practical problems with *sola scriptura* that indicate it could not have been proposed before a certain stage in Church history (see Day 16). The urgency of knowing precisely what belongs in the canon points to another such practical difficulty. That is, nobody would have proposed *sola scriptura* in an age before people thought they knew the boundaries of the canon with precision, making *sola scriptura* again an anachronism of a later age.

Fourth, the reason the canon was able to remain undefined for centuries was precisely because the early Church did *not* employ *sola scriptura*: In addition to Scripture, it relied on apostolic Tradition and the Church's living Magisterium. As long as these were available, the question of the canon's precise boundaries was not critical. Tradition clarified some questions, and the Magisterium could settle new pressing questions as they arose.

Religion as a Human Universal

CHALLENGE

"Okay, religion is a human universal—something that's found in all cultures. That doesn't mean that it's true, and it certainly doesn't mean that Christianity is true."

DEFENSE

Nobody would argue that because religion is a human universal, Christianity must be true. That would be excessively simplistic.

Instead, the argument is that the fact that religion is a human universal points to there *being* a religious dimension to the world.

The starting point for this argument is recognizing the universality of religion in human cultures. There have been no cultures without religion, either now or in the past. Even cultures that have tried to stamp out religion have not been able to do so. Further, as we observe elsewhere, children are naturally predisposed to religious belief (see Day 313). Religion is therefore a basic impulse that is rooted in human nature.

Other, similarly basic impulses tell us something about the world. The human impulses to eat and breathe point to the existence of food and oxygen. The impulses to sex and language point to the possibilities of reproduction and of communicating information in symbolic form.

Any basic impulse representing a human universal is rooted in human nature. Therefore, the religious impulse also tells us something about the world—that it has a religious or supernatural dimension.

This does not tell us much about that dimension. It does not tell us, for example, which God or gods are real or what the afterlife is like. But, in the same way, the mere impulse to eat does not tell us much about what kinds of food exist, and the mere impulse toward language does not tell us much about what kinds of information are out there.

If you want to know about the latter subjects, much more detailed studies have to be done, but the existence of the basic impulses tell us that the subjects are real.

In the same way, if you want to find out the details of the supernatural world, more detailed studies must be made and the whole enterprise of apologetics comes into play to prove or disprove particular religious claims. However, the religious impulse does point to the reality of the supernatural realm.

TIP

For more, see C.S. Lewis's essay "The Weight of Glory."

Catholic Teaching on Merit

CHALLENGE

"Catholic theology of merit is false. We can't earn our place before God."

DEFENSE

The Church does not teach that we can earn our place before God. Everything we receive from him is due to his grace.

When we first come to God and are justified, it is entirely by his grace, for "none of those things that precede justification, whether faith or works, merit the grace of justification" (Trent, Decree on Justification 8).

After our initial justification, God's grace leads us to do good works (Eph. 2:10) and he rewards these (Rom. 2:6–7), but still, "with regard to God, there is no strict right to any merit on the part of man. Between God and us there is an immeasurable inequality, for we have received everything from him, our Creator" (CCC 2007).

In terms of this "strict right," Benedict XVI wrote: "We cannot—to use the classical expression—'merit' heaven through our works. Heaven is always more than we could merit, just as being loved is never something 'merited,' but always a gift" (*Spe Salvi* 35).

On the other hand, Scripture does indicate that we will receive rewards, that our actions can lay up "treasures in heaven," and that God will reward patience in good work with glory, honor, immortality, and eternal life (see Day 312). There is a sense, therefore, in which each of these things is understood in Scripture as a reward for what we have done by God's grace. However, good works receive a reward (i.e., become meritorious) not because we earn our place before God, but because they are done by his grace and because he freely promised to reward them.

"According to the Catholic understanding, good works, made possible by grace and the working of the Holy Spirit, contribute to growth in grace, so that the righteousness that comes from God is preserved and communion with Christ is deepened. When Catholics affirm the 'meritorious' character of good works, they wish to say that, according to the biblical witness, a reward in heaven is promised to these works. Their intention is to emphasize the responsibility of persons for their actions, not to contest the character of those works as gifts, or far less to deny that justification always remains the unmerited gift of grace" (JD 38).

Legislating Religious Views

"People shouldn't legislate their religious views. We live in a democracy, and not everybody has the same religion."

This challenge is problematic on several grounds.

First, it assumes people in a democracy shouldn't vote according to their beliefs. This is false. Democracies exist precisely to allow people to express their will regarding how society should be governed. Saying that they should not vote their will simply because it is informed by their religious views and others disagree with those views, is contrary to the fundamental enterprise of democracy.

We would not accept the same argument in a different field (e.g., people should refrain from voting based on their scientific views because other people disagree with those views), and we should not accept it here.

Second, people voting their religious views has done a great deal of good. In many countries, legal opposition to slavery, racism, and poverty has been motivated by people's religious beliefs. We would not say that people motivated in this way should have refrained from voting because others disagreed with their religious views on these matters.

Third, while others' religious freedom should be respected and protected by law in many situations, this principle is not absolute. Sometimes the religious beliefs of a group are directly opposed to the common good. If the Manson Family believed it was okay to kill random people in Los Angeles, or if jihadist Muslims believe it is okay to attack innocent civilians in New York, that does not mean we are obliged to let them do these things.

Fourth, sometimes it is impossible for the law to accommodate different religious views because what is required by one religion is prohibited by another.

Fifth, the claim something is a "religious issue" is often a dodge used to avoid having to deal with the merits of the case. For example, pro-abortion activists often claim abortion is a religious issue. While—as with any issue—people may hold religious views regarding abortion, the truth is that it is a human rights issue that can be argued without any reference to religion (see Day 70).

In such cases, the claim one should not legislate religious views is a distraction from the arguments at hand. It is a conversation stopper used to prevent the merits of a question from being explored.

Appearance of Age?

CHALLENGE

"The Catholic Church is wrong to express appreciation for scientific studies on the origins of the universe, life, and man (see CCC 283). Contrary to modern scientific ideas, the universe is only a few thousand years old. God created it with the appearance of age, just like he created Adam as an adult."

DEFENSE

This view creates problems for God's truthfulness.

The challenge is based on an overly literal interpretation of Genesis (see Days 90, 290, and 339). However, if we assume for the moment God did create Adam as an adult, there would be a very good reason: Human infants can't survive on their own. If God created the first man directly from the dust, with no caretakers, as an infant, he would have died. Babies can't even eat solid food, such as the fruit of the trees in the Garden. Consequently, God would have had very good reason to create Adam and Eve as adults.

The need to create things in a state of maturity would have extended to things Adam and Eve needed (e.g., trees already bearing fruit), but it wouldn't have extended to other things. For example, there would have been no need to create the earth with fossilized dinosaur bones buried in the ground. Adam and Eve would have had no need of those to survive.

Consequently, creating that kind of appearance of age would be unnecessary, and it would raise the question of God's truthfulness, since he would appear to be deliberately planting false evidence to mislead people about the age of the world.

The problem is especially acute because the night sky appears to show us events that took place much longer ago than a few thousand years, and astronomers regularly see stars go supernova in galaxies millions of light years away. If the universe is only a few thousand years old, and if God created the starlight from these galaxies a few thousand light years away so that it is arriving only now, then the night sky is showing us fictional images of events that never took place in reality.

This is not consistent with the truthfulness of God, who is "the way, the truth, and the life" (John 14:6).

Christianity and Pacifism

CHALLENGE

"For Christians, violence is never permitted. Jesus teaches strict pacifism when he says, 'Do not resist one who is evil. But if any one strikes you on the right cheek, turn to him the other also' (Matt. 5:39)."

DEFENSE

What Jesus teaches in one passage must be read in light of what he teaches elsewhere.

Jesus' statement about turning the other cheek occurs in the Sermon on the Mount (Matt. 5–7), but in the same discourse he draws a distinction between the natural, human response and a supernatural response that goes beyond it. The first is morally acceptable, but it does not result in an eternal reward. The second goes beyond what is morally required and does result in an eternal reward (cf. Matt. 5:43–47).

Self-defense is a human response. It is a morally acceptable but merely human response, and it does not result in a reward from God. Turning the other cheek is a supernatural response and, all things being equal, it can result in a reward from God.

The fact that Jesus is not opposed to self-defense as a human response is indicated in Luke 22 where, in view of mounting danger, Jesus tells his disciples, "And let him who has no sword sell his mantle and buy one" (Luke 22:36). This indicates that Jesus recognized that the use of lethal force in self-defense—for swords were used to kill aggressors—was morally permissible.

Other passages in the New Testament indicate a similar legitimacy for the use of lethal force. Thus Paul states, "If then I am a wrongdoer, and have committed anything for which I deserve to die, I do not seek to escape death" (Acts 25:11a). Similarly, Paul tells his readers:

Would you have no fear of him who is in authority? Then do what is good, and you will receive his approval, for he is God's servant for your good. But if you do wrong, be afraid, for he does not bear the sword in vain; he is the servant of God to execute his wrath on the wrongdoer (Rom. 13:3–4).

Swords were not used to spank but to kill people. Therefore, Paul—like Jesus—recognizes the legitimate use of lethal force in some circumstances.

The Cumulative Case for God

CHALLENGE

"There is no one argument that demonstrates the Christian God exists. At most, each points to only a single aspect of the Christian God."

DEFENSE

The arguments are not meant to be used individually. They're meant to be combined in a cumulative case.

It would be possible to combine all the arguments into a single, highly complex argument, with many subarguments (similar to the way a computer program contains many subroutines). However, such an argument would be excessively difficult to follow. Consequently, apologists through the ages have broken the overall argument for the Christian God into smaller, more easily understandable pieces, which taken together provide a compelling case for the whole Christian vision.

Historical examples of this method are found in St. Thomas Aquinas's *Summa Theologiae* (I:2–43) and *Summa Contra Gentiles* (I:3–102).

This present book is not a systematic treatise on the Christian understanding of God, so it doesn't argue these points one by one. However, the arguments it does provide contribute elements of the Christian view of God:

- The *kalam* argument discusses God as the cause of the universe, who transcends space and time (see Days 46 and 47).
- The change argument discusses God as the ultimate and changeless cause of change in the world (see Days 73 and 74).
- The contingency argument discusses God as the first and necessary cause of all contingent things (see Days 168 and 169).
- The fine-tuning argument discusses God as the designer of the universe (see Days 178 and 179).
- The quantum mechanical argument discusses God as the one whose knowledge of the world makes it actual (see Days 230 and 231).
- Pascal's Wager gives reasons why we should embrace the Christian view of God rather than skepticism (see Days 318 and 319).

Additional arguments in this book address:

- The concept of the Trinity (see Days 28, 39, 137, and 194)
- The status of Jesus as the Messiah (see Day 14)
- The Resurrection of Jesus (see Days 206–215)

Ultimately, everything in the book contributes to defending one aspect of the Christian faith or another, and no single entry is meant to prove the entirety on its own.

Keeping the Sabbath

CHALLENGE

"Why do Catholics worship on Sunday instead of keeping the Sabbath? The (Saturday) Sabbath is part of the Ten Commandments, which Catholics recognize as expressing the moral law (CCC 1962)."

DEFENSE

The Sabbath command is unique among the Ten Commandments in that it incorporates both moral and ceremonial aspects.

The Catechism of Trent states:

> The other commandments of the Decalogue are precepts of the natural law, obligatory at all times and unalterable. Hence, after the abrogation of the Law of Moses, all the commandments contained in the [Ten Commandments] are observed by Christians, not indeed because their observance is commanded by Moses, but because they are in conformity with nature which dictates obedience to them. This commandment about the observance of the Sabbath, on the other hand, considered as to the time appointed for its fulfillment, is not fixed and unalterable, but susceptible of change, and belongs not to the moral, but the ceremonial law.
>
> Neither is it a principle of the natural law; we are not instructed by nature to give external worship to God on that day, rather than on any other. And in fact the Sabbath was kept holy only from the time of the liberation of the people of Israel from the bondage of Pharaoh. The observance of the Sabbath was to be abrogated at the same time as the other Hebrew rites and ceremonies, that is, at the death of Christ (3:4:4).

Consequently, observing the Sabbath isn't required even for Jewish people after the death of Christ, and it was never required for Gentiles (see Day 322).

Paul states: "Therefore let no one pass judgment on you in questions of food and drink or with regard to a festival or a new moon or a Sabbath" (Col. 2:17)—the annual feasts, the monthly new moons, and the weekly sabbaths being the three types of holy days on the Jewish calendar.

The moral principles underlying the Sabbath—devoting adequate time to rest and worship—remain binding, so the first-century Church began honoring the first day of the week—Sunday—as "the Lord's day" (Rev. 1:10; cf. 1 Cor. 16:2), since it was on this day the Lord Jesus was resurrected (Matt. 28:1; Mark 16:2; Luke 24:1, John 20:1). Thus Christians observe Sunday rather than the Jewish Sabbath.

Evolution and the Benefits of Religion

CHALLENGE

"If religion has benefits for individuals and groups, why can't we say that evolution has favored the development of religion, even though it has no bearing on reality."

DEFENSE

Religion does have benefits (see Day 283), but this doesn't lead to the conclusion that religious beliefs are false.

If it were possible to dismiss a belief as having no bearing on reality simply because adopting it has benefits from an evolutionary point of view (i.e., promoting the survival and reproduction of those who hold it), then we would have to dismiss a vast number of beliefs. For example, the belief that arsenic in significant quantities is poisonous would be dismissed, because this belief is beneficial for survival. We would also dismiss the belief that children should be cared for, because that is beneficial for reproduction.

In fact, if we were to dismiss all beliefs that have evolutionary benefit then the result would be an impoverished, dysfunctional belief system that would positively gravely hinder human survival and reproduction. This is because our cognitive faculties, and the beliefs that flow from them, are adapted to allow our survival and reproduction.

This does not mean that every belief we have is adaptive or that it is true. People obviously have maladapted and untrue beliefs. However, we can't simply dismiss the truth of a belief because it is adaptive. Therefore, if we're open to the truth of other adaptive beliefs, we should be open to the truth of religious beliefs. If we're open to arguments that arsenic is poisonous or that children should be cared for, we should be open to arguments that God exists.

To dismiss religious beliefs, you would need to do more than point to their adaptive nature. You would need to show why they, unlike other adaptive beliefs, have no relationship to reality. This would be difficult in the absence of conclusive proof that God does not exist or that there is no afterlife. In the absence of such proof, the believer would be entitled to hold that religious beliefs should be given the same consideration as other adaptive beliefs.

Further, he would be entitled to hold, from his perspective, that the evolutionary process that gave us our cognitive faculties was superintended by divine providence precisely so that we could come to know God.

Homosexual Unions Not Marriages

CHALLENGE

"Why shouldn't people of the same sex be allowed to marry one another?"

DEFENSE

It's not so much a question of what should be allowed as of what is *possible*. Marriage involves a reality that can only exist between a man and a woman.

Marriage is a union of a man and a woman that is oriented toward the good of the spouses and the procreation and education of offspring (CCC 1601). No other kind of union is a marriage.

Since before recorded history, men and women have united to care for each other and to bring up children. That happens in every culture, no matter where in the world. In fact, a culture would die without those unions of men and women. Marriage is thus a human universal, an institution that is built into human nature.

People of the same sex cannot marry one another because any union between them would not have the reality that marriage possesses.

This is particularly obvious when it comes to procreation. Two men or two women cannot procreate. For new children to be brought into the world, biology requires the union of a man and a woman.

But procreation is not the only issue. Men and women are different in ways that go beyond reproduction. Both physically and psychologically, they complement and complete one another in a manner that two people of the same sex do not.

These differences also play an important role in raising children. By setting examples of true fatherhood and motherhood, a husband and wife provide the kind of environment that helps children grow and develop properly.

Even apart from procreation and raising children—as in the case of marriages that do not result in children due to infertility—the physical and psychological differences between men and women enable them to unite and thrive in a way two people of the same sex cannot.

In all these cases, and especially in the case of procreation, it is clear from nature that men and women are designed to be united with each other in a way two men or two women are not. For this reason, same-sex unions do not possess the reality of marriage, and it is simply playing games with words to call them marriages when they lack that reality.

A Multiplicity of Gods?

"Why can't there be a multiplicity of gods?"

The answer depends on what you mean by "gods."

In classical paganism, the gods people typically worshipped were not infinite, eternal beings. Instead, they were understood to be superhuman but finite beings who came into existence at some point. (Thus Osiris's father was Geb, Zeus's father was Chronos, Thor's father was Odin.)

It is possible for there to be multiple superhuman beings. That could be the case even in the natural world. There might be creatures in the physical universe who are more intelligent, more powerful, and longer lived than man.

The same is true of the supernatural world. In fact, the Judeo-Christian view holds that there *are* superhuman, supernatural beings. Angels are immaterial beings who display miraculous abilities. It is therefore possible for there to be a multiplicity of finite, superhuman beings.

This does not provide evidence for the existence of any set of pagan deities. Much less does it provide reason to worship them. On the Judeo-Christian view, whatever respect may be due a finite being, it does not amount to the worship due the infinite Creator.

One might ask whether a more elevated polytheism is possible, whereby there is more than one ultimate, infinite God. It is not clear that any religion proposes this. Not even Zoroastrianism, which is often said to be dualistic, does so. It is ultimately monotheistic because it holds that its fundamental deity, Ahura Mazda, will eventually defeat his opponent, Angra Mainyu.

We have a strong intuition that, whatever the ultimate reality may be, it is one, and thus there could not be more than one ultimate, infinite God.

If one did propose the existence of two such beings, then they would need to exist within some kind of framework that contained them both. This framework would then be more fundamental than either. However, if there is something more fundamental than a being, then that being cannot be the ultimate, infinite God proposed on the Judeo-Christian view but must be a being of a lesser order.

According to Judaism and Christianity, God is the fundamental basis of all that is real, and, properly understood, there cannot be two or more fundamental bases of reality.

Antipopes

CHALLENGE

"There can't be an 'unbroken line' of popes going back to Peter. Look at the vacancies between popes, and at the antipopes."

DEFENSE

The "unbroken line" claim may be found in the writings of individual Catholics, but it is difficult to find it in any official Church documents. Nevertheless, it expresses a truth: There is a line of popes (bishops of Rome) that we can trace in historical succession, going back to Peter.

The statement that it is unbroken must be understood in the sense that those who make the claim intend, otherwise a straw man will result. This means recognizing certain obvious facts, such as the vacancies that occur between the death or resignation of one pope and the election of another.

Similar vacancies are found in offices around the world, including lines of kings, presidents, premiers, and others. Temporary vacancies occur all the time, yet the offices in question still exist. An American thus might speak of an unbroken line of presidents going back to George Washington, though there have been periods between the death of one president and the swearing in of another.

Consequently, the only way to "break" a line would be for the office itself to be abolished—not just be unfilled for a time. For example, if the U.S. Constitution were amended to abolish the office of president and then, at a later date, it was amended again to reintroduce it, there would be a break in the line of U.S. presidents.

Similarly, the only way for the line of popes to be broken in this sense would be for the office of bishop of Rome to be abolished and then reintroduced at a later date. That has never happened, so it is meaningful to speak of an unbroken line of popes going back to Peter.

Neither does the existence of antipopes break the line. An antipope is a person who falsely claims to be the pope. They are the ecclesiastical equivalents of royal pretenders—people who falsely claim a royal office or title. (A presidential pretender would be the same thing in an American context.)

The existence of pretenders—whether to the papacy, a line of kings, or any other office—doesn't mean there is no legitimate occupant of the office or that the office has been abolished and the line broken.

The Cosmic Teapot

CHALLENGE

"As an atheist, I may not be able to prove God doesn't exist, but I also can't prove there isn't, orbiting between Earth and Mars, a teapot too small to be detected by telescopes. If I don't have to believe in the latter, I don't have to believe in the former."

DEFENSE

This argument is subject to a number of objections.

First, it was originally proposed by the philosopher Bertrand Russell as an answer to believers who felt atheists have the burden of proof regarding the existence of God (see "Is There a God?" *The Collected Papers of Bertrand Russell*, vol. 11).

From this perspective, the teapot argument is unnecessary. As we observe elsewhere (see Day 86), the burden of proof is on whoever tries to convince another person of his position. If a believer tries to convince an atheist God exists, the believer has the burden of proof. If an atheist tries to convince a believer God does not exist, the atheist has it.

Second, the teapot argument doesn't tell us anything about abstract cases where we have no evidence for or against something's existence. If we really have no evidence, then the existence of a thing is just as likely as its non-existence, and neither believers nor non-believers can claim an advantage.

The teapot argument masks this by sneaking in evidence, based on our background knowledge, without acknowledging the fact. We already know that a china teapot is an artificial, man-made entity, and since we have not launched any teapots into orbit between Earth and Mars, we *do* have evidence making such a teapot improbable.

The probability would change dramatically if we proposed that there is a small rock orbiting between Earth and Mars. We already know that the solar system is filled with small rocks—from tiny meteoroids to large asteroids. In fact, Mars is near the asteroid belt. Therefore, it is highly probable that there is a small rock (in fact, many small rocks) orbiting between Earth and Mars.

Third, if an atheist wishes to argue that the existence of God is as improbable as Russell's teapot, he will have to engage God's existence on the merits of the case and argue why God is improbable. He will also need to provide reasons to reject the arguments for God's existence.

Ancient Scriptures

"Why should I pay attention to the Bible at all? It's an ancient book written by people of limited understanding. Besides, other religions have their own scriptures, too. Why are they any less important?"

The Christian scriptures are unique and valuable.

The mere fact that the books of the Bible were written a long time ago is no reason to look down on or dismiss them. To do so would be chronological snobbery. Just because a person wrote before you doesn't mean that person was wrong. If it did, we would have to dismiss all works written in the past, obliterating our knowledge of history and preventing knowledge from being passed from one generation to another.

The question is not when a work was written but whether it contains truth. Because of the growth of various fields of knowledge, we may expect more recently written works to contain more of certain types of truth—e.g., truths about math or science—but the information that we seek from Scripture isn't on those topics. Instead, we are seeking truth of a religious nature—e.g., about God and his dealings with man—and this is an area that is largely beyond the powers of natural reason to investigate for itself.

Consequently, for us to have this information, God must take the initiative: He must reveal himself to man. *If* God does so and *when* God does so is entirely up to him. For it to happen at all, it must take place at some point in human history, and—unless God were to make contact with man for the very first time at the end of the world—future ages would look back on that time and view it as ancient. That's not an indication it is false or that he didn't do it. The question, therefore, is what evidence we have that God made contact with man and that the Bible preserves what he revealed to us.

Here apologetics becomes relevant. In particular, the arguments supporting God's existence and the occurrence of miracles, especially the Resurrection of Jesus, play an important role. The first set of arguments support the proposition that there is a God who might choose to contact mankind, and the second support the Bible as the record of the resulting revelation. Other religions do not have comparable evidence.

What This Book Doesn't Cover

"This book doesn't include my objection to the Faith!"

A single book can only do so much. Therefore, let me recommend some more resources that may help.

- *The Handbook of Catholic Apologetics* by Peter Kreeft and Ronald Tacelli: This is an excellent survey of the general evidences for the Christian faith, written by a pair of scholars who communicate in a manner easily accessible to all.
- *Scaling the Secular City* by J.P. Moreland: This was one of the first apologetic books I read when I began studying the field. Dr. Moreland is an outstanding scholar who carries the discussion to a level satisfying for those who want to go deeper.
- *Mere Christianity* by C.S. Lewis: This is another popular-level work that covers the basics of why one should choose to be a Christian, written by one of the greatest Christian authors of the twentieth century.
- *Miracles* by C.S. Lewis: The topic of miracles and how they relate to science is one of the most misunderstood subjects in apologetics. This book contains valuable insights.
- *Hard Sayings* by Trent Horn: There are many books about passages of the Bible that are difficult to accept for one reason or another. Trent's book is written from a Catholic perspective and takes advantage of the current state of magisterial thinking.
- *The Fathers Know Best* by Jimmy Akin: As we've seen in this book, the Church Fathers are an important witness to the teaching of Christ and the apostles. My own book on the subject shows what they taught on numerous subjects and how this corresponds to the teaching of the Church today.
- *The Drama of Salvation* by Jimmy Akin: One of the most sensitive subjects between Protestants and Catholics is how we are saved. This book discusses the subject in what I hope is a calm and constructive manner.

I hope these recommendations help. God loves you; may he reward your further studies and bless you richly!

Your pal,

—*Jimmy Akin*

Alphabetical Index

About the Author

Jimmy Akin is an internationally known author and speaker. As the senior apologist at Catholic Answers, he has more than twenty years of experiencing defending and explaining the Faith.

Jimmy is a convert to the Faith and has an extensive background in the Bible, theology, the Church Fathers, philosophy, canon law, and liturgy.

Jimmy is a weekly guest on the national radio program Catholic Answers Live, a regular contributor to Catholic Answers Magazine, and a popular blogger and podcaster. His books include *The Fathers Know Best* and *The Drama of Salvation*. His personal web site is JimmyAkin. com.